Margaret Ann Palliser, O. P.

Christ, Our Mother of Mercy

Margaret Ann Palliser, O. P.

Christ, Our Mother of Mercy

Divine Mercy and Compassion
in the Theology of
the *Shewings* of Julian of Norwich

Walter de Gruyter · Berlin · New York
1992

CUM APPROBATIONE ECCLESIASTICA
Imprimatur, Rome, 6 May 1991
Vicariato di Roma

⊗ Printed on acid-free paper wich falls
within the guidelines of the ANSI to ensure
permanence and durability.

Library of Congress Cataloging-in-Publication Data

Palliser, Margaret Ann, 1947-
    Christ, our mother of mercy : divine mercy and compassion in
the theology of the Shewings of Julian of Norwich / Margaret
Ann Palliser.
        p.   cm.
    Includes bibliographical references and index.
    ISBN 3-11-013558-2
    1. Julian, of Norwich, b. 1343.   Revelations of divine love.
2. Love — Religious aspects — Christianity — History of doctrines — Middle Ages, 600-1500. 3. God — Mercy — History of
doctrines — Middle Ages, 600-1500. 4. God — Motherhood —
History of doctrines — Middle Ages, 600-1500. 5. Jesus Christ —
History of doctrines — Middle Ages, 600-1500.   I. Title.
BV4831.J83P35   1992
231'.4 — dc20   92-24301
                                                            CIP

Die Deutsche Bibliothek — Cataloging in Publication Data

Palliser, Margaret Ann:
Christ, our mother of mercy : divine mercy and compassion in the
theology of the Shewings of Julian of Norwich / Margaret Ann
Palliser. — Berlin ; New York : de Gruyter, 1992
    ISBN 3-11-013558-2

Printed in Germany
Printing: Arthur Collignon GmbH, Berlin 30
Binding: Lüderitz & Bauer, Berlin 61

To my mother

Norma Brady Palliser

*who taught me
the meaning of compassion*

Preface

On September 12, 1984, chance circumstances led me to spend three hours in the city of Norwich in northeast England. After a visit to the beautiful Norwich Cathedral, I found my way to the tiny Church of St. Julian where I paused to pray at the restored anchorhold of the fourteenth-century mystic, Julian of Norwich. That brief visit was my first encounter with this remarkable woman whose writings have been such an inspiration and consolation to me since that time.

My interest in Julian began to grow when, in 1986, I had the good fortune to study the English mystics with Simon Tugwell, O.P., of Black-friars, Oxford. With his guidance, I discovered Julian to be not only an appealing writer but a most competent theologian as well. Professor Tugwell's approach to Julian's theology has so shaped my own that, during the evolution of this manuscript, I have often and gratefully been aware of his presence as an invisible scholiast. I thank him for his invaluable contribution to my understanding of Julian. Since 1987, my study of Julian has been enriched in countless ways by Paul Molinari, S.J., of the Pontifical Gregorian University, Rome, whose insightful direction has made it possible for me to bring this project to fruitful completion. His enthusiasm for my work has been a constant source of encouragement to me. I am grateful to him for his kindness and unfailing compassion.

I wish to express my deep appreciation to my family, to my friends, to the members of my religious congregation, the Dominican Sisters of Sparkill, New York, and to my Dominican sisters and brothers at the Dominican House of Studies in Rome, for the countless ways they have supported me during my years of study. In a special way, the love and kindness of my sisters at Villa St. Dominic in Glasco, New York, have made it possible for me to complete this study. I thank them for their hospitality, patience, understanding, and encouragement during the past two years. It has been a grace for me to be among them.

I owe a great debt of gratitude to the many people who have aided me in the preparation of this manuscript. For their assistance in locating reference materials, I am very grateful to Mary and Keith Zimmer at the St. Louis Public Library, Jeffrey Bessler and Kathleen Casey at St. Louis University Divinity Library, and Sheila Campbell, M.M.M.; without their generous help, my efforts would have been severely hampered. I wish to thank Peter Gumpel, S.J., Mary O'Driscoll, O.P., John O'Donnell, S.J., Paul O'Leary, O.P., and Donagh O'Shea, O.P., for their challenging observations and wise suggestions for the final draft. For their patience and dedication to the monumental task of proofreading this manuscript in its various stages, I am indebted to Christine Cunningham, I.H.M., Katherine Gaffney, O.P., Julian Guzman, S.D.S., Helen Jacobson, O.S.F., and Pauline Jenner, O.P. For sharing their expertise in computer technology, I thank Gordon Chang, Michael Murphy, Michael A. Hoonhout, William J. Palliser, and Christopher Vender.

I wish to acknowledge the Pontifical Institute of Mediaeval Studies in Toronto for its gracious permission to quote extensively from the critical edition of Julian's *Shewings* by Edmund Colledge, O.S.A., and James Walsh, S.J., *A Book of Showings to the Anchoress Julian of Norwich*, Studies and Texts 35 (Toronto: Pontifical Institute of Medieval Studies, 1978).

As a result of my study, I am firmly convinced that Julian's *Shewings* offers a profound theological basis for understanding divine mercy and compassion. It is my sincere hope that her message will be a source of consolation and hope for all who read these pages.

Margaret Ann Palliser, O.P.

Glasco, New York
May 8, 1992

Table of Contents

Abbreviations

PG   *Patrologia Graeca.* Edited by J.-P. Migne. Paris, 1857-66.

PL   *Patrologia Latina.* Edited by J.-P. Migne. Paris, 1844-64.

Introduction

In May, 1373, a devout thirty-year-old English woman received sixteen 'shewings'[1] from God. We know her today as Julian of Norwich, the medieval anchoress whose extraordinary *Book of Shewings* is the basis for this study on divine mercy and compassion.

While there is no autograph copy extant, Julian's *Shewings* have come down to us in manuscript form in two versions: the Short Text (twenty-five chapters) and the Long Text (eighty-six chapters). Scholars generally agree that the shorter version preceded the Long Text and was probably recorded by Julian sometime soon after her experience of the revelations in May, 1373. By Julian's own comment in chapter 51, we know that her expanded version was not completed until at least twenty years after her actual experience of the shewings.[2] It is this Long Text which will form the basis of our study because it represents the fruit of Julian's many years of theological reflection on the content of the sixteen revelations she had received as a young woman.[3]

As an introduction to the analysis of Julian's teaching on divine mercy and compassion, we shall first explore briefly the little biographical information that has come down to us about this unique mystic and theologian of the fourteenth century. We shall then focus our attention on the character and structure of the text itself. Finally, we shall define the precise nature and scope of this study, indicating the methodology employed.

---

1   Throughout this study we shall use Julian's preferred word 'shewings' to refer to the revelations (or visions) themselves; the italicized form (*Shewings*) will refer to the text of the book she wrote about her experience.

2   51:86.

3   Unless otherwise noted, all quotations used in this study will be taken from the Long Text of the recent critical edition by Edmund Colledge, O.S.A., and James Walsh, S.J., *A Book of Showings to the Anchoress Julian of Norwich*, Studies and Texts 35 (Toronto: Pontifical Institute of Medieval Studies, 1978). This edition will hereafter be referred to as *A Book of Showings*. For the convenience of the reader, references to this edition will be given by chapter and line number and will be included with the actual quotations within the text of this study (e.g., line 86 of the fifty-first chapter has been noted above as 51:86). References to the Short Text will use Roman numerals for the chapter number (e.g., xxii:17). N.b., the chapter numbers from this critical edition are transferable to other editions and translations.

A. Julian and Her *Shewings*

This section will highlight those aspects of Julian's life and personality which offer us some insight into her approach to the mystery of God's mercy and compassion, the mystery so masterfully explicated in her *Shewings*. It will also offer some preliminary comments on the text itself, especially in terms of Julian's literary style and theological method.

1. Who was Julian of Norwich?

Despite the unprecedented level of interest in the theology of Julian of Norwich today, we still know very little about her life.[4] In fact, not even her name is known with certainty.[5] Our primary source of information remains the internal evidence of the *Shewings* itself.[6]

We learn from her own testimony that Julian was born sometime in late 1342. She tells us that, at the age of thirty and a half, she fell sick for three days and three nights; after receiving the last rites of the Church, she lay near death for an additional two days.[7] Just at the point when she felt that she was in fact dying, her pain was suddenly taken from her,[8] and she was given sixteen shewings of God's love; her visions

---

4 Several recent studies provide comprehensive analyses of the historical evidence regarding Julian's life: *A Book of Showings*, 33-59; Brant Pelphrey, *Love Was His Meaning, The Theology and Mysticism of Julian of Norwich*, edited by James Hogg, Elizabethan and Renaissance Studies 92:4 (Salzburg: Institut für Anglistik und Amerikanistik, 1982) 1-52; and Sheila Upjohn, *In Search of Julian of Norwich* (London: Darton, Longman and Todd, 1989) 1-36, 56-73.

5 In fact, 'Julian' may not have been her actual name; she may well have taken it from the church to which her anchorhold was attached.

6 Julian rarely alludes to herself in terms of her historical situation; those few references she does make are limited almost entirely to the circumstances of her illness: the date, the summoning of the curate to administer the last rites, the presence of her mother and some others at her bedside, the times of day when the shewings began and ended, the visit of another cleric after she had already received fifteen shewings, etc. [2:2-4; 3:2-52; 8:25-32; x:29-34; 65:37-40; 66:3-29; 70:11-13] Julian also refers to the fact that it took her fifteen years of reflection to come to an understanding of much of what she was shown [86:14-15] and that an additional five years passed before she was given to grasp the significance of the parable of the lord and the servant [51:86-87].

7 3:2-6.

8 3:5-42; 66:7-10.

took place over the course of little more than twenty-four hours, starting at about 4 a.m. on 8 May, 1373, and lasting until about sunrise the next morning.[9] Julian believed herself to be dying and wondered why such revelations were being bestowed on someone who was not going to be alive since it seemed to her as though their content ought to be shared with other christians who truly needed to know about God's love and mercy.[10] When, after the fifteenth shewing, her pain returned and she realized that she was probably not going to die,[11] Julian began to doubt her experience, attributing what she had been 'shewn' to delirium;[12] God responded to her confusion with a sixteenth revelation to confirm the reality of what she had already seen in the first fifteen shewings.[13] Julian then began what was to be almost twenty years of reflection, processing the meaning of her shewings and trying to reconcile them with what she knew to be true from her own experience and from the teachings of the Church. We have the fruit of Julian's labor in the book which reflects what she felt to be her mission: to comfort her 'even christians' by sharing with them the message of her shewings.[14]

According to the evidence of four wills, Julian became an anchoress at the Church of St. Julian in Conisford (now part of the city of Norwich) sometime before 1393 and was still alive in 1416; these facts are corroborated by the scribe who wrote the preface of the 'Amherst' MS in 1413 and by the testimony of Margery Kempe whose autobiography records a visit to Julian in her anchorhold, c. 1415.[15] Later wills suggest that Julian was no longer alive in 1423, but their evidence is not as easy to interpret.[16] At any rate, it seems likely that Julian lived into her seventies

---

9 65:37-40; 70:11. There is confusion over the date of Julian's shewings. According to the Sloane MSS, Julian had her shewings on 8 [viij] May; the Paris MS records 13 [xiij] May. It remains impossible to determine which of the two dates reflects a scribal error.
10 8:25-32.
11 66:10-15.
12 66:16-17.25-26.
13 66:16-35; 68:2-74.
14 8:22-40; cf. 9:2-5.17-19. 'Evyn christen' is Julian's term for her 'fellow christian.'
15 Other than the internal evidence of the *Shewings* and the testimony of the scribe of the 'Amherst' MS (see p. 18, below), the only external evidence of Julian's existence is found in the terms of four wills (Roger Reed, 1393/4; Thomas Edmund, 1404; John Plumpton, 1415; and Isabel Ufford, 1416) and in Margery Kempe's autobiographical account of her visit with Julian. *A Book of Showings*, 1, 33-36; and Margery Kempe, *The Book of Margery Kempe*, edited by Sanford Brown Meech and Hope Emily Allen, The Early English Text Society 212 (London: Oxford University Press, 1940), 42-43.
16 For a review of these wills, see Brant Pelphrey, *Love Was His Meaning*, 11.

and spent at least twenty of those years as a solitary in her anchorhold in Norwich. Prior to her enclosure, Julian probably had been a lay woman, although some have put forward the theory that she had been a Benedictine nun.[17] Again, we simply do not know; other than the historical information we have already reviewed, we have no way to determine specifics of Julian's personal history except by conjecture.[18]

In order to understand the context of the *Shewings*, we need to say something about Julian's world. While we know little of her particular history, we can know something of her life by the fact that she lived in tumultuous fourteenth century England. Julian's life was circumscribed by the calamitous events that besieged England during that time: the Hundred Years' War, the Black Death, the collapse of the economy, famines, the Peasants' Revolt, as well as various theological controversies that raged within the Church (e.g., Wycliffe's teachings and the Lollard movement, the Avignon papacy and Great Schism, quarrels and moral

---

17 Colledge and Walsh seem convinced that, prior to her enclosure as an anchoress, Julian had been a nun, possibly at Carrow Priory to which the advowson of St. Julian's Church belonged. Glasscoe suggests that this link does indeed connect Julian with the Benedictine tradition, but that there is no evidence to suppose that Julian herself was a Benedictine nun. Tanner notes that Margery Kempe gave the title *Dame* to Julian, but that this fact does not prove that Julian was a nun because that title was sometimes accorded to lay women as well as to nuns and, furthermore, that she was not called *Dame* or *Domina* in references to her in wills. As Tugwell points out, the fact that her mother was at her bedside seems to suggest that Julian was not a nun at the time of her shewings and that, more significantly, her theology as a whole does not reflect the elitist pretensions one might expect from members of religious orders in Julian's day. Ward completely discounts the theory that Julian was a nun on the basis of the lack of evidence in the existing records of Carrow Priory or any other nunnery and the fact that her writings never allude to any monastic practices or formation; Ward suggests instead that Julian was a young widow (and probably mother) whose husband and child(ren) had died in one of the recurring onslaughts of plague in Norwich and who was living in her own house with her servants and her mother when she received the shewings. See *A Book of Showings*, 43-45; Marion Glasscoe, ed., *Julian of Norwich, A Revelation of Love*, rev. ed., M. J. Swanton, gen. ed., Exeter Medieval English Texts and Studies (Exeter: University of Exeter, 1986) vii; Norman P. Tanner, *The Church in Late Medieval Norwich, 1370-1532*, Studies and Texts, 66 (Toronto: Pontifical Institute of Mediaeval Studies, 1984) 60; Simon Tugwell, O.P., "Julian of Norwich," in *Ways of Imperfection: An Exploration of Christian Spirituality* (London: Darton, Longman and Todd, 1984) 187-207; and Benedicta Ward, S.L.G., "Julian the Solitary," in *Julian Reconsidered*, edited by Kevin Leech and Benedicta Ward, S.L.G., Fairacres Publication No. 106 (Oxford: SLG Press, 1988) 19-29.

18 For example, we may presume some things about her life as a medieval anchoress. See Rotha Mary Clay, *The Hermits and Anchorites of England* (London: Methuen and Co., 1914).

decline among the clergy and the religious Orders, etc.).[19] In such a troubled setting, it was not easy for the ordinary christian to believe in a God who allowed disasters to beset humankind and even the Church; as we shall see, Julian herself clearly struggles throughout the *Shewings* with the question of evil and suffering.

The fact that she lived in the busy port city of Norwich, at that time a bustling hub for the international textile trade and a center for theological learning,[20] would account for Julian's obvious familiarity with the theological vocabulary of her day. The people of Norwich would have had access to the preaching of many well-educated clerics in their city. Moreover, because of their proximity to and trade relations with the Continent, they would also have been aware of some of the new theological ideas which were coming from the mystics of the Rhineland and the Low Countries during that period. Of course, none of these facts implies that Julian would have had a formal theological education, although such a possibility cannot be completely ruled out; we just simply cannot know from the scant historical evidence we do have.[21] While we cannot know with certainty what books Julian may have read or even that she read at all, we can be sure that someone with her manifest intellectual curiosity and reputation for holiness (as testified by the witness of Margery

---

19   For a good overview of this general period in England, and in Norwich in particular, see Margaret Deanesly, *The History of the Medieval Church, 590-1500* (London: Methuen and Co. Ltd., 1925) 179-238; William Abel Pantin, *The English Church in the Fourteenth Century* (Cambridge: Cambridge University Press, 1955); Brant Pelphrey, *Love Was His Meaning,* 32-51.

20   Norwich boasted of some fifty parishes, a cathedral priory, a Benedictine monastery and nunnery, several colleges of secular priests and four friaries (Dominican, Augustinian, Franciscan, Carmelite) during Julian's lifetime. Norman P. Tanner, *The Church in Late Medieval Norwich, 1370-1532,* 173-189.

21   Julian refers to herself as 'a simple creature unlettered' at the time of her shewings. [2:2] This may mean that she could not read, or more probably that she was not literate in Latin. Tugwell argues that, based on the tone of authority evident in the Long Text, Julian had certainly acquired some sort of education by the time she wrote the longer version of the *Shewings*. In their analysis of the text, Colledge and Walsh go further, concluding that Julian's intellectual formation must have included an exceptionally good grounding in Latin, in scripture, and in the liberal arts, and that she knew the writings of spiritual masters such as Augustine, Gregory, and William of St. Thierry. Ward rightly refutes the Colledge and Walsh position, pointing out that those very few direct quotations which Julian did use came either from scripture or from popular works easily accessible to the ear; she notes that, beyond those few examples of direct quotations, only parallels may be drawn with other authors. See *A Book of Showings,* 43-45; Simon Tugwell, O.P., *Ways of Imperfection,* 190; and Benedicta Ward, S.L.G., "Julian the Solitary," 25-26.

Kempe)[22] would have been aware of the current theological ideas being preached in Norwich and would have felt to some extent the influence of other mystical writers of her day, if only through her contact with confessors and her spiritual director. We might note here that, although her prayer as a young woman shows indications of typical late medieval English piety with its fundamentally affective character and its distaste for theological learning,[23] she also demonstrates her ability to move beyond the narrow scope of that piety. For example, in the early chapters of the *Shewings*, she is preoccupied with a desire to have a vision of Christ's passion and to suffer 'bodily sickness' in her own body as a way of suffering with Christ;[24] by the end of the *Shewings*, however, she offers a solid theological basis for our ontological union with Christ, both in his sufferings and in his glory.

2. Julian's visions

Julian clearly indicates that her sixteen shewings themselves are the primary basis for her reflections. The unity of Julian's experience is captured in the first chapter of the *Shewings* where we are told that she was given one single revelation of God's love in sixteen shewings,[25] and that all her shewings and insights were grounded in and followed from the first, a vision of the crucified Christ's head crowned with thorns.[26]

Just what was Julian shown? Julian had a vision of the bleeding head of the crucified Christ. As the sixteen shewings progressed, she watched as his skin 'dried,' growing darker as he approached death,[27] and then suddenly saw his face transfigured into glory.[28] Along with this 'bodily sight' of Christ, she also experienced 'ghostly sight'[29] and 'words formed

---

22 See note 15, p. 3, above.
23 Wolfgang Riehle, *The Middle English Mystics*, translated by Bernard Standring (London: Routledge & Kegan Paul, 1981) 5.
24 2:5-39.
25 1:2-3.
26 1:3-7.
27 16:3-30.
28 21:3-9.
29 These included visions of the Trinity [5:5-40; 22:7-23] and of Christ's presence in her soul [68:2-52]. In chapters 4 and 51, we find Julian making a further distinction between 'ghostly in bodily likeness' and 'more ghostly without bodily likeness.' [4:28-29; 51:5-6] For a comprehensive analysis of Julian's own classification of her shewings, see Paul Molinari, S.J., *Julian of Norwich. The Teaching of a 14th Century*

in her understanding.'[30] In addition to the intense but brief experience of her sixteen shewings, Julian was given later 'inward teachings' (inspirations) by which she gradually came to understand more clearly the content of the sixteen original shewings. These 'touchings' of the Holy Spirit came over the course of her long struggle to unravel the meaning of her visions.[31]

Some have raised the question of the authenticity of Julian's visions and their possible relationship to her illness. We have already noted that she experienced no pain during the shewings themselves and that her pain returned when the visions ceased. Colledge and Walsh point out that the physical symptoms (which Julian describes with almost clinical precision) closely resemble those of a person in severe cardiac failure, i.e., chest pains, shortness of breath, difficulty in speech, loss of vision, and finally paralysis.[32] These symptoms, together with the fact that Julian alludes to fever,[33] suggest to Pelphrey that she may have been suffering from the pneumonic plague which ravaged the city of Norwich several times during that period.[34] The suddenness with which her illness appeared in such an advanced and serious stage and the equal suddenness of her cure lead Molinari, however, to conclude that her sickness probably had a preternatural origin.[35]

The nature of the relationship between Julian's illness and her shewings has prompted much debate. Pelphrey goes so far as to speculate that Julian may have been having an after-death experience.[36] Whereas Thouless maintains that Julian's visions were actually hallucinations resulting from her weakened condition,[37] Molinari and others reject

---

English Mystic (London: Longmans, Green & Co., 1958) 32-48.

30 9:29-30; cf. 73:2-4. Julian perceived locutions sometimes as coming directly from Christ on the cross [e.g., 13:6-7; 22:2-7; 25:14-25; 26:6-18] and at other times as spiritual insights given directly to her understanding [e.g., 5:12-16; 82:18-21].

31 E.g., 51:77-78.86-89; 65:35-37; 83:2; 86:13-19.

32 *A Book of Showings*, 68-69.

33 ii:20; 67:15.

34 Brant Pelphrey, "Spirituality in Mission: Lessons from Julian of Norwich," *Cross Currents* 34 (1984) 178.

35 "[It seems] probable that her sickness was due to a temporary abnormal condition of her psycho-physical system, and not to a purely organic and permanent deficiency already affecting Julian." Paul Molinari, S.J., *Julian of Norwich*, 24-25.

36 Brant Pelphrey, "Spirituality in Mission: Lessons from Julian of Norwich," 178.

37 Thouless concludes that, following upon her illness, "her normal mental life was weakened, and the scenes of the Passion with which meditation had stored her mind welled up to the surface of consciousness and presented themselves with hallucinatory vividness." Robert Thouless, *The Lady Julian: A Psychological Study* (London: Society for Promoting Christian Knowledge, 1924) 25.

neurotic hysteria or a state of hypnotic trance as causes, both because of
the witness of her balanced character and personality, and because of the
salutary effects the shewings produced in her spiritual life and in her
doctrine.[38] Moreover, Molinari's thorough analysis of the nature of the
shewings themselves demonstrates their real correspondence to the three
standard categories of mystical experience, i.e., corporeal, imaginative,
and intellectual visions and locutions.[39] Julian's humble, self-effacing
description of her experience of her shewings and the remarkable sound-
ness of the theological insights she draws from them both suggest that
there is no real reason for us to doubt their authenticity. Rather than
focus on the question of the exact nature of Julian's shewings, this study
will probe the theological significance of her vision: she sees and understands in the crucified Christ not only the mystery of his incarnation, but
also truths about the Trinity and about the human person's union with
God. Moreover, as we shall discover, all of Julian's theological insights
flow in some manner from her vision of the crucified Christ.

3. Julian as mystic, theologian, and communicator

An early description of Julian's *Shewings* may be found in an entry in
Pierre Poiret's *Bibliotheca Mysticorum Selecta* (Amsterdam, 1708) which
reads: *Julianae, Matris Anachoretae, Revelationes de amore Dei. Anglice.
Theodidactae* ['taught by God'], *profundae, ecstaticae.*[40] In the introduction to her remarkable 1901 rendering of the text, Grace Warrack adapts

---

38 Paul Molinari, S.J., *Julian of Norwich*, 25-31. See also Paul Renaudin, *Quatre
    Mystiques Anglais* (Paris: Les Éditions du Cerf, 1945) 60; and Anna Maria Rey-
    nolds, C.P., ed., *Julian of Norwich: A Shewing of God's Love* (London: Sheed and
    Ward, 1958) li-liv.
        Pepler admits of the possibility that Julian may have been suffering from an
    acute neurosis, induced perhaps by an overly enthusiastic life of penance and
    solitude; however, he notes that this, in itself, would not be grounds for dismissing
    the authenticity of Julian's visionary experience. He further notes that, in the end,
    hysterical neurosis may be detected by the unbalanced state of the subject; Julian
    did not exhibit any signs of the kind of unbalanced hysteria that might cast doubt
    on the genuineness of her shewings. Conrad Pepler, O.P., "Visions and Shewings,"
    Life of the Spirit 3 (1948/49) 487.
39 Paul Molinari, S.J., *Julian of Norwich*, 32-48, 60-70. See also Roland Maisonneuve,
    L'univers visionnaire de Julian of Norwich (Paris: O.E.I.L., 1987) 43-61; Conrad
    Pepler, O.P., "Visions and Shewings," 486-493; and Anna Maria Reynolds, C.P., ed.,
    Julian of Norwich: A Shewing of God's Love, xlvii-l.
40 *A Book of Showings*, 14.

Poiret's succinct analysis, assigning Julian the titles *Theodidacta, Profunda, Evangelica.*[41] Chambers goes even further than Warrack by altering both the terms and their sequence to *Experiential, Evangelical, Mystical.*[42] Descriptions of Julian as a mystic who is taught by God and by her experience, as a profound thinker, and as an evangelical writer, tell us something about the content and style of the *Shewings* and, consequently, about Julian herself; together they suggest that Julian's *Shewings* are the work of a mystic, theologian, and communicator *par excellence.*

The apparent authenticity of Julian's shewings supports the choice of the title of *mystic* for Julian. Her life and teaching both seem to be the fruit of genuine mystical experience. More significant in this study is the question of her status as *theologian.* The choice of the word 'theologian' to describe Julian is, in fact, a natural one; the *Shewings* is not a book of piety but a work that presents an integrated theological vision.[43] We have already alluded to Julian's sound theological sense. In some ways, it is unfortunate that she has been recognized as a mystic and poet because it has meant that her theology has not always been taken very seriously.[44] More accurately, Julian is a christian mystic whose immediate experience of God led her to use her remarkable intellectual gifts in the service of the science we call theology; her teachings reveal her to be a competent theologian as well as a mystic.[45] Thomas Merton suggests that Julian deserves to be ranked not only as the greatest of the English mystics but also, with John Henry Newman, as the greatest English theologian.[46] Her admirable skill in dealing with complex issues causes Tugwell to charac-

---

41 Grace Warrack, ed., *Revelations of Divine Love* (London: Methuen and Co., 1901) lxxi.

42 Percy Franklin Chambers, ed., *Juliana of Norwich: An Introductory Appreciation and an Interpretive Anthology* (London: Gollancz, 1955) 75-76.

43 The *Shewings* is neither a manual on prayer nor a 'how-to' guide to the spiritual life. As Hanshell points out, Julian is not, in fact, primarily a 'spiritual' writer but a theologian, and it is precisely this fact which lays an incomparable foundation for her spirituality. Deryck Hanshell, "A Crux in the Interpretation of Dame Julian," *The Downside Review* 92 (1974) 78.

44 Critics such as Thouless and Israel have asserted that Julian has no real place among intellectually-based theologians. Martin Israel, "A Meditation on Dame Julian's Revelations of Divine Love," *Fourteenth Century English Mystics Newsletter* 6 (1980) 68; Robert H. Thouless, *The Lady Julian: A Psychological Study,* 9.

45 Edmund Colledge, O.S.A. - James Walsh, S.J. "Editing Julian of Norwich's Revelations: A Progress Report," *Mediaeval Studies* 38 (1976) 421-425; and Paul Molinari, S.J., *Julian of Norwich,* 56, 191.

46 Thomas Merton, "The English Mystics," in *Mystics and the Zen Masters* (New York: Farrar, Straus and Giroux, 1967) 140; *Seeds of Destruction* (New York: Farrar, Straus and Cudahy, 1964) 275.

terize Julian as a *speculative* theologian;[47] in any case, her doctrine extends well beyond the parameters of what is usually considered to be *mystical* theology, incorporating a clearly articulated christology as well as elements of theodicy. Moreover, we would also be justified in calling her theology *pastoral* because it addresses the real need to guide and encourage those who struggle to live the christian life.[48]

Julian's theology is grounded squarely in both realms of her experience, i.e., the mystical and the practical.[49] She is an independent thinker who is never content merely to accept life at face value. With remarkable clarity and order for one who refers to herself as 'unlettered,'[50] Julian uses her vigorous intellect and considerable analytical skills to probe the questions her experience raises, and she does so with an impressive degree of originality in thought and expression. As a result, the *Shewings* represents not so much the quasi-intuitive insight of the mystic as the finely-honed arguments of the natural philosopher who struggles to come to terms with her experience as a whole. Julian seems to understand that mystery is not so much a deterrent to human reason as it is an inexhaustible source of challenge for it; the very ineffability of her shewings actually serves to provoke her intelligence. She values the gift of human reason, seeing it as 'the highest gift we have received.'[51] With her reason, she persistently pursues new depths of understanding in regard to the truths of her faith. Her intellectual curiosity is such that she is determined not to remain in some sort of murky 'mystical darkness' if there is any possibility of enjoying more light. As to her orthodoxy,[52] she takes

---

47   Simon Tugwell, O.P. "Julian of Norwich As a Speculative Theologian," *Fourteenth Century English Mystics Newsletter* 9 (1983) 199-209.

48   Gatta presents a strong argument to support this insight. Julia Gatta, *A Pastoral Art, Spiritual Guidance in the English Mystics* (London: Darton, Longman and Todd, 1987); and "Julian of Norwich: Theodicy as a Pastoral Art," *Anglican Theological Review* 63 (1981) 173-181.

49   Eric Colledge calls Julian's *Shewings* a "singularly pure distillation of her own experiences of mystical rapture." Colledge and Walsh also note that all of her observations represent, not abstract didacticism, but the fruit of her own experience. Edmund Colledge, O.S.A. - James Walsh, S.J. "Editing Julian of Norwich's Revelations: A Progress Report," 426; and Eric Colledge, *Medieval Mystics of England* (London: John Murray, 1961) 83.

50   See note 21, p. 5, above.

51   83:10-13; cf. 80:2-8.

52   Her doctrine on the 'godly will' is viewed as heterodox by Hudleston, Koenig, and Wolters. Dom Roger Hudleston, ed., *Revelations of Divine Love* (London: Burns, Oates and Washbourne Ltd., 1927) xxxiii; Elizabeth K.J. Koenig, "Imagination in Julian of Norwich," *New Catholic World* 225 (1982) 260; and Clifton Wolters, ed., *Revelations of Divine Love* (Harmondsworth: Penguin Books, 1966) 35-38.

great pains to demonstrate her loyalty to Church doctrine, consistently referring her experience to the faith of the Church.[53] She insists that her shewings are not contradictory to but coextensive with that faith,[54] an insight that reflects her right understanding of the nature of private revelation.[55]

We may thirdly characterize Julian as a *communicator,* a woman who felt that her mission was to communicate her insights to other christians for their comfort and encouragement in their daily struggle to live the christian life.[56] Julian understood her own experience as representing the common experience of all christians.[57] She tells us that her shewings were given to her 'generally,' i.e., intended for the whole community of believers, not solely for herself.[58] Thus it was that she came to write the *Shewings,* one of the masterpieces of the early English language. Its literary beauty and unique charm attest to Julian's mastery of the art of communication, an essential skill for any evangelist.

---

53 E.g., 9:21-28; 10:47-61; 29:2-10; 32:37-55; 33:3-25; 45:13-30; 46:50; 47:5-8; 50:10-38. Pelphrey points out that heretics were burned in Norwich in Julian's day (the so-called 'Lollard's Pit' was only a mile or so away from Julian's cell), and that it is not inconceivable that Julian's protestations of loyalty may have been due in part to fear of a possible charge of Lollardy, a charge which fell on other anchoresses of her time. Brant Pelphrey, *Love Was His Meaning,* 37-38.

54 7:65-67.

55 As Molinari points out, the divine purpose in private revelations which, like Julian's, touch on points of doctrine is precisely to give the recipient a clearer understanding of the truths of faith. Paul Molinari, S.J., *Julian of Norwich,* 54.

56 Julian addresses herself to the ordinary 'even christian,' not to the theologically learned or the spiritually 'proficient.' As Tugwell points out, the two references that suggest she identifies herself with an elite audience of 'contemplatives' only appear in the earlier Short Text [iv:40-46; vi:40-52] and are conspicuous by their absence in Julian's later version. It is evident that, by the time she wrote the Long Text of the *Shewings,* Julian had dropped such pretensions and directed her attention to the ordinary christian. Simon Tugwell, O.P., *Ways of Imperfection,* 188-189; cf. Marion Glasscoe, "Means of Showing: An Approach to Reading Julian of Norwich," in *Spätmittelalterliche Geistliche Literatur in der Nationalsprache* 1, edited by James Hogg, Analecta Cartusiana 106:1 (Salzburg: Institut für Anglistik und Amerikanistik, 1983) 157. For a differing opinion, see Julia Gatta, "Julian of Norwich: Theodicy as a Pastoral Art," 174-175.

57 40:33; 41:8-9.

58 "Alle that I say of me I mene in person of alle my evyn cristen, for I am lernyd in the gostely shewying of our lord god that he meneth so." [8:32-34] Cf. 8:22-24.34-40; 27:3-6; 37:2-9; 79:3-8. Julian also uses the word 'general' in another related sense, telling us that her shewings are to be understood 'in general,' i.e., while her shewings do not exclude particularities, we cannot know about them specifically. [35:7-14; cf. 11:32.]

Julian writes little to call attention to herself and never poses as a model of sanctity to be imitated; on the contrary, her concern for the spiritual welfare of her readers even prompts her to make an example of her own failure in faith so that others might learn from her mistake.[59] In humility, what she earnestly seeks is to communicate the content of her shewings, not to win the reader's admiration.[60] Of course, she had to deal with the problem of the ineffability of her shewings. While she recognized the ultimate poverty of language to convey the content of her mystical experience, Julian nevertheless worked hard at expressing what she could, but in trust she left to God the actual task of imparting the full meaning to her readers.[61]

This brings us to the matter of Julian's considerable skill as a writer, a fact which prompted Underhill to name Julian as 'the first English Woman of Letters.'[62] While we cannot know with certainty if she was, in fact, literate or if she actually wrote the *Shewings* without the aid of an amanuensis, the text itself does give some support to that conclusion. For example, the many cross references suggest that the final version is the result of Julian's personal editing and revising of the text, a task which would have been considerably more complicated and unlikely in the event that she herself had been unable to read.[63] On the other hand, as Glasscoe points out, the rhythms and inflections of her use of language, as well as some of her examples of rhetorical control, are quite consistent with an oral tradition.[64] In any case, even if Julian produced the text of the *Shewings* by dictation, its exquisitely beautiful prose remains a remarkable testament to her skill with the English language. As Riehle notes, Julian had the ability to combine abstract thought with language and imagery derived from everyday experience, i.e., language that is concrete, concise,

---

59   66:20-35; cf. 8:28-30.
60   She sees herself as the 'lowest of those who shall be saved' [78:28-29; cf. 8:36; vi:40-52]; her humility is further evidenced by her insistence that love, not visions, is the measure of one's goodness [9:2-10].
61   26:11-18; 73:6-8.
62   Evelyn Underhill, "Medieval Mysticism," in *The Cambridge Medieval History*, Vol 7, edited by J. R. Tanner *et al* (Cambridge: University Press, 1932) 807.
63   E.g., 17:4-5; 55:30-31; 59:13-19. Although Pelphrey considers the question of Julian's literacy to be unresolvable from the evidence, he notes that her 'forward' references (i.e., references to ideas which would appear later in the text) present one of the more convincing arguments for her ability to read. Brant Pelphrey, *Love Was His Meaning*, 26-28.
64   Glasscoe notes Julian's habit of interrupting herself and the frequent compression of structure in thought sequences, suggesting that they point to an author's thinking aloud rather than polishing pre-formulated ideas. Marion Glasscoe, ed., *Julian of Norwich*, A Revelation of Love, xv-xvi.

and easily remembered.[65] Her examples, images, and observations are practical, realistic, and 'to the point.'[66] A keen observer, she demonstrates great concern for precision and accuracy. Julian's respect for her readers reveals itself in her meticulous attention to details. Her vividly realistic descriptions are not designed to evoke an emotional reaction but to present a wealth of data from which readers might be able to learn as much as possible from her experience, perhaps even something that she herself had missed.[67] Similarly, the obvious intention of her imagery is always to give the substance of faith, not to excite emotions; any emotional uplift we may experience comes from her message rather than from her descriptions. Her realism in details is matched by a pastoral realism. She understands the limitations we experience in our attempts to progress along the path of christian holiness, telling us to do what we can while we are yet unable to reach the ideals we pursue.[68] In all, Julian makes the connections between doctrine and real problems of the spiritual life, i.e., sin, discouragement, and impatience.

As a final comment on Julian's skill as a writer, we note her superb use of language and imagery to convey complex theological concepts.[69] A competent theologian and writer, Julian uses imagery as a key element in her theologizing about divine mercy and compassion. Two images in particular, her masterful allegory, the parable of the lord and the servant,

---

65 Wolfgang Riehle, *The Middle English Mystics*, 81, 88.

66 E.g., 5:2-6.9-33; 6:35-46; 7:12-30.35-45; 10:21-31; 12:3-12; 14:3-12.

67 We see this attention to detail particularly evident in Julian's careful descriptions of Christ's bleeding head [e.g., 12:3-12; 16:3-30; 17:2-49], in her analysis of the parable of the lord and the servant [e.g., 51:7-53.90-114.120-133.153-173.185-210. 299-331], and in her description of the devil [67:2-11].

68 E.g., 23:25-29; 61:4-14; 65:27-30.

69 Colledge and Walsh are convinced that Julian was a master rhetorician, citing examples of no less than forty-seven different types of rhetorical figures within the *Shewings*. In their own analyses, Homier and Stone also assess Julian's *Shewings* to be a most accomplished example of early English mystical prose. Moreover, Glasscoe and Vinje each suggest that Julian may have been writing as a 'spiritual exegete,' i.e., she may have been consciously interpreting both her experience and the images of her shewings in terms of their multi-level possibilities of meaning: literal, allegorical, and tropological, and anagogical (or mystical). See *A Book of Showings*, 47-52, 134-139, 735-748; Marion Glasscoe, "Means of Showing: An Approach to Reading Julian of Norwich," 158; Donald F. Homier, "The Function of Rhetoric in Julian of Norwich's Revelations of Divine Love," *Fourteenth Century English Mystics Newsletter* 8 (1982) 162-178; Robert Karl Stone, *Middle English Prose Style, Margery Kempe and Julian of Norwich* (The Hague: Mouton and Co., 1970) 52-156; and Patricia Mary Vinje, *An Understanding of Love According to the Anchoress Julian of Norwich*, edited by James Hogg, Elizabethan and Renaissance Studies 92:8 (Salzburg: Institut für Anglistik und Amerikanistik, 1983) 72-84.

and her image of Christ as our tender, compassionate mother, shed
significant light on the christological nature of divine mercy and compassion and reveal the centrality of Christ's incarnation to Julian's
thought. Since neither of these rich images appears in the Short Text, it
may be suggested that Julian did not come to her full understanding of
divine mercy and compassion until after she had spent many years in
prayerful, theological reflection on her experience of her shewings. These
same images, the fruit of Julian's mystical insight and her skills as a
theologian and communicator, continue to offer us much food for our
own meditation and reflection.

4. 'Take everything together . . . .'

Even a cursory reading of the *Shewings* reveals that it is not a systematic
treatise, i.e., Julian does not lead us through a step-by-step exposition of
her theology. On the contrary, the *Shewings* is much closer to being a
narrative account of Julian's experience, but one into which she inserts
many later reflections and explanations as they seem appropriate to
her.[70] We find that she tends to be somewhat repetitious, highlighting
important insights by coming back to them again and again, each time
with a different nuancing. For this reason, the scribe's colophon at the
end of the Sloane manuscripts may well provide us with the best advice
for approaching a study of Julian's *Shewings*.

---

70 As we have already noted, the Long Text reflects twenty years of prayerful reflection on the content of the shewings and, therefore, contains much material of real
theological import which the earlier, more narrative Short Text did not include.
      Maisonneuve notes that the structure itself reflects Julian's own process of
coming to understanding: "Such a texture of later cross-references to earlier
showings embodies in literary form the way in which Julian's text has undergone
a superimposition of later layers of understanding while it still depends on being
seen entire. Memory of the past visions is both maintained and modified in a
present of continuing meditation. In the way that it carries the authenticating
visions forwards [sic] within itself by cross-reference to their words and details,
striving to pierce beyond them spiritually while acknowledging the essential limits
of contemplation, Julian's text presents a state of understanding which is now a
whole complex state of mind no longer susceptible to the constraints of linear
narrative expression." Roland Maisonneuve, "The Visionary Universe of Julian of
Norwich," in *The Medieval Mystical Tradition in England*, Exeter, 1980, edited by
Marion Glasscoe (Exeter: University of Exeter, 1980) 66.

And be ware *thou* take not on thing after thy affection *and* liking *and* leve another, for that is the conditio*n* of an heretique; but take every thing with other, *and* trewly vnderstonden: all is according to holy scripture, *and* growndid in the same.[71]

While the scribe's obvious intention here is to guard Julian's orthodoxy by warning us against a selective reading of the text,[72] the admonition also recommends itself to a broader application: the complex nature of the organization of the *Shewings* requires that it be read and studied as a whole, that its insights be recognized as mutually informing. Pelphrey points out that the very shape of the *Shewings* reveals this characteristic of <u>interrelatedness</u>, demonstrating Julian's approach as <u>thematic</u> rather than deductive, her thought as 'relational' thought rather than sequential or 'compartmental' thought.[73] Maisonneuve aptly describes Julian's organizational approach in terms of the technique of musical composition, i.e., introduction of a theme, its development and nuancing, its modifications in new modes, its interpenetration of other themes, all taking place within the parameters of the harmonic structure.[74]

Given the 'relationality' of the text, we might do well to follow Maisonneuve's suggestion that we employ what Julian describes as her own methodology, based on the 'inward teaching' that invited her to examine all the elements of her vision and to consider each element both in itself and in its relationship with the whole.[75] In order to grasp the full meaning of her theological insights, we must examine carefully each individual point Julian makes, trying to see its interconnections with and interdependence on every other element she presents in the *Shewings*. As Jantzen rightly insists, even several straightforward linear readings of the text cannot take the place of patient study; a careful, non-linear approach is essential if we are to uncover the full richness of her doctrine because so many of the individual points she raises assume a prior understanding of insights and concepts she only explains elsewhere, often later, in the text.[76]

---

71 *A Book of Showings,* notes, p. 734.
72 Some aspects of Julian's thought (e.g., her understanding of the 'godly will' in chapter 53), if taken in isolation from the whole of her doctrine, could indeed suggest heterodox interpretations.
73 Brant Pelphrey, *Love Was His Meaning,* 81-84.
74 Roland Maisonneuve, *L'univers visionnaire de Julian of Norwich,* 267-271.
75 51:86-92. Roland Maisonneuve, "The Visionary Universe of Julian of Norwich," 89.
76 Grace Jantzen, *Julian of Norwich: Mystic and Theologian* (London: Society for Promoting Christian Knowledge, 1987) 89-90.

In order to 'take everything together' in regard to the *Shewings,* we must also acknowledge that Julian's thought reflects some external theological influences, most notably that of scripture. Living as she did within a culture that was steeped in biblical language and allusions, Julian absorbed both its doctrine and vocabulary; this is evidenced especially in her use of Pauline and Johannine themes throughout the *Shewings.*[77] Margery Kempe's account of her visit with Julian further attests to Julian's use and knowledge of New Testament themes.[78] Although she does not adopt a scholastic approach, the very fact that the Long Text demonstrates an increasingly doctrinal tone suggests that Julian may have had access to some of the many theologians in Norwich at that time. Recent authors (most notably, Colledge and Walsh) have theorized at great length in terms of specific influences on Julian's theology (e.g., Augustine, Anselm, Gregory, Pseudo-Dionysius, William of St. Thierry, Walter Hilton, Meister Eckhart, and others), and Julian's thought has been variously described as Franciscan, Dominican, Augustinian, Benedictine, and Carmelite.[79] Nevertheless, with the exception of a single direct non-scriptural quotation from Gregory's the *Life of St. Benedict,*[80] there is no firm evidence in the *Shewings* to indicate that Julian consciously borrowed from any specific theological writings; therefore, we must admit of the possibility that she simply drew her theology directly from the insights of the shewings, albeit against the background of the rich spiritual tradition available to her in the Church's preaching, teaching, and praxis at that time.

Two additional cautions are also in order for a right assessment of the work of this remarkable mystic, theologian, and communicator. First, one must keep in mind that Julian's intended audience is always her beloved 'even christians.'[81] What Julian has entrusted to writing is the fruit of a mystical experience, the content of which she struggles to de-

---

77 The influence of scripture on Julian will be considered in an excursus to chapter 4, p. 211-217, below.

78 Margery Kempe reports that Julian cited both Jerome and Paul and gave various examples from 'Holy Writ.' Margery Kempe, *The Book of Margery Kempe,* edited by Sanford Brown Meech and Hope Emily Allen, 42-43.

79 See *A Book of Showings,* 45, 71-197; Roland Maisonneuve, *L'univers visionnaire de Julian of Norwich,* 66-68; Brant Pelphrey, *Love Was His Meaning,* 16-17, 66-79; Sr. Anna Maria Reynolds, "Some Literary Influences in the Revelations of Julian of Norwich," *Leeds Studies in English and Kindred Languages* 7-8 (1952) 24-27.

80 "For a soul that seth the maker of all thyng, all that is made semyth fulle lytylle." [8:11-13] See Sr. Anna Maria Reynolds, "Some Literary Influences in the Revelations of Julian of Norwich," 23.

81 See note 14, p. 3, and also p. 11, above.

scribe and convey. Even though at times she herself could not understand the full implications of some aspects of what had been shown to her, Julian was given the grace to grasp God's loving plan of salvation as it applies to all christians. By her careful and consistent use of this term throughout the *Shewings*, she obviously wishes to be understood as addressing those truly repentant sinners who, like herself, are seeking to receive God's mercy; she makes it very clear that her intent and purpose is to help those christians who, because of their desire to serve the Lord, are both saddened and distressed by the awareness of their shortcomings.

Our second caution refers to the historical context of Julian's theologizing. Julian's longer version of the *Shewings* was written only after twenty years of reflection. As she pondered the content of her revelations over the course of those long years, Julian gave gradual expression to an exposition which became more elaborated and more theologically developed. Her theology, however, must always be situated within the context of the period during which the *Shewings* were written, i.e., in the late fourteenth century. At that time theology had not yet addressed and refined some issues closely linked with what Julian had perceived in her shewings. Hence, her use of some theological terms does not reflect the same precision and clarity as subsequent doctrinal developments would permit in the centuries that followed her.

These two cautions must be borne in mind throughout this study. We must not read Julian as applying her teachings on salvation indiscriminately, nor may we accurately assess her insights if we interpret them in terms of later developments in theological doctrine and vocabulary.

5. The manuscripts

As we have already noted, Julian's *Shewings* have come down to us in two versions, the Short Text and the Long Text. Scholars are in general agreement that the shorter version preceded the longer version and was probably recorded by Julian sometime soon after her experience. Julian herself tells us that the Long Text was not completed until 'twenty years save three months' after her experience of the shewings in May 1373.[82]

We have knowledge of the *Shewings* through six extant manuscripts and one early printed version, each of which represents a fairly late stage in the manuscript tradition:

---

82 51:86.

London, MS British Museum, Additional 37790 ('Amherst')
Paris, MS Bibliothèque Nationale, Fonds anglais 40
London, MS British Museum, Sloane 2499
London, MS British Museum, Sloane 3705
London, Westminster Archdiocesan Archives MS
MS St. Joseph's College, Upholland
Cressy, R. F. Serenus, Benedictine. *XVI Revelations of Divine Love, Shewed to a Devout Servant of our Lord called 'Mother Juliana' An Anchorete of Norwich: Who lived in the Dayes of King Edward the Third.* 1670, copy in Trinity College Library, Cambridge.

Sometimes given the name 'Amherst' (after its last private owner), the British Museum Additional MS 37790 is the oldest manuscript and the only full copy of the Short Text which has survived. As we have already noted, in its preface the scribe indicates that, when it was copied in 1413, Julian was 'still alive,' a 'recluse at Norwich.' In the opinion of Colledge and Walsh, the manuscript itself dates from the mid-fifteenth century.[83]

Three complete manuscripts of the Long Text have survived: the Paris MS (c. 1650); Sloane MS 2499 (c. 1650); and Sloane MS 3705 (eighteenth century).[84] Additionally, we have the early printed version of the Paris MS which was published by Cressy in 1670. The two remaining manuscripts, the Westminster and Upholland MSS, contain only extracts from the *Shewings* and date from c. 1500 and c. 1650, respectively.[85]

Colledge and Walsh have concluded that there are two manuscript traditions for the Long Text: the Paris MS (from which the Cressy edition derives, and thereby probably the Upholland MS) and the Sloane MS 2499 (from which the Sloane MS 3705 derives directly, and which shares a common ancestor with the Westminster MS).[86] The fact that the Paris MS and the Sloane MS 2499 exhibit separate characteristics suggests that they both derive from a yet different fourteenth century original;[87] however, until that lost original is recovered, it will remain impossible to tell which of the two traditions is closer to that original (although, as both Glasscoe and Reynolds note, the Sloane MS 2499 does show a greater resemblance to fourteenth century English).[88]

83 *A Book of Showings,* 1.
84 *A Book of Showings,* 6-9.
85 *A Book of Showings,* 9-10.
86 *A Book of Showings,* 25-27.
87 *A Book of Showings,* 26.
88 Marion Glasscoe, *Julian of Norwich, A Revelation of Love,* viii; Sr. Anna Maria Reynolds, "Some Literary Influences in the Revelations of Julian of Norwich," 19.

To date, the most complete edition of all the available manuscripts is the recent critical edition by Colledge and Walsh which includes both the Short Text and the Long Text;[89] unfortunately, in terms of its rendering of the Long Text, it represents not so much a true critical edition as an editing of the Paris MS with occasional emendations from the Sloane MSS. Besides the version of the Short Text in the Colledge and Walsh edition, the 'Amherst' Additional MS 37790 is also available in an edition by Beer,[90] and the Sloane MS 2499 has been published recently in the form of an excellent study text edited by Glasscoe.[91]

---

89 As previously noted, Edmund Colledge, O.S.A. - James Walsh, S.J., eds., *A Book of Showings to the Anchoress Julian of Norwich,* Studies and Texts, 35 (Toronto: Pontifical Institute of Mediaeval Studies, 1978).

90 Frances Fitzgerald Beer, ed., *Julian of Norwich's 'Revelations of Divine Love': The Shorter Version,* M. Gorlain, gen. ed., Middle English Texts 8 (Heidelberg: Carl Winter Universitätsverlag, 1978).

91 As previously noted, Marion Glasscoe, ed., *Julian of Norwich, A Revelation of Love,* rev. ed., M. J. Swanton, gen. ed., Exeter Medieval English Texts and Studies (Exeter: University of Exeter, 1986).

B. Purpose and Scope of This Study

This study has been motivated by the belief that there is no message more needed in today's world than the good news of God's mercy and compassion. All too many christians find themselves falling prey to depression, discouragement, and even despair over the evil and suffering they experience in themselves and in the world; disconsolate, they simply lose heart and give up the battle against sin and injustice. In Julian's *Shewings* we can find that good news of mercy, that message of comfort for sinners,[92] which provides us with real reason for confidence in God's love. We who receive this message of mercy hear the reassuring voice of a compassionate Christ whose fidelity calls forth our absolute trust and confidence that, indeed, 'all shall be well.'[93] Moreover, once we have experienced God's mercy, we ourselves become messengers of that same mercy by our own exercise of compassion, messengers of God's comfort to all who are oppressed by sin and suffering.

The serious reader will grasp the importance of assenting to Julian's theological argument before resting in such beautiful phrases as 'all shall be well.' One must grapple with Julian's intellectual struggle and its ramifications before taking the comfort her words offer. For this reason, this investigation will approach Julian's spirituality by addressing itself to her theological doctrine. Theology is always the basis of spirituality, i.e., one's understanding of God determines how one relates to God. This study is born from the conviction that Julian's theology offers the basis for a profoundly rich understanding of God's mercy and compassion, an understanding which can transform one's way of relating to God by giving the christian reason to live in confidence, gratitude, trust and joy, even in the midst of the pain we suffer in this world.

1. Methodology

The specific task of this present study is to make explicit the rich theology implied in Julian's use of the words *mercy* and *compassion*. This task will necessarily involve an examination of aspects of Julian's trinitarian theology, her christology and soteriology, and her anthropology, including her

---

92 34:22-23; 79:22-26.
93 27:11-14.

unique understanding of the relationship of mercy to both nature and grace. Our methodological approach will be to root our reflections in the theological implications which arise from Julian's remarkably consistent usage of six key words: *mercy, keep, save, compassion, ruth,* and *pity.* Seen within the framework of her doctrine of the *oneing*[94] of the soul to God, these six words will provide the basis for a systematic analysis of her christological vision of divine mercy and compassion.

As an internal analysis of the text, one of the major features of this study is its exhaustive references to the middle English text of the *Shewings*. By using only the middle English text, we avoid the considerable problem of editorial interpretation inherent in translations; for the convenience of those readers who may not have access to the middle English text, we shall make extensive use of quotation. Unless otherwise noted, all quotations will be taken from the Long Text of the critical edition by Colledge and Walsh, cited by chapter and line.[95] Because this longer version of the *Shewings* is the fruit of her twenty years of probing analysis and prayerful reflection on her shewings, the decision to limit our discussion primarily to Julian's Long Text represents a conscious choice to pursue her theology rather than her historical experience (which finds more immediate expression in the Short Text).

2. Outline of this study

The first three chapters of this study will present Julian's theology of divine mercy in all its facets. Chapters one and two will relate Julian's doctrine on *mercy* to her understanding of *kind* (nature) and *grace,* respectively. In these two chapters, we shall find that Julian's consistently christocentric treatment of divine mercy is situated within the context of a well-formed trinitarian theology which, although never fully delineated in strict scholastic terms, is inseparable from and necessarily implicit in all that Julian has to say about divine mercy. We shall explore various aspects of Julian's understanding of the working of divine mercy within the framework of her trinitarian doctrine of the soul's being oned to God. We shall see that Julian's christology and anthropology are based on her understanding of the oneing of the human person to God in Christ by kind, mercy, and grace, all in virtue of Christ's oneing our sensuality to our substance by his incarnation. Our analysis will demonstrate that, for

---

94 'Union' or 'uniting.'
95 See note 3, p. 1, above.

Julian, divine mercy is the event of our salvation in Christ and is the key to understanding the relationship between nature and grace: <u>nature is defined by mercy, and grace is the extension of mercy in time</u>.

Since a discussion of divine mercy necessarily includes an understanding of the nature of sin and salvation, our investigation will include a careful examination of Julian's parable of the lord and the servant, the 'answer' which was given to her in her struggle to see how God views our sin. We shall see how Julian struggled to understand the divine, eternal perspective of salvation within human categories of thought, reflected specifically in her use of the word *keeping* to denote the existential *working of mercy and grace* in time.

The understanding of divine mercy which emerges from the first two chapters will provide the basis for chapter three which will explore Julian's powerful image of Christ as our mother of mercy. Christ's motherhood of mercy will be considered from three perspectives: Christ as our mother in kind, mercy, and grace; Christ's passion as our spiritual birthing; and divine revelation as Christ's comforting word of mercy to his children.

In chapter four we shall consider Julian's understanding of compassion. Again, the christocentric nature of Julian's theology will become evident: she situates divine compassion properly in Christ by virtue of his incarnation. This fourth chapter will also examine the *wound of compassion,* i.e., the relationship between divine compassion and that human compassion which marks the life of the christian. Finally, in chapter five we shall synthesize the findings of our study in terms of their significance for the ordinary christian's spiritual life.

As a final word of introduction, we note that the mysterious parable of the lord and the servant in chapter 51 holds the key to our understanding the *Shewings,* just as it did for Julian herself. During the course of our study, we shall come to appreciate its centrality, both within her theology and within her own process of coming to understand the meaning of her shewings. We shall also find that the image of Christ as mother is best approached as the culminating insight of Julian's christology and anthropology. We shall, therefore, locate our understanding of mercy and compassion within the broad framework of the christology implied in the parable; that process will, in turn, lead us to grasp the real theological significance of Christ's compassionate motherhood of mercy.

1 Divine Mercy: God Saves Us in Christ

How does one reconcile the presence of sin and suffering within a world view which posits an all-powerful, all-loving God?[1] This paradox is Julian's basic theological dilemma, the problem with which she struggles throughout the *Shewings*. As early as chapter 11, Julian questions the meaning of sin in a world wherein all happens by the 'foreseeing wisdom' of God,[2] i.e., all that is done is done by God and must, therefore, be good.

> I saw god in a poynt,[3] that is to say in my vnderstandyng, by which syght I saw that he is in althyng. I beheld *with* avysement, seeyng and knowyng in that syght that he doth alle that is done. I merveyled in that syght *with* a softe drede, and thought: What is synne? [11:3-7][4]

Initially Julian's answer came in the form of the enigmatic revelation recorded in the most familiar and oft-quoted line from the *Shewings*:

> Synne is behouely, but alle shalle be wele, and alle shalle be wele, and alle maner of thynge shalle be wele. [27:13-14][5]

---

1 Theodicy was a particularly relevant issue in fourteenth century England. Medieval scholastic doctrine taught that God is the 'cause' of all, acting in all the acts of nature, of creatures, etc. (e.g., Thomas Aquinas, *Summa Theologiae* 1a, q.44, a.1-4; q.105, a.5). Julian lived at a time when both the Black Death and famines ravaged Europe, decimating the population. Because of the sheer magnitude of the epidemic and the speed with which it took its toll, many of the plague's victims died in despair, without benefit of the Church's sacraments. The ordinary christian of Julian's day had a difficult time relating to a God who allowed and even 'caused' such devastation and despair.

2 11:8-9.44-49.

3 For Julian, the phrase 'I saw God in a point' seems to suggest the notion of God's active presence in all created reality as its origin, its source of continued existence, and its final end. Cf. 35:15-19. Reynolds suggests that Julian's use of this expression illustrates her affinity with the thought of Pseudo-Dionysius who, in *Divine Names*, predicates existence of God and uses the image of the centre of a circle as the starting point from which all the radii are concentrated into a single unity. See Sr. Anna Maria Reynolds, C.P., "Some Literary Influences in the *Revelations* of Julian of Norwich," 24; cf. Dionysius, *Divine Names,* V (*PG* 3, 821).

4 Cf. 11:16-19.48-49.

5 The best-known borrowing of this line is found in T.S. Eliot's "Little Gidding," *Four Quartets* (New York: Harcourt, Brace and Company, 1943) 36-39.

Here we see the kernel of the mystery which occupied Julian for those twenty years of prayerful theological reflection that bore fruit in the Long Text of her *Book of Shewings*. It is in the context of this paradox that we must situate her doctrine on divine mercy, the mercy which makes 'well' all that which is 'not well' in our eyes.[6]

---

6   Julian equates all that is 'not good' with sin, i.e., with Christ's sufferings on account of our sins [27:14-18; cf. 40:41-42]. Her specific doctrine on sin will be explored more fully in chapter 2 (see p. 91-106, below).

A. Divine Mercy and Julian's Christocentric Theology of Salvation

1. The mercy of God: the ground of mercy is the Trinity

For Julian, mercy is truly a divine attribute. The word 'mercy'[7] appears 107 times in the *Shewings*, always with reference either to God[8] or, more often, to Christ;[9] not once does Julian speak of mercy in the realm of solely human relationships or activity.

Not surprisingly Julian grounds the mystery of divine mercy in the love and goodness of the Trinity.[10] For Julian, divine mercy stands in special relationship to the 'rightfulness' of the Trinity,[11] in which rightfulness all God's creatures participate.[12] By definition, what is rightful is both 'right' and 'full' (i.e., having no manner of defect), thus needing neither the working of mercy nor of grace to bring it to perfection.[13] Only when sin makes its appearance does God's goodness provide for the

---

7 Included here are such derivative forms as *merciful, mercifully,* two instances of *gramercy* (a contraction of 'grant mercy'), as well as the Latin phrase *cuius anime propicietur deus.*

8 2:18.30; 3:9.25; 38:29; 39:7; 47:6.7.12.34.35; 48:48; 49:21.33; 52:80.91; 61:33; 63:13; 67:13; 74:10; 79:7; and 86:29 (*propicietur*); Julian also refers more specifically to the mercy of the Father in the symbolism of the parable of the lord and the servant [51:123.136.139].

9 Of the 107 usages of *mercy* in the Long Text, only 25 refer explicitly to God or to the Father (see note 8, above). The other 82 instances of *mercy* have at least implicit christological reference: *mercy* appears 28 times in clear reference to Christ; 44 additional times within the christological context of 'the working of mercy and grace' (see p. 82-87, below); and 10 times in reference to 'the lorde,' which usage, given the overall context of the *Shewings*, seems to point to a christological interpretation (e.g., see note 33, p. 28, below).

10 Cf. 35:37; 47:33-35; 48:13-18.26-32; 56:29-31; 59:2-8. The theology of the *Shewings* is thoroughly (and very often explicitly) trinitarian in scope. Thus, when Julian uses the word 'God,' the Trinity is implied. E.g., see 35:26-31 (note 11, below).

11 "Ryghtfulhed is that thyng *that* is so good *that* may nott be better than it is, for god hym selfe is very ryghtfulhed, and all hys werkes be done ryghtfully, as they be ordeyned fro *without*ought begynnyng by hys hygh myght, hys hygh wysdom, hys hygh goodnesse. And ryght as he hath ordeyne(d) it to the best, ryght so he werkyth contynually, and ledyth it to the same ende." [35:26-31]

12 11:25-28.

13 11:25-48.

working of mercy,[14] to bring all that is not fully 'right' into that rightfulness proper to God's creation.

> Alle *the* soules that shalle be savyd in hevyn wi*though*t ende be made ryght-
> fulle in the sy*gh*t of god and by hys awne goodnesse, in whych ryghtfullnes we
> be endlessly kepte and marvelously aboue all creatures.
>   And marcy is a werkyng *that* comyth of the goodnes of god, and it shall
> last wurkynge as long as synne is sufferyd to pursew ryghtfulle soules. And
> whan synne hath no lenger leue to pursew, than shalle the werkyng of mercy
> cees. And than shalle alle be brought into ryghtfulnes and ther in stonde
> wi*though*t ende. . . . And thus in ryghtfulnes and in mercy he wyll be known
> and lovyd, now and wi*though*t ende. [35:33-41.43-45]

In a real sense, it is God's rightfulness that dictates mercy: all that is 'not
well' shall be made well, i.e., rightful, by the working of mercy. Mercy is
the effecting, the 'working' of God's rightfulness.

Inherent within the idea of rightfulness is the concept of God's loving
fidelity, the unchangeability of God's loving purpose.[15] God is 'ever in
the one same love' towards us.[16] The notion of God's fidelity is a crucial
component of Julian's doctrine of mercy. Indeed, God's rightfulness and
fidelity constitute our only source of security in the face of our continual
need for divine mercy on account of our sins. God's promise to make all
things 'well' stands at the basis of our hope in mercy.[17]

For Julian, God's promise of mercy also provides the source of our
joy in this life. We delight in the fact that it is God who will make all
things to be 'well,' i.e., that we are not expected to conquer sin by our
own powers.[18] In fact, we shall 'do right nought but sin' while we live
on this earth.[19] It is God alone who effects the triumph of divine rightfulness; not even our sin can hinder God's goodness from working. In
this revelation lies our hope and our greatest joy. The entire situation is
in God's hands. We do not have to depend on our own strength, nor do

---

14 Julian often uses the phrase 'the working of mercy and grace' (e.g., 11:27); for now,
    however, our discussion will be limited to the 'working' of mercy. The relationship
    of grace to mercy will be examined in chapter 2 (see p. 72-90, below).

15 "I saw fulle truly that he channgyd nevyr hys purpose in no manner of thyng, ne
    nevyr shalle wi*th*out end." [11:44-45] Cf. 49:54-55; 51:239; 79:16.

16 43:33; 46:17-18.36; 49:4-13; 61:26-27; 78:12-14; 79:16.

17 "And thus our good lorde answeryd to alle the questyons and dow*gh*tys that I myght
    make, sayeng full comfortabely; I may make alle thyng wele, and I can make alle
    thyng welle, and I shalle make alle thing wele, and I wylle make alle thyng welle:
    and thou shalt se thy selfe *that* all maner of thyng shall be welle." [31:2-6]

18 36:4-6.34-39.

19 36:4-7.39-40; 82:4-15; cf. 37:2-9; 52:57-58; 79:2-13.

we need to worry about the power of the devil whose might is 'locked in God's hand.'[20]

There is one final observation that should be made before we move to a consideration of the trinitarian theology of the *Shewings*. Directly linked to the working of mercy implied in God's making all things to be 'well' is a promise of 'sight,' i.e., knowledge. God assures us not only that 'all shall be well,' but also that we ourselves shall *see* that it is so.[21] This allusion to sight suggests the notion of union with God because perfect vision or knowledge is acquired when the soul is fully united with God. Once we have been completely *oned*[22] to God, we shall have no further need to trust God's word that all is indeed 'well'; we shall see and know it for ourselves.[23] Since union with God is the condition of possibility for full knowledge, Julian's linking of the promise of sight to the working of mercy points to the close connection between divine mercy and our being oned to God.

2. Julian's trinitarian theology

Even a cursory reading of the *Shewings* reveals the thoroughly trinitarian faith which forms the theological context within which Julian reflects.[24] Although Julian does not explicitly develop a theology of the Trinity in the *Shewings*, her choice of vocabulary and even her prose style show her dependence on the traditional trinitarian theology of the Church.[25] In

---

20 13:18; cf. 65:23. Cf. *The Ancrene Riwle*, translated by M. B. Salu (London: Burns & Oates, 1955) 102.

21 "Thou shalt se thy selfe, I vnderstond the (onyng) of alle man kynde that shalle be sauyd in to the blyssedfulle trynite." [31:10-12] Cf. 31:2-6 (note 17, p. 26, above); 36:29-30; 72:6-9.

22 As we have noted in the *Introduction*, Julian's term for 'union' is 'oneing.'

23 We shall return to the relationship between sight and union in chapter 3 (p.144-145, below); for now, it is sufficient to note that the promise of sight is clearly linked to the working of mercy.

24 The *Shewings* are punctuated by explicit trinitarian references (e.g., Julian speaks of God as 'might, wisdom, and goodness' (or 'love'), using an Augustinian trinitarian appropriation which was a commonplace in the medieval scholastic doctrine of Julian's day). See Thomas Aquinas, *Summa Theologiae* 1a, q.39, a.8.

25 Julian employs multiple trinitarian analogies: might, wisdom, love; truth, wisdom, goodness; maker, keeper, lover; fatherhood, motherhood, lordship; charity unmade, charity made, charity given; etc. Moreover, she shows a preference for classifying things in groups of three (e.g., three heavens; three 'motherhoods' in Christ; three ways of beholding the passion, etc.), often suggesting allusions to the Trinity. For

fact, it might even be argued that the Trinity is never the specific object of Julian's thought because, as Pelphrey points out, it is a basic assumption which underlies the content of every chapter of the *Shewings*.[26]

While Julian employs the language and insights of the tradition to interpret the content of her shewings, she does so within her own strongly christological framework. The christocentricity of the *Shewings* cannot be overemphasized.[27] Julian seems relatively unconcerned about probing the inner secrets of the intratrinitarian life, preferring instead to concentrate on the economic trinity, i.e., the Trinity's working of our salvation in and through Jesus Christ.[28] In so doing, she demonstrates a greater affinity with the biblical understanding of the relationship between the Father, Son and Holy Spirit than with the more abstract speculation of medieval scholasticism.[29]

Just as Julian often exploits the ambiguity of various middle English words,[30] she also retains a certain ambiguity in her language about the Trinity. For Julian, God is always 'Three-in-One';[31] she often makes identical affirmations about God and about the Trinity, interchanging the two terms.[32] One complicating factor is her lack of consistency in the use of the term 'lorde,' sometimes used for God, but more often for Christ, the 'shewer' of her revelations.[33] Much of this seemingly imprecise and

---

more detailed studies of Julian's trinitarian doctrine, see Brant Pelphrey, *Love Was His Meaning,* 102-125; J.P.H. Clark, "Nature, Grace and the Trinity in Julian of Norwich," *The Downside Review* 100 (1982) 203-220.

26   Brant Pelphrey, *Love Was His Meaning,* 103.

27   As we have noted in the *Introduction* (see p. 6-8, above), all of Julian's theological insights find their basis in the shewing of the crucified Christ. All is revealed in the shewing of Christ's passion; even sin ('our fowle blacke dede') was shown to her there in the figure of darkness [10:36-37].

28   Julian does make some references to the mutual indwelling of the three persons of the Trinity, usually in the context of God's work *ad extra,* i.e., in the human soul: 1:51; 4:11-15; 7:54-55; 51:328-331; 54:5-6; 57:19-20; 58:64; 61:39; 68:5-14; 83:22-23.

29   E.g., Julian posits the Father as ground of all being, the Son as working the will of the Father, and Holy Spirit as perfecting and confirming the Son's work in us [59:23-30].

30   E.g., she uses 'suffer' as meaning both 'to allow' and 'to experience pain' [35:20]; she predicates 'truth' both of God and of the human person, suggesting perhaps a more nuanced meaning of truth as 'faith' in reference to the human person [44:8-21].

31   "For the trinitie is god, god is the trinitie." [4:11]

32   E.g., compare 4:11-14 to 5:17-19.

33   E.g., Julian tells us that 'God brought to mynde that I shuld synne' [37:2]. A few lines later, she rephrases her statement: 'Oure lorde shewyd me that I shuld synne' [37:8]. In 78:31, she repeats that 'he shewed me *that* I shuld synne,' this time with a clear antecedent 'lorde' who is 'oure blessyd savyour' [78:24-30; cf. 78:2; 79:2-3].

even ambiguous usage actually results from one of the most fundamental insights of the *Shewings*: the location of the mystery of the trinitarian Godhead in the crucified Christ. Julian speaks with remarkable clarity on this point. Whereas other medievals such as Bernard begin with the humanity of Christ and move on, as it were, to the Godhead, Julian locates the Trinity in the cross of Christ.[34] In the very first shewing she recognizes that to look at Christ is to see the Trinity; in other words, Christ cannot be considered outside the context of his relationship to the Father and the Holy Spirit.

> The trinitie is our endlesse ioy and our bleisse, by our lord Jesu Christ, and in our lord Jesu Christ. And this was shewed in the first syght and in all, for wher Jhesu appireth the blessed trinitie is vnderstand, as to my sight. [4:13-16]

For Julian, our only access to the mystery of the Trinity is through the revelation that is Christ. The Trinity is 'comprehended' in Christ.[35]

This insight makes sense of Julian's use of parallel assertions about Christ and about the Trinity (or God). For example, in telling us that Jesus takes his place permanently in our soul, she also says that the soul in which Christ dwells is thus 'occupied' by the Godhead (sovereign might, sovereign wisdom and sovereign goodness).[36] In a similar parallelism, Julian explains that trinitarian love is our ground[37] and, elsewhere, that Christ[38] (or 'our lorde')[39] or God[40] (or, even more specifically, the Father)[41] is the ground of our being. Her parallel assertions about Christ and the Father ought to be interpreted in the light of her statement that

---

34 E.g., see Bernard of Clairvaux, Sermon 20:6-9, in *Bernard of Clairvaux: On the Song of Songs I,* translated by Kilian Walsh, O.C.S.O., Cistercian Fathers Series 4 (Kalamazoo: Cistercian Publications, Inc., 1979) 152-155.

35 57:19-20. Julian speaks not only of the fullness of trinitarian attributes in Christ [61:38-39], but of the Father and the Holy Spirit as being present in Christ [58:63-64; 83:22-23]. Cf. 1:51-54; 7:53-58; 51:328-331.

36 68:9-17; cf. 51:328-329; 55:24-29; 61:38-39. For an example of a direct parallelism between Christ and the Trinity, compare 4:13 to 77:44.

37 "Oure lyfe is alle grounded and rotyd in loue, and without loue we may nott lyve." [49:5-6] "For or that he made vs he louyd vs, and when we were made we louyd hym; and this is a lo(u)e made of the kyndly substanncyall goodnesse of the holy gost, myghty in reson of the myghte of the fader, and wyse in mynde of the wysdom of the son. And thus is mannys soule made of god, and in the same poynte knyte to god." [53:36-40]

38 28:29; 53:32; 58:43; 59:10; 63:28.

39 39:44; 42:19; 78:7.

40 49:54; 56:12-16; 59:21-23; 62:13-15.

41 58:56.

it is only in Christ that she is able to see the Father.[42] In making identical assertions about Christ and the Father, Julian seems more to emphasize the unity of Christ with the Father rather than a strict notion of trinitarian appropriation.

The christocentricity of Julian's trinitarian vision is thus the backdrop against which we must interpret all of her theology. While she may seem to be somewhat imprecise in her terminology at times, the very ambiguity of her language is an aspect of the relationality[43] of her thought, actually serving to preserve the richness of her doctrine. Although we are not yet considering the specifically and markedly christological nature of her doctrine of divine mercy, it is clear even now that, when Julian uses the phrase 'the mercy of God' or alludes to the Father's mercy in the parable of the lord and the servant,[44] that same divine mercy can never be considered apart from Christ.

3. A trinitarian appropriation of salvation

Any doctrine of divine mercy necessarily includes the notion of salvation, i.e., God's saving us from sin.[45] This aspect of Julian's theology is absolutely unambiguous. She tells us clearly who our 'savior'[46] is: Christ Jesus alone saves us.[47] Our salvation is accomplished by virtue of the 'sweet incarnation and passion of Christ';[48] we are saved by the blood of Christ.[49] For Julian, Jesus Christ *is* our salvation.[50]

---

42   "Crist shewyd me his father, in no bodely lycknesse but in his properte and in hys wurkyng. That is to sey, I saw in Crist that the father is." [22:12-14] See also note 155, p. 137, below.
43   We cannot assess any one statement of the *Shewings* in isolation from the rest of her theology (see *Introduction*, p. 14-17, above).
44   See note 8, p. 25, above.
45   Whereas we might tend to equate divine mercy with God's *forgiving* our sins, Julian's concept of mercy would be more accurately represented by the idea of God's *saving* us from sin. She refines the notion of divine forgiveness to exclude any interpretation which might imply a change of attitude on God's part. See p. 33-37, below, for Julian's understanding of wrath and forgiveness.
46   Julian gives the title of 'savior' only to Christ: 1:52; 2:13; 7:55; 10:55; 16:13; 24:18; 30:2.26; 36:48; 51:306; 52:5; 57:48.49.49; 58:27; 59:27; 61:66; 70:23; 78:25; 83:23.
47   80:14-15; cf. 22:19-20.53-55; 61:70-71.
48   51:255-256; cf. 6:26; 13:13; 51:239-240; 62:29-31.
49   12:20-31.
50   In an interesting use of a derivative form of 'salvation,' Julian tells us that Christ is 'oure salue of oure lyfe' [79:39].

The christocentricity of Julian's doctrine is evident in her treatment of the concept of the 'working' of salvation. While maintaining the unity and inseparableness of the three divine persons,[51] she stresses that our salvation is worked in and through Christ. Julian provides us with a straightforward trinitarian formula to explain this appropriation of the working of salvation to Christ: the Father *wills* and ordains the salvation of humankind from all eternity; the incarnate Son, always doing the will of the Father, *works* our salvation definitively in time and space by virtue of his passion; that same salvation is *confirmed* and perfected existentially in us by faith through the power and gift of the Holy Spirit.

> Oure hye fader, almyghty god, whych is beyng, he knowyth vs and louyd vs fro before ony time. Of whych knowyng in his full mervelous depe charyte by the forseeng endlesse councell of all the blessdyd trynyte, he woulde that the seconde person shulde become oure moder, oure brother and oure savyoure. . . . Oure fader wyllyth, oure mother [Christ] werkyth, oure good lorde the holy gost confyrmyth. [59:23-27.29-30][52]

The confirmation or perfecting, that 'gracious according'[53] of the individual soul to God through the gift of faith, is the existential completion of Christ's merciful working of our salvation; saved by Christ from the death of sin, the soul is brought by grace, i.e., the life of the Holy Spirit dwelling in the soul, into that heavenly peace and bliss to which it has been ordained by God from all eternity.[54] Thus, while the whole Trinity is involved in the work of our salvation, the actual 'working' is appropriated properly to Christ.[55]

The christocentricity of Julian's understanding of the trinitarian roles in the working of our salvation is further emphasized in the operative word 'working.' Whenever 'working' is specifically attributed to the Father or to the Holy Spirit, the content of that working always has a christological reference. Julian's single reference to the Father's 'working' reveals it to be intratrinitarian: the rewarding of the Son.[56] Similarly,

---

51 "I vnderstonde for the vnyte of the blessyd trinite, thre persons and oon truth." [31:9-10] Cf. 4:13-16 (p. 29, above); note 28, p. 28, above; note 35, p. 29, above.

52 Cf. 22:53-55; 35:29-31; 51:237-241.250-253; 80:13-18.

53 54:33-36.

54 48:2-4; 72:20-21.

55 This appropriation echoes what Julian has already said in reference to Christ's passion: "Alle the trinyte wrought in the passion of Crist, mynystryn habonndance of vertuse and plente of grace to vs by hym; but only the maydyns sonne sufferyd werof alle the blessed trynyte enjoyeth." [23:30-32]

56 "For the furst hevyn, Crist shewyd me his father, in no bodely lycknesse but in his properte and in hys wurkyng. That is to sey, I saw in Crist that the father is. The

even though Julian's few direct references to the 'working' of the Holy Spirit are *ad extra*, she identifies grace as the completion of Christ's work of mercy.[57] More often, however, she uses the phrase 'the working of mercy and grace,' once again implying a christological reference: Christ's definitive working of mercy is continued in time through grace, the gift and power of the Holy Spirit.[58]

Thus, Julian's trinitarian formula for the working of salvation (i.e., the Father ordains, the Son works, the Holy Spirit confirms) provides an important key for understanding divine mercy as proper to Christ. Christ is necessarily implied in the phrase 'the mercy of God,' not only by reason of his being our only access to God, but also because of his role within the economic Trinity: our salvation is worked in and through Jesus Christ.

---

werkyng of the father is this: that he geavyth mede to hys sonne Jh*e*su Crist." [22:12-15] Cf. 55:5-6.

Julian does refer to God's 'working' in terms of its property of rightfulness [11:24-28; 35:26-31], but without reference to the specific content of the working; moreover, even in that context, she uses a trinitarian formula which further supports a christological interpretation of 'working': "And ryght as he hath ordeyne(d) it to the best, ryght so he werkyth contynually, and ledyth it to the same ende." [35:29-31]

57 40:18; 58:68; cf. 48:32; 58:50-55; 60:59; 62:2-18. In one passage, Julian even defines the work of the Holy Spirit in terms of mercy. [48:2-6 (p. 84, below)].

58 We shall explore Julian's understanding of 'the working of mercy and grace' in chapter 2 (see p. 82-87, below).

B. Salvation: We Are Oned to God in Christ by Virtue of the Incarnation

In order to understand Julian's doctrine on the nature of divine mercy, we must explore the relationship between mercy and salvation. Having considered the trinitarian appropriation which forms the backdrop for her treatment of the working of our salvation, we are now ready to examine Julian's understanding of the nature of that salvation and to establish the role which mercy plays in its working.

1. Mercy and forgiveness: salvation from divine wrath?

Prior to her revelations, Julian had understood divine mercy as God's forgiving our sins, i.e., God's 'giving up' (the original sense of 'forgive') an attitude of wrath in our regard. In such a scenario, mercy would necessarily play a key role in our salvation: as a result of divine mercy, the sinner would be saved from the painful consequences of God's wrath.

> I behelde and merveylyd gretly what is the mercy and forgevenesse of god; for by the techyng that I had before, I vnderstode that the mercy of god shalle be forgeuenesse of hys wrath after the tyme that we haue synned. For me thought that to a soule whose menyng and desyer is to loue, that the wrath of god were harder than ony other payne. And therfore I toke that the forgevenesse of his wrath shulde be one of the pryncypall poyntes of his mercy. [47:5-12]

Since, both from the teaching of the Church and from her own experience, Julian knew herself to be blameworthy for her sins, it is no surprise that she 'marvelled' when she could find no trace of blame or wrath in God in any of her shewings.[59] On the contrary, Julian was shown nothing of divine wrath, no sight of hell or purgatory (although, as she tells us, she desired such sight as a way of learning the truth of what was taught by the Church), no divine condemnation of sinners, not even of those who had put Jesus to death.[60] This contradiction between her prior understanding of God's mercy and the content of her shewings was

---

59 50:7-15; cf. 45:22; 46:29-39; 48:7-16; 77:17. We shall consider the scriptural theme of divine wrath in chapter 4 (see p. 215-217, below).
60 33:2-5.21-23.

the source of much confusion for her.[61] In the course of the *Shewings*, Julian adjusts her earlier notion of the meaning of God's mercy in relation to our sinfulness. Whereas previously she had seen herself as blameworthy and divine mercy as God's 'giving up' a justified wrath, the content of her shewings taught her that mercy has more to do with God's unity and rightfulness, the unchangeability of God's loving purpose, than with any change of attitude on God's part.[62]

Julian tells us that God may not be wroth because wrath is a 'contrariousness' to peace and love, coming from a failing either of might, of wisdom, or of goodness.[63] In God there is no such failing, for God is sovereign might, wisdom and goodness.

> I saw verely that oure lorde was nevyr wroth nor nevyr shall. For he is god, he is good, he is truth, he is loue, he is pees; and hys myght, hys wysdom, hys charyte and his vnyte sufferyth hym nott to be wroth. For I saw truly that it is agaynst the propyrte of hys myght to be wroth, and agaynst *the* properte of hys wysdom, and agaynst the propyrte of hys goodnes. God is that goodnesse that may nott be wroth, for god is nott but goodnes. [46:29-36][64]

Thus, God may not 'forgive' (in the sense of turning from wrath) because God's unity does not allow wrath; there is no wrath in God, only unchanging love and peace.[65]

Likewise, any concept of forgiveness which might suggest that God turns away from anger in our regard is incompatible with divine immutability or, in Julian's terminology, God's unchangeability[66] because the presence of any wrath in God would imply that, in forgiving, God does indeed change from one attitude to another, i.e., from wrath to love. On the contrary, Julian insists most forcefully on God's fidelity, that God loved us 'from without beginning'[67] and that mercy is the working of that unchanging love.[68] Changeability and wrath belong to men and women, not to God.[69] Human beings are the ones who are unmighty, unwise,

61 50:15-28.
62 See p. 26, above.
63 48:7-10.
64 Cf. 13:18-23; 68:13-14.
65 49:3-15.40-45.
66 49:54-55.
67 "We haue been in *the* forsyght of god lovyd and knowyn in his endlys purpose fro *with*out begynnyng, in whych vnbegonne loue he made vs." [85:7-9] Cf. 53:26-40; 55:40-41; 59:23-24; 86:21-27.
68 48:13-18.
69 47:16; 48:6; 49:54-55.

and who fall prey to sin (that which is 'not good');[70] this sin causes in us a wrath and 'continuing contrariousness to peace and love.'[71] The human condition of changeability is a weakness at the basis of our sinning and the cause of all our tribulation and woe; the resulting wrath is on our part.[72] Seeing ourselves to be so foul and blameworthy, we think that God is wroth with us because of our sin.[73] Julian's insight allows us to see that we mistakenly attribute our wrath to God.

Julian's prior notion of mercy as a 'giving up' of God's wrath gives way to a new understanding: divine mercy works in us to 'give up' *our* wrath, not God's.[74] Consequently, divine forgiveness can only be properly understood as God's forgiving *our* wrath, our contrariness to peace and love. The peace that we experience in being forgiven comes from the removal of our own wrath, not from a cessation of any kind of divine wrath on account of our sins.

These insights shed light on Julian's doctrine that divine mercy proceeds from God's rightfulness, i.e., that all God does is rightful and that all God's works participate in that same divine rightfulness.[75] Julian concludes that, by virtue of God's rightfulness, even our sinfulness (that which is 'not well' in our sight and which is the cause of our wrath) must also somehow be 'well' in God's sight. Because sin holds no power in the face of God's loving fidelity, we find ourselves living in the midst of a paradox: what we experience as evil and blameworthy cannot controvert the rightfulness of God's creatures and is, therefore, no obstacle to God's loving us. Herein lies the mystery of the working of mercy: having no lack of might, wisdom and goodness, in rightfulness God forgives our wrath (our contrariness to peace and love) and somehow turns it to good, making 'well' all that is 'not well' and leading us into peace and love, into a participation of that same rightfulness.[76]

This dramatic shift in Julian's understanding of divine mercy and forgiveness brings her back to the heart of her dilemma: what is the meaning of sin if indeed 'all is well'? Is our wrath a mere by-product of our own sincere but faulty judgment about the nature of sin, or does God

---

70 47:16-18.
71 48:6-12.
72 76:29-30. Julian notes that when we are brought up into heaven, God shall make us unchangeable as God is. [49:54-55]
73 40:5-6.
74 "And whan I saw all thys, me behouyd nedys to grannt that *the* mercy of god and the forgyuenesse slaketh and wastyth oure wrath." [48:47-49] Cf. 49:10-13.20-22.26.31-32.
75 See p. 25-26, above.
76 1:33-40; 35:26-31.

perhaps give up our wrath by simply nullifying sin and its effects in our lives?[77] For Julian, neither of these two possibilities seems acceptable. On the one hand, if our judgment of sin as evil and ourselves as culpable (a judgment confirmed by the teaching of the Church) be mistaken, we would be forced to conclude that we may not trust our experience of reality.[78] If, on the other hand, sin and human culpability be real but somehow nullified by God, then our earthly lives would seem to have no meaning at all, i.e., our actions would have no real consequences.[79]

Julian formulates this dilemma in terms of two judgments: God's and ours (which coincides with that of the Church).[80] She seeks to reconcile God's judgment that 'all is well' with the universal human experience that there are many things in this world that are most definitely 'not well.' The questions Julian asks are ones whose answers will provide the basis for her doctrine on divine mercy: how does God see the sin which causes our wrath? how does God forgive our wrath, our contrariness to peace and love? is there some way of our viewing our sinful condition as 'well' while still allowing that sin, evil, and suffering are both quite real and truly 'not well'? In chapter 50, we find Julian's plea for understanding stated in its clearest terms:

> Goode lorde, I see the that thou arte very truth, and I know truly *that* we syn grevously all day and be moch blame wurthy; and I may neyther leue the knowyng of this sooth, nor I se nott the shewyng to vs no manner of blame. How may this be? For I knew be the comyn techyng of holy church and by my owne felyng that the blame of oure synnes contynually hangyth vppon vs, fro *the* furst man in to the tyme that we come vppe in to hevyn. Then was this my merveyle, that I saw oure lorde god shewyng to vs no more blame then if we were as clene and as holy as angelis be in hevyn. . . . For eyther me behovyd to se in god that synne were alle done awey, or els me behovyd to see in god how he seeth it, wher by I myght truly know how it longyth to me to see synne and the manner of oure blame. [50:7-15.19-21][81]

---

77 Pelphrey presents a similar analysis of Julian's dilemma in his discussion of human guilt, blameworthiness, and responsibility. Brant Pelphrey, *Love Was His Meaning*, 298-299.

78 Throughout the *Shewings* Julian insists that sin is vile, horrible, and the greatest harm. [29:8; 40:37; 63:14; 76:5.11-12; 78:3.22]

79 Tugwell offers a comprehensive analysis of the logical and metaphysical implications of Julian's perceptions. See Simon Tugwell, "Julian of Norwich As a Speculative Theologian," 199-209.

80 45:13-30.

81 For Julian, to probe this mystery of sin does not constitute a mere exercise in speculation on ontology; she seeks enlightenment in order that she might know how to deal practically with the problem of sin. [50:32-35]

God's answer to Julian's request for enlightenment takes the form of a mysterious parable of a courteous lord and his devoted servant. As we shall discover, Julian's twenty years of prayerful reflection on the meaning of this parable brought her to an understanding of divine mercy as God's 'keeping' us safe from all dangers, even from the harm we know to be sin.

2. The parable of the lord and the servant

Julian's account of the fourteenth shewing begins with the parable of the lord and the servant.[82] This parable occupies the central literary position in the *Shewings* and also stands at the heart of Julian's theological vision.

In essence, the story of the parable is that of a courteous and dignified lord and a beloved servant who stands ever ready to perform the lord's will. The lord, sitting in state, dispatches the servant on an errand. In his hurry to accomplish the lord's will, the servant falls into a ravine. He is badly bruised, unable to rise or help himself in any way, and there is no one around to help him. Frightened, the servant meekly suffers his pain, fear, and woe while, from afar, the lord watches the whole episode with a most tender regard for the servant, addressing no blame to him for the unfortunate situation. Rather, the lord sees that it was the servant's very desire to please the lord that led to the tragic fall; accordingly, the lord looks upon the servant not only with compassion and pity, but also with rejoicing because of the high honor and blissful reward he plans to give the servant in return for his suffering for the lord's sake, a reward above that which he would have given had the servant never fallen. The servant, however, unable to see the lord's loving regard, remains without comfort. His pain and distress overwhelm him to such a degree that his whole attention is focused on his own situation; he scarcely remembers his love for his lord.

While Julian easily identified elements of the story of the fall of Adam in the parable, there were other parts of the story which left her confused, aspects of the servant that did not seem to fit the historical figure of Adam.[83] For example, Julian certainly would not have attributed Adam's fall to his good will and desire to please God, nor would she have associated honor and reward from God with the consequences of

---

82 51:9-44.
83 51:67-69.100-101.

that fall.[84] Such incongruities between the parable and the story of Adam's fall puzzled Julian until she eventually realized what had not been so immediately obvious: the parable is also an account of Christ's 'fall' to earth in his incarnation. Only after many long years of reflection on the meaning of the elements of the parable did Julian come to understand the essential unity between the first and the second Adam.

> In the servant is comprehendyd the seconde person of *the* trynyte, and in the seruan*n*t is comprehendyd Adam, that is to sey all men. And therfore whan I sey the son*n*e, it menyth the godhed whych is evyn *with* the fader, and when I sey the servannt, it menyth Crystes manhode whych is ryghtfull Adam. . . . When Adam felle godes sonne fell; for the ryght onyng whych was made in hevyn, goddys sonne myght nott be seperath from Adam, for by Adam I vnderstond all*e* man. Adam fell fro lyfe to deth, in to the slade of this wrechyd worlde, and aftyr that in to hell. Goddys son fell *with* Adam in to the slade of the meydens wombe, whych was the feyerest doughter of Adam, and that for to excuse Adam from blame in hevyn and in erth; and myghtely he fechyd hym out of hell. [51:211-215.218-225]

Julian first came to see that the servant of the parable represents not simply individual Adam, but all men and women.[85] The eventual realization that the servant also represents the incarnate Son of God provided her with a key insight into the mystery of sin and, consequently, the mystery of the working of divine mercy: when God looks on Adam, God sees Christ.[86] Thus Julian comes to the rather startling conclusion that,

---

84 Julian's understanding of the sin of Adam would certainly have been shaped by the Augustinian tradition which dominated christian doctrine after the fourth century. According to Augustine, original sin involved human guilt and merited a state of wretchedness because of God's justice. See Augustine of Hippo, *Contra secundam Iuliani responsionem opus imperfectum* 1, 3 (*PL* 45, 1052); cf. *De peccatorum meritis et remissione et de baptismo parvulorum ad Marcellinum libri tres* 1, 11[13]-39[70]; 2, 28[45-46] (*PL* 44, 116-152; 178-179).

85 "The seruannt that stode before hym [the lord], I vnderstode that he was shewed for Adam, that is to sey oone man was shewed that tyme and his fallyng to make there by to be vnderstonde how god beholdyth alle manne and his fallyng. For in the syghte of god alle man is oone man, and oone man is alle man." [51:100-104] Cf. 51:254-256.

86 Pelphrey tells us that Julian "concludes that humanity is *comprehended* in the Son; when God looks upon humanity, [God] 'sees' the life of Christ." Brant Pelphrey, *Love Was His Meaning,* 166. While Julian does go beyond the Pauline christology of Christ as the second Adam, she does not *identify* Christ with Adam. Cf. 1 Cor 15:20-50. As Pelphrey notes, even though both Adam and Christ are *comprehended in* the servant of the parable, Julian's vision "does not allow simple identifications because it has been shown on two levels, mystically depicting the Son of God dwelling in mankind." *Ibid.,* 311.

when God looks on us in our fallen state (i.e., in our sinfulness), God sees Christ in his suffering, and God's response is one of pity and love, not wrath.[87]

The parable of the lord and the servant answers Julian's plea for an understanding of the divine perspective on sin at two levels. At one level, the blindness of the servant explains why we do not see God's unfailing love for us, the love that determines the divine judgment of our situation. At another level, the fact that the servant represents both Adam and Christ explains why God's judgment *is* that judgment of unfailing love: in God's sight, human sinfulness is viewed in the light of Christ's incarnation.

Before we turn our attention to the heart of Julian's insight, i.e., her understanding of the meaning of Christ's incarnation as the event of our being oned to God in Christ, we need to explore briefly the notion of the servant's blindness in the midst of his ordeal because, in a certain sense, the problem of human blindness (our inability to view things as God sees them, i.e., as they really are) is Julian's starting point.[88] As we have already seen, Julian is struggling to save both the 'lower judgment' of the Church (and of human reason) which finds sinners blameworthy and deserving of the punishment of God's wrath, and the 'higher judgment' which belongs to God's rightfulness, that divine perspective which addresses no manner of blame to us.[89] The parable leads Julian to see that, because of the fall, human judgment is a 'blind deeming.'[90] In relating the sufferings that result from the fall, she tells us that the greatest 'mischief' is the fact that we are prevented from seeing our true situation: sin blinds our reason and deprives us of the comforting sight of God's unfailing love for us.[91] Moreover, like the servant, we are not only blinded to the fact that God still looks on us with love, but we even fail to see our

---

87 This same insight is found in the Church's liturgical prayer: "Father, . . . you sent [your Son] as one like ourselves, though free from sin, that you might see and love in us what you see and love in Christ." Preface VII for Sundays of Ordinary Time, *Roman Missal.*

88 We shall examine this idea of *blindness* in greater depth within the context of Julian's understanding of divine revelation (see p. 145-149, below).

89 45:13-30; cf. 11:36-40.

90 11:35.

91 "And anon he fallyth in a slade, and takyth ful grett sorow; and than he gronyth and monyth and wallowyth and wryeth, but he may nott ryse nor helpe hym selfe by no manner of weye. And of all this the most myschefe that I saw hym in was feylyng of comfort, for he culde nott turne his face to loke vppe on his lovyng lorde, whych was to hym full nere, and in whom is full comfort." [51:15-20] Cf. 52:13-16.

own deepest truth, i.e., our profound and continuing orientation to full union with God.

> This man was hurte in his myghte and made fulle febyll, and he was stonyd in his vnderstandyng, for he was turnyd fro the beholdyng of his lorde, but his wylle was kepte in gods syght. For his wylle I saw oure lorde commende and aproue, but hym selfe was lettyd and blyndyd of the knowyng of this wyll. And this is to hym grett sorow and grevous dysses, for neyther he seeth clerly his lovyng lorde whych is to hym full meke and mylde, nor he seeth truly what hym selfe is in the syght of his louyng lord. [51:104-111][92]

The servant's will (his deepest truth, i.e., his love for his lord, his total *being for* his lord) was 'kept,' preserved in the lord's sight in spite of the fact that the servant himself was so taken up in his problems that he barely remembered his love for the lord. Indeed, in his pain and suffering, the servant was only able to see the hopelessness of his immediate situation. However, this wrath, this contrariness to peace, was only on the servant's part; the lord addressed no blame to the servant, only pity and love.

Admittedly, the notion of our blindness does provide an answer to Julian's plea to know how God views our sin. It would seem that we are simply blinded to the reality of God's unfailing love, a love which cannot be broken by our sin. The tragic flaw in the human perspective, reflected in the experience of the servant of the parable, is our concentration on our experience of falling rather than on God's love. God's judgment on our sinning is grounded, not in our logic of failure and punishment, but in the truth of God's endless, faithful, unchangeable love. However, the fact that sin causes a blindness on our part does not really resolve Julian's basic dilemma, i.e., what is the meaning of sin if indeed 'all is well'? We are brought back to the fact that the divine perspective or judgment makes sense to us only when we view the servant as Christ, the beloved Son, the one whose 'falling' is the perfect fulfilling of the Father's will. We can see that the will of the Son was ever 'kept' as Christ learned obedience through suffering,[93] that the bond of loving communion between the Father and the Son was never broken, not even in the darkest moment of the cross when Christ experienced the ultimate human suffering caused by sin, feeling himself to be totally abandoned by God, deprived of the awareness of the loving presence of his Father.[94] When we

---

92 Cf. 51:25-27.
93 Heb 5:8-9.
94 Mark 15:33-34. Julian also uses the imagery of darkness and night to speak of sin as the cause of our pain and our blindness. [52:13-16; 83:18]

try to apply this judgment to our own situation, however, we find that we still cannot understand how our will is 'kept in God's sight' when we experience ourselves as sinful and blameworthy.

Thus we are still left with the fundamental question in regard to the divine judgment: *why* does God see Christ when God looks at us in our sinfulness? In other words, what so unites us with Christ that God looks at us sinners with that love reserved for the beloved Son? The answer to this question lies in Julian's understanding of Christ's incarnation and forms the heart of her doctrine of the working of divine mercy.

3. Christ's incarnation, the event of our salvation: our oneing in Christ

As we have already seen, Julian appropriates the working of our salvation to Christ.[95] In the parable of the lord and the servant she specifically links our being saved to the mystery of Christ's incarnation. As she so clearly tells us, Christ 'would be man to save man.'[96] For Julian, it is the 'fall' of Christ, his becoming incarnate,[97] that somehow makes sense of God's response to our human sinfulness, our 'falling.' The mercy of God, that God who addresses no blame to us but brings us to a reward of joy and endless bliss, can only be properly understood in the light of the Christ event, i.e., the event of our salvation.

One of the distinctive marks of Julian's theology is her ability to think beyond the restrictions of time and space. Whereas we normally speak about our salvation in terms of a temporal sequence of historical events (i.e., the creation, the fall of Adam, and finally our redemption through the incarnation, life, death and resurrection of God's own Son), she seems to grasp the unity, indeed timelessness, of the deed by which our salvation is wrought. For Julian, the accomplishing of our salvation is a single event which was realized in the totality of the life, death, and resurrection of Jesus of Nazareth. She tells us, for example, that Christ's dying for us lasted from his incarnation until he was raised to glory.[98] Moreover, she accents a certain timelessness of the Christ event from the divine perspective. Stressing that we were known and loved 'from without

---

95 See p. 30-32, above.

96 51:239-240.

97 51:222-223.242-243.

98 "He dyed in our manhede, begynnyng at the swete incarnation, and lastyng to the blessyd vprysyng on Ester morow. So long duryd the cost and the charge abowt our redempcion in deed." [23:21-23]

beginning' in Christ who is our ground and head,[99] Julian echoes the Pauline doctrine of predestination in Christ.[100] As Pelphrey aptly remarks, the parable of the lord and the servant serves to highlight the fact that there is no 'pre-salvation' history for God who always views Adam in terms of the humanity of Christ.[101]

The mystery of Christ's incarnation holds the real key to the soteriology of the *Shewings*. Julian understands Christ's passion as the central and definitive moment in his working of our salvation.[102] Her insistence that our salvation takes place 'by virtue of Christ's passion'[103] does not contradict her basic theological premise that we are saved by Christ's taking on flesh;[104] rather, Julian sees the incarnation of the Son of God as an historical event which only truly reaches its definitive moment in time on the cross, when Christ took on the whole of what it means to be human.

Before we examine the nature of the working of our salvation in Christ's incarnation and its meaning within Julian's doctrine of divine mercy, we need to establish what Julian means by 'salvation.' It is clear from many parallel statements in the *Shewings* that she equates salvation with full union with God. She uses the terms 'salvation,' 'oneing,' and 'blessydfulle chere'[105] equivalently in relationship to the true peace and joy which will be found only in heaven.[106] We are *saved* when we are completely oned to God in 'homely'[107] love, the union identified with the bliss of heaven.[108] Only complete union with God brings us to the full sight of God's blessydfulle chere, i.e., the blissful vision of God's face.[109] While we are able to know something of God's blissful chere here on earth by grace, only in heaven do we come to that intimate, face-to-face vision and knowledge of the 'glorious chere of the Godhead' which necessarily brings us that perfect joy which we equate with the bliss of heaven.[110] For Julian, the beatitude which we shall enjoy in heaven

99 53:26-40.51-56; cf. 45:40-42; 58:2-6; 59:23-27; 63:28-30; 85:6-9.
100 See Eph 1:3-12; cf. Col 1:13-20.
101 Brant Pelphrey, *Love Was His Meaning*, 99.
102 See chapter 3 (p. 124-126, below) for a discussion of the centrality of the passion of Christ within Julian's doctrine of divine mercy.
103 E.g., 13:6-10; cf. 68:60-65.
104 More precisely, we are saved by Christ's taking on 'sensuality.' See p. 44-46, below.
105 'Chere' may be translated as *face, mien, demeanor, manner,* etc.
106 Cf. 5:19-21; 14:7-12; 49:29-30.
107 'Intimate' or 'familiar.'
108 "For till I am substantially vnyted to him [God] I may never haue full reste ne verie blisse." [5:19-20]
109 43:49-56; 72:6-9; see also p. 144, below.
110 14:11-12; 43:53-54; 47:30-31; 56:49-51; 71:30-32.36-38; 72:6-13.29-31.40-50.

is not some kind of resultant by-product added to us following upon union; rather, oned to God, we enter into God's own 'blessydfulness,' God's own joy. The fullness of heavenly bliss is God's very 'homeliness' with us, i.e., the relationship of intimate love that *is* union.[111]

The fact that Julian defines salvation in terms of an intimate, interpersonal[112] relationship of union sheds further light on her teaching that there is no wrath in God. When we are oned to God, our relationship to God is that of friendship and loving communion, not separation or wrath. Ultimately, this is the reason why God may not be wroth with us: when God, who is 'ever in one love' (i.e., never changing in love), establishes a relationship of love towards us, that divine love cannot be contraried by wrath.[113]

> And therfor to the soule that . . . seeth so ferforth of the hye marvelous goodnesse of god, that we be endlesly onyd to hym in loue, it is the most vnpossible that may be that god shulde be wrath, for wrath and frenschyppe be two contrariese; for he that wastyth and dystroyeth oure wrath and makyth vs meke and mylde, it behovyth vs nedys to beleue that he be evyr in one loue, meke and mylde, whych is contrary to wrath. For I saw full truly that where oure lorde aperyth, pees is takyn and wrath hath no stede. [49:6-14]

If we are oned to God in homely love, nought can come between us and God;[114] divine wrath is impossible — and we are saved from our sins.

We are now ready to look at Julian's doctrine of the Incarnation as the event of our salvation, i.e., the definitive event of humanity's being oned to God. It is Christ's becoming incarnate that establishes our relationship of oneness with God. We are oned to God in Christ. By his incarnation, Christ joins humanity to God definitively and irrevocably.

Julian's theology of incarnation employs the vocabulary of her day, but she defines terms in her own way. She speaks of the human person as being composed of 'substance' and 'sensuality.'[115] Our *substance* is our

---

111 7:52-56.
112 Julian indicates the interpersonal character of the union by describing it in terms of *homeliness, courtesy,* and *face to face* vision. [7:52-56; 43:53-54]
113 Moreover, as Julian points out, were God to be wroth with us, even for a moment, we would cease to be. [49:14-16]
114 "Oure soule is onyd to hym, vnchanngeable goodnesse. And betwen god and oure soule is neyther wrath nor forgevenesse in hys syght. For oure soule is so fulsomly onyd to god of hys owne goodnesse that betwene god and oure soule may be ryght nought." [46:36-39] Cf. 53:47-49; 54:2-8.
115 Julian's complete doctrine on substance and sensuality can be found within chapters 53-59 of the *Shewings*. See Brant Pelphrey, *Love Was His Meaning*, 89-91, for an analysis of Julian's use of these terms as it compares with that of other medieval theologians such as Thomas Aquinas, Walter Hilton, the author of the *Cloud of*

created nature as rooted in God who is the ground of our being, i.e., Being itself. Our substance is in God, indefectible, unchangeable, outside the limitations of space and time.[116] According to Pelphrey's analysis, by 'substance' Julian means the being of something in its nature (i.e., as God intends it), that which it is in God's eyes, regardless of how it may actually appear to us. While not unlike our understanding of 'essence,' this 'being as it is in God's eyes' must not be confused with the philosophical concept of an immaterial essential idea; the *truth* of a thing must also somehow include its material being.[117] In the case of humanity, substance is not the immaterial soul, but rather the truth of our being as whole persons, body and soul — who we are in God's plan. For Julian, the substance of humanity can only be truly identified in the fulfilled human nature of Christ who is himself the perfection of humanity, at once proceeding from God and perfectly united to God in all his being. *Sensuality,* on the other hand, is that which constitutes our separateness from our Creator — our individual consciousness, our physicality, our life as it is lived in terms of bodily existence here on this earth, our way of experiencing our substance;[118] as such, sensuality accounts for our changeability, our failing, our sin.[119]

Sensuality and *substance* ought not to be interpreted in terms of a body/soul dualism. Speaking of substance and sensuality as our 'higher' and 'lower' parts, Julian teaches that both may rightly be called our *soul.*

> God is more nerer to vs than oure owne soule, for he is grounde in whome oure soule standyth, and he is mene that kepyth *the* substannce and the sensualyte to geder, so that it shall nevyr departe. For oure soule syttyth in

---

Unknowing, and Duns Scotus.

116 While it could appear that Julian is approaching a pantheism in her doctrine on substance, she actually makes an important distinction between our substance and God: "And I sawe no dyfference betwen god and oure substance, but as it were all god; and yett my vnderstandyng toke that oure substance is a creature in god." [54:17-20] Cf. 45:2-3. Likewise, while our substance (our human nature) has its existence in the timelessness of God's purpose, one may not interpret the creation of humanity to be an eternal creation, coexistent with the Godhead; rather, it is God's loving purpose which gives our substance an eternal reference. Our individual creation, on the other hand, retains its temporal reference in Julian's theology. See p. 48-51, below.

117 Brant Pelphrey, *Love Was His Meaning,* 90.

118 Our 'separateness' in our sensuality is not to be confused with our creatureliness. Sensuality does not represent the only difference between humanity and divinity. While our substance is *in God,* it does not share the divine nature but is rather a *creature in God.* [54:17-20] God remains wholly Other than all created reality. See note 116, above.

119 45:4; 48:6; 57:8-9.

god in very rest, and oure soule stondyth in god in suer strenght, and oure soule is kyndely rotyd in god in endlesse loue. . . . And as ane*mptis* oure substannce it may ryghtly be callyd oure soule, and ane*mptis* oure sensualite it may ryghtly be callyd our soule, and that is by the onyng that it hath in god. [56:11-16.20-22][120]

Our soul has a higher *substantial* part (or 'godly will'), which has been oned to God 'from without beginning' when God willed to create it;[121] and our soul has a lower part, the *sensual soul* (the spiritual reality of our particular, bodily existence) in which God dwells from the moment that the soul becomes incarnated.[122] Substance may not be identified with the soul, nor sensuality with the body. (While it is true that sensuality cannot be identified with the body, there cannot be any sensuality without the body; our being made sensual consists precisely in the union of the body with the soul.)[123]

In Christ's incarnation, our sensuality is oned to our substance by virtue of his passion, i.e., his assuming the full consequences of the condition of human sensuality.[124] Taking on the fullness of sensuality, Christ becomes the coincidence of opposites, the impossible possibility, i.e., the oneing of divinity to humanity, of God to God-separateness. In his own person, Christ unites sensuality (that part of the human structure which constitutes our separateness from God but which, therefore, allows for the possibility of *separatedness,* i.e., sin) to substance (the truth of our being which is never separated from God). Christ accomplishes this oneing without sin[125] and, in so doing, defines humanity in its perfection.[126] Julian is careful to make the distinction that, for Christ, substance (the truth of his being always one with the Father) is that of incarnated divinity itself, while our substance is not God, but a creature in God.[127] This distinction, however, does not alter her conclusion that humanity is defined as the perfect oneing of sensuality to substance. It is true that we are not 'at one' with God in the same way as Christ is (i.e., we are not the only-begotten Son, equal with the Father); nonetheless, our substance

---

120 When speaking of the soul of Christ, Julian describes the same 'higher' and 'lower' parts as forming but one soul. [55:44-52]
121 53:11-50; cf. 58:2-11.
122 55:22-29; cf. 57:28.43.
123 55:16-17.
124 As we have already noted, the passion of Christ is the definitive moment of his incarnation (see p. 42, above).
125 10:56-58.
126 For Julian, Christ is 'perfect man' by reason of this oneing. [57:41-46; 58:56-58] See also note 173, p. 55, below.
127 54:17-20 (note 116, p. 44, above).

is a creature in God, eternally oned to God, and the fullness of our humanity is only truly realized when our sensuality is fully integrated with that deepest truth of who we are in God's eyes.

Having seen that the incarnation of Christ is the definitive event of humanity's *at-one-ment*[128] with God, Julian is once again faced with the challenge of accounting for our existential experience of not yet being 'together with' or fully oned to God, i.e., our experience of sin. She finds herself confronting the paradox of salvation as having been already accomplished in Christ, but not yet fully realized in us—the 'already' and the 'not yet' of our salvation. We must explore further her teaching on substance and sensuality before we may proceed to a consideration of how this oneing to God in Christ, while taking place once for all in Christ's incarnation, is accomplished in each of us existentially by grace.

4. Our two makings: our substance and sensuality mirror Christ

In the context of Julian's doctrine on salvation, oneing must be understood to have three distinct but inseparable facets or moments,[129] each of

---

128 Within the context of Julian's theological perspective, 'atonement' (although Julian herself never actually uses the word) might be considered a most appropriate way of speaking about Julian's understanding of the salvation wrought by Christ in his incarnation. The incarnation of the Son of God is the saving deed of atonement, not in an Anselmian sense of 'satisfaction' made to God for the sin of Adam, but in the more original sense of that word as 'at-one-ment,' the act of bringing together that which had been apart. In Christ, what was separate is oned. In comparing the various meanings of 'atonement' to Julian's theology of oneing, however, Pelphrey points out that the word itself carries such numerous interpretations that any equivalence between 'atonement' and Julian's 'oneing' must be approached cautiously. For example, we must be careful not to impose upon Julian's theology any sense of 'again' in connection with oneing (or at-one-ment). Whereas our usual sense of 'atonement' is that of healing a breach, in middle English it is not essential to the meaning of 'oneing' that what is brought together is necessarily being reunited. Julian's doctrine of oneing does not imply any notion of reconciliation, repentance, amends-making, or forgiveness (the more psychological aspects of our own experiences of being brought together again after an offense which caused a separation); rather, Julian emphasizes the *being together*, the relationship of loving communion. Within this understanding, at-one-ment could be considered both as an event (of coming together) and as a state (of being together). Brant Pelphrey, *Love Was His Meaning*, 132-137.

129 Pelphrey describes kind, mercy, and grace as three 'ways' in which the reflection of trinitarian love into humanity takes place, three 'stages' in the development of humanity into God. *Ibid.*, 130-131.

which is necessary for salvation: (a) **kind**:[130] our *first making*, the creation of our substance in God in Christ; (b) **mercy**: our *again-making* or second creation in Christ — the incarnation of the Son of God; and (c) **grace**: our existential perfecting — our *according* or conforming to Christ's life within us. In kind, our capacity and desire for God are established; in mercy, that potential which *is* human nature is fully actualized in Christ; in grace, this same actualization is realized in us — our longing is fulfilled. Thus, we are oned to God in love by our very nature as *capax dei*, by the actual union of humanity with divinity in the person of Jesus Christ, and by the work of the Holy Spirit in our souls, enabling us to respond in love to God.

> In oure fader almyghty we haue oure kepyng and oure blesse, and a nemptys oure kyndely substannce whych is to vs by oure makyng fro *with*out begynnyng; and in the seconde person in wytt and wysdom we haue oure k(e)pyng, and anemptys oure sensuallyte, oure restoryng and oure savyng, for he is oure moder, broder and savyoure; and in oure good lorde the holy gost we haue oure rewardyng and oure yeldyng for oure lyvyng and oure traveyle, and endlessly ovyrpassyng alle that we desyer in his mervelous curtesy of his hye plentuous grace. For alle oure lyfe is in thre: in the furst (we haue) oure beyyng, and in the seconde we haue oure encresyng, and in the thyrde we haue oure fulfyllyng. The furst is kynde, the seconde is mercy, the thyrde is grace. [58:22-33][131]

All our life is in these three; we cannot be saved (i.e., fully oned) without all three — kind, mercy, and grace.[132]

As we shall discover, while Julian speaks in trinitarian terms (kind, mercy, and grace as expressions of the involvement of the Father, the Son, and the Holy Spirit in the working of our salvation), she also preserves the christocentric focus of her doctrine on oneing by giving both nature (i.e., kind) and grace a strong christological reference, highlighting the centrality of mercy within her understanding of salvation. We shall now focus on kind and mercy, our two 'makings,' the first two moments of our at-one-ment in Christ.[133]

---

130 In middle English, 'kind' means *nature* or, more specifically, *human nature*. In its adjectival form, it means *human* or *natural*. Hence, to be 'kind' is to be properly human, i.e., loving, sympathetic, gracious; conversely, to be 'unkind' is to be inhuman or unnatural, i.e., to fail to be true to one's nature. Julian uses the word in all of the above senses.

131 Cf. 55:21-23.35-38; 56:39-46.51-56; 57:8-16.38-40; 58:56-59; 59:21-35.

132 56:53-56.

133 The third moment, our oneing by grace, will be considered in chapter 2 (see p. 68-90, below).

a. Kind: our first oneing in the Trinity

Julian is perfectly in line with the standard christian doctrine that we are made in the image and likeness of God.

> And thus was my vnderstandyng led of god to se in hym and to wytt, to vnderstonde and to know that oure soule is a made trynyte lyke to the vnmade blessyd trynyte, knowyn and lovyd fro with out begynnyng, and in the makyng onyd to the maker. [55:39-42][134]

We were loved before we were made ('from without beginning') in the rightfulness of God's endless purpose.[135] Our substance ('kind made') is rightfully oned to God, its maker ('substantial kind unmade'), who 'keeps' it whole and safe in endless love.[136] This 'being in God's loving purpose' constitutes our first making, our substantial oneing to God.

> For that ech kynde that hevyn shall be fulfyllyd with behovyd nedys of goddys rygh(t)fulnes so to be knytt and onyd in hym that there in were kepte a substannce whych myght nevyr nor shulde be partyd from hym, and that thorow hys awne good wyll in his endlesse forse(ing) purpose. [53:18-22]

Since our first oneing takes place in God's eternal purpose, our substance is indefectible, resting unalterably in God's unchangeable love;[137] our substance is in God.[138] This first oneing in God determines the very nature of humanity: our kind is to be a capacity for at-one-ness with God, which capacity never changes because it belongs to God's rightfulness, God's loving purpose. (This is the fundamental sense in which Julian speaks of the 'godly will' which, in all who are destined to be saved, is never separated from God.)[139] In our first making, God 'knit us

---

134 Cf. 10:47-49.53-54. Julian echoes standard post-Augustinian doctrine, applying various trinitarian analogues to the soul: might, wisdom, love [53:37-40]; truth, wisdom, love [44:8-21]; and (specifically in virtue of our first making) reason, mind, love [53:37-40; 55:14-16; 56:51-53].

135 "For I saw that god began nevyr to loue mankynde: for ryghte the same that mankynd shall be in endlesse blesse, fulfyllyng the joy of god as anemptis his werkys, ryghte so the same mankynd hath be in the forsyghte of god knowen and lovyd fro without begynnyng in his ryghtfull entent." [53:26-30] Cf. 58:2-3; 86:24-27.

136 53:46-49; cf. 45:2-3.40-42; 53:17-18; 59:40-42.

137 As we saw in 53:26-30 (note 135, above), Julian identifies God's eternal purpose with God's unchangeable love. Cf. 86:20-27. N.b., Julian posits our substance in God in terms of the divine loving purpose rather than as a 'divine idea' within some system of essential idealism. See p. 44, above.

138 45:40-42; 54:9-20; 55:8-9.16-18.23-24; 57:59; cf. 56:3-6.

139 53:11-22; cf. 38:17-20.

and oned us [to God], by which oneing we be kept as clean and as noble as we were made.'[140] In God's sight (i.e., in our substance), humanity is created rightful, in which rightfulness we are endlessly 'kept.'[141] Although we do not perceive this substantial oneing in ourselves, it is how God sees us, i.e., in the divine perspective we are oned to God in mutual love from the first moment of our existence, however obscured our love for God may be in our own eyes.

> For or[142] that he made vs he louyd vs, and when we were made we louyd hym; and this is a lo(u)e made of the kyndly substanncyall goodness of the holy gost, myghty in reson of the myghte of the fader, and wyse in mynde of the wysdom of the son. And thus is mannys soule made of god, and in the same poynte knyte to god. [53:36-40][143]

While Julian tells us that our 'kindly substance' belongs to us by this first making by our 'father almighty,' the Creator whose love endlessly preserves our kind (our capacity to be one with God),[144] she gives this first oneing a strong christological reference. We rest in the love of God our maker in our first making—but in Christ, in whom humanity has dwelt eternally in the Trinity. Because the Second Person of the Trinity accepted to become human *ab aeterno*,[145] the mutuality of love between God and humanity which that acceptance accomplishes must be under- stood as outside the limits of time; therefore, the loving response of the human element of the hypostatic union must be understood as somehow present in the eternal intratrinitarian love in the person of the Son, even while not realized in time until the actual coming of the historical person of Jesus Christ. It is Julian's genius not only to find the Trinity present in humanity (in the person of Jesus of Nazareth) but also to discover the presence of humanity in the Trinity (in the person of God's eternal Son).[146] Christ *is* our true nature, defining in himself the substance of

---

140 58:6-8; cf. 57:17-18.
141 35:33-36.
142 'Before.'
143 Cf. 86:24-26.
144 58:22-24 (p. 47, above). Elsewhere, Julian tells us that our substance is whole in each person of the Trinity. [58:59-63]
145 "And by the endlesse entent and assent and the full acorde of all the trynyte, *the* myd person wolde be grounde and hed of this feyer kynde out of whome we be all come, in whom we be alle enclosyd, in to whom we shall all goo, in hym fyndyng oure full hevyn in everylastyng joy by the forseyeng purpose of alle the blessyd trynyte fro *without* begynnyng." [53:30-35] Cf. 51:234-241.
146 See Brant Pelphrey, *Love Was His Meaning,* 129.

perfect humanity, humanity as God intends it. The substance of our
humanity finds its place in the Trinity, 'treasured in God' *in Christ*.

> And right the same *that* we shulde be so end, the same we ware tresured in
> god and hyd, knowen and lovyd fro wi*though*t begynnyng. Wherfore he wyll
> we wytt *that th*e nobelest thyng that evyr he made is mankynde, and the
> fulleste substannce[147] and the hyest vertu is *the* blessyd soule of Crist. And
> ferthermore he wyll we wytt that this deerwurthy soule was preciously knytt
> to hym in the makyng, whych knott is so suttell and so myghty that it is onyd
> in to god. In whych onyng it is made endlesly holy. Farthermore he wyll we
> wytt that all the soulys *that* shalle be savyd in hevyn *with* out ende be knytt in
> this knott, and onyd in this oony*ng*, and made holy in this holynesse. [53:54-
> 64]

We dwell in God, *in the soul of Christ*:

> Ande for the grete endlesse loue that god hath to alle mankynde, he
> makyth no depertyng in loue betwen the blessyd soule of Crist and the lest
> soule that shall be savyd. For it is full esy to beleue and truste that the
> dwellyng of the blessyd soule of Crist is full hygh in *the* glorious godhede; and
> truly as I vnderstode in oure lordes menyng, where the blessyd soule of Crist
> is, there is the substance of alle the soules that shall be savyd by Crist. [54:2-8]

This is the 'rightful oneing accomplished in heaven' by which God's Son
may not be separated from all who share humanity with him.[148] Our

---

147 Julian's use of the word 'substance' here (in reference to Christ's soul) is a bit
     misleading. She is not identifying Christ's immaterial human soul with *substance*
     as we have defined it; rather, it would seem that she is simply using 'substance'
     here in a broad, non-technical sense as meaning the created spiritual reality of the
     human element of the hypostatic union. As we have already seen, for Julian, the
     human *soul* is a spiritual reality with two parts: our 'substantial' soul, the truth of
     our being always oned to God in God's loving purpose; and our 'sensual' soul, that
     which we are in our sensuality, the spiritual reality which comes into being only
     when we assume flesh (see p. 44-45, above). Thus, the 'soul of Christ' would
     include his substance (the truth of his being with the Father as the eternal Son
     incarnated), but would also include the spiritual (non-material) reality of his
     incarnated existence, i.e., his sensual soul: "And these two pertyes were in Crist,
     the heyer and *the* lower, whych is but one soule. The hyer perty was evyr in pees
     wi*th* god in full joy and blysse. The lower perty, whych is sensualyte, sufferyd for
     the saluacion of mankynd." [55:49-53] Perfectly oneing sensuality to substance,
     Christ is the ground of our human soul. [56:11-25; cf. 28:29; 53:30-34 (note 145, p.
     49, above); 63:28-30.]
148 51:219-221; cf. 51:301-302; 53:18-22. We are so oned to God in Christ that nothing
     can come between God and our soul. [46:38-39; 53:47-49; 54:2-8]

kindly substance is beclosed in Jesus, with the blessed soul of Christ sitting in rest in the Godhead.[149]

Thus, Julian can say that we were made 'all at once' in Christ.

> God the blyssydfull trynyte, whych is evyr lastyng beyng, ryght as he is end-lesse fro *with*out begynnyng, ryghte so it was in his purpose endlesse to make mankynde, whych feyer kynd furst was dyght to his owne son, the second person; and when he woulde, by fulle accorde of alle the trynyte he made vs alle at onys. [58:2-6][150]

Our substantial making, i.e., the creation of our true nature, is in Christ, in whom humanity is defined as a capacity for at-one-ness with God. We are included in Christ's incarnation by virtue of sharing his human nature. In that sense, we are created 'all at once' in God's eternal plan. In God, the substantial creation of humanity is a single 'moment' because God's loving regard for all human beings is eternal, i.e., beyond the limits of time.[151] In other words, humanity itself has one simultaneous creation in Christ by which all who share human nature are ordained and predes-tined to union with God.[152] Humanity is created for the eternal Son, and we participate in that same humanity at the time of our own individual creation.[153] We must abandon our sense of time-framed chronology and adopt a more Pauline view, seeing all of these events as one great act of divine love: we are created in Christ, in whom and for whom all things were created.[154] This insight leads Julian to comment that, while it is a great source of joy for us that our humanity is made to be God's dwelling place, it is reason for even greater joy that we dwell in 'God unmade' in Christ by virtue of his humanity.[155] This truth places a sharp focus on the christological reference of our first making: our substantial oneing is by virtue of Christ's incarnation.

---

149 56:23-24; cf. 56:2-18.

150 Cf. 51:328-331; 57:21-22; 62:29-32.

151 See 53:26-30 (note 135, p. 48, above).

152 As Pelphrey notes, Julian's position is quite different from the heretical doctrine that all souls were created at once and were then 'released' at different times, a view that was put forward by Origen or his students and that tended to recur in medieval neoplatonism. See Brant Pelphrey, *Love Was His Meaning,* 117.

153 Our own individual creation in time, that moment in history when the soul is joined to the body, is not the same 'moment' as our simultaneous creation in Christ. Cf. 86:24-26.

154 Col 1:15-17.

155 54:9-11; cf. 51:328-331; 58:59-64.

b. Mercy: our second oneing in Christ's incarnation

In our first making, our substance mirrors the Trinity, i.e., in the person of Jesus Christ;[156] however, for Julian our first making is only one aspect of the story. God wills that we be made double, i.e., substance and sensuality.[157] In addition to our substantial oneing in Christ, we are oned in 'deed,'[158] the deed of Christ's sensuality-taking, his incarnation. In Julian's terminology, the higher part of human nature (our substance) is eternally oned to the Trinity in the person of the eternal Son; this is our first making. The lower part of human nature (sensuality) is oned to God in our second making, the taking of sensuality by the Son. We were knit to God in the first oneing, and God was knit to us in the second oneing of Christ's incarnation.

> Oure kynde,[159] which is the hyer party, is knytte to god in *the* makyng, and god is knytt to oure kynde, whych is the lower party in oure flessch takyng. And thus in Crist oure two kyndys be onyd, for the trynyte is comprehendyd in Crist, in whom oure hyer party is groundyd and rotyd; and oure lower party the second parson hath taken, whych kynd furst to hym was adyght. [57:18-22]

By virtue of humanity's second making in Christ's taking on flesh, our sensuality mirrors Christ who defines it in himself: our sensuality was 'dyght' (prepared) for the indwelling of the Son of God,[160] i.e., our sensuality was created for Christ. Once again, Julian overturns our time-framed concepts. The eternal Son did not assume *our* 'fallen humanity' in becoming incarnate; rather, it is we who, in becoming sensual at the moment of our individual creation in time, are given a participation in *Christ's* humanity.[161] By sharing in human nature, then, we participate in the two oneings of humanity to God accomplished in Christ. Just as our

---

156 To mirror Christ *is* to image the Trinity in that Jesus is the perfect image of God. Cf. Col 1:15.

157 56:59; cf. 55:44-50; 58:39-40.

158 23:19-24.

159 Julian's use of the word 'kynde' is not absolutely consistent. In most instances, she uses 'kynde' to indicate the true nature of humanity as God intends it; thus, while she tends to identify it with *substance* (e.g., our 'kyndely substannce' [58:22-24]), there is a sense in which our kind or nature, like the soul, can also be said to include sensuality as an essential aspect of that which is truly human 'being.' Cf. 56:11-22 (p. 44-45, above) and note 147, p. 50, above.

160 57:21-22; cf. 51:328-331; 58:3-4; 62:29-32.

161 "For all mankynde that shall be savyd by the swete incarnacion and the passion of Crist, alle is the manhode of Cryst. For he is the heed, and we be his membris." [51:254-256]

substance is an at-one-ness with God (a participation in the mutuality of love between God and humanity, a mutuality eternally present in the Trinity by reason of Christ's substantive union with the Father and the Holy Spirit),[162] so too our sensuality is a share in the humanity of the Son of God. When our soul is joined to flesh at the moment of our own individual creation in time, we are oned anew to God by virtue of Christ's own sensuality-taking; not only is our substance enclosed in Christ within the Trinity, but Christ is also enclosed in the 'worshipful city' of our sensuality.[163]

Whereas we are a 'made trinity'[164] in our first making, our again-making gives us our sensuality, our embodied being-in-the-world of time and space, a 'being' which only finds its full realization in the life of Jesus Christ. Christ is 'perfect man,'[165] i.e., full human life without sin.

> And ryght as we were made lyke to the trynyte in oure furst makyng, our maker would *that* we should be lyke to Jhesu Cryst oure sauiour in hevyn *with*ought ende by the vertu of oure (geyn) makyng. Then betwene thes two he would for loue and for worshipe of man make hym selfe as lyke to man in this deadly lyfe in our fowlhede and in our wretchednes as man myght be *with*out gylt; wherof it menyth, as is before sayd, it was the ymage and the lyknes of owr fowle blacke dede wher in our feyer bryght blessyd lorde hyd his godhede. [10:53-61]

It is important to note that Julian equates neither flesh nor sensuality with evil.[166] By oneing our sensuality with his divinity, Christ actually demonstrates the goodness of the flesh.[167] It is only for those of us who are not yet fully oned (i.e., not yet enjoying the full bliss of heaven) that

---

162 See p. 48-51, above.

163 "That wurschypfull cytte *that* oure lorde Jhesu syttyth in, it is oure sensualyte, in whych he is enclosyd; and oure kyndly substance is beclosyd in Jhesu, *with the* blessyd soule of Crist syttyng in rest in the godhed." [56:23-25] Our soul is a kingdom in which Christ is enthroned, never to depart. [68:15-17; cf. 51:145-146; 55:30-31; 57:55-56; 81:9-12.]

164 "Oure soule is a made trynyte lyke to the vnmade blessyd trynyte, knowyn and lovyd fro *with* out begynnyng, and in *the* makyng onyd to the maker." [55:40-42]

165 The perfection or fullness of humanity becomes ours in Christ 'in whom oure partys be onyd and all made perfyte man.' [58:57-58]

166 We have already seen that, although sensuality implies flesh, it is not identified with it. See p. 45, above.

167 Pelphrey points out that Julian's use of the term 'flesh' cannot be interpreted as meaning that the human body is somehow opposed to God. On the contrary, God loves the human body so much that the Son of God took it on unreservedly in assuming human nature in his incarnation. See Brant Pelphrey, *Love Was His Meaning*, 155-156.

sensuality is still in some way apart from God, marred by the scourge of sin.

We can see that Christ's incarnation truly holds the key to Julian's soteriology and anthropology. We may only understand ourselves in the light of that perfection of human nature which is Jesus Christ. Humanity is saved in the impossible possibility of the God-man who defines it in himself as the oneing of *in-God-ness* with God-given *God-separateness*. By virtue of Christ's incarnation, our first oneing takes place within the Trinity in the endless purpose of God's love. By taking on flesh, Christ accomplished our second oneing (or 'again-making'), the oneing of our sensuality to our substance, i.e., our God-separateness to our being-in-God.[168] For Julian, this second oneing (or remaking) constitutes mercy proper, the mercy which works our rightfulness in God's sight even when we fail in our sensuality.[169] In his own person, Jesus Christ reveals to us our indefectible 'godly will,' our 'rightful' substance. In his substance (i.e., the truth of his being as the incarnate Son of God), Christ remains in continual union with the Father and the Holy Spirit. The same is true for us who are created in Christ's image; in our substance we remain oned to God even while, in our sensuality, we fail because our existential oneing to God is not yet complete.[170] (Because he oned sensuality perfectly to his substance, Christ did not fail in his sensuality, i.e., he did not sin.)[171]

Julian does not talk about the remaking of humanity in terms of any kind of a break with the first making, i.e., in the sense of correcting a faulty first attempt. Our first making in God is not flawed or imperfect; rather, our second making in Christ is an 'increase' over the first.[172] By our second making, we are given our being-in-the-world; we enter the realm of space and time through our sensuality. Of course, sin also enters the picture while we live in the tension of our as yet incomplete, personal existential oneing of sensuality and substance. Only in the person of Christ is this oneing complete; we shall share existentially in the perfection of his oneing when we come to the bliss of heaven. Until that time, however, the fact that our humanity does not separate us from God becomes our hope, our joy.

---

168 57:42-46; 58:56-58.
169 Cf. 35:37-39.
170 57:8-9.
171 Christ assumed the burden of our sin, but without guilt. [10:56-58 (p. 53, above)]
172 58:22-33. Pelphrey agrees that our original creation is not to be seen as imperfect, and he sees remaking as a step in the continuous creation of humankind; 'increasing' and 'remaking' describe one same aspect of human development. Brant Pelphrey, *Love Was His Meaning*, 132.

At this point in our study, the christocentricity of Julian's doctrine on salvation is evident from the centrality of Christ's incarnation in her understanding of kind and mercy. Kind and mercy are two distinct but inseparable moments in our being oned to God, each of which has a clearly christological reference. We have identified mercy proper as the second moment of our oneing to God, which oneing we perceive in the historical person of Jesus Christ, the incarnate Son of God; in him, humanity is oned definitively to the Trinity by virtue of his taking on sensuality. Perhaps not so easily perceived is Julian's concept of kind or nature as humanity's first oneing to God in the person of the eternal Son, by virtue of whose incarnation humanity is not only defined but present in the Trinity without reference to space or time.

In one sense, Julian's doctrine on kind and mercy provides her with the key to understanding salvation, i.e., why God looks at us sinners with that love properly reserved for Christ. Sin is overcome in Christ, the only true 'rightful' humanity, the 'perfect man' in whom all who are to be saved are oned.[173] By virtue of Christ's incarnation, in our first making our substance mirrors the Trinity in the person of the Son, while in our second making we mirror Christ's embodied being-in-the-world, i.e., his human life without sin. Our rightfulness depends upon our being oned to God in Christ, not upon the merits of our own actions. This is the meaning of salvation: to be oned so completely in Christ that we are fully and definitively incorporated into his own rightfulness, his own sinlessness.[174] Oned to God in Christ, we too participate in the divine peace and love, and wrath has no place in us—and we are saved.[175] In another sense, however, Julian's teaching on kind and mercy still does not resolve her basic dilemma regarding sin: if humanity is indeed saved definitively by reason of Christ's incarnation, and if, consequently, 'all is well,' then what is sin? How are we to understand our experience of sin

---

173 In the parable of the lord and the servant, Julian identifies the humanity of Christ as 'ryghtfull Adam.' [51:214-215] Cf. 57:41-46; 58:56-58.

174 Cf. 58:57-58 (note 165, p. 53, above).

175 Not only is there no wrath between God and us because of our oneing and because of the intimacy of our interpersonal union with God (see p. 43, above), but our own wrath is also destroyed in this oneing: "And therfor to the soule that of his speciall grace seeth so ferforth of the hye marvelous goodnesse of god, that we be endlesly onyd to hym in loue, it is the most vnpossible that may be that god shulde be wrath, for wrath and frenschyppe be two contrariese; for he that wastyth and dystroyeth oure wrath and makyth vs meke and mylde, it behovyth vs nedys to beleue that he be evyr in one loue, meke and mylde, whych is contrary to wrath. For I saw full truly that where oure lorde aperyth, pees is takyn and wrath hath no stede." [49:6-14] Cf. 48:47-49 (note 74, p. 35, above).

and suffering, i.e., our very real experience of being not yet oned fully to God in bliss? This question leads us to a consideration of Julian's doctrine on grace, the third moment in our oneing. Only the 'working of mercy and grace' finally explains our personal, existential oneing in time, a oneing that takes place in the context of a sinful world.

2 The Working of Mercy and Grace: God 'Keeps' Us in Christ

Having looked at the first two moments of our oneing, we are ready to face the question of sin, i.e., our experience of being not yet fully oned to God. Divine mercy is not only the definitive oneing of humanity to God in the Christ event, but also a process of our being oned in Christ existentially, an experience which we find best described by Julian's term 'keeping.' This existential oneing is accomplished by Christ's working in us by the Holy Spirit, i.e., by the 'working of mercy and grace.' Julian's understanding of the relationship between grace (the third moment of our being oned in Christ) and mercy provides us with a way to understand the paradox of salvation as having been already accomplished in Christ, but not yet fully realized in us sinners.

Just as nature and mercy are inextricably bound together (i.e., our kind is determined 'from without beginning,' outside time, by virtue of Christ's oneing humanity to God in himself by his incarnation), so too grace cannot be understood outside the context of divine mercy. Indeed, Julian consistently links them together in her phrase 'the working of mercy and grace.'[1] As we shall see, mercy works our 'keeping in love' (i.e., our protection, our preservation in time from any lasting harm from sin) by grace; grace is the extension of mercy in time.[2]

---

1 Julian explicitly links 'mercy' with 'grace' no less than 53 times. She uses the actual phrase 'the working of mercy and grace' [or its equivalent] in 15 places: 11:27.30; 35:25; 40:42; 48:17.32; 49:42; 55:17; 57:10.11-12.13.29-30.40; 58:50; 77:21. Aside from her use of this specific phrase, she links the two words 38 additional times: 33:26; 35:43.44-45; 37:4; 38:29-31; 40:5.16; 41:21; 42:23.24.64; 45:9-10; 46:10; 48:4-5.27.28-29; 50:2-3; 52:17; 55:22.37; 56:30.37.40.44.54-55; 57:15-16; 58:57-59; 59:2.6.22-23; 60:4.33; 61:49-51; 63:13-14; 77:5; 78:43; 83:19.

2 See chapter 3 (p. 111-122, below) on Christ's 'motherhood of grace' as the extension of the working of mercy in time.

A. Two Perspectives: Time and Eternity

In her doctrine on mercy, Julian grapples with the problem of finding a way to speak about our personal experience of divine mercy (the event of our existential salvation, willed by God 'from without beginning' and accomplished definitively, once for all, in Christ) within the human categories of time. We have already said something about Julian's insight into the 'timelessness' of God's perspective[3] and her struggle to reconcile the two judgments, i.e., the temporal human perspective with the eternal divine perspective. To appreciate Julian's doctrine on mercy as it is experienced in time, we must begin by considering her efforts to overcome the limitations inherent in human language when one tries to speak of the divine perspective, a perspective outside the reference of time altogether.

1. Human language and timelessness

The fact of our salvation is revealed to Julian,[4] but her own experience tells her that in this life we are not yet fully 'saved.' Her task is to find a way to talk about the mercy which 'saves' us within the human category of time. She struggles with the problem of the *to be* of salvation within a theological framework which posits salvation as an event already accomplished in Christ. Her dilemma is reflected in her frequent use of the phrase 'those that are to be saved.'[5] In the simultaneity of God's eternal

---

3   E.g., the creation of humanity, be it the humanity of Christ, of Adam, or of any one of us, is a single 'moment' in God's loving purpose (see p. 51, above). See also p. 41-42, above.

4   All of Julian's insights have to do with salvation and the 'saved': "I speke of them that shalle be savyd, for in this tyme god shewde me no nother." [9:20-21] When she later questions the meaning of hell, damnation, and purgatory, her answer is that there is no answer to be given her. [33:2-23; cf. 35:2-6] It is salvation alone that is revealed, and Julian accepts the revelation as it is given. [33:28-36; 35:6-11] She does not deny the possibility of damnation; rather, she is clarifying what it is that is revealed, i.e., salvation. Her approach leads us to reflect on the parameters of revelation: damnation itself is not part of the good news of God's revelation; it only finds its place in doctrine as the logical *that from which we are saved.* What is revealed is salvation; all else is hidden.

5   4:26; 9:11.15.20; 12:30; 13:13.21.45; 15:32; 20:5.19; 24:7; 25:15; 27:32; 28:5; 31:12. 16.40; 35:33; 36:35; 37:15.16; 39:29; 50:5; 51:255.264.265.265; 52:8; 53:3.12.62; 54:4.

now, our salvation is already accomplished (that at-one-ment which is complete in Christ); however, in a certain sense, the event of our salvation remains yet 'to be' (that existential oneing which is still in progress in us). Julian's vocabulary simply reflects the paradox and tension experienced in every christian life: the 'already' and the 'not yet' of salvation.[6]

Julian's whole theological approach reflects her sensitivity to this tension between the eternal reality and that same reality as experienced in time. For Julian, eternity does not rob time of meaning; on the contrary, time manifests and incarnates the eternal truth of God's loving purpose. In Julian's experience of the shewings, the two realities are held in tension: her heart was filled with joy at the sight of the Trinity (eternal reality) in the vision of Christ's bleeding head (temporal phenomenon).[7] Each reality has its own truth: the phenomenon maintains its reality, albeit in the limited sphere of the spatio-temporal world; the eternal truth of the love of the Trinity (the sight of which love accounts for Julian's joy) remains the higher truth, the ultimate reality. Christ's pain was the 'deed' in time; the love was without beginning and is and ever shall be.[8]

To deal with this tension, Julian adopts the standard theological convention of paradoxical language. She uses terms such as 'ever,' 'never,' 'continually,' 'endless,' and 'without end' in her struggle to speak from an eternal reference.[9] For Julian, God's 'endless purpose'[10] is eternal, i.e., it is neither before time nor a never-ending prolongation of time; rather, it is outside the human category of time. While our being-in-the-world has its beginning in time, we are 'in God's endless purpose' within the mystery of God's timelessness.[11] In the language of paradox, Julian tells us

---

8; 55:4; 57:4.49; 58:11; 59:8; 75:17; 78:29. We may also point to the significance of this expression in terms of countering accusations of universalism in her theology by noting that Julian qualifies what she has to say about salvation by limiting its application to 'those who are to be saved.'

6   E.g., she speaks of our lives as having two parts: an outward part that is in pain and woe in this life; an inward part that is a high, blessydfulle life, all in peace and love. [19:26-32]

7   4:3-16.

8   "The loue that made hym to suffer it passith as far alle his paynes as hevyn is aboue erth; for the payne was a noble precious and wurschypfulle dede done in a tyme by the workyng of loue. And loue was without begynnyng, is and shall be without ende." [22:46-49]

9   Roland Maisonneuve, L'univers visionnaire de Julian of Norwich, 281.

10   As we have seen, Julian identifies God's purpose with God's love. [53:26-37; cf. 58:2-3; 86:24-27] See p. 48, above.

11   See p. 49-51, above.

that God loves us 'from without beginning,'[12] a phrase which combines the notion of time ('from' as signifying a beginning point) with the notion of timelessness ('without beginning').

Julian's paradoxical use of tenses further demonstrates her attempt to reconcile God's eternal now with our human experience of chronological time. Whereas we perceive reality as historical (i.e., events follow one another sequentially), in God's perspective all reality is apprehended at once without reference to time. For example, the Lord reveals to Julian that all 'was made well' (past),[13] 'all is well' (present),[14] and 'all shall be well' (future).[15] Even though these three statements imply a certain degree of contradiction for us because of the mutual exclusivity of past, present and future, they may be reconciled if understood as an expression of the divine perspective.[16] Similarly, the concept of the eternal now of God's perspective sheds light on some seeming inconsistencies in Julian's imagery as it relates to time. For example, she speaks of our being 'endlessly borne' in Christ our mother, i.e, carried in the womb of Christ from whom we 'never come out.'[17] (The middle English word 'borne' may also be translated as 'born,' in which case Julian would be speaking about an eternal birthing process.) At the same time, however, she tells us that we are children already born and needing the motherly care of Christ who feeds us,[18] guides us,[19] and protects us from dangers[20] as we grow to maturity. Here again we meet the problem of the limitations of human language. We have no language other than that which we learn from creatures; however, whenever we try to use language drawn from our own

12   53:26-40; 55:40-41; 85:7-9; cf. 59:23-24; 86:21-27.
13   22:53-57; 29:4-5.16-17.
14   11:18-19; 34:23-24; 85:15-17.
15   1:39-40; 27:13-14.34; 29:16-17; 31:3-6; 32:8.17-18.20-21.35-37.47-57; 34:25 26; 35:13; 63:46-47; 68:73.
16   This same aspect of God's timelessness also helps to explain Julian's interpretation of the parable of the lord and the servant. Her understanding of the events of salvation history (i.e, the creation, the fall of Adam, Christ's incarnation, his passion and death, etc.) is stretched far beyond the boundaries of chronological time; Julian sees them as they are in God's perspective, as one single *event* which we, limited as we are, perceive as played out sequentially in time. The juxtaposition of the creation of Adam and Christ's incarnation allows Julian to grasp the essential unity between Christ, Adam, and each one of us. See p. 37-39, above.
17   "Oure savyoure is oure very moder, in whome we be endlesly borne and nevyr shall come out of hym." [57:49-50]
18   60:29-33.
19   60:51-57.
20   61:35-40.66-69.

experience to talk about God, we find it to be inadequate.[21] Julian seems to understand that things which are mutually exclusive in human terms may not be so when applied to God; all is unified within the simplicity of God. Because Christ is himself the coincidence of opposites, reconciling all dichotomies in himself, Julian is able to call him 'mother'; moreover, Christ is always 'he' (never 'she') who is mother because his motherhood transcends masculine/feminine linguistic categories.

Lastly, when Julian tells us that God is 'our maker, our keeper, and our lover,'[22] she necessarily implies God's loving, active involvement in our spatio-temporal world. God, who is outside the created order of time and acts freely in regard to it, is nevertheless actively present in temporal reality.[23] Julian's distinctive use of the word 'keeping' will be explored later in this chapter;[24] for now, it is sufficient to note that the word 'keep' itself implies a reference to time in terms of continuity.

2. Salvation and time

In chapter 49, Julian gives a description of the existential experience of salvation:

> For we may nott be blesfully savyd tyll we be verely in pees and in loue, for that is oure saluation.

---

21 32:49-50. In his study on Julian's 'visionary' language, Maisonneuve gives a penetrating analysis of three literary devices Julian employs in her attempt to express the ineffable content of her shewings: the antithetical paradox, hyperbole, and symbolic figuration. For a more complete analysis of Julian's use of language, see Roland Maisonneuve, L'univers visionnaire de Julian of Norwich, 79-120, 280-283.

22 4:12; 5:19. Julian makes two additional references to God as our 'keeper' [39:45; 49:40], and also specifies Christ as our 'keeper' [52:31; 77:45].

23 "See, I am god. See, I am in all thyngs. See, I do all thyng. See, I nevyr lefte my handes of my workes, ne never shalle without ende. See, I lede all thyng to the end that I ordeyne it to, f(ro) without begynnyng, by the same myght, wysdom and loue that I made it with; how shoulde any thyng be a mysse?" [11:51-56]

In commenting on this passage, Pelphrey suggests the uniqueness of Julian's insight into the nature of divine activity with regard to the created world: "Her concept is not a Platonic one, in which there is a dualism between the realms of spirit and matter, nor an Aristotelian one in which God remains outside an orderly universe which he has created. The image which Julian suggests is of an intimacy between God and creation, in which God acts freely without regard to time — because it is part of the created order." See Brant Pelphrey, "'Uncreated Charity': The Trinity in Julian of Norwich," Sobornost 7, Series 7 (1978) 531.

24 See p. 68ff, below.

And though we be wrath, and the contraryousnes that is in vs be nowe in tribulacion, deseses and woo, as fallyng in to oure blyndnesse and oure pronyte, yett be we suer and safe by *the* mercyfull kepyng of god that we perysch nott. But we be nott blyssefully safe in havyng of oure endlesse joye tyll we be all in pees and in loue, that is to sey full plesyd w*ith* god and w*ith* alle his werkes and w*ith* alle his domys, and lovyng and plesabyll w*ith* oure selfe and w*ith* oure evyn criste*n* and w*ith* alle that god louyth, as loue lykyth. And this doth goddes goodnes in vs.

Thus saw I that god is our very peas; and he is oure suer keper when we be oure selfe at vnpeas, and he contynually werkyth to bry*n*g vs in to endlesse peas. And thus when by the werkyng of mercy and grace we be made meke and mylde, than we be full safe. Sodenly is the soule onyd to god, when she is truly peesyd in her selfe, for in hym is founde no wrath. [49:29-45]

While Julian clearly identifies salvation with that full union with God which is the timeless bliss of heaven,[25] her concept of salvation as oneing also implies progressivity and continuity, aspects necessarily associated with temporality. We shall now explore briefly these aspects as well as her understanding of salvation as healing and as deliverance, each of which suggests a temporal reference.

a. Salvation as oneing

As we have seen, Julian's notion of salvation as our oneing must always be understood in terms of an interpersonal communion;[26] this implies the progressivity and continuity associated with interpersonal relationships. Julian indicates the interpersonal character of the union by describing it in terms of homeliness, courtesy, and face-to-face vision.[27] We are oned to God in Christ,[28] oned to Christ,[29] oned to each other in Christ.[30] Also inherent in the concept of at-one-ment is a prior condition of separate-

---

25 Julian uses the terms *salvation, blessydfulle chere, sight* (beatific vision), *oneing,* and *heaven* equivalently. E.g., our being 'truly in peace and in love' [49:30] is only fully realized in the bliss of heaven, i.e., in substantial union with God. [5:19-20; 40:20-24; 51:112-114] We await the vision of Christ's blessydfulle chere in the endless joy and bliss of heaven. [72:6-9.18-20] Full 'sight' and knowledge of God is the bliss of heaven, the fruit of our being fully oned to God in Christ; in this life we see and know only in part. [72:6-9; 31:10-12; 47:30-31; 80:11-12] See also p. 42-43, above.
26 See p. 42-43, above.
27 7:52-55; 43:53-54.
28 53:56-64; 54:2-8.
29 71:19-24; 78:14.25-30.
30 71:19-24; cf. 31:34-36; 51:254-257; 75:5-8.

ness. What had been apart is brought together.[31] This oneing, our move-ment towards communion, is progressive, begun now and completed in heaven. In time, we move by degrees towards ever greater communion with God until we are at last brought to that fullness of union marked by beatitude;[32] in being oned to God, we are necessarily brought into full rightfulness (delivered from sin),[33] and we enjoy sight of God's blessyd-fulle chere. This progression must be seen in terms of a love relationship that deepens or 'wholes' to include each human person existentially in Christ.[34]

To say that oneing is an interpersonal love relationship is not, howev-er, to say that this relationship is primarily affective; in Julian's theology, our relationship with God has an ontological basis.

> Ande for the grete endlesse loue that god hath to alle mankynde, he makyth no departyng in loue betwen the blessyd soule of Crist and the lest soule that shall be savyd. For it is full esy to beleue and truste that the dwellyng of the blessyd soule of Crist is full hygh in *the* glorious godhede; and truly as I vnderstode in oure lordes menyng, where the blessyd soule of Crist is, there is the substance of alle the soules that shall be savyd by Crist.
>
> Hyely owe we to enjoye *that* god dwellyth in oure soule; and more hyly we owe to enjoye that oure soule dwellyth in god. [54:2-10]

Since in the soul of Christ there is 'the substance of all the souls that shall be saved,' we find an ontological basis for saying that we are oned to each other in Christ. Moreover, when we are fully oned, our sensuality is brought up into our substance which is beclosed in Christ within the Godhead.[35] Our being oned to God in Christ is not only a communion with God and with each other, but also a communion between ourselves and our truest 'self' — our self in Christ.[36]

---

31 See note 128, p. 46, above.

32 In speaking about Julian's doctrine on prayer, Molinari points out that prayer has always to be seen in the light of our progressive unification with God. The prayer that 'ones the soul to God' [43:2; cf. 41:30-32; 42:6-12], itself a high degree of union with God (e.g., a higher degree than mere longing or aspiration [5:35-40]), constitutes the necessary stage preceding the highest forms of union. Paul Molinari, S.J., *Julian of Norwich*, 99-100.

33 35:37-41.

34 We shall explore Julian's notion of our growth in relationship more fully in our consideration of salvation as 'healing' (see p. 64-66, below); for now, it is sufficient to note that growth, by its very nature, implies the passage of time.

35 56:23-25.

36 "That wurschypfull cytte *that* oure lorde Jhesu syttyth in, it is oure sensualyte, in whych he is enclosyd; and oure kyndly substance is beclosyd in Jhesu, with *the* blessyd soule of Crist syttyng in rest in the godhed. And I saw full suerly that it

b. Salvation as healing

Julian returns to the original meaning of the word 'salvation' (from the
Latin *salus*) as 'health' or 'wholeness.' Our existential salvation will be
complete when we are fully healed,[37] i.e., brought into wholeness in
Christ on the final judgment day ('domys day').

> For thys is the goostly thyrst of Cryst, the loue longyng *that* lastyth and evyr
> shall tyll we see that syght at domys day; for we that shalle be safe, and shalle
> be Crystes joy and hys blysse, ben yet here, and some be to come, and so
> shalle some be in to that day. Therfore this is his thurste and loue longyng
> of vs, all to geder here in hym to oure endlesse blysse, as to my syght. For we
> be nott now fully as hole in hym as we shalle be than. [31:14-20]

The *Shewings* abounds with images of health, healing, and wholeness.
Mercy works our healing.[38] Christ himself is our 'kind nurse,'[39] our medicine,[40] our 'salve.'[41] He cures us[42] and heals us by his wounds.[43] He is the
health and life of the sacraments.[44] By being oned, we are brought into
Christ's own 'holiness' (a form of the word 'wholeness').[45] But perhaps
Julian's clearest image of salvation as wholeness is one that also implies
the passage of time: the image of our progressive growth, our maturing
to wholeness, i.e., full stature in Christ.

> And all the gyftes that god may geue to the creature he hath gevyn to his son
> Jh*es*u for vs, whych gyftes he wonnyng in vs hath beclosyd in hym in to the
> tyme that we be waxyn and growyn, oure soule *with* oure body and oure body
> *with* oure soule. Eyther of them take helpe of other tylle we be broughte vp
> in to stature as kynde werkyth; and than in the ground of kynd *with* werkyng

---

> behouyth nedys to be that we shulde be in longyng and in pen*n*ance into the tyme
> that we be led so depe in to god that we verely and trewly know oure owne soule."
> [56:23-28]

37 Although Julian's notion of healing necessarily implies the problem of sin, we shall
   defer our discussion of sin until later (see p. 91-106, below).
38 48:30-31; cf. 55:16-18.
39 61:68.
40 82:14.
41 79:39.
42 78:25.
43 61:66; cf. 39:30-31. Christ's blood is a 'flood of mercy' [61:64] that will 'heele vs
   fulle feyer by processe of tyme' [63:22].
44 60:35-37.
45 53:56-64; cf. 28:19-20. In Julian's day, 'hole' was synonomous with 'health' [3:36],
   and 'holy' was used both as an adjective meaning 'saintly' [33:13; 75:6] and as an
   adverb meaning 'wholly' [52:57].

of mercy *the* holy gost gracyously enspirith in to vs gyftes ledyng to endlesse lyfe. [55:31-38]

Julian's understanding of the process of oneing as our growth towards wholeness in Christ is reflected in both her imagery and her vocabulary. For example, she describes the work of mercy and grace as 'perfecting,' 'fulfilling,' and 'increasing,'[46] and she depicts us in various stages of a process of growth, both as Christ's children who need to be guided and disciplined towards growth in the ways of love,[47] and as Christ's beloved wife who has reached the maturity of reciprocal love in spousal union.[48]

In speaking of our earthly existence as a process of growth and maturation, Julian echoes not only Paul,[49] but also that early christian tradition exemplified in the writings of Irenaeus. For Irenaeus, Adam was not endowed at his creation with supernatural perfections; rather, Adam was created 'weak and untrained,' but with a childlike aptitude for growth towards perfection.[50] Within such a scenario, sin is not unlike a debilitating illness or an immaturity that evokes pity, not wrath, from God.[51] Our growth to full maturity, the process of becoming wholly ourselves in Christ, is the healing of that immaturity and weakness that is sin. In the language of the *Shewings*, as we are oned, we are progressively healed of our sin, growing into the likeness of Christ in all things; in this oneing lies our salvation and true bliss.[52]

This concept of growth has implications for Julian's understanding of oneing as an interpersonal relationship of love between God and the soul. Remembering that, for Julian, this interpersonal relationship has an ontological basis, we can see that our growth is, in fact, a growth in love. When God is, God loves, i.e., God communicates self. God as trinity reveals that love is, by its nature, interpersonal relationship. As a result of God's free and gratuitous love in our regard, we have been created as those creatures with a capacity to return God's interpersonal love. The

---

46 46:7-10; 55:16-21; 56:43-44; 57:8-13; 58:30-32.
47 61:35-57; 63:30-40.
48 51:326-328; 58:15-16.
49 Eph 4:4-16; cf. 1 Cor 3:1-2.
50 Irenaeus of Lyons, *Adversus Haereses* IV, 37, 1-4; 38, 1-3 (*PG* 7, 1099-1102, 1105-1108). The author is indebted to Simon Tugwell, O.P., who has pointed out to her similarities between the thought of Julian and theology of Irenaeus.
51 Irenaeus of Lyons, *Adversus Haereses* III, 23, 5-6 (*PG* 7, 963-4). See also Pelphrey, *Love Was His Meaning*, 84-85, 157.
52 "And the blessyd creatures *that* shalle be in hevyn *with* hym *with* out ende, he wylle haue them lyke vnto hym selfe in alle thyng, and (to) be lyke to oure lorde perfetly, it is oure very saluacion and oure fulle blysse." [77:55-58] Cf. 2 Cor 3:18; Phil 3:20-21; 1 Pet 2:21.

more we are oned to God in love, the more we become that which God communicates in that interpersonal relationship of love: we further incarnate God's own love for us and, having grown in love, are able to love more fully in return. Our truest 'self' (Christ) is God's love incarnate; thus, our growth ('increasing') is growth in love and in relationship.

The notion of continuity is also reinforced by Julian's concept of oneing as growth and healing. Growth, healing, and even transfiguration necessarily imply that what one is now (or what one shall be finally) is substantially what one has been from the beginning. Julian clearly maintains continuity between our immature (i.e., sinful) selves and ourselves wholly mature in Christ.[53] Our weakness is healed, not destroyed; and our wounds are turned to 'worships' in the bliss of heaven.[54]

c. Salvation as deliverance

The passage of time is also suggested in the notion of salvation as deliverance inasmuch as deliverance implies the existence of a 'before,' i.e., a prior state or condition from which one is delivered. Julian gives us a marvelous image of our salvation as deliverance in the fifteenth shewing:

> And in thys tyme I sawe a body lyeng on the erth, whych body shewde heuy and feerfulle and with oute shape and forme, as it were a swylge stynkyng myrre; and sodeynly oute of this body sprong a fulle feyer creature, a lyttle chylld, full shapyn and formyd, swyft and lyfly and whytter then the lylye, whych sharpely glydyd vppe in to hevyn. . . . It is fulle blesfulle man to be taken fro payne, more than payne be taken fro man; for if payne be taken from vs, it may come agayne. Therfore this is a souereyne comfort and a blesful beholdyng in a longyng soule, that we shall be taken fro payne. For in this behest I saw a mercyfulle compassion that oure lorde hath in vs for oure woo, and a curtesse behytyng of cleene delyuerance; for he wylle that we be comfo(r)tyd in the ovyr passyng joy. [64:31-35.40-46]

Julian marvels at God's goodness in delivering us from pain rather than simply removing pain from our life. We are truly saved from pain when we are removed from the painful situation; if, on the other hand, it is pain which is removed, there is always the possibility that pain may return (as did Julian's pain at the conclusion of her visions).[55] The image of

---

53 The servant of the parable is transfigured into a mighty lord, while ever remaining who he is: Christ, Adam, and 'alle man.' [51:211-231; 299-330]

54 "Though that he [the sinful soul] be helyd, hys woundys be sene before god, nott as woundes but as wurshyppes." [39:31-32] See p. 129-131, below.

55 3:36; 66:10-15.

deliverance, then, symbolizes our soul's continuity of identity in the movement from the realm of time (in which pain may reappear) into the realm of eternity (in which we shall be in bliss, unchangeable as God is unchangeable).[56]

---

56 49:54-55.

B. Mercy, Grace, and 'Keeping'

Grace, the third moment of our oneing, is the event of our individual existential salvation in time, the effecting and unfolding of God's rightfulness in our regard. Julian's doctrine of grace is shaped by her understanding of divine mercy: we are 'kept' in God's love, even in the time of our sinning, as we struggle in time towards the wholeness that is our truest 'self,' our self in Christ.

Our existential experience of oneing requires a way of speaking about the event of salvation as progressive. We have already seen how Julian uses the images of healing, growth, interpersonal relationship, and deliverance, all of which reflect the progressivity and continuity of our experience of salvation in time. We shall now turn our attention to the most distinctive word in her vocabulary of mercy: mercy as 'keeping.'

1. Mercy works our 'keeping'

Like much of her imagery, Julian's choice of the word 'keeping' has to do with the human category of time. The Christ event (Christ's incarnation, life, death, and resurrection) is the event of our salvation, i.e., our being oned to God in Christ. This oneing, although realized historically in the person of Jesus Christ, stands ultimately outside the human category of time, grounding our relationship to God from all eternity. We live, however, in time and space, and we experience ourselves as not yet saved, not yet fully oned. We struggle with the same paradox that faced the early Church: the 'already' and the 'not yet' of salvation. We are already saved — but not yet. This paradox gives birth to Julian's unique doctrine of divine mercy as 'keeping.'

a. 'Keeping': our existential experience of salvation

As Julian tells us in her description of salvation, we are not 'blesfully saved' until heaven, but we are 'sure and safe by the merciful keeping of God that we perish not.'[57] Here we encounter the most significant and

---

57 49:29-34 (p. 62, above).

characteristic phrase in her vocabulary of mercy: 'merciful keeping'[58] is Julian's expression for our existential experience of being oned or saved in Christ. We are 'kept' by the mercy of God. 'Keeping' is the working of mercy, our oneing in Christ, as experienced in time:

> For the ground of mercy is in loue, and the werkyng of mercy is oure kepyng in loue; and this was shewed in such a manner that I culde not perceyve of the properte of mercy other wyse but as it were all loue in loue.
> That is to sey, as to my syght, mercy is a swete gracious werkyng in loue, medlyd with plentuous pytte, for mercy werkyth vs kepyng, and mercy werkyth turnyng to vs all thyng to good. [48:13-19]

The working of mercy is our 'keeping in love.'

We have already seen how, for Julian, mercy (i.e., mercy proper, our again-making in Christ) works our salvation. Now we may expand her definition of mercy to include 'keeping,' our protection and preservation: we are 'kept' in God's sight by virtue of that oneing accomplished by Christ's incarnation.[59] Mercy works our 'keeping,' our existential salvation, that rightfulness into which we mature, in time, as a result of our being oned in Christ.[60] We are 'saved' and 'kept' by the mercy of God.

Julian's use of the word 'keep' parallels her use of 'save.' We are 'saved by Christ'[61] and 'kept by Christ';[62] we are 'saved by mercy'[63] and 'kept by mercy';[64] we are 'saved/safe in Christ'[65] and 'kept in Christ.'[66] We have our 'keeping' and our 'saving' in Christ[67] who is our 'savior,'[68] our 'salvation,'[69] and our 'keeper.'[70] While 'saving' and 'keeping' are

---

58 49:33; cf. 38:29-30; 47:35-37; 78:7-11.
59 Julian speaks both of our will and of our soul as being 'kept' whole in Jesus Christ. [53:16-22.46-49; 59:40-42; cf. 51:106-107.]
60 "Alle the soules that shalle be savyd in hevyn withought ende be made ryghtfulle in the syght of god and by hys awne goodnesse in whych ryghtfullnes we be endlessly kepte and marvelously aboue all creatures." [35:33-36] Cf. 45:2-4; 53:17-22.
61 1:51-54; 20:19; 22:19-20.53-55; 51:239-240.255-256; 54:6-8; 55:4.52; 61:66; 74:38; 77:50-51; 80:14-15.
62 1:51-54; 37:10-13; 39:18; 40:2-3.54; 52:11-12; 59:9-11; 61:2-3.72-73; 71:34 35; 72:32-39; 77:42; 78:8; 79:15-17.32; 80:32-33.42-43; 82:20-21; cf. 60:51-53.
63 2:18; 56:53-54; 67:13.
64 47:34; 48:14.18.30-31; 55:17-18; 67:13.
65 53:17-18; 51:265.265; 53:62-63; 59:41.
66 35:42; 53:19-21; 58:44-46.
67 58:24-25.
68 1:52; 2:13; 7:55; 10:55; 16:13; 24:17-18; 30:2.26; 36:47-48; 51:306; 52:5; 57:48.49.49; 58:24-27; 59:27; 61:65-66; 70:23; 78:25; 83:23.
69 30:2-3; 36:47-48; 79:39.
70 52:31; 77:45.

paralleled in Julian's vocabulary of mercy, there emerges one clear distinction between them: 'keeping' bears an inherent reference to time or
duration and is associated with our life as lived here on this earth. Our
salvation, while accomplished ontologically in Christ, is only existentially
complete in our individual regard with the event of our being fully oned
to Christ in peace and in love in the endless joy of heaven.[71] Mercy works
our 'keeping' here on earth; we are 'kept whole in God's sight' until that
fullness of salvation in heaven. We are 'kept' on earth (in time) and
'saved' in heaven (outside time), and both the saving and the 'keeping'
are by God's mercy.

For Julian, 'keeping' is a way of speaking about our salvation. To be
'kept' by Christ is to be 'saved' by Christ. It is Christ's office to save us,
and that saving work is the meaning of his words, 'I keep thee full surely.'

> It is [Christ's] office to saue vs, it is his worshyppe to do it, and it is hys
> wylle we know it; for he wyll we loue hym swetely and trust in hym mekely
> and myghtly. And this shewde he in these gracious wordes: I kepe the fulle
> suerly. [61:70-73]

Moreover, 'keeping' (like 'salvation') maintains a consistent christological
reference in the *Shewings*.[72] It is Christ, the 'shewer' of Julian's revelations, who comforts and reassures her with the words, 'I keep thee full
surely';[73] and, although Julian does tell us that we are 'kept by God,'[74]
it is also clear that, based on her christology, we must infer that to be
'kept by God' is to be 'kept by God *in* Christ.'[75] Similarly, to be 'kept
in God'[76] is to be 'kept in God in Christ.'[77]

---

71 49:29-55.
72 1:51-54; 35:42; 37:10-13; 39:18; 40:2-3.54; 52:11-12.31; 53:19-21; 58:24 25.44-46;
    59:9-11; 61:2-3.72-73; 71:34-35; 77:42.45; 78:8; 79:15-17.32; 80:42-43; 82:20-21; cf.
    60:51-53.
73 37:10-13; cf. 40:54; 61:70-73; 82:20.
74 1:22; 4:22-23; 5:18.43-46; 15:24; 18:24; 38:29; 44:21; 47:35; 49:33-34; 54:20-21; 56:12-
    13; 72:34.39; 85:9; cf. 'kept by Trinity' [49:17-20; 62:5-12].
75 We must remember that, for Julian, God (i.e., the Trinity) is comprehended in
    Christ [57:19-20; cf. 4:13-16; 58:63-64; 83:22-23], and when she refers to God, she
    often means Christ in his divinity. E.g., she tells us that "the blessed trinitie our
    maker in Christ Jesu our sauiour endlessly dwelleth in our sowle, worschippfully
    rewlyng and commanding all thing*es*, vs mightly and wisely sauyng and kepyng for
    loue." [1:51-54] Cf. 68:2-14. Thus, there is no contradiction when Julian tells us
    that the Trinity is our 'keeper' and Christ is our 'keeper.' The Trinity 'keeps' us
    in and through Christ. Cf. note 22, p. 61, above.
76 45:2-3; 49:18-20; 53:19-21; 54:20-21; 58:22-27; cf. 10:25-26.
77 See p. 49-51, above.

b. 'Sureness of keeping' implies fidelity

Julian's concept of 'keeping' carries with it the temporal characteristic of continuity, especially the continuity implied in a loving, interpersonal relationship. The working of mercy never ceases;[78] we are 'kept' continually.[79] 'Continual keeping' is Julian's way of speaking about divine fidelity, God's faithfulness in loving, personal relationship with us. As we have seen, divine fidelity is best understood within the context of God's rightfulness and unchangeability.[80] God's fidelity is God's rightfulness translated into terms of time. It is our experience of relating to God in time which gives us our notion of divine fidelity; we perceive God's unchangeability as faithfulness. Because God is faithful and is 'ever in one same love' towards us,[81] we are 'kept full surely' in that love. Our relationship with God is marked by 'sureness of keeping,'[82] a security not unlike that security characteristic of any interpersonal relationship which is grounded in loving fidelity; and, for Julian, this 'sureness of keeping' springs from mercy.

> The seconde manner of chere, it is pitte and ruth and compassion, and this shewyth he to all his louers *with* sekernesse of kepyng that hath nede to his mercy. [71:28-30]

Because God's mercy is a rightful mercy, it cannot be controverted. God remains true, faithful to a stance of mercy in our regard, even in the face of our sinning.[83] This fidelity is the 'sureness of keeping that hath need to God's mercy.'

Finally, Julian further highlights the continual and interpersonal nature of divine faithfulness when she speaks in terms of Christ's fidelity. She tells us that Christ never removes from the place he takes up in our soul;[84] there, he 'treasures' our gifts within himself continuously until we reach the maturity necessary for using those gifts.[85]

---

78 48:13-26.
79 46:17-18; 49:40-41; 51:136-139; cf. 11:52-53; 49:24-27; 80:32-43.
80 See p. 25-26, 33-35, above, for a discussion of the relationship between divine rightfulness, divine unchangeability, and divine mercy.
81 43:33; 46:17-18.36; 49:4-13; 61:26-27; 78:12-14; 79:16.
82 15:24; 37:11.13; 46:17-18; 53:4; 71:29-30; 72:34.39; cf. 15:24.
83 38:29-30; 40:2-3; 49:24-25; 53:4-5; 62:2-8; 71:34-36; 75:3-4; 78:8-11; 80:32 34.38-43; 82:28-29. Julian tells us that God's love 'may nott nor wyll not be broken for trespas.' [61:27] Cf. 39:41-42; 40:49.
84 55:30-31; 68:15-17; 81:9-12; cf. 51:328-331; 52:39-40; 56:23-25; 57:53-56; 80:14-18.
85 18:18-20; 51:264-267; 55:30-35; 57:38-41; 75:21-23; cf. 56:3-4.

2. Grace: the extension of mercy in time

Julian's theology of mercy cannot be separated from her understanding of grace as the third moment in the event of our being oned to God in Christ. We must consider the relationship between mercy and grace in order to appreciate fully the uniqueness of her vision of mercy. For Julian, grace is the extension of the working of mercy (our again-making by Christ's incarnation) in time. The Holy Spirit confirms in us that oneing which is ours in Christ; by virtue of this confirming we are saved existentially. By grace, we become events of divine mercy.

We have seen how our humanity itself is a participation in Christ's incarnation.[86] The oneing of our substance to our sensuality, although completed historically in Christ (the 'perfect man,' i.e., fulfilled human nature, proceeding from God and in perfect communion with God), must still take place existentially in us.[87] When we are completely oned, our whole self is fully integrated in God in Christ, the ground of our being.[88] Living as we do in time, we experience this oneing progressively as we grow to maturity in Christ, which growth is reflected in our life of virtue. In shifting her attention from God's eternal perspective,[89] Julian necessarily introduces the traditional theological concept of grace, the basis of the christian life of virtue initiated at baptism.

For Julian, grace provides the explanation for the paradox we experience as we live in this world: we are not yet fully oned, but we are 'kept' safe and sure by God's merciful 'keeping,' i.e., through the working of mercy and grace.[90] Grace allows for our being oned in time and for the tension involved in that oneing, answering one of Julian's basic questions: what is the meaning of our earthly life, our life lived in the shadow of sin? We experience the tension, the 'contrariousness' between our lower, 'outward' part (our sensuality which is bound up with time), and our higher, 'inward' part (our substance *sub specie aeternitatis*).[91] Our life on

---

86 See p. 48-56, above.

87 56:33-37; Julian also speaks of Christ as 'perfyte man' and ourselves as being fulfilled in his perfection by grace. [58:56-59] Cf. 57:44-46.

88 For Julian, Christ is the ground of our life [28:29; 53:32; 63:28-30], the divine 'mene that kepyth *the* substannce and the sensualyte to geder' [56:11-18].

89 In God's sight, the human person mirrors Christ both in substance and in sensuality: substance mirrors the Trinity in the person of Christ; sensuality mirrors Christ's embodied being-in-the-world. See 10:55-61 (p. 53, above).

90 "And though we be wrath, and the contraryousnes that is in vs be nowe in tribulacion, deseses and woo, as fallyng in to oure blyndnesse and oure pronyte, yett be we suer and safe by the mercyfull kepyng of god that we perysch nott." [49:31-34]

91 Although we are ever like God in our substance, we are often unlike God in our

earth *is* the process of our being oned, the inward part's mastering of the outward by grace.[92] God, acting in our sensuality by grace, gives meaning to our existence in this world, gives a point to human history.[93] We are 'mercifully kept,' preserved and protected by grace as we struggle towards maturity in Christ.

a. Mercy as 'keeping' is the domain of grace: the indwelling Christ

To understand Julian's doctrine on grace,[94] we must view grace in terms of its role in the economy of salvation. We are saved because we are oned in Christ by the working of mercy; however, while we are in this 'changeable' life, Christ's mercy takes the form of our being 'kept' by the Holy Spirit.

> But oure good lorde the holy gost, whych is endlesse lyfe dwellyng in oure soule, full truly kepyth vs and werketh ther in a pees, and bryngyth it to ees by grace, and makyth it buxom and accordyth it to god. And this is the mercy and the wey that oure good lord contynually ledyth vs in, as longe as we be in this lyfe whych is channgeable. [48:2-6]

The salvation effected by Christ is communicated to us through the life of grace, i.e., the presence of the Holy Spirit in our souls.[95] Here Julian is speaking about life in our temporal world (our 'changeable' life). God works in time by grace, and the working of that grace cannot be separated from Christ: although grace finds its source in the Trinity,[96] it is in

---

condition, i.e., by our sins. [43:2-4; cf. 41:40-41] The tension of christian life, which tension we experience as wrath or 'unpeace,' results from the 'contrarying' of sin to the presence of grace. [49:45-49]

92 "I saw truly that the inward party is master and souereyne to the outward, nought chargyng nor takyng hede of the wylles of *that*, but alle the intent and the wylle is sett endlesly to be onyd to our lorde Jhesu. That the outward party sholde drawe the inward to assent was not shewde to me; but that the inwarde party drawyth the outward party by grace, and both shalle be onyd in blysse *without* ende by the vertu of Christ, this was shewde." [19:33-39] Cf. 71:19-24; 2 Cor 4:16.

93 Our 'higher part,' our substance, has no *history*. [55:50-51]

94 Although Julian herself does not actually use the terminology of 'uncreated grace' and 'created grace,' her doctrine does not contradict such terms. Her vocabulary clearly points to the notion of 'uncreated grace' when she tells us that grace is God, as unmade kind is God' [63:10-11]; moreover, those gifts which the Holy Spirit breathes into us [55:36-38; cf. 57:38-41] may easily be understood as 'created grace' (or charisms). See also note 144, p. 81, below.

95 E.g., God teaches us by grace [10:78-81] and enables us to pray by grace [43:49-55].

96 62:5-12; cf. 49:17-20.

and through Christ that divine grace enters the world.[97] Grace is the
mode of Christ's continual working of mercy in our existential lives, i.e.,
where sin is still allowed to pursue us.[98] In this earthly life, we seek for
help and grace from Christ[99] in our struggle against sin because grace is
Christ's to bestow.[100]

The *Shewings* contains many examples of Julian's christological view
of grace: Christ gives us his grace in order that we might understand and
choose rightly;[101] his word itself is grace to us;[102] he reforms our judgment by grace;[103] he 'mercifully and graciously' sustains and nourishes us
with the sacraments, i.e., the life of grace in the Church;[104] and he draws
us to himself and to each other by grace.[105] The 'wounds' of contrition,
compassion, and willful longing for God ('means' by which we are saved)
are Christ's work in us by grace.[106] Christ 'touches' us[107] and 'keeps' us by
his touch,[108] and that 'touching' is grace.[109]

We are 'kept by grace'[110] and 'kept by Christ' through grace (or by
his 'gracious inwardly keeping').[111] There is no contradiction in saying

---

97   "Alle the trinyte wrought in the passion of Crist, mynystryn habonndance of vertuse
      and plente of grace to vs by hym." [23:30-31]
98   60:57-59; cf. 35:37-40.
99   7:51-52; 21:10-14; 46:23-25; 61:51; cf. 41:52. The 'help and grace' we seek from
      Christ is the Holy Spirit. [59:33]
100   While she sometimes refers to God's grace [43:45-55; 51:44.151.160], Julian usually
      speaks of grace as Christ's: 23:17-27; 39:21-25; 41:64-67; 52:12-14; 59:37-48; 60:33-
      37; 60:58-59 [cf. 60:55-57]; 61:10-14; 68:48-50; 70:17-19; 78:31-34.
      Julian also speaks of Christ's gracious presence [65:13], his gracious hands
      [61:66], his gracious words [61:72], his gracious comfort [79:4-5], his gracious
      teaching [79:23]. Christ is our 'gracious mother' [60:7; 61:48-49; 63:44] who teaches
      us and shows us our sin by the 'sweet gracious light of himself' [42:32-33; 78:2-5;
      cf. 82:25-26]. (N.b., for Julian, the adjective 'gracious' always has a theological
      context; our modern connotations of 'gracious' derive from the more primary
      theological sense it had in medieval English literature.)
101   37:3-4 (cf. 78:34); 61:12-14.
102   41:64-66; cf. 60:36; 61:72.
103   45:9-10.
104   60:30-37.
105   71:21-24.
106   39:22-29; see chapter 4, p. 192-198, below, for a more complete discussion of the
      'wound' of compassion.
107   36:46; 40:4; 52:12; 61:10-11; 71:39; 79:31-32; 81:14.
108   "And whan we be fallen by freelte or blyndnes, than oure curtesse lord touchyng
      vs steryth vs and kepyth vs." [79:31-32] Cf. 52:11-13.
109   1:19-20; 20:29; 39:6; 40:31-32 [cf. 52:54]; 43:45-49; 52:62; 74:11-12.
110   48:2-3; 52:67; 62:5-12; 80:2-6.
111   79:15-19; cf. 71:38-43; 59:37-42.

that Christ 'keeps' us by grace (i.e., the Holy Spirit) because, although 'keeping' lies in the domain of grace in terms of its temporal reference, it remains nevertheless Christ's 'keeping.'[112] (In her christological view of grace, Julian resonates with John, for whom the Holy Spirit is always the spirit of Christ in the economy of salvation.)[113]

When we look at Julian's understanding of the role of grace in our lives, we find that the working of grace itself has a strong christological reference. We are already united ontologically to Christ by his incarnation in the first two moments of our oneing, i.e., kind and mercy;[114] the task of grace is to unite the soul existentially with Christ. Just as the Holy Spirit *is* the bond of love between the Father and the Son,[115] so

---

112 Clark suggests that Julian appropriates 'keeping' to the Holy Spirit by the fact that in the Short Text she refers to God as 'the maker, the lover, the keeper' [iv: 16-18] and follows that by the traditional Augustinian trinitarian appropriation of God as 'all mighty, all wise and all good' [iv:48]. Clark holds, moreover, that Julian is probably simply following common medieval doctrine in positing 'keeping' (or conservation) as the special domain of the Holy Spirit, citing Thomas Aquinas (*Summa Theologiae* 1a, q.39, a.8). See J.P.H. Clark, "Nature, Grace and the Trinity in Julian of Norwich," 203-204.

The Long Text of the *Shewings,* however, does not readily support such a straightforward appropriation. Julian does modify the word order in the Long Text (God is 'the maker, the keper, the louer' [5:19; cf. 4:11-12] and adds that the Trinity is our maker, 'keeper,' and lover 'by our lord Jesu Christ, and in our lord Jesu Christ' [4:12-14]), even though she retains the original order in her explanation: "In this little thing I saw iij propreties. The first is *that* god made it, the secund that god loueth it, the thirde that god kepyth it." [5:17-18] Julian's inconsistency in this instance, coupled with her specific references to Christ as our 'keeper' [52:31; 77:45], seems to suggest that God's 'keeping' retains a christological reference. Moreover, as Clark also points out (p. 204), to refer the middle term 'lover' to Christ presents the complication that it ascribes to Christ that which is conventionally appropriated to the Holy Spirit.

113 Christ sends the Spirit [John 14:16-17; 15:26; 20:22; 1 John 4:13]; the Spirit makes present in us the work of Christ [John 14:26; 16:7-15]; cf. 2 Cor 3:17 (the Lord is the Spirit).

114 See p. 46-47, above.

115 Julian makes frequent use of the traditional Augustinian appropriation of trinitarian love to the Holy Spirit: 1:10; 8:7-8;11:53-55; 35:15-17; 46:31-32; 58:13-14.36; 59:13-16; 61:39-40; 62:5-6; 73:28-31. She also indicates something of the nature of that love as originating in the Father and the Son: "Truth seeth god, and wisdom beholdyth god, and of theyse two comyth the thurde; and that is a meruelous delyght in god, which is loue. Where truth and wysedom is, verely there is loue, verely comyng of them both, and alle of goddes makyng. For god is endlesse souereyne truth, endlesse souereyne wysdom, endlesse souereyne loue vnmade." [44:8-12] Julian amplifies this insight in her explanation of the parable of the lord and the servant: "The lorde is god the father, the servant is the sonne Jesu Cryst,

in our life grace[116] is the unbreakable bond of loving union between
Christ and the soul.

> For or that he made vs he louyd vs, and when we were made we louyd hym;
> and this is a lo(u)e made of the kyndly substanncyall goodnesse of the holy
> gost, myghty in reson of the myghte of the fader, and wyse in mynde of the
> wysdom of the son. [53:36-39]

Grace is the 'ground of love' in us,[117] the bond of love that stands at the
heart of Christ's 'gracious inwardly keeping' of our souls.

> Also oure curteyse lorde, in that same tyme he shewde fulle swetly and fulle
> myghtely the endleshed and the vnchanngeabylte of his loue, and also his
> grete goodnesse and his gracious inwardely kepyng, that the loue of hym and
> of oure sowlys shalle nevyr be depertyd vnto withouten ende. [79:15-19]

The existential bonding in love constitutes the 'royal lordship' of the
Holy Spirit. In an original trinitarian ternary (viz., Father, Mother, and
Lord), Julian attributes the property of lordship to the Holy Spirit.

> I beheld the werkyng of alle the blessyd trynyte, in whych behblldyng I saw
> and vnderstode these thre propertes: the properte of the faderhed, and the
> properte of the mother hed, and the properte of the lordschyppe in one god.
> [58:19-22][118]

This lordship is the lordship of love, of grace.

> For the furst I saw and vnderstode that the hygh myght of the trynyte is
> oure fader, and the depe wysdom of the trynite is oure moder, and the grete
> loue of the trynyte is oure lorde. [58:34-36]

> I it am, the myght and the goodnes of faderhode, I it am, the wysdom and the
> kyndnes of moderhode, I it am, the lyght and the grace that is all blessyd loue;
> I it am, the trynyte, I it am, the vnyte. [59:14-16]

> the holy gost is the evyn loue whych is in them both." [51:217-218] The Holy Spirit
> is the 'ground of love' in the servant: "And inward in hym was shewed a ground
> of loue, whych loue he had to the lorde, that was evyn lyke the loue that the lord
> had to hym." [51:173-175]

116 Here we speak of uncreated grace. We shall return to the idea of created grace,
i.e., gifts or charisms (see p. 79-82, below).

117 See 51:173-175 (note 115, p. 75-76, above).

118 Julian goes on to identify these properties with the three persons. [58:22 27] Cf.
54:20-23; 58:59-72; 59:13-16.29-30; 83:14-16.

Grace belongs properly to God's 'lordship of love';[119] it is that 'sovereign uncreated love'[120] which reigns in our soul and which 'keeps' us safe by virtue of uniting us in love to Christ. Our lives are grounded in that bond of love without which we may not live: grace 'keeps' us in love.[121] Our 'keeping' lies within the domain of grace because the bond that 'keeps' us, the bond of love that is our oneing in Christ, *is* the Holy Spirit.

We have already seen how Julian appropriates the work of salvation to Christ alone.[122] Christ is with us even now, mercifully working our existential salvation.

> Christ aloone dyd alle the grett werkes that longyth to oure saluation, and none but he; and ryghte so he aloone doth now in the last end, that is to sey he dwellyth here in vs, and rewlyth vs, and ge(m)yth vs in this lyvyng, and brynggyth vs to his blesse. [80:14-18][123]

---

119 "Grace is a wurshypfull properte, whych longyth to ryall lordschyppe in the same loue. . . . [And] grace werkyth *with* mercy, reysyng, rewarding, endlesly ovyr passyng that oure lovyng and our traveyle deseruyth, spredyng abrode and shewyng the hye plentuousnesse, largesse of goddes ryall lordschyppe in his mervelouse curtesy." [48:29-30.32-35]

   Julian also describes the Holy Spirit as the goodness of the Trinity [e.g., 1:38-41; 32:15-16; 35:28-29; 36:67; 46:33-35; 48:9-11; 49:17-20; 53:36-39; 54:20-27; 58:12-14.59-62; 63:28-30; 77:17-19]; however, she further explains that God's love for us springs from God's goodness [cf. 53:36-39] and that this same goodness works through grace [62:11-12].

120 See 44:8-12 (note 115, p. 75, above); cf. 63:10; 84:10-15.

121 5:45; 35:42; 44:20-21; 48:14; 53:49-51; 75:3; 82:28-29; 85:9; cf. 49:5-6. Because Julian links grace to the love and goodness of the Holy Spirit, she can also say that we are 'kept' by God's love [8:14; 59:11; 84:8] and by God's goodness [49:24-29].

122 See p. 30-32, above.

123 Julian makes multiple references to Christ's dwelling in the soul, especially in reference to the sixteenth shewing: "And then oure good lorde opy*n*nd my gostely eye and shewde me my soule in *the* myddys of my harte. I saw *the* soule so large as it were an endlesse warde, and also as it were a blessyd kyngdom; and by the condicio*ns that* I saw there in I vnderstode *th*at it is a wurschypfulle cytte, in myddes of that cytte (sitts) oure lorde Jh*e*su, very god and very man, a feyer person and of large stature, hyghest bysschoppe, most solempne kynge, wurschypfullest lorde. . . . He syttyth in *the* soule evyn ryghte in peas and rest, and he rulyth and ye(m)yth hevyn and erth and all that is. The manhode *with* the godhed syttyth in rest, the godhede rulyth and ye(m)eth with*out*yn ony instrument or besynesse. And *the* soule is alle occupyed *with the* blessyd godhed, *that* is souereyne myghte, souereyne wysdom and souereyn goodnesse. The place that Jh*e*su takyth in oure soule he shall nevyr remoue with*out*en ende, as to my syght, for in vs is his homelyest home and his endlesse dwellyng." [68:2-17] Cf. 1:51-54; 51:328-331; 52:39-40; 54:34-35; 55:30-31; 56:23-25; 57:53-56; 81:9-12; cf. 77:42; 80:37-39; 81:2-15.

It is Julian's understanding of grace which provides the explanation for this saving presence of Christ in the soul which is not yet fully oned in him. The soul is 'occupied' with grace,[124] and Christ's presence in the soul is effected by this 'occupation' of the Holy Spirit. In a sense, the Holy Spirit is the condition of possibility for sharing Christ's divine life. Here again, Julian echoes John for whom divine indwelling is directly linked to the presence of the Holy Spirit.[125] Christ indwells by grace until we are brought into the full bliss of perfect union in heaven. In time, Christ works his mercy in our existential lives because we are oned in him through the bond of love that is the Holy Spirit. This bond of love 'keeps' us; we are safe because we are united to Christ. By the Holy Spirit we are able to touch Christ. As we are 'kept' by Christ's 'touch' (grace),[126] so too we are 'kept' by touching Christ: to 'cleave' to Christ through grace is to be sure and safe from all perils.[127]

The fruit of the Holy Spirit's lordship of love is the christian life, the life of Christ lived in us.[128] By grace, Christ dwells with us in time.[129] Christ is present in the soul, 'mercifully working' in us, and we are enabled to respond to Christ's presence by the 'gracious according' of the Holy Spirit.[130] We 'accord' by grace to Christ's working in us, and this correspondence to Christ constitutes our personal development, i.e, the growth of our 'virtues' (our powers). This is the 'buxomness'[131] wrought in us by grace.

---

124 23:17-18; cf. 7:9-11.

125 1 John 4:13-17; cf. John 14:15 -17:26.

126 See p. 73-74, above.

127 "Flee we to oure lorde, and we shall be comfortyd. Touch we hym, and we shalle be made cleene. Cleve we to hym, and we shalle be suer and safe from alle manner of peryllys." [77:49-51] Here we may find allusions to the Holy Spirit as 'comforter' and to the cleansing waters of christian baptism. Cf. 77:14-16; 86:9.

128 In this, Julian recalls the Pauline doctrine on faith and the grace of baptism. Cf. Rom 6:1-4; Gal 2:20-21; Col 2:12.

129 "Oure lord is *with* us, kepyng vs and ledyng in to fulhed of joy." [77:42-43] "He shewde hym in erth thus, as it were a pylgrymage, that is to sey he is here *with* vs ledyng vs, and shalle be tylle when he hath brought vs alle to his blysse in hevyn." [81:6-8] Cf. 52:29-40; 79:40-41; 80:14-18.38-43; and note 123, p. 77, above.

130 "Cryst marcifully is werkyng in vs, and we gracyously accordyng to hym thorow the yefte and the vertu of the holy gost." [54:34-36]

131 Julian used words such as 'buxom' (pliant) [48:4] and 'soft' [74:8], typical expressions used by the English mystical writers of her day for describing the passive promptitude of the soul to the movements of the Spirit, a promptitude characteristic of the gifts of the Spirit. See Conrad Pepler, "The Ground of Union," *Life of the Spirit* 4 (1949) 253.

But oure good lorde the holy gost, whych is endlesse lyfe dwellyng in oure soule, full truly kepyth vs and werketh ther in a pees, and bryngyth it to ees by grace, and makyth it buxom and accordyth it to god. [48:2-4]

Grace makes us 'supple' to Christ's merciful work in us.[132]

In our existential oneing, we 'accord' to our kind, our truest 'self' in Christ.[133] What Christ is by nature, we are by participation, i.e., by grace.

For the same vertuse *that* we haue receyvyd of oure substannce gevyn to vs in kynd of the goodnes of god, the same vertuse by the werkyng of mercy be gevyn to vs in grace, throw the holy gost renewed; which vertuse and gyftys are tresoured to vs in Jhesu Criste. [57:38-41][134]

Although we are like Christ in substance or kind, we are unlike Christ in condition because of our sin.[135] It is only by grace that we are brought into our true identity.[136] For example, we realize existentially by grace the natural hatred for sin that is proper to our kind.[137] While we grow to maturity, Christ 'treasures' in himself the virtues which become ours by grace.

And all the gyftes that god may geue to the creature he hath gevyn to his son Jhesu for vs, whych gyftes he wonnyng in vs hath beclosyd in hym in to the tyme that we be waxyn and growyn, oure soule *with* oure body and oure body *with* oure soule. Eyther of them take helpe of other tylle we be broughte vp in to stature as kynde werkyth; and than in the ground of kynd *with* werkyng of mercy *the* holy gost gracyously enspirith in to vs gyftes ledyng to endlesse lyfe. [55:31-38]

---

132 58:48-50; cf. 43:30-33.

133 See p. 49-50, above.

134 The life and virtue we have in the lower part come from the higher by grace. [52:88]

135 43:2-4.

136 Grace makes us like Christ 'in condition as we are in kind.' [41:40-41] Cf. 72:20-21.

137 "Here may we see that we haue verely of kynd to hate synne, and we haue verely of grace to hate synne, for kynd is all good and feyer in it selfe, and grace was sent oute to saue kynde and dystroy synne, and bryng agayne feyer kynde in to the blessyd poynt from thens it cam, that is god, *with* more noblynes and wurschyppe by the vertuse wurkyng of grace." [63:2-7]

'Hating of sin and wickedness' is ours through the lordship of the Holy Spirit; it belongs properly to virtue to hate sin and wickedness. [59:30-36] Cf. 40:31-32; 52:26-27.53-56; 76:4-8.

Christ is our treasury. All that is wanting in us is found in him.[138] Our will is 'kept' whole and safe in him.[139] Moreover, it is the bond of love, i.e., grace, which 'keeps' us safe in Christ and makes his virtues our own.

> For Jhesu is in all that shall be safe, and all that (shall) be sa(fe) is in Jhesu, and all of the charyte of god, with obedience, mekenesse and paciens and vertuous that longyth to vs. [51:265-267][140]

Once again we see the strong christological focus of Julian's doctrine: all our virtues are Christ's.[141] To 'come again into our substance' is to be brought into the 'virtue of Christ.'[142] It is not until we are completely oned in Christ that we become 'holy,' i.e., in full possession of our 'mights' (our powers or faculties).[143] In our earthly condition, we are enabled to participate in Christ's life through the working of grace, which participation constitutes our existential oneing. In a real sense, the Holy Spirit's personal identity remains undisclosed in the work of our 'gracious according' to Christ; in the process of our becoming holy, it is the person of Christ that becomes ever more manifest. Made supple by grace to the life of Christ within us, we reflect that life by becoming more and more Christlike. The fact of the progressive nature of our oneing becomes apparent whenever we take on further likeness to Christ.

To speak of our christian life in grace is, necessarily, to speak of faith. For Julian, faith is the first fruit of the 'gracious according' of the Holy Spirit; it is the beginning of the christian life, the virtue (or 'power') from which all other christian virtues flow.

> And oure feyth is a vertu that comyth of oure kynde substannce in to oure sensuall soule by the holy gost, in whych vertu alle oure vertues comyn to vs, for without that no man may receyue vertues, for it is nought eles but a ryght vnderstandyng with trew beleue and suer truste of oure beyng, that we be in god and he in vs, whych we se nott.
>
> And this vertu with all other that god hath ordeyned to vs comyng ther in werkyth in vs grete thynges; for Cryst marcifully is werkyng in vs, and we gracyously accordyng to hym thorow the yefte and the vertue of the holy gost. This werkyng maykyth that we be Crystes chyldren and cristen in lyvyng. [54:27-37]

---

138 42:64-65.
139 53:16-22; 59:40-42; cf. 45:2-3.40-42; 53:46-49.
140 Cf. 10:69-71.80-81; 77:20-21.
141 Julian tells us, moreover, that the powers of all creatures, even the heavens and the earth, stand in Christ. [18:16-20]
142 55:19-21.
143 "For in to the tyme that it [our soul] is in the full myghtis, we may nott be alle holy." [56:33-34] Cf. 43:37-38; 75:21-23.

As we have already seen, the 'virtues' which flow from faith are the gifts of grace[144] which are given to us through the Holy Spirit as we mature in Christ, those same gifts which are treasured in Christ until we be fully grown, i.e., until we come into our full powers.[145] Julian consistently attributes our life of virtue (our 'good living') to the help and grace of the Holy Spirit.[146] The life of faith, with all the virtues that follow from faith, evidences our existential oneing by manifesting the presence of the Holy Spirit in our soul; faith is our participation in divine life, our existential 'according' to kind.[147] For Julian, every aspect of christian life, including prayer, witnesses to this oneing by grace.[148]

Julian's concept of faith cannot be fully understood except within the context of the life of the Church. Faith is our 'sight' while we remain on earth.[149] By faith, we see who we truly are in Christ.[150] Identifying this gift of sight with the faith of the Church (i.e., its doctrine and teachings), she tells us that 'faith keeps the sight by grace.'[151] Faith is the ground of all the 'goods' by which we are guided to salvation: the commandments, the sacraments, the virtues.[152] In other words, we are 'kept' and saved by the

---

144 Here we speak of 'created grace' which takes the form of virtues or charisms. Julian clearly uses 'grace' to mean a gratuitous gift which God bestows on us. [51:49-53; cf. 41:24-25.]

    Julian describes the virtue of charity (our response of love by grace) as 'charity given': "Charyte vnmade is god, charyte made is oure soule in god, charyte gevyn is vertu, and *that* is a gracious gyfte of wurkyng, in whych we loue god for hym selfe, and oure selfe in god, and alle *that* god lovyth for god." [84:13-15] Colledge and Walsh point out Julian's consonance with the Thomistic doctrine which distinguishes between uncreated charity (the Holy Spirit who dwells in the soul), created charity (our participation in the love between the Father and the Son, which love is the Holy Spirit), and charity as an infused virtue, a 'given' grace (Thomas Aquinas, *Summa Theologiae* 2a2ae, q.23, a.2; q.24, a.2 and 3). See *A Book of Showings,* 84:10, notes, p. 727; cf. note 94, p. 73, above.

145 See 55:31-38 (p. 79, above); see also note 143, p. 80, above.

146 35:4-5; 41:51-53.

147 54:27-28, above; cf. 57:26-28.

148 For Julian, any movement of the will towards God is the work of grace (e.g., 39:21-23; 52:58-68; 61:11-14; 65:2-4). She defines prayer as the true and lasting union of wills (the soul's with God's) wrought in us by the working of the Holy Spirit. [41:30-32] Cf. 40:7; 41:52-53.61-64; 42:18-20; 43:45-49. Our prayer is a witness that we will as God wills. [43:4-5]

149 For Julian, 'sight' is always a gift of grace. We shall return to the link between sight and faith in chapter 3 (see p. 155-159, below).

150 46:2-5; 62:26-27.

151 7:60-67; 70:16-40; cf. 1:40-41; 2:40; 30:5-7; 34:18-20.

152 57:26-41.

life of faith as it is taught and lived in the Church.[153] By actively embracing this life of faith, we fulfill Christ's desire that we be his 'helpers' in his work of oneing us.[154] Julian further indicates the participative nature of our existential oneing by exhorting us to 'keep ourselves in the faith' by grace in order to be saved.[155] If we 'keep' ourselves in the 'sight' that faith gives, we shall not be overcome,[156] for our faith is 'grounded in God's word,' which word shall never be broken.[157]

Thus, we have our 'gracious keeping' in the life of faith. We are 'kept in true faith' (and in the other 'virtues') by Christ through the working of grace.

> By gracyous toucchyng of swete lyghtenyng of goostly lyfe, wher by that we ar kept in true feyth, hope and charite, *with* contrycion and devotion and also *with* contemplacion and alle manner of tru joyes and swete comfortes. The blessydfull chere of oure lorde god werkyth it in vs by grace. [71:39-43][158]

> For a boue the feyth is no goodnesse keppt in this lyffe, as to my syght; and beneth the feyth is no helth of soule. But in the feyth, there wyll oure lorde we kepe vs, for we haue by his goodnesse and his owne werkyng to kepe vs in the feyth; and by his suffra*n*nce throw goostely enmyte we are asayde in *the* fayth and made myghty. [71:12-16]

It is Christ's own working in us by grace that enables us to 'keep' ourselves in the faith of the Church.

b. The 'working of mercy and grace'

Throughout the *Shewings,* mercy and grace are consistently and inextricably linked.[159] Their interconnectedness is seen, first of all, within the context of Julian's understanding of the three moments of our oneing: kind, mercy, and grace are 'three properties in one goodness.'

---

153 80:2-8; cf. 39:6-13; 52:58-60; 61:61-64.
154 57:56-59.
155 1:40-41; 9:23; 32:50-53; 33:24-27; 70:5-8.26-40; 71:38-43.
156 70:16-40.
157 32:37-40.50-56.
158 For Julian, 'alle manner of tru joyes and swete comfortes' is a natural way to describe the effect of grace on our life. Comfort and joy are sure hallmarks of the working of the Holy Spirit. [1:19-20; 23:15-29; 36:36-50; 37:5-6; 40:31-32; 48:2-4.36-37; 74:8; 79:4-5.22-24]
159 See note 1, p. 57, above.

Of this substancyall kyndnesse mercy and grace spryngyth and spredyth in to vs, werkyng all thyn*ges* in fulfyllyng of oure joy. Theyse be oure groundys, in whych we haue oure beyng, oure encrese and oure fulfyllyng. For in kynde we haue oure lyfe and oure beyng, and in mercy and grace we haue oure encres and oure fulfyllyng. It be thre propertes in one goodnes, and where that one werkyth alle werkyn in the thynges whych be now longyng to vs. [56:39-44][160]

While Julian's understanding of kind, mercy, and grace is clearly trinitarian,[161] she does indicate a special relationship between mercy and grace, almost over against kind. While mercy and grace spring from the 'kindly ground' we have in God,[162] we cannot be saved by our kind without the working of mercy and grace.[163] Moreover, this 'working of mercy and grace' is specifically related to our being 'kept' in time.

And what tyme oure soule is enspyred in oure body, in whych we be made sensuall, as soone mercy and grace begynne to werke, havyng of vs cure and kepyng *with* pytte and loue. [55:16-18]

This expression, 'the working of mercy and grace,'[164] is probably the most significant phrase in Julian's language of 'keeping.' Not only is the work of mercy paralleled with the action of grace, but they are jointly credited with the existential accomplishing of our salvation in Christ. We have our 'keeping' by the working of mercy and grace.[165] Julian further clarifies the unity between mercy and grace when she describes our 'keeping' by mercy and grace as 'two workings in one love.'

But yet in all this the swet eye of pytte and of loue departeth nevyr from vs, ne the werkyng of mercy cesyth nott. For I behelde the *properte* of mercy, and I behelde the properte of grace, whych haue ij maner of workyng in one loue. Mercy is a pyttefull properte, whych longyth to moderhode in tender loue; and grace is a wurshypfull properte, whych longyth to ryall lordschyppe in the same loue. [48:25-30][166]

In some ways, perhaps, it may seem that Julian actually identifies mercy with grace. For example, she practically defines mercy in terms of

---

160 Cf. 56:36-38.
161 See p. 46-47, above.
162 56:39-41.
163 56:51-55.
164 35:19-25; 40:42; 49:42; 55:16-18; 57:10.11-12.13.29-30; 77:21; cf. 11:27.30; 35:43; 40:16; 45:9-10; 46:8-10; 48:17.32; 55:37; 56:30-31.37; 57:39-40; 58:50; 59:2.22-23; 60:33; 77:5-6; 78:42-43; 83:19-21.
165 55:16-18.
166 Cf. 52:81-92; 59:44-48.

the working of grace while we are in time, i.e., in a condition of changeableness.

> But oure good lorde the holy gost, whych is endlesse lyfe dwellyng in oure
> soule, full truly kepyth vs and werketh ther in a pees, and bryngyth it to ees
> by grace, and makyth it buxom and accordyth it to god. And this is the mercy
> and the wey that oure good lord continually ledyth vs in, as longe as we be
> in this lyfe whych is channgeable. [48:2-6][167]

The role of the Holy Spirit (or grace) is described as effecting the working of mercy in time until we are brought to the fullness of salvation in heaven, the unchangeableness of God.[168] The working of mercy in time, our 'keeping in love,' is gracious,[169] i.e., we are saved *by* mercy *through* grace.

We can see not only that mercy is 'gracious,' but also that grace acts as the extension[170] of mercy in time. Mercy (our oneing to God in Christ) is effected existentially by the bond of the Holy Spirit, i.e., grace. Christ ones us, and the bond of union is the Holy Spirit. This existential oneing is the completion or confirming of the working of mercy (our ontological or substantial oneing to God in Christ). Thus, by grace, the working of mercy continues unceasingly in time.[171] Existentially, we become events of God's mercy by grace. It is all one work of Christ;[172] grace ones us existentially, making mercy (the salvific work of Christ) present in the soul.[173]

Julian's vocabulary also indicates that the role of grace is to complete or extend the work of mercy: grace works with mercy,[174] rewarding,[175]

---

167 Cf. 47:13-21; 48:13-35.

168 Cf. 49:54-55.

169 "For the ground of mercy is in love, and the werkyng of mercy is oure kepyng in loue. . . . That is to sey, as to my syght, mercy is a swete gracious werkyng in loue, medlyd *with* plentuous pytte, for mercy werkyth vs kepyng, and mercy werkyth turnyng to vs all thyng to good." [48:13-14.17-19]

170 At one point when she was speaking of Mary, Julian attributes to grace the activity of extension in the actual expression 'continued by grace': "For in this I saw a substance of kynde loue contynued by grace that his creatures haue to hym, whych kynde loue was most fulsomly shewde in his swete mother." [18:4-6]

171 48:4-6.

172 Julian consistently maintains her christological focus: mercy and grace work in our lives by the power of Christ's passion. [45:8-11; 56:30-31]

173 80:14-21.

174 48:32; 58:50.

175 7:58-59; 48:32-44; 58:27-30.52-55. 'Raising up to greater joy' is another expression Julian uses for 'rewarding': 38:30-33; 52:95-96; 56:37-44; 59:5-8; 62:8-12; 63:4-7; 74:15-16.

confirming,[176] fulfilling it;[177] grace renews the working of mercy[178] and spreads mercy abroad.[179] In her most clearly elaborated reflection on the relationship between mercy and grace, Julian tells us that mercy works our 'keeping' and that it is grace that does the actual rewarding or gifting. In other words, mercy suffers our 'falling,' and grace picks us up again.

> For the ground of mercy is in loue, and the werkyng of mercy is oure kepyng in loue; and this was shewed in such a manner that I culde not perceyve of the *properte* of mercy other wyse but as it were all loue in loue.
>
> That is to sey, as to my syght, mercy is a swete gracious werkyng in loue, medlyd *with* plentuous pytte, for mercy werkyth vs kepyng, and mercy werkyth turnyng to vs all thyng to good. Mercy for loue sufferyth vs to feyle by mesure; and in as moch as we fayle, in so moch we falle, and in as much as we falle, in so moch we dye. For vs behovyth nedys to dye in as moch as we fayle syghte and felyng of god that is oure lyfe. Our faylyng is dredfulle, oure fallyng is shamfull, and oure dyeng is sorowfull.
>
> Yet in all this the swet eye of pytte and of loue departeth nevyr from vs, ne the werkyng of mercy cesyth nott. For I behelde the *properte* of mercy, and I behelde the properte of grace, whych haue ij maner of workyng in one loue. Mercy is a pyttefull properte, whych longyth to moderhode in tender loue; and grace is a wurshypfull properte, whych longyth to ryall lordschyppe in the same loue. Mercy werkyth kypyng, sufferyng, quyckyng and helyng, and alle is of tendyrnesse of loue; and grace werkyth *with* mercy, reysyng, rewarding, endlesly ovyr passyng that oure lovyng and our traveyle deseruyth, spredyng abrode and shewyng the hye plentuousnesse, largesse of goddes ryall lordschyppe in his mervelouse curtesy. And this is of *the* habundannce of loue, for grace werkyth oure dredfull faylyng in to plentuouse and endlesse solace; and grace werkyth oure shamefull fallyng in to hye wurschyppefull rysyng; and grace werkyth oure sorowfull dyeng in to holy blyssyd lyffe. [48:13-39][180]

Grace, in 'raising us up,' actually rewards us with a higher 'nobility' than would be ours had we not fallen.[181] Grace fulfills, i.e., 'fills full' the failing.[182] This 'fulfilling' wrought by grace is described as 'rewarding':

---

176 59:29-30.

177 55:21; 56:43; 57:16; 58:31-33.52-55.58-59.

178 "The same vertuse by the werkyng of mercy be gevyn to vs in grace, throw the holy gost renewed." [57:39-40]

179 48:34; 56:40-41; 59:45-48; cf. 60:2-6.

180 Cf. 35:19-25.

181 Cf. 38:30-33; 46:24-25; 52:46-50.95-96; 63:4-7; 77:5-6. Julian speaks of 'the profytes of oure trybulacion that oure lorde shall make vs to gett by by mercy and grace.' [56:36-37] Cf. 35:43; 59:2-4.22-23.

182 48:37-38; 57:8-11.

> And in oure good lorde the holy gost we haue oure rewardyng and our yeld-
> yng for oure lyvyng and oure traveyle, and endlessly ovyrpassyng alle that we
> desyer in his mervelous curtesy of his hye plentuous grace. . . . In [this] we
> haue oure fulfyllyng. [58:27-30.31-32]

Grace rewards us for our travail,[183] giving us the encouragement and
strength we need to rise from our falling. Rewarding is the 'raising up'
accomplished by grace,[184] the changing of our falling and dying into
surety of life.[185] This rewarding stands at the heart of the relationship
of grace to mercy.

> And grace werkyth *with* mercy, and namely in two propertes, as it was shewde,
> whych werkyng longyth to the thurde person, the holy goste. He werkyth,
> rewardyng and gevyng. Rewardyng is a gyfte of trust that *the* lorde doth to
> them that hath traveyled; and gevyng is a curtesse werkyng whych he doth
> frely of grace, fulfyllyng and ovyr passyng alle that is deservyd of creaturys.
> [58:50-55]

An understanding of the working of grace as 'rewarding' helps us to
make sense of what seem to be duplicate attributions to mercy and to
grace. For example, there is no inconsistency in saying that 'mercy turns
all to good,'[186] 'grace turns all to goodness and worship,'[187] and 'mercy and grace turn all to goodness and worship';[188] on the contrary, the
transformation of all things to good *is* the working of mercy by grace, i.e.,
mercy 'travails,' and grace rewards that travail.[189] Parallel attributions
to mercy (or Christ) and to grace may be similarly interpreted.[190] In

---

183 Cf. 14:3-20; 83:17-21.
184 39:21; 46:24-25; 48:32.37-38; 52:11-13; 62:8-9.
185 48:38-39.
186 48:19.
187 48:32-45; 52:95-96; 62:9-12; 74:15-16.
188 59:5-8.
189 In the parable, the Son, by grace, brings his 'city' (the soul) to a 'noble fairness' by
     hard travail. [51:151-152] Cf. 35:19-25.
190 Christ teaches [34:18; 40:47; 71:8; 73:2; 78:31-35; 79:22-24] and grace teaches [30:7;
     40:32; 32:51-52; 39:13; 63:18; 79:22-24]; Christ leads us [81:6-8] and grace leads
     [35:30; 45:36-37; 56:9; 83:15-16]; Christ is our 'savior' (see note 46, p. 30, above)
     and our 'keeper' [52:31; 77:45], and grace saves [63:2-7] and 'keeps' [71:38-43] us.
     We may understand these statements by realizing that, for Julian, Christ works in
     time by grace.
        While Julian properly attributes our restoring to mercy [57:15-16; 58:46-47.56-
     57], she also speaks about our being restored ('brought again') by grace [51:43-
     44.151-152.159-160; 62:16-18; 63:4-7]; similarly, our 'increasing' is properly attribut-
     ed to mercy [56:38-44; 58:31-33.46], but also to grace [46:24; 55:21; 58:31.68].
     Mercy gives us 'sight' [61:33-34; 63:12-15; 70:30-35; 78:2-5], a role Julian generally

addition, the concept of rewarding helps us to understand why Julian ascribes so many things jointly to the working of mercy and grace.[191]

c. Mercy: the key to the relationship between nature and grace

As we have seen, our salvation is an event both outside of time (our
'kindly substance' is oned to God in the Trinity in the person of Christ)
and within the realm of time, i.e., both once-for-all historically in the
Christ event and throughout time in the continuing process of our being
individually, existentially oned in Christ by the working of grace. For
Julian, our oneing (or, as we experience it in time, our 'keeping') is one
single event of divine love, albeit in three aspects or moments: our 'first
making' (kind), our 'again-making' in Christ (mercy), and our existential
'according' to the indwelling Christ (grace).

We may summarize Julian's teaching on our oneing by kind, mercy,
and grace in terms of the Trinity: the Father wills our salvation, the Son
works it, and the Holy Spirit confirms it.[192] In *kind,* our salvation is
ordained and willed by the Father who creates us and is our 'keeper' in
kind. This first making is by virtue of Christ's incarnation: our kind or
nature is defined by Christ, first prepared for him as a capacity for at-
one-ness with God. We are saveable because of our nature, not in spite
of it. Our nature is oned to God in the person of Christ, in whom humanity is not only defined but is also present in the Trinity without
reference to space and time. In *mercy,* salvation enters the realm of time,
'mercifully worked' by Christ who perfectly accomplishes the will of the
Father. By virtue of his passion and death, the Son defines humanity
(our kind) in himself in his incarnation; oneing substance to sensuality,

---

assigns to grace [6:53-54; 7:55-58; 10:16.77; 20:26-30.35-36; 35:32-33.45; 36:49-50;
43:18-19.35-36.45-59; 45:36-38; 49:7-8; 52:53-54.80; 53:10-11; 64:49-51; 65:35-37;
72:23-24; 78:2-3.15].

191 E.g., we are 'kept in faith' by mercy and grace [33:24-26; 57:28-30]; we are raised
to joy by mercy and grace [35:43; 59:2; 77:4-6]; mercy and grace work all things to
good in fulfilling our joy [56:39-41; 59:6-8]; we 'increase and wax' by the furthering
and speeding of mercy and grace [46:9-10]; mercy and grace restore and fulfill our
kind [57:9-10.14-16; 60:3-5]; we have our virtues by the helping and speeding of
mercy and grace [59:21-23]; we are made meek and mild by the working of mercy
and grace [49:42]; we are enabled to give our intent to love and meekness by the
working of mercy and grace [40:41-43]; our sins are forgiven by mercy and grace
[40:16]; Jesus reforms our judgment by mercy and grace [45:8-11]; Christ 'bought'
us by mercy and grace [56:30-31]; we 'see' by the 'sweet light of mercy and grace'
[40:3-5]; we know, believe, and walk in the light with mercy and grace [83:19-21].

192 59:21-30; see also p. 30-32, above.

Christ becomes the coincidence of opposites, the impossible possibility
which unites *in-God-ness* with *God-separateness*. Humanity is oned definitively to the Trinity by virtue of Christ's taking on sensuality. Mercy
proper, the event of our again-making in Christ's oneing of substance to
sensuality, represents an 'increasing' over our first making. By his incarnation, Christ gives us our embodied being-in-the-world. By mercy, we
are saved 'in deed' in the Christ event, historically once-for-all. Christ is
our 'keeper' in mercy. In *grace*, salvation is existentially realized or confirmed in the individual soul by the gracious 'according' of the Holy
Spirit. In time, we are united to Christ in the bond of love which is the
Holy Spirit. Christ dwells with us and, by grace, we are enabled to respond in love to his merciful working in us. This correspondence to the
life of Christ in us is experienced as progressive and is evidenced by
growth in the christian life of virtue. Grace is the working of mercy in
time, protecting us and leading us to full maturity in Christ, i.e., full
union. We experience this progressive oneing as 'keeping'; we are 'kept'
whole and safe in Christ by grace (even while we yet fail in our sensuality) until that time when we are completely oned to God in Christ in the
bliss of heaven. Here on earth, we are enabled to participate in Christ's
life in us through the working of grace, which participation constitutes
our existential oneing. Mercy proper (our oneing in Christ) works our
'keeping' by grace; grace is the extension of divine mercy in time. By the
'working of mercy and grace,' the human subject becomes an event of
God's mercy.

We can see that these three dimensions of the event of our salvation,
while distinct, may not be separated; rather, the 'moments' of our oneing
must be seen as facets of a whole, not in isolation. In their unity, they
disclose the unity of the Trinity's involvement in our salvation.[193] Kind,
mercy, and grace are 'three properties in one goodness'; where one
works, all work.[194] Even while her understanding of salvation is clearly
trinitarian, the role of Christ remains Julian's central focus: it is Christ
who 'works' our salvation.[195] Christ defines our kind in himself and
ones us existentially to himself through the working of grace. Mercy is
Christ, the definitive event of our salvation; by grace, *we* become events
of divine mercy, i.e., Christ's saving us. Thus, the first moment of our
oneing (kind or nature) and the third moment (grace) each find their

---

193 56:39-46.53-56; 57:38-41; 58:19-33.56-59; 59:13-16.21-36.

194 56:39-46; see also p. 82-83, above.

195 This 'working' of Christ does not lose its trinitarian reference: where the Son
'works,' the whole Trinity is involved; it is the Father's will that Christ works, and
his working is confirmed by the Holy Spirit. [59:29-30]

meaning in the second central moment (mercy). Our nature is defined by mercy, and grace is the extension of mercy in time. Mercy is thus the keystone in Julian's doctrine on our salvation by kind, mercy, and grace; it is mercy which gives nature and grace their meanings and establishes the relationship between the two.

Julian's doctrine on nature and grace demonstrates the continuity between our sinful selves and ourselves as fulfilled in Christ. The Spirit completes what we already are. Our human nature is neither repudiated nor altered; rather, its failing[196] is 'filled-full' by the working of mercy and grace, by which working all is turned to good. We are 'ordained' to full union with God in Christ by kind, and we 'get there by grace.'[197] Kind and grace are not opposed;[198] they are 'of one accord,' and we 'accord' ourselves to both by the mercy of God.[199]

The harmony between nature and grace has a clearly christological basis: the proper goodness of Christ.[200] Our nature flows from God and is restored by Christ's saving us through the working of grace.[201] This harmony between nature and grace is further accented in Julian's theology of 'keeping.' In kind, we have our ontological 'keeping': God is the ground of our kind.

> I saw that oure kynde is in god hoole, . . . whose kynde kepyth and mercy and grace restoryth and fulfyllyth. [57:14-16]

Our kind has its origin in God, who is 'substantial kindness.'[202] (Even mercy and grace, which restore and fulfill our kind, spring from the

---

196 57:8-11.

197 72:20-21; cf. 63:2-7.

198 Our human capacities belong to us both by kind and by grace [46:5-15; 59:40 42; 63:2-7; 74:20-23; 75:35-38]; we are bound to God for kind and for grace [62:22-23; cf. 72:55-56].

199 63:10-16.

200 Julian tells us that Christ is our 'mother in kind' and our 'mother in grace': "And thus is Jhesu oure very moder in kynd of oure furst makyng, and he is oure very moder in grace by takyng of oure kynde made. Alle the feyer werkyng and all the swete kyndly officis of dereworthy motherhed is in propred to the seconde person, for in hym we haue this goodly wylle, hole and safe without ende, both in kynde and in grace, of his owne propyr goodnesse." [59:37-42]

201 62:13-18.22-23; cf. 57:11-13.

202 As 'substantial kind unmade' [53:47], God is the source of all that is: "God is kynd in his being; that is to sey that goodnesse that is kynd, it is god. He is the grounde, he is the substannce, he is the same thyng that is kyndnesse, and he is very fader and very modyr of kyndys. And alle kyndes that he hath made to flowe out of hym to werke his wylle, it shulde be restoryd and brought agayne in to hym by saluacion of man throw the werkyng of grace." [62:13-18]

'kindness' that is God.)[203] In the Father, we have our 'keeping' regard to our 'kindly substance.'[204] We are 'kept' safe and whole in God.[205] In grace, on the other hand, we have our existential 'keeping': by grace, we become events of God's mercy, i.e., the oneing accomplished by Christ. What Christ is by nature, we are by grace; we participate in his humanity through the bond of the Holy Spirit. We have our 'keeping' in Christ by grace. Christ suffers our human living, and grace accords us to Christ's living in us in such a way that our true nature is fulfilled. The natural order is ordained to reach its perfection through the grace of Christ. Our task is to recognize and embrace our true nature in Christ, becoming Christ's 'helpers' in the work of our salvation.[206] Far from being a passive experience on our part, grace is that active embracing of our true nature, that 'according' to the life of Christ in us; all else is 'unkindness' (sin), which unkindness or 'contrarying' is the source of our pain, our suffering.

Thus, mercy is the key to Julian's christological understanding of the relationship between nature and grace. Mercy is our salvation, the event of our being oned in Christ by virtue of his incarnation. The Christ event defines nature as the oneing of substance and sensuality; we identify our truest 'self' in Christ. Mercy is also our existential 'keeping,' the same event of our salvation as experienced in time: we are oned to God in Christ existentially by the 'working of mercy and grace.' By the bond of the Holy Spirit, Christ extends his working of mercy in time. Grace is never an intervention into nature; rather, grace realizes the potential of the natural order. Because we live in the context of sin, we experience our existential oneing as a 'being kept safe' in Christ.[207]

---

203 56:38-56; cf. 57:14-16 (p. 89, above).

204 "In oure fader almyghty we haue oure kepyng and oure blesse, and a nemptys oure kyndely substannce whych is to vs by oure makyng fro without begynnyng." [58:22-24]

205 We have our ground in God *in Christ*, i.e., in the Wisdom that is the second person of the Trinity. See p. 48-51, above.

206 57:53-59.

207 While Julian does speak in trinitarian terms, our 'keeping' in kind, mercy, and grace retains a strong christological reference: in kind, we are 'kept in God' in Christ; we are 'kept by Christ' by the working of mercy; we are 'kept in Christ' by grace, that bond of love which is the Holy Spirit, by which bond Christ lives in us, mercifully working our salvation.

C. The Mystery of Sin

We have seen that mercy works our 'keeping,' the existential experience of the event of our salvation, our oneing in Christ. However, to say that we are 'kept' or 'saved' is necessarily to imply the existence of sin, that peril from which we are preserved and protected. We perceive our 'keeping' as a preservation from an ultimate triumph of sin over us, a protection which 'keeps' us safe until we are fully oned.[208] Even when we fall, we are secure because God's merciful 'keeping' never allows us to perish.[209] The divine pledge, 'I keep you full surely,' is an expression of God's continuing fidelity in the role of protector. Even the imagery of the *Shewings* speaks of protection: all being is fragile but is preserved and protected because God made it, loves it and 'keeps' it;[210] Christ is our 'clothing,' enfolding and protecting us;[211] Christ is our protective mother.[212] Indeed, the very notion of Christ as our 'savior' is rendered meaningless outside the context of sin and suffering; if all were indeed 'well,' we would have no need to be saved.

We find, then, that the notion of mercy as 'keeping' or protection brings us back to Julian's original dilemma: if 'all is well,' what does the human experience of sin mean? Not only does our experience tell us that all is 'not well' in our world, but the very presence of divine mercy in our world actually signals the presence of sin, that evil from which we must be protected.[213] If 'all is well,' what is the peril of sin?

1. The light of mercy and grace

When Julian is shown her sin, she is immediately consoled and reassured by God's promise of merciful 'keeping.'

---

208 "For the soule that shalle come to hevyn is so precyous to god and the place so wurshypfulle that the goodnes of god sufferyth nevyr that soule to synne fynally *that* shalle come ther." [38:8-10] Cf. 51:126-139; 53:6-8.51-52; 72:21-22.
209 38:29-30; 49:24-25.33-34.
210 5:9-16.
211 5:4-6.
212 61:35-73.
213 "And marcy is a werkyng *that* comyth of the goodnes of god, and it shalle last wurkynge as long as synne is sufferyd to pursew ryghtfulle soules. And whan synne hath no lenger leue to pursew, than shalle the werkyng of mercy cees." [35:37-40]

God brought to mynde that I shuld synne; . . . . And in thys I conceyvyd
a softe drede; and to this oure lorde answeryd: I kepe the fulle suerly. Thys
worde was seyde *with* more loue and suernes of gostly kepyng than I can or
may telle. [37:2.9-11][214]

Julian is never shown sin except within the context of divine mercy precisely because sin is never allowed to pursue us unchecked by the working
of mercy and grace.[215] In the course of her shewings, Julian learns that
the question of sin can only be answered in the light of Christ, i.e., the
light of mercy.

Owre lorde of his mercy shewyth vs oure synne and oure feblynesse by the
swete gracious lyght of hym selfe, for oure synne is so foule and so horryble
that he of his curtesy wylle not shewe it vs but by *the* lyght of his mercy.
[78:2-5][216]

In the light of Christ himself (our true nature), we make the startling
discovery that sin is unnatural, an 'unkindness.'[217] Sin lies within the
realm of our changeableness, our inconsistency with our nature.[218] When
we sin, we act against our true will, that 'godly will' which is 'kept whole
and safe in Christ.'[219] In other words, sin is our experience of not yet
being fully oned, the tension in which we live in this world. The opposite
of oneing, sin is the fracture between substance and sensuality, which
fracture distorts the human wholeness that is holiness.[220] The true nature
of this fracture is most clearly revealed in the pain Christ endured for us
in his passion and death.[221] Therein we see sin for what it is: the cause
of Christ's sufferings and, indeed, of all human pain.[222] Only within the

---

214 Julian's fear at the sight of her sin stems from her unsureness of herself and her
     inability even to know the measure of her sin. [79:11-14]
215 35:37-40 (note 213, p. 91, above); cf. 11:26-30.
216 Cf. 78:21-22. Elsewhere, Julian speaks of our being shown our sin by the 'sweet
     light of mercy and grace.' [40:2-5] Cf. 11:24-30; 37:2-4; 78:15-16.31-43; 82:11-26.
217 "We shall se verely that synne is wurse, vyler and paynfuller than hell without ony
     lycknesse. For it is contraryous to our feyer kynde; for as verely as synne is vn-
     clene, as trewly synne is vnkynde." [63:14-16]
218 76:29-30; cf. 47:16-17.
219 53:16-22; 59:40-42; cf. 45:2-3.40-42; 53:46-49. Our true will is our deepest truth,
     our orientation towards God. See p. 39-40, above.
220 We have already seen how grace helps us in our struggle to bring our sensuality
     into harmony with our 'godly will.' [19:33-39] See p. 72-73, above.
221 20:4-21; 27:15-34.
222 "And thus we haue mater of mornyng, for oure synne is cause of Cristes paynes."
     [52:51-52] Our sin is the cause of Christ's pain, but Christ's pain becomes our own
     by virtue of our oneing: "Here I saw a grett onyng betwene Crist and vs, to my
     vnderstondyng; for when he was in payne we ware in payne, and alle creatures that

mystery of the Christ may we comprehend sin's real meaning, both its horror and its ultimate powerlessness in the face of God's love incarnate in Jesus Christ. Moreover, the gracious knowing of the truth about sin is itself a moment of mercy and grace for us.[223]

Our natural instinct to view the work of mercy in relationship to sin is correct: mercy belongs to the domain of fallenness, i.e, our sensual existence. For Julian, however, the fallenness of sin is not primarily a matter of a moral defect; rather, simply by being created as this type of creature (sensual), we operate within the realm of mercy and grace.[224] Ultimately, sin is not a falling in the sense that something has gone irrevocably awry in God's plan, but a falling that may be likened to a serious injury or wound that weakens us and causes us pain. In our fallen state, we cannot keep from sinning,[225] but we are continually preserved and protected by God, even in our very sinning.[226] We are not 'kept' *from* falling, but 'kept' *in* our falling and rising, preserved from the harm of an ultimate triumph of sin.

> Iff any such lyver be in erth, whych is contynually kepte fro fallyng, I know it nott, for it was nott shewde me. But thys was shewde, that in fallyng and in rysyng we are evyr preciously kepte in o(ne) loue. For in the beholdyng of god we falle nott, and in *the* beholdyng of oure selfe we stonde nott; and boyth theyse be soth,[227] as to my syght, but the beholdyng of oure lord god is the hygher sothnes. [82:27-32]

Our misjudgment of our situation stems from the fact that, from our temporal perspective, we are unable to see our sin as God sees it. The integrity of our 'godly will' is preserved in God's sight, even when we ourselves cannot see it.[228] Even in the midst of our sinning, we are protected from the ultimate harm of sin ('endless death') by God's merciful 'keeping.'[229]

---

myght suffer payne sufferyd *with* hym." [18:14-16] Cf. 18:36-37; 27:14-18.28-34.

223 "He wylle hym selfe for loue shewe it [sin] vs, in tyme of mercy and of grace." [78:42-43] Cf. 78:15-16. See p. 143-150, below, for a discussion of our need to know the truth about sin.

224 "And what tyme oure soule is enspyred in oure body, in whych we be made sensuall, as soone mercy and grace begynne to werke, havyng of vs cure and kepyng *with* pytte and loue." [55:16-18]

225 36:4-7.39-40; 37:2-9; 52:57-58; 79:2-13; 82:4-15.

226 Julian tells us that we are 'kept' in the time of our sinning (which she further identifies with the time of our need). [40:2-5; 49:24-25; 53:2-5; 62:2-7; 71:34-36; 75:3-4; 78:8-11; 79:31-32; 82:28-29; cf. 39:45-48.]

227 'True.'

228 39:18-20; 51:106-111; cf. 62:6-11.

229 51:127-139; cf. 38:29-30; 39:45-46; 49:24-25.33-34.

We can see that Julian's insight is based on her understanding of oneing: mercy (Christ's taking on sensuality) is the condition of possibility for sin. If we speak in temporal terms, we can say that oneing (which is mercy) presumes a prior separation: sin is precisely our condition of being separated from God. Here Julian reflects a Pauline theme: by taking on sensuality, Christ experienced a certain separation from the Father, i.e., Christ became 'sin' for our sake.[230] By virtue of our humanity we share both in Christ's condition of separation from the Father and in his oned existence with the Father.[231] So, while the context of our sensual existence is sin, the context of sin is always divine mercy, our oneing in Christ.

Julian's understanding of sin derives from her unique ordering of the event of our salvation in terms other than our usual chronology of salvation history. Julian does not adopt the familiar, temporally-ordered scenario of the Creation, followed by the fall of Adam and, consequently, by the Redemption. In the *Shewings*, Julian's doctrine of kind, mercy, and grace replaces the creation/fall/redemption scenario with that of a first making and an again-making.[232] Our first making is in God, and our again-making is in Christ, which second making takes place definitively in the Christ event and existentially in us through the working of grace. As we have seen, there is no 'fall' outside the context of that 'fall' which is Christ's in his incarnation, by virtue of which falling we are 'kept' by the working of mercy and grace as we struggle in the process of maturing to full conformity to and union with Christ. Moreover, because she saw separatedness from God as part of God's picture from the beginning, Julian's perspective bypassed the popular medieval controversy regarding the Incarnation and the Redemption (i.e., whether Christ would have come had Adam not sinned), a theological question which prompted heated debate in her own day.[233] For Julian, Christ's incarnation may

---

230 "For our sake he made him to be sin who knew no sin, so that in him we might become the righteousness of God." [2 Cor 5:21]

231 Julian even refers to Christ's journey into hell (the most extreme form of separation from God) in order to unite all humanity with God. [51:299-301]

232 Swanson captures something of Julian's insight about our creation as our first and second making in Christ: "Mother Julian's main theological concern, unlike that of almost all others, is *not* the redemption, but (if you will allow it) the 'demption' — that is, not the *re*-purchase of humankind in the crucifixion, but the original 'purchase' of humankind in the creation." John-Julian Swanson, "Guide for the Inexpert Mystic," in *Julian. Woman of our Day*, edited by Robert Llewelyn (London: Darton, Longman and Todd, 1985), 78-79.

233 Clark claims Julian's affinities with the nuanced position of Duns Scotus, i.e., that 'God willed the end before the means' and that the Incarnation was not simply 'occasioned' by the fall, but was for its own sake part of God's purpose from all

only be properly understood within the context of sin and salvation, i.e., the oneing of God-separatedness to God in Christ.

2. Julian's metaphysics of sin

Julian adopts a traditional metaphysics in regard to sin.[234] Sin is a nought, a 'no deed,' having no kind of substance, no part of being;[235] sin is a 'nothing' because the power of evil has been broken.[236] By definition, sin is all that is 'not good,' i.e., all that is separated from God;[237] however, by virtue of Christ's passion, the devil ('fiend') is overcome,[238] and all his evil efforts are turned to good by the working of mercy and grace.[239] Consequently, even though we may experience ourselves as separated from God by sin, the separation is not complete be-

---

eternity. However, it would seem that, in having the incarnation of Christ *define* humanity, Julian is actually closer to the insight of Irenaeus: "*Verbum Dei, Jesum Christum Dominum nostrum . . . propter immensam suam dilectionem factus est quod sumus nos, uti nos perficeret esse quod est ipse.*" Without the Incarnation, the human person could not reach the glorious destiny ordained under the dispensation of grace, i.e., a *saved* sinner. God wished to save exactly this type of humanity, a fallen humanity, a humanity that struggles with sin. Moreover, by relating her doctrine to the actual dispensation of grace in Christ, Julian also shows some similarity to the position of Aquinas. In holding that, given what we know by divine revelation, the Incarnation would not have happened if Adam had not sinned, Aquinas was simply saying that we cannot presume to *know* anything about the Incarnation within the context of any world other than the one we know. In other words, the Incarnation must be seen in the context of sin and salvation; conclusions about any other scenario cannot be valid. See J.P.H. Clark, "Predestination in Christ according to Julian of Norwich," *The Downside Review* 100 (April 1982) 88-89; Irenaeus, *Adversus Haereses* V, *praef.* (*PG* 7, 1120); and Thomas Aquinas, *Summa Theologiae* 3, q.1, a.3, *corp.*

234 See, for example, Thomas Aquinas, *Summa Theologiae*, 1a, q.48, a.1 and 3.
235 xxiii:26-30; 11:21-23; 27:26-27. Moreover, Julian even suggests that damnation amounts to a form of non-being. [33:8-15]
236 The devil's might is 'locked in God's hand.' [13:18; 65:23-24; cf. 67:10-11.] In chapter 13 Julian further clarifies the elements of the problem. The devil's 'unmight' is no match for God. Christ does not react to the devil, for to react would be to admit that the devil had some power to affect Christ. [13:24-35]
237 27:14-24; cf. 40:41-42.
238 13:7.10.37.39-40; 68:61-62; 70:14-16; cf. 1:54.
239 1:36-37; 13:10-49; 20:30-32; 38:17-21; 39:39-40; 48:19-45; 49:31-53; 59:2-11; 62:9-10; cf. Rom 8:28.

cause total separation from God would be equivalent to non-being.[240] While we may no longer feel God's life in us because of our sins, in God's sight we are not dead.[241] The separation which results from our sin is more like our falling into a chasm or ravine: our experience is one of pain and loss, but in reality God is ever near and never loses sight of us.[242]

Julian again takes into account the human perspective on sin by telling us that sin's non-being will only be fully manifested to us at the end of history, on that eschatological 'last day' when we shall see that truly 'all is well.'[243] Here she highlights the fact that, although sin is non-being on the ontological plane, its very real impact on our lives attests to its influence within the realm of history. Our existential experience of sin on the historical plane brings us to an appreciation of its real dangers.[244] Vile and horrendous,[245] sin is the 'sharpest scourge' to the soul,[246] a wound that causes us only sorrow and pain.[247] Sin harasses us[248] and imprisons us.[249] Contrary to our nature, sin defiles us and 'befouls' the image of God in us[250] whenever we allow its nothingness (its untruth, its 'unkindness') to replace truth in our lives.[251] Distinguishing between sin itself and sin's effects in our spatio-temporal world, Julian concludes that sin has real significance historically, but not ultimately: however sin may distort the image of God in us on the historical plane, ontologically we are still *capax dei*. The more we become our true selves, the less sin has its reality in our lives.

As separation from God, sin is the antithesis of oneing. At the existential level, this condition of being not yet fully oned is experienced as the pain of deprivation: we know the pain of separation from God

---

240 "We may nott stonde a twynglyng of an ey but *with* kepyng of grace." [52:66 67] Cf. 33:8-15; 49:5-6.15-20; 56:12-16; Rom 8:38-39.
241 50:3-6; 72:14-22.
242 See 51:15-53 for an account of the servant's painful experience of separation from his lord. Cf. 62:2-8.
243 32:17-60.
244 Julian often speaks of sin in terms of perils, temptations, and threatening enemies and 'fiends' who attack us: 1:54; 4:20-27; 13:7-46; 39:45-48; 40:27-30; 41:62; 65:23-25; 67:2-26; 68:61-62; 69:2-4; 70:2-16; 76:30-43; 77:2-13.51; 78:9-11.39-40; 79:24-31.
245 29:8; 40:37-38; 63:14-15; 72:12; 76:5-6; 78:3-5.21-22.
246 39:2-4; cf. 29:8-9.
247 38:2-8; 39:35-36; 47:40-45; 72:15.
248 Sin 'pursues' rightful souls [35:37-39] and 'travails' them [47:44].
249 40:12; cf. 77:41; 81:16-25.
250 10:57-61; 39:10-11; 40:5-6; 43:2-4; 63:16; 73:35-36; cf. 61:49-51; 64:31-45.
251 Julian herself speaks of her 'great sin' and 'great unkindness' in doubting the truth, the reality of her shewings. [66:30-35]

(which is the greatest pain to the soul)[252] as well as those sufferings which result from the lack of any of the goods which God has ordained to our kind.[253] Within this ontology, Julian quite naturally characterizes sin as immaturity or as a debilitating sickness which weakens its victims. She describes our immature or weakened state in terms of deprivations: we fall because sin has made us blind, foolish, feeble and frail, deprived of our full powers.[254] Each of these various deprivations will inevitably manifest itself as pain, whether that pain be the pain inherent to the deprivation itself[255] or the growing pains of our immaturity (the sufferings and woe brought about by our mistakes and failures). Thus, while holding that sin is a nought, Julian does provide us with a basis for an epistemology of sin: we can know sin by knowing the very real pain it causes us,[256] the suffering caused by the lack of the good, our experience of being not yet fully oned. Moreover, Julian places the passion of Christ at the heart of our knowledge of sin by identifying the pain of sin with the sufferings Christ endured for us in his passion and death.[257]

3. God's mercy, God's justice

We must not consider sin solely from our temporal perspective, albeit in the light of mercy and grace. While we are shown everything we need to know in regard to our salvation,[258] nevertheless we still do not see the

---

252 64:7-9; 76:11; cf. 72:2-11.
253 Evil is not merely the neutral absence of a good, but the absence of a good which ought to be there, a *remotio boni privative*. Thomas Aquinas, *Summa Theologiae*, 1a, q.48, a.3, *corp.*
254 36:64-65; 40:27; 41:8-9; 47:16-21; 51:105-106.228-231; 52:15.28.60-61.66; 61:18-20; 66:6; 72:14-17.57; 73:41; 74:36; 76:8-12.24.31-32; 77:4-6; 78:2.37; 79:31-32; cf. 41:45. As was the case with our sense of being separated from God by sin (see p. 95-96, above), the deprivations we experience are also more apparent than real because the goods we seem to lack are treasured in Christ. [55:31-35; 57:38-41]
255 E.g., we live in painful longing for God: 31:43; 40:23-24; 42:57; 45:39; 51:260-265; 71:20; cf. 46:13.
256 "But I saw nott synne, for I beleue it had no maner of substannce, ne no part of beyng, ne it myght not be knowen but by the payne that is caused therof." [27:26-28] Cf. 27:33-34; 51:15-31; 72:14-15.
257 "In *th*is nakyd worde: Synne, oure lorde brough*t*e to my mynde generally alle that is nott good, and the shamfull despyte and the vttermost trybulation that he bare for vs in thys lyfe, and hys dyeng and alle hys paynes, and passion of alle hys creatures gostly and bodely." [27:14-18] Cf. 52:51-52.
258 30:2-13; cf. 36:26-27.

whole of God's working of rightfulness in our regard.[259] What we do
know is that, within the divine perspective, all is 'well' (i.e., rightful) and
that what we experience in time as not fully rightful is made 'well' by the
working of mercy and grace.[260]

Divine mercy (our 'sureness of keeping') clearly derives from God's
rightfulness. Because divine rightfulness necessarily implies that God's
loving purpose in our regard be unchanging, it also dictates that we be
'kept' in love, even while we are still sinners. In other words, divine
justice (God's fidelity to Godself) manifests itself as divine mercy. Thus,
God's way of dealing with our sin has to do with rightfulness, fidelity, and
love rather than with wrath.[261] It is precisely in rightfulness and mercy
that God wills to be known and loved.[262] The working of mercy and grace
is the expression of God's fidelity. Our sinfulness is overcome by God's
unchanging love. Sin is treated as God's rightfulness requires: mercy
slakes our wrath.

> For I saw full truly that evyr as oure contraryousnes werkyth to vs here in
> erth payne, shame and sorow, ryght so on the contrary wyse grace werkyth to
> vs in hevyn solace, wurschyp and blysse, ovyr passyng so ferforth that when we
> come vppe and receyve that swete reward whych grace hath wrought to vs,
> there we shall thanke and blysse oure lorde, endlessly enjoyeng that evyr we
> sufferyd woo; and that shalle be for a properte of blessyd loue that we shalle
> know in god, whych we myght nevyr haue knowen withoughte wo goyng
> before. And whan I saw all thys, me behouyd nedys to grannt that the mercy
> of god and the forgyuenesse slaketh and wastyth oure wrath. [48:40-49]

To say that God's mercy overcomes our wrath is not to say that sin
has no significance. On the contrary, Julian's existential experience of sin
showed her that sin does, in fact, hinder the soul's union with God.

> Oure lorde brought to my mynde the longyng that I had to hym before; and
> I saw nothyng lettyd[263] my but synne. [27:2-3]

---

259 Julian is insistent that God has the right to maintain 'privy counsels' in peace
     [30:12-16], e.g., the 'great deed' by which all shall be made well, the nature of
     which will only be revealed at the end of time [32:23-40.55-60; 34:2-5; 36:57-58].

260 "And so be all the workes of our lorde, and therto nedyth neyther workyng of
     mercy ne grace, for they be alle ryghtfulle, wher in feylyth ryght nought. And in a
     other tyme he shewde for beholdyng of synne nakedly, as I shall say after, when he
     vsyth workyng of mercy and of grace." [11:26-30]

261 We have already seen that there is no wrath in God; therefore, God's response to
     our sinning is never a response of wrath. See p. 25-26, 34-35, above.

262 35:43-45.

263 'Hindered.'

Sin stands as a hallmark of our creaturely condition.[264] Yet, while we are indeed hindered by sin, sin itself is powerless to hinder God's loving purpose in our regard. God's faithful love cannot be thwarted by our infidelity.[265] God loves us endlessly and 'keeps' us tenderly, even while we are sinning.[266] We rejoice because God's rightfulness cannot be controverted. God will make all things 'well,' regardless of our sinning.

> Owre lorde god shewde that a deed shalle be done and hym selfe shalle do it, and it shall be wurschypfulle and mervelous and plenteuous, and by (me) it shall be done, and hym selfe shalle do it. And this is the hyghest joy that the soule vnderstode, that god hym selfe shall do it, and I shalle do ryght nought but synne; and my synne shall nott lett his goodnes workyng. [36:2-7]

We take comfort in the fact that it is God who accomplishes our rightfulness; it does not depend on us.[267] Our rightfulness depends on our being oned in Christ, not on our own merits. We are 'kept' and protected from an ultimate triumph by sin because we are oned to God in Christ.

We must be careful to distinguish between moral and ontological levels when we speak about Julian's doctrine on sin. For Julian, moral failure[268] is real, an indication of our existential condition of separation from God, our not-yet-fully-oned condition. 'Keeping,' however, is an ontological relationship, not merely a moral one. We are 'kept' in God's love whether we perceive it or not, 'in weal and in woe.'[269] The fact that we continue to fall does not indicate a change in God's stance towards us; whether we sin or not, God loves us and 'keeps' us.[270] Moreover, ontologically, we do not fully assent to sinfulness because our will

---

264 Dickman further suggests: "In highly schematic terms we can say that sin serves a double function in Julian's theology: it prevents her from transcending her immanentist and Christo-centric perspective, but in that way it also provides for a firm distinction between Creator and created being and thus helps to protect her vision from spilling over into pantheism or some version of Pelagianism." Susan Dickman, "Julian of Norwich and Margery Kempe: Two Images of 14th-Century Spirituality," in *Spätmittelalterliche Geistliche Literatur in der Nationalsprache*, 1, edited by James Hogg, Analecta Cartusiana 106 (Salzburg: Institut für Anglistik und Amerikanistik, 1983) 184.

265 "Hard and mervelous is that loue whych may nott nor wyll not be broken for trespas." [61:26-27] Cf. 39:41-42; 40:49; 76:28-29.

266 40:3; 82:11.

267 Cf. 36:37-39.

268 While Julian does not address the issue of sin within the framework of moral theology, she clearly implies guilt on our part by saying that Christ became like us except in our guilt. [10:56-58]

269 "He kepyth vs evyr in lyke suer, in wo and in wele." [15:24] Cf. 1:22-23; 62:2-12.

270 "For whether we be foule or clene, we are evyr one in his lovyng." [76:28-29]

is preserved whole and safe in Christ.[271] Sin falls to us against our will.[272] In Christ, we truly hate sin even while we continue to fall.[273] Our hatred of sin is, in a certain sense, the sign that all is indeed 'well,' i.e., that our will is oned to God's will even while we continue to sin because of our feebleness.[274] Even when we feel most broken by our sins, at our deepest level, we 'abide God.'[275] Notwithstanding our feelings of woe, God wills that we understand that we are more truly in heaven than on earth.[276] Since we, like the servant of the parable,[277] cannot see that our will is preserved, we ought not to be deceived by our feelings of pain or fear.[278] The 'grudging' of our outward sensuality does not indicate the inward assent of the soul.[279] Losing or gaining the feeling of comfort has nothing to do with one's ontological state (and may even be unrelated to one's moral condition).[280]

The relationship between the divine and the human judgments on sin now becomes more understandable. While we experience ourselves as quite blameworthy on account of our sins,[281] in rightfulness God re-

---

271 53:11-22; cf. 52:21-33. As Hanshell rightly suggests, the real key to interpreting Julian's doctrine on sin lies in the fact that she situates our 'godly will' in Christ. See Deryck Hanshell, "A Crux in the Interpretation of Dame Julian," 87.

272 82:8; see also note 219, p. 92, above.

273 As we have seen, our hatred of sin is the fruit of our existential oneing by grace and, like prayer, witnesses to the oneing of our will to God's. See note 137, p. 79, above; cf. 45:3-5.

274 "Whenn [a mann or womann] loves nought synne, botte hates it and luffegh god, alle is wele. And he that trewlye doegh thus, thowgh he synn sum tyme by frelty or vnkunnyge in his wille, he falles nought, for he wille myghtely ryse agayne and behalde god, whamm he loves in alle his wille." [xxiii: 50-54]

275 "And by Adams fallyng we be so broken in oure felyng on dyverse manner by synne and by sondry paynes, in whych we be made derke and so blynde that vnnethys we can take any comforte. But in oure menyng we abyde god, . . . and this is his owne werkyng in vs." [52:13-17]

276 55:12-14.

277 51:107-111.

278 "Fulle preciously oure good lorde kepyth vs whan it semyth to vs that we be neer forsaken and cast away for oure synne." [39:18-19] Cf. 27:25-26; 49:20-22.31-34; 50:3-6; 72:14-22.

279 19:23-39; cf. 28:31-32.

280 In chapter 15 Julian relates her experience of rapidly alternating feelings of ecstatic joy and of terrible depression. [15:2-20] Ever practical, she tells us that the changes were so sudden that they could not have been due to her sinning because there had been no time to sin! [15:26-27]

281 39:18-20; 46:26-29; 50:8-13; 77:16-17; cf. 40:5-6. Moreover, the teaching of the Church reinforces our own judgment of our sinning as blameworthy. [45:20-21; 50:10-13] See also note 268, p. 99, above.

sponds to our sinful state with endless, constant love and 'sureness of keeping.'[282] God's rightful judgment is based on our substance which is 'kept whole and safe in Christ, whereas we judge ourselves on those changeable, outward appearances of our sensual existence.[283] In light of Julian's doctrine of the 'godly will,' we can now see how both judgments are preserved: in our own eyes, we stand not; in God's eyes, we fall not.[284] In other words, at the moral level we do indeed sin, and sin grievously, but sin's triumph is overturned by God's love and rightfulness.[285] Even while our own judgment on the gravity of our sin does have its truth, God's rightful judgment is the higher truth.[286] The two judgments, although accorded and oned,[287] are not identical; they will both be known in heaven.[288]

Finally, we need to consider the question of guilt. Wherever we find the word 'blame' used in the *Shewings,* we tend to interpret it as meaning 'guilt,' i.e., our culpability or accountability for our misconduct. However, as Pelphrey suggests, in context Julian's use of the word 'blame' seems to refer to the act of blame, i.e., to adjudge the person guilty.[289] Therefore, the fact that we are accountable for our individual sins is not really at issue when she tells us that God addresses no manner of blame to us for our falling.[290] Her insight is not that we are guiltless, but rather that God does not judge us as our guilt deserves.[291] On the contrary, whereas we see that we deserve blame for our sins, God seems to address comfort, not blame to us.[292] Thus, Julian again reconciles the human

---

282 46:17-18.
283 45:2-11.
284 See 82:27-32 (p. 93, above). Here, 'fall' is obviously used in the sense of a total and irrevocable separation from God and, therefore, from the possibility of conversion and salvation.
285 "For we shalle verely see in hevyn without ende *that* we haue grevously synned in this lyfe; and not withstondyng this we shalle verely see that we were nevyr hurt in his loue, nor we were nevyr lesse of pryce in his syght." [61:22-25]
286 82:29-32 (p. 93, above).
287 Jesus reforms our judgment by mercy and grace by virtue of his passion, and so brings it into rightfulness. [45:9-11]
288 45:11-12.
289 Brant Pelphrey, *Love Was His Meaning,* 299-300.
290 27:35-38; 28:32-35; 39:35-37; 45:14-16.20-22; 50:9-15; 51:34; 52:94-96; 80:42-43; 82:9-10; cf. 19:23-24; 53:6-8; 63:7-9.
291 Because we are guilty, we ought meekly accuse ourselves [52:69-72.75-81] yet 'not busy ourselves greatly about our accusing' [79:32-36]. See also note 268, p. 99, above.
292 51:117. God's compassionate response to our situation will be the subject of chapter 4 (see p. 167-174, below).

and the divine judgments: our guilt and blameworthiness (our human judgment which is consonant with the Church's teaching)[293] and the divine judgment of God's love and mercy, the judgment that is ours in Christ in whom there is no guilt.[294] We need to see and know both judgments.

> For other wyse is the beholdyng of god, and other wyse is the beholdyng of man. For it longyth to man mekely to accuse hym selfe, and it longyth to the propyr goodnesse of oure lorde god curtesly to excuse man. . . . Thus wylle oure good lorde *that* we accuse oure selfe wylfully, and truly se and know (our fallyng *and* all *the* harmes *that* cum therof, seand *and* witand *that* we may never restoren it; *and* therwith, if we wilfully *and* truly sen *and* knowen,) his evyrlastyng loue that he hath to vs and his plentuous mercy. And thus gracyously to se and know both to geder is *the* meke accusyng that oure good lorde askyth of vs. [52:69-72.75-81]

To learn the truth of both judgments, our blameworthiness and the sureness of God's gracious 'keeping,' is to discover the meaning of divine mercy. Oned to God in Christ, we are 'kept' in love, even while we continue to sin.

4. Sin is 'behovely'

Knowing sin to be the cause of Christ's passion as well as a real hindrance to the soul's full union with God, Julian quite naturally wondered why God allows sin at all. Why had not God kept humanity sinless from the very beginning? We have already seen the answer given her:

> Synne is behouely, but alle shalle be wele, and alle shalle be wele, and alle maner of thynge shalle be wele. [27:13-14]

For Julian, sin is a strange anomaly: a scourge to us and yet somehow 'behovely.'[295] As we have seen, she struggles with the anomaly of sin

---

293 See note 281, p. 100, above.
294 "Goddys son fell *with* Adam in to the slade of the meydens wombe, whych was the feyerest doughter of Adam, and that for to excuse Adam from blame in hevyn and in erth; . . . . And thus hath oure good lorde J*he*su taken vppon hym all oure blame; and therfore oure fader may nor wyll no more blame assigne to vs than to hys owne derwurthy son J*he*su Cryst." [51:222-224.232-234] Cf. Heb 4:15.
295 One meaning of the word 'behovely' in middle English may range from a weak 'useful' to a strong 'necessary.' Although it is ambiguous here, there is no reason to exclude the strong meaning. Saying that sin is 'necessary' places Julian's doc-

throughout the *Shewings*, trying to understand how evil and the pain it brings into our world can be behovely for us.

As she reflects upon the nature of our oneing, Julian realizes that the more we are oned, the more we hate our sin, and the greater the pain our falling causes us. The greater our pain, the more we cling to Christ. Thus, sin actually defeats itself: just as a child's illness or fear sends the child to the mother for help and safety,[296] so our sin sends us to Christ.

> And thys payne [caused by sin] is somthyng, as to my syghte, for a tyme, for it purgyth and makyth vs to know oure selfe and aske mercy. [27:28-30][297]

A sharp scourge, sin is nevertheless a purifying scourge which purges us of pride and presumption.[298] We learn our need for mercy, our inability to repair the harm done by our sins.[299] Without the self-knowledge sin occasions, we risk falling prey to the kind of recklessness which proceeds a distorted perception of safety.[300] While the assurance of God's loving 'keeping' comforts us and protects us from despair, our falling brings us the meekness we need in order to be Christ's 'helpers' in the process of our existential oneing, our moving toward wholeness in him.[301]

For Julian, all profit comes through the working of mercy and grace.[302] She is shown that our falling is to our profit because mercy and grace enable us to rise to greater bliss.[303] Moreover, in our falling, we experience a property of divine love which we could not know otherwise: we learn that God's love may not nor will not be broken by our offenses. Thus, we need to fall, and we need to see our falling.

---

trine in line with the orthodox theology of the *felix culpa* of the Easter vigil liturgy's *Exsultet*: "*O certe necessarium Adae peccatum, quod Christi morte deletum est! O felix culpa, quae talem ac tantum meruit habere Redemptorem!*" Easter Vigil, *Missale Romanum.*

A second meaning of 'behovely' is 'befitting.' To say that sin is befitting is to suggest that sin does indeed have an appropriate place within the whole divine plan of our salvation.

296 61:41-51.
297 Cf. 61:41-51; 77:14-16.49-51; 79:32-39.
298 28:11-20; 39:2-7; 78:15-18; cf. 27:18-21; 63:39; 79:19-20.
299 52:77-78.
300 52:56-68; cf. 79:26-31. We shall return to Julian's insistence on our need for self-knowledge (see p. 143-150, 206-210, below).
301 79:11-21; cf. 57:56-57. We shall take up the theme of meekness in our discussion of the nature of presumption and despair. See chapter 4, p. 207-210, below.
302 59:22-23; cf. 56:36-37.51-55.
303 "And we haue of oure febylnesse and oure foly to falle, and we haue of mercy and of grace of *the* holy gost to ryse to more joye." [77:4-6] Cf. 35:41-43; 38:30-33; 48:40-47; 52:46-49; 59:2-8; 63:4-7.

For it nedyth vs to falle, and it nedyth vs to see it; for yf we felle nott, we shulde nott knowe how febyll and how wrechyd we be of oure selfe, nor also we shulde not so fulsomly know *the* mervelous loue of oure maker.

For we shalle verely see in hevyn wi*th*out ende *that* we haue grevously synned in this lyfe; and not wi*th*stondyng this we shalle verely see that we were nevyr hurt in his loue, nor we were nevyr the lesse of pryce in his syght. And by the assey of this fallyng we shalle haue an hygh and a mervelous knowyng of loue in god wi*th*out ende; for hard and mervelous is that loue whych may nott nor wyll not be broken for trespas.

And this was one vnderstandyng of profyte; and other is the lownesse and mekenesse that we shall get by the syght of oure fallyng, for therby we shall hyely be reysyd in hevyn, to whych rysyng we my*gh*te nevyr haue comyn wi*th*out that meknesse. And therfor it nedyt vs to see it; and if we se it not, though we felle it shuld not pr*o*fyte vs. And comonly furst we falle and sethen we se it; and both is of the mercy of god. [61:18-34][304]

Falling brings us the profit of knowing the graciousness of the love of God which 'keeps' us even though we sin. This higher reward is ours, however, only because we see the grievousness of our sinning; if we do not understand the gravity of our sin, we cannot rejoice in the lavishness of God's love. The meekness we gain from our experience of falling is the true beginning of our profit.[305] The greater our awareness of our sinfulness, the greater the appreciation of the depth of God's love for us. Thus, Julian can say that both our falling and the sight of our fall derive from the mercy of God which works this higher rewarding.

In speaking of our eternal reward, Julian tells us that we also benefit from our painful existence as sinners. We are given a higher joy than would be ours had we not fallen; God will reward us for the travail sin caused us.[306] This heavenly reward will be so wonderful that we shall rejoice that we suffered woe here on earth.[307] This bliss that we shall enjoy in heaven by mercy and grace is ours precisely because of the fact that sin has been allowed to afflict us here on earth.

And all this blysse we haue by mercy and grace, whych manner blysse we myght nevyr haue had and knowen, but yf that properte of goodnesse whych is in god had ben contraryed, wher by we haue this blysse. For wyckydnesse hath ben sufferyd to ryse contrary to *that* goodnesse; and the goodnesse of mercy and grace contraryed agaynst that wyckydnesse, and turnyd all to goodnesse and wurshyppe to all that shalle be savyd. [59:2-8][308]

---

304 Cf. 21:24-26; 48:45-47; 59:2-8.
305 Cf. 38:31-33.
306 14:3-4.14-20.
307 48:41-45.
308 Cf. 21:24-26; 35:41-43; 48:40-47; 51:49-61; 52:46-49; 56:35-37; 61:19-32; 77:4-6.

Not only will our reward be proportionate to our sufferings,[309] but that reward is intrinsically related to our pain.

> And god shewed that synne shalle be no shame, but wurshype to man, for ryght as to every synne is *answeryng a payne by truth, ryght so for every synne to the same soule is gevyn a blysse by loue. Ryght as dyuerse synnes be ponysschyd *with* dyuers paynes after that it be greuous, ryght so shalle they be rewardyd *with* dyvers joyes in hevyn for theyr victories, after as the synne haue ben paynfulle and sorowfulle to the soule in erth. [38:2-8]

The 'token of sin,' i.e., the pain it brings and even our shame itself, is turned to worship and joy by the working of mercy and grace.[310] By virtue of his passion, Christ turns all our blame into endless worship.[311] Moreover, in heaven where we are healed of our sin, our wounds will be seen not as wounds, but as 'worships.'[312] In other words, sin is the context of our personal history, which history will be glorified, not nullified; the deficiency that is our sin will be gloriously transformed. We shall examine further Julian's understanding of the exact nature of this transformation from woundedness to 'worship' when we consider her teaching on Christ's passion.[313] For now, it is sufficient to note that our continuity of identity between earthly existence and heavenly fulfillment has to do with our sinfulness: just as on earth there is for every sin an answering pain in reality, so there shall be a bliss in heaven to correspond to each of those pains. Our reward is, therefore, intrinsically related to those sufferings caused by sin.

Finally, we need to take note of Julian's caveat in regard to sin, lest we be tempted to sin more in order to receive a greater reward (a problem of misinterpretation that has plagued the Church since the time of Paul).[314]

> But now because of alle thys gostly comfort that is before seyde, if any man or woman be steryd by foly to sey or to thynke: if this be tru, than were it good for to synne to haue the more mede, or elles to charge the lesse to synne, beware of this steryng. For truly, if it come, it is vntrue and of the enemy.
>
> For the same tru loue that touchyth vs alle by hys blessyd comfort, the same blessyd loue techyth vs that we shalle hate syn only for loue. And I am suer by my awne felyng, the more that ech kynde soule seeth this in the

---

309   21:26-28.
310   38:20-21; 48:19-45; 59:6-8; cf. 13:15-16.46-49; 39:31-40; 56:36-37.39-41.
311   1:36-37; 52:95-96; cf. 20:31-32; 24:23-25; 28:26-29; 49:46-53.
312   39:31-32.
313   See p. 129-131, below.
314   Cf. Rom 6:1-2.

curtesse loue of our lorde god, the lother is hym to synne, and the more he
is asschamyd. For if it were leyde before vs, alle the payne *that* is in hell and
in purgatory and in erth, deed or other, than synne we shulde rather chese
alle that payne than synne. [40:27-37]

We have seen that it is true that our sin actually serves to reveal God's
love: the greater our failing, the more we understand the depth of God's
love for us. However, the more we understand God's love, the worse our
sins will seem and the more we will seek to avoid them.[315] God's love
in the face of our sinning teaches us to hate sin, not to presume upon
God's mercy. While she tells us that sin is behovely, we find that Julian
never loses sight of the horror of sin, insisting on our need to see its true
nature. Sin is inhuman, an 'unkindness' which distorts the image of God
in us and causes us only pain. We therefore hate sin because it hinders
us from ourselves, from what we truly will: the union with God for which
we long. Only in the light of God's mercy can we endure the horrible
sight of our sin. To take a falsely optimistic view of sin (i.e., that sin is
not really the evil it seems to be) is to reject the truth that sin is the
cause of Christ's passion, and indeed of all human pain. Ultimately, sin
is behovely because it is the occasion for the working of mercy and grace.
By God's sufferance we fall, in God's love we are surely 'kept,' and by
God's mercy and grace we shall be raised to everlasting joy.[316]

---

315 When we have 'sight' of God's love, we hate sin. [52:16-29; cf. 76:4-8.]
316 35:41-43.

3 Christ, Our Mother of Mercy

The first chapter of the *Shewings* begins by telling us that all of Julian's shewings are the revelation of divine love, a love that is revealed to us in three distinct but inseparable aspects: the trinitarian love which is God; that same divine love which is poured out to us in Christ; and our own experience[1] of that trinitarian love as we are oned to God in Christ.

> This is a reuelacion of loue that Jhe*su* Christ our endles blisse made in xvi shewynges, of which the first is of his precious crownyng of thornes; and ther in was conteined *and* specified the blessed trinitie *with* the incarnacion and the vnithing between god and mans sowle, *with* manie fayer schewynges and techynges of endelesse wisdom and loue, in which all the shewynges that foloweth be grovndide and ioyned. [1:2-7]

These three elements — the Trinity, Christ's incarnation, and the uniting of the soul with God — make up a single mystery of love: we are given to participate in the intratrinitarian love of God in and through Christ by virtue of his incarnation and his indwelling in our soul by grace.[2]

When Julian summarizes her triple understanding of divine love near the conclusion of the *Shewings*, she returns to the same three themes of trinitarian love, incarnation, and oneing.

> I had iij manner of vnderstondyng*es* in this lyght of (c)ha(r)ite. The furst is charite vnmade, the seconnde is charyte made, the thyrde is charyte gevyn. Charyte vnmade is god, charyte made is oure soule in god, charyte gevyn is vertu, and *that* is a gracious gyfte of wurkyng, in whych we loue god for hym selfe, and oure selfe in god, and alle *that* god lovyth for god. [84:10-15]

---

1 The primary sense of 'experience' here is objective rather than subjective: we stand in God's love by virtue of the objective, ontological relationship we have to God in Jesus Christ, which relationship may not always be *felt* subjectively at the empirical level.

2 In a beautiful, oft-quoted passage from the final chapter of the *Shewings*, Julian reiterates the unity of the shewings, telling us that their meaning may be distilled into a single word — love: "And fro the tyme *that* it was shewde, I desyerde oftyn tymes to wytt in what was oure lords menyng. And xv yere after and mor, I was answeryd in gostly vnderstondyng, seyeng thus: What, woldest thou wytt thy lordes menyng in this thyng? Wytt it wele, loue was his menyng. Who shewyth it the? Loue. (What shewid he the? Love.) Wherfore shewyth he it the? For loue. Holde the therin, thou shalt wytt more in the same. But thou schalt nevyr witt therin other *with*outyn ende." [86:13-19]

Julian refers to divine love as it is revealed (the 'light of charity') and speaks in clear, trinitarian terms: 'charity unmade' is God, the Father as the source of the mystery of trinitarian love; 'charity made' is our soul in God, our ontological status in Christ by virtue of his incarnation; and 'charity given' is our life of love, our practice of the virtue of charity, made possible by the action of the Holy Spirit in our lives. As we have already seen, it is possible to read 'charity' as referring to the Holy Spirit (both as uncreated intratrinitarian love and as the love which is the fruit of the working of grace in our lives);[3] however, Julian's summary statement is more properly understood when situated within the context of her christology. Jesus Christ *is* the ground of the oneing in love between the Trinity and humanity, and our life of virtue is the evidence of that oneing, the manifestation of Christ's working of love within us by grace. As Maisonneuve puts it, Julian's vision of divine love is christo-trinitarian: trinitarian in nature, but unified within the economy of love, that revelation of divine love which is Jesus Christ.[4]

In the two previous chapters of this study, we have seen how Julian's christo-trinitarian vision of divine love lies at the basis of her understanding of divine mercy. For Julian, divine mercy is God's loving plan for our salvation, our being oned in Christ. While trinitarian in scope, oneing by kind, mercy, and grace is grounded in the mystery of the Christ event.[5] The mercy of God cannot be separated from Christ's working of it. Divine mercy proper is Christ's oneing of our sensuality to our substance in himself in his incarnation. Christ's incarnation is the definitive event of our salvation; and we, in turn, become existential events of God's mercy (i.e., Christ's saving us) by the working of mercy and grace. We have also seen how Julian uses words and images to highlight the centrality of Christ in the economy of salvation. Christ is our savior, our 'salve' who heals and 'wholes' us;[6] he is himself our salvation, our reward, our heaven. Christ is our 'keeper' who defines us in himself as oned to God; our salvation rests on Christ's being the true identity of the human person, our truest 'self.' He is our treasury: our will is 'kept' whole and safe in Christ (in whose holiness we participate), and in him all our powers and virtues are 'kept' and preserved until we reach our full maturity. Having examined the doctrinal foundation on which Julian builds, we are

---

3   See chapter 2, notes 94 (p. 73, above) and 144 (p. 81, above).

4   Roland Maisonneuve, *L'univers visionnaire de Julian of Norwich*, 180.

5   As we have seen, mercy defines our nature, and grace is the extension of mercy in time.

6   79:39. See also p. 64-66, above.

ready to explore additional aspects of her portrayal of Christ which complete her unique theology of divine mercy.

In a striking metaphor by which she attempts to convey something of the intimacy of the love with which Christ 'keeps' us, Julian speaks of our being 'clothed' in Christ.

> He is oure clothing, that for loue wrappeth vs and wyndeth vs, halseth vs and all becloseth vs, hangeth about vs for tender loue, *that* he may never leeue vs. [5:4-6]

Julian further highlights the intimate nature of this 'beclosing,' telling us that, just as the body is clad in cloth and the flesh in skin, so are we, soul and body, clad and enclosed in the goodness of God.[7] As Julian develops this image, its christological focus becomes even more clear: we all come from Christ, are enclosed in him, and go to him, finding our heaven in him.[8] Here we find the first hint of the image with which Julian crowns her doctrine of divine mercy: Christ, our mother[9] of mercy, in whom we are enclosed in endless love, our tender mother who brings us to birth by his passion and who comforts us by the light of himself, the revelation of God's mercy.

---

7   6:41-44; cf. 6:33-34; 49:20-22; 54:21-24; 56:16-18. Moreover, Julian tells us that all bliss, all joy, and the whole heavens are beclosed in God. [51:155-157]
8   53:32-35; cf. 54:21-22; 55:3-4; 56:24-25; 57:41-46.49-53; 72:25-27.
9   As we have already noted, Julian never confuses the issue of gender in Christ's regard; Christ is always 'he' (never 'she') who is our mother.

A. Christ's Motherhood of Mercy

The christocentric focus of her theology of mercy is probably nowhere more evident than in Julian's image of Christ as our tender mother of mercy. Like the parable of the lord and the servant, Julian's image of the divine motherhood[10] is the fruit of years of reflection on her shewings, appearing only in the Long Text. Both its length and the centrality of its placement within the text suggest the theological importance of the motherhood theme in the *Shewings*.[11] The image of Christ as mother is not simply an interesting curiosity within her theology; rather, the motherhood imagery represents the very heart of Julian's mature theology.

---

10 While Julian's treatment of this theme is exceptionally well-developed and integrated, it is not unique within the christian tradition. Aside from obvious scriptural allusions to God as mother [Deut 32:11; Isa 49:1.14-15; 66:11-13], Christ as mother [Heb 5:12; Matt 23:37], and wisdom as mother [Sir 15:1-2; 24:24; Matt 11:19; Luke 7:35], there are various examples of this theme in such authors as Clement of Alexandria, Hilary of Poitiers, Ambrose, John Chrysostom, Jerome, Anselm, William of St. Thierry, and Bernard. For the most complete discussion available to date on the *divine motherhood* theme in the tradition, see Caroline Walker Bynum, *Jesus as Mother: Studies in the Spirituality of the High Middle Ages* (Berkeley: University of California Press, 1982). See also Ritamary Bradley, "Patristic Background of the motherhood similitude in Julian of Norwich," *Christian Scholar's Review* 8 (1978) 101-113; and Valerie Lagorio, "Variations on the Theme of God's Motherhood in Medieval English Mystical and Devotional Writings," *Studia Mystica* 8 (1985) 15-37.

11 Julian introduces the idea of Christ as our 'true mother' near the conclusion of chapter 57 [57:49-50] and then devotes most of the following six chapters to developing the concept Christ's role as our mother.

The christocentric nature of the divine motherhood becomes evident even in the use Julian makes of the word 'mother.' The word 'mother' (and its derivative 'motherhood') appears 85 times in the *Shewings*: 9 times in reference to Mary [1:31; 6:16; 8:6; 18:6; 25:7.10; 57:47.48.48]; 3 times in reference to the Church [46:50; 61:58.63; cf. 62:25]; 4 times in reference to God as our mother [59:43; 60:5.48; 62:15]; and 60 times explicitly or implicitly referring to Christ as our mother [48:29; 57:49; 58:13.21.35.38.39.42.44.44.46.49.57.60; 59:9.10.12.15.27.29. 29.32.37.38.39.45.46; 60:4.7.7.8.14.19.29.30.39.45.47.58.62; 61:38.44.48.49.49.53.67; 62:25.29; 63:20.28.34.35.37.39.40.42.44.48; 83:15]. Moreover, she uses the word 'mother' 9 times in reference to human motherhood as a reflection of Christ's motherhood [60:18.38.52; 61:35.38.46.47.56; 74:35].

1. Christ, our mother in kind and in grace

Julian offers three ways of contemplating the 'motherhood' of divine love.

> I vnderstode thre manner of beholdynges of motherhed in god. The furst
> is grounde of oure kynde makyng, the second is takyng of oure kynde, and
> ther begynnyth the moderhed of grace, the thurde is moderhed in werkyng.
> And therin is a forth sp(r)edyng by the same grace of lengt and brede, of hygh
> and of depnesse without ende; and alle is one loue. [59:43-48]

Julian predicates motherhood of the entire Trinity, but *in* and *through*
Christ. First, as the 'wisdom of God,' the Eternal Word is the mother of
our substantial nature, our kind.[12] Secondly, in assuming our sensuality,
the Word made flesh becomes our 'mother of mercy.'[13] In his incarnation, our 'mother Christ'[14] brings us to birth in his oneing of our substance and sensuality by the power of his passion, death and resurrection.[15] We are thus 'grounded and rooted' in the motherhood of Christ:
our substantial mother becomes our mother sensually by his incarnation.[16] It comes as no surprise, moreover, that Christ's motherhood of
grace also begins with his incarnation[17] because grace begins to work with

---

12 58:12-13.24-27.42-49; 60:58; cf. 60:5.15; 63:33-34. Julian associates the three persons of the Trinity with three properties: *fatherhood* (the Father almighty), *motherhood* (Christ, the Wisdom of God), and *lordship* (the Holy Spirit). [58:12-14.19-30]
While she states that we have our being (our 'kyndely substannce') in the Father
[58:22-24], she holds that the whole Trinity is involved in that substantial making,
appropriating the property of motherhood in our creation to the Second Person as
the 'wisdom of God': "For alle oure lyfe is in thre: in the furst (we haue) oure
beyng . . . . For the furst I saw and vnderstode that the hygh myght of the trynyte
is oure fader, and the depe wysdom of the trynyte is oure moder, and the grete
loue of the trynyte is oure lorde; and alle these haue we in kynde and in oure
substanncyall makyng." [58:30-31.34-37] Cf. 63:28-30.

13 58:44.49.57. Julian also calls Christ 'oure moder of mercy and pytte' [59:32-33].
We shall examine Julian's understanding of pity and compassion in chapter 4 (see
p. 165ff, below). For now, it is sufficient to note that she does not use the term
'mercy' as identical with 'compassion' or 'pity'; her concepts of mercy and compassion remain distinct, even if inseparable. Cf. 48:17-18; 55:17-18; 59:32-33.

14 58:46.

15 58:43-48.

16 "And ferthere more I saw that the seconde person, whych is oure moder, substann-
cyally the same derewurthy person, is now become oure moder sensuall, for we be
doubell of gods makyng, that is to sey substannciall and sensuall . . . . [And] the
seconde person of the trynyte is oure moder in kynd in oure substanncyall makyng,
in whom we be groundyd and rotyd, and he is oure moder of mercy in oure sensualyte takyng." [58:37-40.42-44]

17 59:45.

mercy when sensuality enters the picture.[18] Consequently, as a 'forth spreading by that same grace,'[19] the 'motherhood of working' is the extension in time of Christ's motherhood of mercy and corresponds to our 'keeping' in love by the working of mercy and grace in our existential lives, which 'keeping' Julian explicitly appropriates to Christ our mother.

> Thus Jhesu Crist . . . is oure very moder; we haue oure beyng of hym, where the ground of moderhed begynnyth, with alle the swete kepyng of loue that endlesly folowyth. [59:9-11]

Julian's description of Christ's motherhood in kind and in mercy reflects her understanding of the first two moments of our oneing in Christ, and her explanation of the motherhood of grace or 'working' corresponds to the third moment, our 'keeping' or existential oneing by the working of mercy and grace. Moreover, her teaching on these three divine motherhoods provides us with the most clearly christocentric formulation of her doctrine on kind, mercy, and grace, especially in her explicit reference to the relationship of grace to mercy: the motherhood of grace begins with Christ's incarnation (i.e., his motherhood of mercy) and continues in the form of the motherhood of working. In other words, the working of grace is situated in a christological context within the motherhood imagery; the motherhood of grace (our 'keeping' in love) is the natural follow-up in time to Christ's motherhood of mercy.[20]

The three motherhoods in God are thus appropriated to Christ as the Eternal Word (the motherhood of kind), as the Word made flesh (the motherhood of mercy), and in his existential working of our salvation in us by grace (his 'keeping' us by the motherhood of working). Just as kind, mercy, and grace are three properties in one goodness, so the three divine motherhoods are diverse aspects of the one same maternal love.[21] While trinitarian in its scope,[22] the divine motherhood is properly

---

18 55:16-18.
19 59:45-48.
20 59:9-11.38-42; cf. 60:51-53.
21 58:44-50; 59:43-48; cf. 56:41-46.
22 As Maisonneuve rightly suggests, Christ's motherhood is a total motherhood with a trinitarian character: it creates us, recreates us, and transfigures us in that creation. See Roland Maisonneuve, *L'univers visionnaire de Julian of Norwich,* 232.

Sr. Mary Paul holds that Julian's theology is really more in line with the biblical tradition which links Wisdom with the Holy Spirit. There is, however, no evidence in the text to support Sr. Mary Paul's suggestion that, equating Wisdom with 'God the Mother,' Julian illogically appropriates motherhood to the Son simply because she follows the post-Justinian tradition of linking Wisdom to Christ rather than to the Spirit. On the contrary, Julian clearly appropriates motherhood to the Son by

Christ's, a motherhood in kind and in grace by virtue of his making and taking of our kind.

> And thus is *Jhesu* oure very moder in kynd of oure furst makyng, and he is oure very moder in grace by takyng of oure kynde made. Alle the feyer werkyng and all the swete kyndly officis of dereworthy motherhed is in propred to *the* seconde person, for in hym we haue this goodly wylle, hole and safe wi*th*out ende, both in kynde and in grace, of his owne pr*o*pyr goodnesse. [59:37-42][23]

Here again, Julian deftly fashions the imagery of divine motherhood to elucidate her doctrine on oneing. Just as mercy is the central moment of our oneing by kind, mercy, and grace, so too Christ's motherhood of mercy makes sense of all other designations of God as mother. Christ's motherhood of mercy (his oneing of our sensuality to our substance in his incarnation) is the basis both of his motherhood of kind and of his motherhood of grace which begins with our being made sensual and overflows into the existential motherhood of working. The motherhood of mercy stands in the same relationship to the motherhoods of kind and of grace (or working) as does the working of mercy to nature and grace.

Julian further highlights the theological meaning of Christ's motherhood of mercy by telling us that the ground of Christ's work as mother is his incarnation.

> Oure kynde moder, our gracious modyr, for he wolde alle hole become oure modyr in alle thing, he toke the grounde of his werke full lowe and full myldely in the maydyns wombe. [60:7-9]

Only by virtue of his incarnation does Christ become our mother in the fullest sense: our mother who truly suffers the pains of labor in his passion[24] and who, because he shares our humanity, is able to bring us to birth with that tenderness of love proper to the intimate mother-child relationship.[25]

---

the Spirit. On the contrary, Julian clearly appropriates motherhood to the Son by virtue of his incarnation and passion, and lordship to the Holy Spirit. See Sr. Mary Paul, *All Shall Be Well, Julian of Norwich and the Compassion of God* (Oxford: SLG Press, 1976) 31-38. See note 11, p. 110, above.

23 Cf. 59:9-11; 60:11-14.
24 60:18-27; 63:31-32. See also p. 132-134, below.
25 For Julian, the word 'tender' seems to be reserved as somehow proper to humanity (e.g., in speaking of Christ's passion she refers to his 'tender body' or 'tender flesh' [1:13; 12:5; 17:9-10.17; 20:15-16.18; 51:291]; she also refers to John of Beverley's 'tender age' [38:27]). When Julian predicates tenderness of God, it usually has an explicit or implicit christological reference [5:6; 27:31.35; 72:26; 77:19; 80:42; 81:18],

> The kynde lovyng moder that woot and knowyth the neyde of hyr chylde, she kepyth it full tenderly, as the kynde and condycion of moderhed wyll. [60:51-53]

We have our 'tender keeping'[26] in our mother Christ precisely because Christ shares with us the capacity for human tenderness. The image of Christ's motherhood of mercy thus serves to reveal the tender, homely way God relates to our humanity through Christ's incarnation.

> Mercy is a pyttefull properte, whych longyth to moderhode in tender loue;
> . . . . Mercy werkyth kypyng, sufferyng, quyckyng and helyng, and alle is of tendyrnesse of loue. [48:28-32]

For Julian, Christ is the archetypal mother, our true mother from whom all motherhood derives. While Julian's moving description of Christ's motherhood of working reflects her own personal understanding of various aspects of human motherhood,[27] she never speaks of Christ's being *like* a mother.[28] On the contrary, mothers are like Christ. Christ alone may rightly be called 'mother.'[29]

> Thys feyer louely worde: Moder, it is so swete and so kynde in it selfe that it may not verely be seyde of none ne to none but of hym and to hym that is very mother of lyfe and of alle. To the properte of moderhede longyth kynd, loue, wysdom and knowyng, and it is god. [60:45-48]

---

primarily in terms of Christ's motherhood of working [36:45; 40:3; 48:29.31-32; 60:31.38.38.53; 61:2; 62:6; 77:23] or of his passion (see above). Only two exceptions to this pattern of christological reference appear in the *Shewings* [6:52-53; 12:14], suggesting that Julian makes a connection between the presence of the quality of tenderness in God and the fact that Christ shares our humanity.

26 40:3; 48:31-32; 61:2-3; 62:6; 80:42-43.

27 See p. 118-120, 186-189, below.

28 Heimmel points out that, although Julian shows her ability to create striking similes (e.g., 28:6-8), she never states anywhere that Christ is 'like' a mother, or does things 'as' a mother would. She has deliberately chosen metaphor over simile for the motherhood imagery, employing three forms to express this relationship: the direct and equating verb 'is' (e.g., 'oure savyoure is oure very moder' [57:49]), the appositive (e.g., 'our moder, Cryst' [83:15]), and the substitution of the word 'mother' in place of Christ (e.g., 'oure mother werkyth' [59:29]). There are only two examples of simile within Julian's motherhood imagery, and in both instances the 'as' refers not to Christ but to the 'we' of the relationship and is concerned with our role as child rather than Christ's as mother. See Jennifer P. Heimmel, "God is our Mother": Julian of Norwich and the Medieval Image of Christian Feminine Divinity (Unpublished dissertation, Fordham University, 1980) 60-61.

29 Cf. 60:14-17; Matt 23:9.

Just as all fatherhood takes its name from God the Father, so does all motherhood take its name from Christ.[30] Human parenthood is the reflection of the divine reality. We learn something of what fatherhood and motherhood mean by our human experience of them, but we do not 'apply' the terms to God; rather, God is fatherhood and Christ is motherhood. All that is maternal finds its origin in Christ. Julian goes so far as to say that Christ is the true subject of all human motherhood.[31]

Christ's motherhood thus grounds the full cycle of our human life, from before our birth until after our death. Moreover, Christ as mother not only reveals a maternal love at the heart of the Godhead but also brings us into that love. We are endlessly borne in Christ our mother, from whose womb we come and to whose womb we return.[32] Christ's motherhood of mercy, i.e., his taking on sensuality, stands at the heart of his working of our salvation: for Christ, to be our brother *is* to be our mother, and to be our mother is to be our savior.

> Oure hye fader, almyghty god, whych is beyng, he knowyth vs and louyd vs fro before ony time. Of whych knowyng in his full mervelous depe charyte by the forseeng endlesse councell of all the blessyd trynyte, he woulde that the seconde person shulde become oure moder, oure brother and oure savyoure. Where of it folowyth that as verely as god is oure fader, as verely god is oure mother. [59:23-29][33]

Whereas the order of creation reveals the love of God the Father, the working of our salvation is revealed as maternal in nature: divine mercy, Christ's saving and 'keeping' us, is the expression of God's maternal love.

2. Christ's motherhood of working

Within Julian's motherhood imagery, divine mercy as our 'keeping' in love finds its counterpart in Christ's motherhood of working.[34] As we have already seen, the motherhood of mercy is the ground of the motherhood of grace which has its continuation in the motherhood of working.

---

30 Cf. Eph 3:14-15.
31 "For though it be so *that* oure bodely forthbryngyng be but lytle, lowe and symple in regard of oure gostely forth bryngyng, yett it is he that doth it in the creaturys by whom that it is done.... Thys werkyng [of human motherhood] *with* all *that* be feyer and good, oure lord doth it in hem by whome it is done." [60:49-51.57-58]
32 53:30-35; 57:49-50; 64:3-4; cf. 62:14-18.
33 Cf. 52:2-5.
34 59:9-11.38-42; 60:51-53; see also p. 111-112, above.

Moreover, the image of the motherhood of working identifies Christ as subject of the working of mercy and grace. Christ protects and preserves us with all the tenderness of a loving mother; for our part, there is no higher stature in this life than that of our childhood in that tender 'keeping' of our gracious mother of mercy.[35]

a. Christ's unceasing labor: our spiritual 'forth bringing'

It is not difficult to understand why Julian connects the concept of motherhood with Christ's incarnation and passion. Our humanity is defined, given to us in Christ. Just as God is our Father in creation by giving us our being in that first making, Christ is our mother in our again-making by virtue of his giving us our embodied being-in-the-world, our sensuality. Christ's incarnation and his passion and death can be understood as the labor by which he brings us to birth.[36] What may come as a surprise is the fact that Julian presents Christ's motherhood of working as a *motive* for his incarnation: Christ took on our poor flesh in order to be able to perform the office of motherhood in every way, even the most humble.[37] The tender, compassionate service of a mother who suffers for and with her children becomes the primary image Julian uses to portray the work of Christ's motherhood of mercy. His motherhood is not confined to the historical events of his incarnation and his passion and death; rather, Christ our mother works unceasingly within the full context of our existential lives.

Deliberately juxtaposing life and death in order to point out the perfection of Christ's motherhood of mercy, Julian tells us that, unlike our natural mothers who bear us to pain and dying, Christ bears us to joy and endless living.[38] We are borne in Christ's maternal womb through

---

35 63:42-45.

36 This aspect of Christ's passion will be examined more fully in a later section of this chapter (see p. 132-134, below).

37 "Oure kynde moder, oure gracious modyr, for he wolde alle hole become oure modyr in alle thyng, he toke the grounde of his werke full lowe and full myldely in the maydyns wombe. And that shewde he in the furst, wher he broughte *that* meke maydyn before the eye of my vnderstondyng, in *the* sympyll stature as she was whan she conceyvyd; that is to sey oure hye god, the souereyn wysdom of all, in this lowe place he arayed hym and dyght hym all redy in oure poure flessch, hym selfe to do the servyce and the officie of moderhode in alle thyng." [60:7-14]

38 "We wytt that alle oure moders bere vs to payne and to dyeng. A, what is that? But oure very moder Jhe*s*u, he alone beryth vs to joye and to endlesse levyng, blessyd mot he be." [60:18-20] Cf. 63:31-32.

an endless cycle of life, without beginning or conclusion, never coming out of him.[39] In Christ we are carried to the Father[40] in whom the bliss that is ours by virtue of Christ's motherhood begins anew.

> And I vnderstode none hygher stature in this lyfe than chyldehode in febyl-nesse and faylyng of myght and of wytte in to *the* tyme *that* oure gracious moder hath brought vs vpp to oure fadyrs blysse. And ther shall it verely be made known to vs, his menyng in the swete woordes wher he seyth: Alle shalle be welle, and thou shalt see it thy selfe, that alle manner thyng shall be welle. And than shalle *the* blysse of oure moderheed in Crist be new to begynne in the joyes of oure fader god, whych new begynnyng shall last, *with*out end new begynnyng. Thus I vnder stode that all his blessyd chyldren whych be come out of hym by kynd shulde be brougt agayne in to hym by grace. [63:42-50; 64:3-4][41]

Our mother Christ remains, as it were, in unceasing labor until we come to full spiritual birth in him in the bliss of heaven.

> And of this swete feyer werkyng he shalle nevyr ceese nor stynte, tylle all his deerwurthy chyldren be borne and brought forth; and that shewde he where he gaue the vnderstandyng of the gostely thurst that is the loue longyng that shalle last tylle domys day. [63:23-27][42]

For Julian, Christ's unceasing labor constitutes the 'working' of his motherhood, which working she calls a 'forth spreading' by grace; by his motherhood of mercy and grace, Christ works our endless spiritual birth.

> Now me behovyth to seye a lytyll more of this forth spredyng, as I vnderstode in *the* menyng of oure lord: how that we be brought agayne by the moterherd of mercy and grace in to oure kyndly stede, where *that* we ware in, made by *the* moderhed of kynd loue, whych kynde loue nevyr leevyth vs. [60:2-6]

Here we find the clear parallel to Julian's understanding of our 'keeping' in Christ by the working of mercy and grace: by the motherhood of working we have our restoring and reforming until we reach the fullness

---

39 "Oure savyoure is oure very moder, in whome we be endlesly borne and nevyr shall come out of hym." [57:49-50] Cf. 53:30-35; 62:14-18; 64:3-4.
40 55:2-6.
41 Colledge and Walsh have chosen to designate the final sentence of this passage [64:3-4] as the opening to chapter 64, whereas none of the manuscripts shows this division. The Sloane MSS place the whole passage at the end of chapter 63, while the Paris MS and the Cressy edition place it at the beginning of chapter 64. See *A Book of Showings,* notes, p. 619.
42 Cf. 60:20-27.

of our identity in our mother Christ.[43] Christ, our mother of mercy and grace, tenderly 'keeps' us, nourishing us with his own life[44] until we are brought to full spiritual birth (our 'ghostly forth bringing').[45]

b. A debt of love: the tender service of the motherhood of working

The selfless nature of mother's love will inevitably imply that she suffer inconvenience, even real pain, in order to provide her children with all that is needed for their safety and full development. This suffering extends beyond that of childbirth itself; in compassion,[46] the mother continues to suffer with her children for their greater good. This is the 'debt' of motherhood which Christ assumes.

> Wherfore hym behovyth to fynde[47] vs, for the deerworthy loue of moder-
> hed hath made hym dettour to vs. [60:28-29]

The image of Christ as our 'debtor' is a strong one. However, the debt of Christ's motherhood does not denote any indebtedness to us; rather, the obligation deriving from his motherhood is freely chosen by Christ 'because of love' (i.e., not in return for anything we do for him). For love, Christ suffers for us in his motherhood of working until he has borne us to the full bliss of heaven.[48]

Even though a mother may allow the child's falling and distress if it will be to the child's profit, the mother's love will never allow any peril to harm the child.[49] She sees the child's need and 'keeps' the child ten-

---

43 "In oure moder of mercy we haue oure reformyng and oure restoryng, in whom
    oure partys be onyd and all made perfyte man." [58:57-58]
44 "The moder may geue her chylde sucke hyr mylke, but oure precyous moder Jhesu,
    he may fede vs wyth hym selfe, and doth full curtesly and full tendyrly with the
    blessyd sacrament, that is precyous fode of very lyfe." [60:29-32]
45 "Ande in oure gostly forth bryngyng he vsyth more tendernesse in kepyng without
    ony comparyson." [61:2-3]
46 The theme of Christ's motherly compassion will be treated more extensively in
    chapter 4 (see p. 186-189, below).
47 'Nourish' or 'feed.'
48 60:20-27.
49 61:35-37. We find a similar image in the Ancrene Riwle, a thirteenth century rule
    for anchoresses, a rule which Julian is likely to have known well; however, whereas
    Julian speaks of Christ's 'allowing' us to fall for our greater good, the Ancrene
    Riwle suggests that Christ is simply 'playing with us' as a mother, 'withdrawing his
    grace' and 'leaving us alone' to be tempted. Clearly, Julian's vision of the responsi-
    ble love of a mother is the superior image theologically. See Part IV of The
    Ancrene Riwle, translated by M. B. Salu, 102.

derly.[50] Even should our earthly mother allow her child to perish, Christ's motherhood of working will never let us perish,[51] but raises us from our falling and strengthens us.[52] Our compassionate 'mother of mercy' not only protects us from harm, but even turns our falling into good.[53] Consequently, we come to trust in his motherly love. Julian points out the natural reliance of the child on the mother.[54] When distressed or afraid, the child runs hastily to the mother, crying for help; in our case, it is the sight of our sin which sends us to Christ our mother for mercy.

> But oft tymes when oure fallyng and oure wrechydnes is shewde vs, we be so sore adred and so gretly ashamyd of oure selfe that vnnethis we witt wher *that* we may holde vs. But then wylle nott oure curtesse moder that we flee away, for hym were nothing lother; but he wyll than that we vse the condicion of a chylde. For when it is dissesyd and a feerd, it rynnyth hastely to the moder; and if it may do no more, it cryeth on the mother for helpe *with* alle *the* mygtes. So wyll he that we done as *the* meke chylde, seyeng thus: My kynd moder, my gracyous moder, my deerworthy moder, haue mercy on me. I haue made my selfe foule and vnlyke to thee, and I may not nor canne ame*n*de it but *with* thyne helpe and grace. [61:41-51][55]

We are to flee to the arms of our 'mother of mercy and pity'[56] when we are suffering or afraid, trusting him to 'keep' us safe in his love.[57] We neither despair of Christ's love nor presume on our own strength.[58]

The unselfish, loving service of Christ's motherhood of working is the paradigm for understanding the working of mercy and grace, i.e., the motherhood of 'keeping': Christ suffers for us, nourishes us, guides us, and even allows our chastisement when necessary,[59] all in the tender service of a mother's love so that we might be brought to full spiritual birth in him. Christ's 'keeping' of us is in the mode of that unsentimen-

---

50 60:51-53.
51 61:37-40.
52 61:10-12.
53 "Mercy is a swete gracious werkyng in loue, medlyd *with* plentuous pytte, for mercy werkyth vs kepyng, and mercy werkyth turnyng to vs all thyng to good." [48:17-19]
54 "For kyndly the chylde dyspeyreth nott of the moders loue, kyndely the chylde presumyth nott of it selfe, kyndely the chylde louyth the moder and eche one of them other." [63:38-40]
55 Cf. 28:33-35; 77:14-16.49-51; 86:7-10.
56 59:32-33.
57 74:33-38; cf. 61:43-51; 63:20-23.
58 Cf. 63:38-40 (note 54, above).
59 "And when it [the child] is wexid of more age, she sufferyth it that it be cha(s)tised in brekyng downe of vicis, to make the chylde receyve vertues and grace." [60:55-57]

tal, wise, and loving understanding of one's child, an understanding which enables the mother to support true growth. We increase, wax, and are strengthened and healed existentially by the working of our mother Christ who gives all his intent to our salvation.

> The swet gracious handes of oure moder be redy and diligent a bout vs; for he in alle this werkyng vsyth the very office of a kynde norysse, that hath not elles to done but to entende about the saluation of hyr chylde. [61:66-69][60]

In his motherhood of working, Christ is our gracious guide who patiently teaches us,[61] our diligent nurse who tenderly heals us.

c. Christ's motherhood of working in the Church

Finally, we need to say a word about the image of the Church as our mother. Just as Christ is the ground of our humanity, so he is the ground of the Church, both the teacher and the teaching.[62]

> Oure precyous moder Jhesu, he may fede vs wyth hym selfe, and doth full curtesly and full tendyrly with the blessyd sacrament, that is precyous fode of very lyfe; and with all the swete sacramentes he systeynyth vs full mercyfully and graciously, and so ment he in theyse blessyd wordys, where he seyde: I it am that holy chyrch prechyth the and techyth the. That is to sey: All the helth and the lyfe of sacramentys, alle the vertu and the grace of my worde, alle the goodnesse that is ordeynyd in holy chyrch to the, I it am. [60:30-37]

Christ is the Church; consequently, the Church is our mother.[63] We have our 'keeping,' our safety, in the faith of the Church because therein we are fastened to Christ himself.

> And he wylle that we take vs myghtly to the feyth of holy chyrch, and fynd there oure deerworthy mother in solas and trew vnderstandyng with all the blessyd commonn. For one singular person may oftyn tymes be broken, as it semyth to the selfe, but the hole body of holy chyrch was nevyr broken, nor nevyr shall be with out ende. And therfore a suer thyng it is, a good and a

---

60   Cf. 61:12; 63:20-23.
61   For a complete analysis of Julian's use of the image of Christ as teacher, see Ritamary Bradley, "Christ the Teacher in Julian's Shewings, The Biblical and Patristic Traditions," in The Medieval Mystical Tradition in England, Dartington, 1982, edited by Marion Glasscoe (Exeter: University of Exeter, 1982) 127-142.
62   34:17-18; cf. 26:10-11.
63   46:50; 61:58-63.

gracious to wylle mekly and myghtly be fastenyd and onyd to oure moder holy
church, that is Crist Jhesu. [61:57-64][64]

When we find ourselves in need, we fly to the Church and find there the
solace and comfort of our mother Christ.

Julian's imagery of the motherhood of working further nuances our
understanding of the integral relationship between Christ's 'keeping' us
and the life of grace in the Church. We are treasured in Christ our
mother who sustains us within himself until we are brought to full spiritual birth.[65] As we grow in the christian life, the working of Christ's motherhood of mercy adapts to each new level of maturity.[66] (This is our 'spiritual forthbringing' in which Christ uses such tenderness.)[67] We are nur-
tured by his tender 'keeping' during the time of the growth that is ours
by grace. In other words, Christ's nurturing *is* grace. As we grow, we
take on his features. Just as the child has from birth a certain resemblance to the parents, a resemblance which becomes more marked as he
or she matures and sometimes even takes on the idiosyncratic traits of
the parents, so do we have our resemblance to Christ by 'inheritance'
(our participation in his humanity)[68] and by environment (our upbring-
ing, i.e., the life of grace within the Church). We take on our mother
Christ's characteristics, which are none other than the reverberations of
the working of mercy and grace in us.[69] By grace, our human will is
accorded with Christ's, i.e., we assume existentially the 'godly will' that is
already ours in Christ our mother. The motherhood of working perfects
and confirms our human nature as Christ's, and we begin to reflect more
and more the life of Christ in us.[70]

Within Julian's vision, the Church is thus the channel of Christ's
mercy, the mode in which Christ continues his motherhood of working.
In the Church we find our *mater et magistra,* a true mother who 'keeps'
us safe by her teaching[71] and who nourishes us and heals our wounds

---

64   Cf. 62:24-26; 67:22-24.
65   60:20-23.
66   "The kynde lovyng moder that woot and knowyth the neyde of hyr chylde, she
      kepyth it full tenderly, as the kynde and condycion of moderhed wyll. And evyr as
      it waxith in age and in stature, she channgyth her werkes, but nott her loue."
      [60:51-55]
67   61:2-3 (note 45, p. 118, above).
68   Our virtues belong to us 'in kind' as Christ's 'children.' [63:37-38]
69   As we shall see in chapter 4, these characteristics include Christ's woundedness
      which, in us, takes the form of the three 'wounds' of contrition, compassion, and
      willful longing for God (see p. 197-198, below).
70   See p. 79-80, above.
71   80:3-4.

by word and sacrament.[72] As humble sons and daughters of our mother Church while we are here on earth, we fulfill our highest calling, that of the simple stature of children who are 'kept' by their mother Christ.[73]

---

72 39:7-9.31-32; 60:30-37.
73 63:42-45; cf. 46:50.

B. The Passion: Christ Brings Us to Birth

The mystery of Christ's incarnation includes his life, passion, death, and resurrection and occupies the central place in every truly christian spirituality; however, different periods within the Church's history have tended to highlight diverse aspects of that one mystery.[74] In Julian's day, meditation on the suffering Jesus formed the core of English popular piety.[75] The sacred art, the mystery play cycles, and the religious poetry of medieval England provided even the ordinary, uneducated peasant with an eloquent vocabulary with which to reflect on the events of Calvary.

Living in fourteenth century England, Julian could not have escaped the pervasive influence of medieval popular devotion to the passion of Christ. Given the devotional climate of her day, it should come as no surprise that, many years prior to her shewings, Julian had asked for the gift of a 'mind of the passion,' i.e., a true 'knowing' of Christ's sufferings; she wished to know Christ's agony as those who had been at the foot of the cross knew it so that she might 'suffer with' Christ as they had.[76] Julian's sincere desire to know Christ crucified is the backdrop against which she experienced her shewings.[77] Indeed, as Julian lay dying, a curate set a crucifix before her eyes, and the image of the crucified Christ became the actual physical focus of her visions.[78] Thus, we must situate

---

74 E.g., in the period following the fourth century Arian crisis, the Church emphasized the divinity of the glorified, living Christ, whereas the *devotio moderna* of the fourteenth and fifteenth centuries focused attention on the earthly Jesus whose humility of life serves as a model for our imitation.

75 Devotion to the suffering humanity of Christ was fostered by the writings of such medieval spiritual masters such as Anselm, Bernard, and Bonaventure, while Francis of Assisi's devotion to the crucified Christ spread throughout Europe and the whole Church through the influence of the Franciscans. This devotional current is exemplified in the beautiful Meditations on the Passion by Julian's contemporary Richard Rolle or in the *Ancrene Riwle*'s many prescriptions regarding devotion to Christ's passion. See Part I of *The Ancrene Riwle,* translated by M. B. Salu, 7-20; Richard Rolle, "Meditations on the Passion," in *Richard Rolle, the English Writings,* translated by Rosamund S. Allen (New York: Paulist Press, 1988) 90-124; cf. Roland Maisonneuve, *L'univers visionnaire de Julian of Norwich,* 71-74; and Mary Frances Walsh Meany, "The Image of Christ in the Revelations of Divine Love of Julian of Norwich," Unpublished dissertation (Fordham University, 1975) 131-149.

76 2:5-20. The Long Text makes it clear that Julian's desire for this gift was among the religious aspirations of her youth. Cf. 2:38-39.

77 3:43-47; 17:50-52; 55:52-54; 61:7-8; 77:30-32; cf. 1 Cor 2:2; Phil 3:10.

78 3:20-32; 4:3-8; 7:12-21; 10:3-10; 12:3-12; 16:3-30; 17:2-49; 19:2-5; 20:2-4; 21:3-7;

Julian's theology of mercy within the context of her understanding of Christ's passion.

1. Christ's passion as the ground of all the shewings

For Julian, it is the sight of the crucified Christ which reveals the Trinity, the Son's incarnation, and the uniting of the soul to God, and which grounds and joins all the 'many fair shewings and teachings of endless wisdom and love' that followed her initial vision of Christ's bleeding head.[79] Christ's passion is the ground of all the shewings; the revelation of divine love is made in and through his passion and death on the cross.

a. Christ's passion reveals the Trinity

As we have already said, Julian locates the Trinity in the cross of Christ.[80] As she looked at Christ's bleeding head in the first shewing, she was shown the Trinity.[81] Julian's only access to the mystery of the Trinity is Christ: where Jesus appears, the Trinity is understood.[82] For Julian, the love which is the Trinity is not an abstraction. God's love is revealed in very personal terms, manifest in the face of the crucified Christ. The mystery of the cross is *the* revelation of the merciful love of the Father whose will Christ carries out in his passion and death;[83] moreover, Christ's passion, death, and resurrection reveal the Holy Spirit as the bond of love by which Christ remains ever united to the Father, even in his experience of the utter desolation of the cross. In fact, for Julian, the love between the Father and the Son is the most understandable aspect of the Trinity.[84]

While clearly involving the power of the whole Trinity, the passion remains properly Christ's by virtue of his humanity.

      24:3-7; 25:3-5.
79   1:2-7 (p. 107, above); cf. 6:62-64.
80   See p. 29, above.
81   4:9-16.
82   4:15.
83   59:23-30; cf. 51:234-243.
84   "Though the thre persons of *the* blessyd trynyte be alle evyn in the selfe, the soule toke most vnderstandyng in loue." [73:25-27]

And as aneynst Cristes manhode, it is knowyn in our feyth and also shewde
that he *with* the vertu of the godhede for loue to bryng vs to hys blysse
sufferyd paynes and passion and dyed. And theyse be the workes of Cristes
manhed, wher in he enjoyeth. [31:26-30]

Christ alone suffered the pains of the passion.

Alle the trinyte wrought in the passion of Crist, mynystryn habonndance
of vertuse and plente of grace to vs by hym; but only the maydyns sonne
sufferyd, werof alle the blessed trynyte enyoyeth. [23:30-32]

The 'enjoying' (rejoicing) of the whole Trinity is yet another dimension
of God which is revealed in the sufferings of Christ; as we shall see,
Julian's understanding of heaven itself (i.e., the endless joy, bliss, and
delight of the Trinity) is so intimately bound to Christ's cross that she
sometimes identifies the two.[85] The joy of the Trinity, which joy constitutes the bliss of heaven, lies in the accomplishment of our again-making
in Christ, the working of our salvation by virtue of Christ's passion.

b. Christ's passion reveals humanity

The cross of Christ also reveals who we are as human beings and what sin
is. In the cross we are shown the true nature of our sin by the light of
God's mercy and grace,[86] i.e., by the light of the salvation we have by
virtue of Christ's passion and death. While we are yet on earth, Christ
shows us his suffering, the suffering caused by our sin.[87] We come to
understand something of the horror of sin when we look upon the blood-
stained face of the crucified Jesus.[88] There we see sin for what it truly
is: the cause of Christ's pain and of all human suffering.[89] It is Christ's
experience of suffering which defines our own.

By his act of total self-emptying on the cross, Jesus also shows us
what it means to be truly human: to give oneself utterly in love and in

---

85 22:7-23; 23:2-14; cf. 19:15-20. This identification of the joy of heaven with the
    passion of Christ will be explored more fully later in this chapter (see p. 136-142,
    below).
86 40:2-5; 78:2-5.15-16.31-43; see also p. 91-95, above, and note 27, p. 28, above.
87 While we are on earth, we see the 'chere' of Christ's passion; in heaven, we shall
    have full sight of his 'blessydfulle chere,' i.e., his bliss and joy. [21:18-26] See
    chapter 4, p. 178-180, 189-191, below, for the development of this point.
88 For Julian, the bleeding head of Christ is 'a fygur and a lyknes of oure fowle blacke
    dede, which that our feyre bryght blessed lord bare for oure synne.' [10:36-38]
89 52:51-52; cf. 18:14-16.36-37; 27:28-34.

trust. Sin, on the other hand, is that which contradicts love and which is, therefore, most inhuman or 'unkind.'[90] The mystery of Christ's passion, death, and resurrection reveals to us the triumph of love over sin. In the context of a sinful world, Jesus definitively realizes in himself the human capacity to be 'at one' with God. Ultimately, sin is absolutely powerless over humanity that is oned to God in love. It is by love, the love that is stronger than death, that the 'fiend' is overcome.[91] Our truest 'self' is Christ in whom humanity reaches the perfection of love and in whom sin is overcome by that same love. In Christ's humanity lies our salvation, our happiness, our eternal bliss. The revelation of the triumph of divine love in Christ's passion is the revelation of that love which defines us as oned to God.

2. 'By virtue of Christ's passion'

'By virtue of Christ's passion' sounds as a continual refrain throughout the *Shewings*.[92] The passion of Christ stands at the center of Julian's theology: all that Christ has done and continues to do for us is done by the power of his cross. We are saved, oned to God in Christ 'by virtue of his passion.'[93] In his dying on the cross, Christ our mother bore us to endless life.[94]

a. Christ's passion as the definitive moment of his incarnation

In his incarnation, Christ took on the human condition and the burden of suffering and death which belongs to that condition. As the parable of the lord and the servant illustrates so clearly, suffering *is* the human condition.[95] In that sense, Christ's whole life is his passion, his dying. For as long as he was on earth, Christ suffered for us.[96]

---

90 63:14-16.
91 13:7-10.13-14.37-41; 68:60-62; 70:14-16.
92 1:15-16; 5:44-45; 13:7-10.13-14.39-40; 20:30-32; 28:26-28; 40:16-19; 45:9-11; 52:44-46; 56:29-31.35-36; 58:47-48; 70:14-15; cf. 12:20-26; 23:47; 31:28-29; 51:255-256; 63:31-32; 68:61-62.
93 5:44-45; 51:255-256; 56:35-36; 58:47-48; cf. 13:13-14; 70:14-15.
94 63:31-32; cf. 31:28-29; 40:16-19.
95 "The soore that he toke was oure flessch, in whych as sone he had felyng of dedely paynes." [51:280-282] Cf. 51:15-31.
96 20:24-25.

> He dyed in our manhede, begynnyng at the swete incarnation, and lastyng to
> the blessyd vprysyng on Ester morow. So long duryd the cost and the charge
> abowt oure redempcion in deed. [23:21-23]

The kenosis of Christ's incarnation does, however, reach its historical
climax in the events of Calvary. The passion of Christ is the definitive
moment of his incarnation, the moment in which he accepted the full
consequences of his humanity. Nowhere is his suffering of the pain[97]
of the human condition more evident than in his passion and death when,
carrying the full burden of our sin, he experienced the ultimate in human
suffering.

> He sufferd more payne than all man of saluacion that evyr was from the furst
> begynnyng in to the last day myght telle or fully thynke, havyng regard to the
> worthynes of the hyghest worshypful kyng and the shamfulle and dyspyteous
> peynfull deth. For he that is hyghest and worthyest was foulest co(n)dempnyd
> and vtterly dyspysed; for the hyest poynt that may be seen in his passion is to
> thynke and to know that he is god that sufferyd. [20:5-11][98]

Here we see the crux of Julian's insight into the passion: it is *God* that
suffered.[99] Because our lives are the cross he bears, Christ in his passion
ones the totality of the human condition to God in himself; in Christ, the
God-separatedness of our sensuality is brought into God. Christ's passion
stands as the moment of at-one-ment, the moment when Christ ones in
himself all that is separated from God by sin.[100] Christ suffers our pain
(the unmistakable evidence of the scourge of sin) in order to give birth
to a humanity oned to God in love.

In the parable of the lord and the servant we are told that Christ
suffered 'the greatest labor and the hardest travail that is' in order to
recover the 'treasure' of humanity for God.[101] This again-buying or

---

97 The word 'payne' derived from the word 'penalty.' In middle English, the meaning
is ambiguous, including both penalty and pain (in the modern sense). The pain of
the passion was the 'penalty' of sin, the price to be paid because of the context of
sin. Here 'penalty' does not connote divine punishment; rather it is the pain
inflicted by sin itself.

98 Cf. Phil 2:5-11.

99 Cf. 31:27-29. We shall explore Julian's understanding of divine impassibility in
chapter 4 (see p. 176-178, 185-186, below).

100 Christ reconciles all dichotomies in himself, nobility and lowliness, might and
homeliness: "For verely it is the most ioy that may be, as to my syght, that he that
is hyghest and myghtyest, noblyest and wurthyest, is lowest and mekest, hamlyest
and curtysest." [7:46-48]

101 For Julian, humanity is the 'treasure that was in the earth' which the servant of the
parable is sent to obtain for the lord. [51:185-210]

'asseeth'[102] was the saving work, the 'travail' of his passion. It is 'by virtue of his passion' that Christ restores us,[103] buys us again,[104] and saves us.[105] His passion is our comfort,[106] our security against sin: it saves us from the 'fiend' because sin is rendered powerless by love.[107] By his suffering, Christ 'bought' us from hell (eternal separation from God) and brings us into communion with the Trinity.[108] Moreover, because our sensuality is oned to our substance in him, the triumph of love which is effected by his passion restores us from 'double death,'[109] i.e., it restores both our 'fallen' life (the separation of our sensuality from our substance) and, consequently, our mortal life (the separation of the soul from the body).

The passion of Christ is central to Julian's understanding of our oneing by divine mercy. Mercy proper is the 'redemption in deed'[110] of our remaking in Christ's incarnation: by virtue of his passion, we are oned to our substance in our mother of mercy.

> He is oure moder of mercy in oure sensualyte takyng. And thus oure moder is to vs dyverse manner werkyng, in whom oure pertys be kepte vndepertyd; for in oure moder Cryst we profyt and encrese, and in mercy he reformyth vs and restoryth, and by the vertu of his passion, his deth and his vprysyng onyd vs to oure substannce. Thus workyth oure moder in mercy to all his belovyd chyldren whych be to hym buxom and obedyent. [58:43-50][111]

---

102 29:11-14; cf. 60:24. Logarbo points out that 'asseeth' has its roots in the Latin expression *ad satis* and is best translated as *that which makes sufficient*, in the sense of making up for something which is lacking. The 'satisfaction' which Christ makes is not so much a satisfying of God's offended dignity, but rather Christ's bridging with love the fracture that is sin. In this sense, Julian's use of the term 'asseeth' differs sharply from Anselm's satisfaction through atonement and emphasizes instead the ontological meaning of the 'redemption in deed' as the oneing of God and humanity in and by Christ's freely given love in his passion and death. See Mona Logarbo, "Salvation Theology in Julian of Norwich: Sin, Forgiveness, and Redemption in the Revelations," *Thought* 61 (1986) 374. See also note 128, p. 46, above.

103 5:44-45.

104 56:29-31; cf. 22:20.

105 51:255-256.

106 27:30-31; see p. 178-180, below, for the development of this point.

107 13:7-10,13-14.37-41; 68:60-62; 70:14-16.

108 23:49; 56:29-31. cf. 12:20-31; 51:299-311.

109 55:44-54.

110 23:21-23 (p. 127, above).

111 Cf. 56:35-37.

Julian consistently attributes our oneing by mercy and grace to the power of Christ's passion: we are 'bought' again in love by mercy and grace through the power of Christ's passion;[112] we are healed and washed clean by his blood, a 'flood' of mercy;[113] we are forgiven our sins and brought into the joys of heaven by mercy and grace by the power of the passion;[114] the rewarding of grace is ours by virtue of his passion;[115] even the oneing which reforms our judgment by mercy and grace is accomplished by virtue of Christ's passion.[116]

b. Our wounds become our 'worships'

In the parable of the lord and the servant, the servant's love for his lord was the motive that sent him running to do his lord's will. For love, the servant ran (and eventually suffered much pain and travail) in order to do that 'one thing' that would be worship to his loving lord.

> The wysdom of the seruannt sawe inwardly that ther was one thyng to do whych shuld be wurschyppe to the lord; and the servannt for loue, havyng no regarde to hym selfe nor to nothyng that myght fall of hym, hastely deed sterte and rynne at the sendyng of his lorde, to do that thyng whych was hys wylle and his wurshyppe. [51:175-180]

Since Christ's incarnation and passion is the 'one thing' which the Father willed and which Christ undertook in love for the Father's glory, the wounds of Christ's passion are, in a real sense, his worship of the Father.

> For the payne was a noble precious and wurschypfulle dede done in a tyme by the workyng of loue. [22:47-48]

Moreover, because it is our pain, i.e., the pain of our sins, that Christ bore in his passion, we can say that *our* wounds are *Christ's* worship. Our pain is his pain by virtue of our oneing; we ourselves are the form which Christ's worship of the Father takes.[117]

---

112 56:29-31.
113 12:20-26; 61:64-66; 63:20-23.
114 40:16-19; cf. 31:28-29; 52:44-46.
115 Our pains are 'turned in to everlastyng joy by the vertu of Cristes passion.' [20:31-32] Cf. 23:47; 28:26-28.
116 45:9-11.
117 "Here I saw a grett onyng betwene Crist and vs, to my vnderstondyng; for when he was in payne we ware in payne, and alle creatures that myght suffer payne sufferyd *with* hym. . . . Thus was oure lord Jhesu payned for vs; and we stonde alle in this maner of payne *with* hym, and shalle do tylle that we come to his blysse." [18:14-

When Julian says that what Christ suffers in us by his cross is his worship of the Father, we must not interpret her to mean that sin itself is worship; rather it is Christ's suffering of our sin that transforms its evil into good.

> Alle *that* oure lorde doyth is ryghtfull(e), and alle that he sufferyth is wurschyp-fulle; and in theyse two is comprehendyd good and evylle. For alle that is good oure lorde doyth, and *that* is evyll oure lord sufferyth. I say nott that evylle is wurschypfulle, but I sey the sufferannce of oure lorde god is wurschy-pfulle, wher by hys goodnes shalle be know *without* ende, and hys mervelous mekenesse and myldhed by thys werkyng of mercy and grace. [35:19-25]

In accepting the suffering of the cross, Jesus turns the 'token of sin' (i.e., the pain sin causes) into worship of the Father by making our sin the opportunity for his love to be demonstrated.[118]

For Julian, 'worship' has a second meaning in relationship to Christ's passion. Christ's wounds represent not only his worship of the Father, but they also become Christ's own 'worships' (his glory, his honors). The pain of Christ's passion is turned to everlasting joy for him and for us.

> Now is all my bitter payne and alle my harde traveyle turnyd to evyrlasting joy and blysse to me and to the. [24:23-25]

Because it is oned to Christ's pain, the pain we suffer also becomes our glory in Christ.[119] We are given a 'high nobility and endless worship' by virtue of the passion and death of Christ.[120] Our pains and tribula-tions, our wounds, are turned to worship, joy, and profit by the working of mercy and grace through the power of Christ's passion.[121]

Julian comes to understand that the true glory of God is to be found in the face of the crucified Christ. When she was shown the figure of Christ dying on the cross, Julian was not given to see an actual moment of death; rather, Christ's agonized face was suddenly transfigured before her eyes.[122] This transfiguration from pain to joy highlights the continu-ity between the suffering Jesus of the passion and Christ, the glorious

---

16.36-37] Cf. 17:52-53. See also chapter 4, p. 177, below.

118 38:20-21. Christ's worship is to save us. [61:70 (p. 70, above)]

119 "And for this lytylle payne that we suffer heer we shalle haue an hygh endlesse knowyng in god, whych we myght nevyr haue *without* that. And the harder oure paynes haue ben *with* hym in hys crosse, the more shalle our worsch(y)ppe be *with* hym in his kyngdom." [21:24-28]

120 52:44-46.94-96; cf. 40:16-19.

121 56:35-37; cf. 13:15.46-48; 20:31-32; 28:26-28; 49:48-53.

122 21:3-7.

king of heaven. In his risen state, Christ still bears the marks of his passion; his wounds are his glory, his 'worships.'[123] In Christ, the death caused by sin is itself transfigured into endless life. Because of our oneing, the same holds true for us.[124] Our wounds are transfigured by the power of Christ's passion.[125] The wounds of our sins are a fundamental part of our personal history and will remain in us; but in God's sight they will be seen in glory not as sins, but as honors, i.e., the worship of Christ's suffering them in us.[126] Since Christ suffered their pain in us, we share in the reward that our oned suffering merits.[127] Our painful wounds, the 'token' of sin, will be our worship, our glory;[128] we shall rejoice in the love that suffered them for our sake.

3. Three 'beholdings' of Christ's motherhood of mercy

Julian tells us that she was given three ways to understand Christ's passion.

> It is gods wylle, as to my vnderstandyng, that we haue iij maner of behold-yng of his blessyd passion. The furst is the harde payne that he sufferyd *with* a contriccion and compassion. [20:33-35]

> And heer saw I for the seconde beholding in his blessyde passion. The loue that made hym to suffer it passith as far alle his paynes as hevyn is aboue

---

123 As we shall see in the next section, we are Christ's reward and bliss as well as his wounds because his wounds are turned to worship (see p. 138-139, below).

124 The implication for us may be seen most clearly in the parable of the lord and the servant; the transformation of Christ into glory is also the transformation of humanity into the likeness of Christ. [51:280-331]

125 In chapter 4 (see p. 197-198, below), we shall see how the wounds of our sins are transfigured into the three 'wounds' of contrition, compassion, and willful longing for God.

126 38:2-3.19-21; 39:31-32 (note 54, p. 66, above); 52:94-96; cf. 1:36-37.

127 Our reward is intrinsically related to our pain: "And god shewed that synne shalle be no shame, but wurshype to man, for ryght as to every synne is *answeryng* a payne by truth, ryght so for every synne to the same soule is gevyn a blysse by loue. Ryght as dyuerse synnes be ponysschyd *with* dyuers paynes after that it be greuous, ryght so shalle they be rewardyd *with* dyvers joyes in hevyn for theyr victories, after as the synne haue ben paynfulle and sorowfulle to the soule in erth." [38:2-8] Cf. 21:26-28 (note 119, p. 130, above).

128 The sin we suffer in this life will be made known in heaven by a reward of exceeding glories [38:11-12]; there, 'the tokyn of synne is turnyd to worshyppe.' [38:20-21] Cf. 38:17-20.

erth; for the payne was a noble precious and wurschypfulle dede done in a tyme by the workyng of loue. [22:45-48]

And heer saw I for the thyrde beholdyng in hys blessydfulle passion, that is to sey the joy and blysse that makyth hym to lyke it. [23:6-8]

These three 'beholdings' of Christ's passion may be understood as three views of true maternal love: (a) the pain that the mother is willing to suffer for the sake of the child; (b) the depth of love which causes the mother to suffer for the child; and (c) the great joy of the mother because of the benefit her own suffering will bring to the child.

a. The passion as *suffering*: Christ suffers the pains of labor

The first way of viewing the passion is to see the suffering Christ bore for us. Julian provides a graphic account of the many sufferings of Christ in his passion. She describes in vivid detail the tearing of his flesh by the crown of thorns and the scourging, the copious bleeding of his head and his body, the discoloring of his face, the slow and painful 'drying' of the flesh as his body was drained of life.[129] Because of his divinity, the pain Christ suffered in his passion surpasses all other pains on earth.

And thus saw I oure lorde Jhesu languryng long tyme, for the vnyng of the godhed gaue strenght to the manhed for loue to suffer more than alle man myght. I meene nott oonly more payne than alle man myght suffer, but also that he sufferd more payne than all man of saluacion that evyr was from the furst begynnyng in to the last day myght telle or fully thynke, havyng regard to the worthynes of the hyghest worshypful kyng and the shamfulle and dyspyteous peynfull deth. For he that is hyghest and worthyest was foulest co(n)dempnyd and vtterly dyspysed. [20:2-9][130]

Christ's suffering includes all the pain due our sins.[131] Because we are his members, oned to him, Christ is the true subject of our pain.[132] This first 'beholding' of Christ's passion, i.e., the sight of Christ's suffer-

---

129 4:2-8; 7:12-34; 10:2-10; 12:2-13; 16:2-30; 17:2-62; 20:2-9; 23:9-13; 27:16-18.23; cf. 51:289-298.303-505.
130 Cf. 27:22-24; 51:287-288.
131 "And for every mannys synne that shal be savyd he sufferyd; and every mannes sorow, desolacion and angwysshe he sawe and sorowd, for kyndnes and loue." [20:19-21] Cf. 27:15-19.
132 See note 117, p. 129, above.

ing, evokes our contrition and compassion when we realize that our sins are the cause of his pain.[133]

By suffering, Christ 'rightfully' earns his glory and our salvation.[134] We are brought into 'noble fairness' by the 'hard travail' of Christ's passion.[135] Seeing the connection between Christ's death on the cross and our own birth to new life in Christ, Julian describes Christ's suffering of his passion in terms of the labor pains of a mother.[136]

> The moders servyce is nerest, rediest and suerest: nerest for it is most of kynd, redyest for it is most of loue, and sekerest for it is most of trewth. This office ne mygh nor coulde nevyr none done to the full but he allone. We wytt that alle oure moders bere vs to payne and to dyeng. A, what is that? But oure very moder Jhesu, he alone beryth vs to joye and to endlesse levyng, blessyd mot he be. Thus he susteyneth vs with in hym in loue and traveyle, in to the full tyme *that* he wolde suffer the sharpyst thornes and grevous paynes that evyr were or evyr shalle be, and dyed at the last. And whan he had done, and so borne vs to blysse, yet myght nott all thys make a seeth to his mervelous loue. [60:14-24]

Christ's passion gives birth to a humanity oned to God in love. We are borne to bliss in our mother Christ.

Julian's reflection on the wound in Christ's side also suggests motherhood themes.

> Wyth a good chere oure good lorde lokyd in to hys syde and behelde *with* joy, and *with* hys swete lokyng he led forth the vnderstandyng of hys creature by the same wound in to hys syd *with* in; and ther he shewyd a feyer and delectable place, and large jnow for alle mankynde that shalle be savyd and rest in pees and in loue. And ther *with* he brought to mynde hys dere worthy blode and hys precious water whych he lett poure out for loue. And *with* the swete beholdyng he shewyd hys blessyd hart clovyn on two. [24:3-9]

Once again, we find imagery which alludes to childbearing. Christ's wound (a symbol of suffering and death) becomes his womb (the place of birth and life).[137] The flow of blood and water suggests a symbolic

---

133 See 20:33-35 (p. 131, above).
134 51:285-286.
135 51:149-152.
136 Julian was not the first to understand Christ's passion in terms of motherhood. E.g., in his *Prayer to St. Paul*, Anselm compares Christ's death to the labor of the mother in bringing forth life. See Anselm, "Prayer to St. Paul," in *The Prayers and Meditations of St Anselm*, translated by Sr. Benedicta Ward, S.L.G. (Harmondsworth: Penguin, 1973) 153-6.
137 Panichelli holds that Julian's imagery of Christ's wound suggests a 'displaced womb,' citing Jonathan Goldberg's study on the literature of the English Renais-

reference both to the biological birth process and to the birth of our
ecclesial life through the sacraments of baptism and eucharist.[138] In this
symbolism, Christ's wound is the womb which gives birth to the Church
and the womb which *is* the Church. As mother, Christ brings us to birth
in the womb of the Church through the waters of baptism and nourishes
us in that womb by his own blood.

> The moder may geue her chylde sucke hyr mylke, but oure precyous moder
> Jhesu, he may fede vs wyth hym selfe, and doth full curtesly and full tendyrly
> with the blessyd sacrament, that is precyous fode of very lyfe; and with all the
> swete sacramentes he systeynyth vs full mercyfully and graciously, and so ment
> he in theyse blessyd wordys, where he seyde: I it am that holy chyrch prech-
> yth the and techyth the. That is to sey: All the helth and the lyfe of sacra-
> mentys, alle the vertu and the grace of my worde, alle the goodnesse that is
> ordeynyd in holy chyrch to the, I it am.
>
> The moder may ley hyr chylde tenderly to hyr brest, but oure tender
> mother Jhesu, he may homely lede vs in to his blessyd brest by his swet opyn
> syde. [60:29-40]

Here Julian further suggests that Christ's motherhood in the Church is
truly the fruit of his suffering when she points out that he leads us into
his breast by the wound of his side.[139]

---

sance: "Birth from the womb is displaced to the side, and thus to the heart and
breast, suggesting childbirth as a spiritual idea rather than as a physical fact." See
Debra Scott Panichelli, "Finding God in the Memory: Julian of Norwich and the
Loss of the Visions," *The Downside Review* 104 (1986) 312-313, citing Jonathan
Goldberg, "The Mothers in Book III of *The Faerie Queene*," *Texas Studies in Literature and Language* 17 (1975) 8. Of course, for Julian, Christ's motherhood encom-
passes both the spiritual and the physical in the sense that even our physical birth
by our human mothers is the work of Christ. [60:49-51.57-58 (note 31, p. 115,
above).]

138 Watkins goes further in her interpretation of the symbolism of the blood in the
Shewings. For Watkins, Julian's statement that Christ's blood that continues to
flow for us in heaven as long as we have need of it [12:26-31] "suggests the menstrual blood of women in general, related as it is to the mystery of generation; and
menstrual blood as the tears of the spinster, because she is barren; as well as the
tears of the Virgin who, though fruitful while pure, bore her child for sorrow."
Renée Neu Watkins, "Two Women Visionaries and Death. Catherine of Siena and
Julian of Norwich," *Numen* 30 (1983) 181.

139 Elsewhere, she tells us to go 'to holy church into oure moders brest.' [62:24-25]

b. The passion as *love*: Christ our mother suffers for love of us

The second 'beholding' of the passion is perhaps the one most easily related to motherhood: we see the love which made Christ to suffer for us. The passion of Christ is a 'worshipful deed worked by love.'

> And heer saw I for the seconde beholding in his blessyde passion. The loue that made hym to suffer it passith as far alle his paynes as hevyn is aboue erth; for the payne was a noble precious and wurschypfulle dede done in a tyme by the workyng of loue. And loue was *with*out begynnyng, is and shall be *with*out ende. For whych loue he seyde fulle swetely thys worde: If I myght suffer more, I wolde suffer more. He seyde nott: yf it were nedfulle to suffer more, but if I myght suffer more; for though it were nott nedfulle, and hye myght suffer more he wolde. [22:45-53][140]

The ground of Christ's passion is his love for us, a 'marvelous love' which Julian clearly situates within the motherhood imagery.

> Thus he susteyneth vs *with* in hym in loue and traveyle, in to the full tyme *that* he wolde suffer the sharpyst thornes and grevous paynes that evyr were or evyr shalle be, and dyed at the last. And wha*n* he had done, and so borne vs to blysse, yett myght nott all thys make a seeth to his mervelous loue. And that shewd he in theyse hye ovyrpassyng wordes of loue: If I myght suffer more I wold suffer more. He myght no more dye, but he wolde nott stynte werkyng. [60:20-27]

The passion of Christ is the expression of the perfection of maternal love, a love which does all that is possible, not simply that which is necessary. If Christ could suffer more, for love he would suffer more.[141]

Christ's pierced heart, his thirst, and his blood also serve to symbolize the love he bears us as our mother. Julian is led into Christ's wounded side; there his heart 'cloven in two' reveals his endless love.[142] The 'drying' of his tender body results in not only a bodily thirst, but a ghostly thirst: the longing of his love which desires to gather us all into him.[143]

---

140 Cf. 20:19-21.26-28; 31:27-29; 82:18-19.

141 "And in these wordes: If I myght suffer more I wolde suffer more, I saw truly *that* as often as he myght dye, as often he wolde, and loue shulde nevyr lett hym haue rest tille he hath done it." [22:25-28] Cf. 22:32-45.

142 "And *with* the swete beholdyng he shewyd hys blessyd hart clovyn on two, and *with* hys enjoyeng he shewyd to my vnderstandyng in part the blyssydfulle godhede as farforth as he wolde that tyme, strengthyng the pour soule for to vnderstande as it may be sayde, that is to mene the endlesse loue that was *with*out begynnyng and is and shal be evyr. And *with* this oure good lorde seyde well blessydfully: Lo how I loue the." [24:9-16]

143 "For thys is the goostly thyrst of Cryst, the loue longyng *that* lastyth and evyr shall

Finally, it is by the power of Christ's love that his precious blood continues to flow over us.[144] In an interesting counterpoint to the image of
Christ's dryness or thirst, Julian emphasizes the plenteous flow of Christ's
blood.[145] The power of the blood of Christ is such that it overflows both
earth and heaven,[146] a veritable 'flood of mercy'[147] by which our mother
Christ we are cleanses and heals us.

> But mekely make we oure mone to oure derewurthy mother, and he shall
> all besprynkyl vs in his precious blode, and make oure soule full softe and
> fulle mylde, and heele vs fulle feyer by processe of tyme, ryght as it is most
> wurschype to hym and joye to vs without ende. And of this swete feyer werk-
> yng he shall nevyr ceese nor stynte, tylle all his deerwurthy chyldren be borne
> and brought forth; and that shewde he where he gaue the vnderstandyng of
> the gostely thurst that is the loue longyng that shalle last tylle domys day.
> [63:20-27][148]

A similar passage in the *Ancrene Riwle* suggests that maternal love may
also be the premise upon which Julian bases her image of Christ's healing
us by washing us in his blood.[149]

c. The passion as *joy*: we are our mother's joy, bliss, and delight

The third way of 'beholding' Christ's passion is to see the joy that is
Christ's in his suffering for love of us.

---

tyll we se that syght at domys day; . . . . Therfore this is his thurste and loue
longyng of vs, all to geder here in hym to oure endlesse blysse, as to my syght. For
we be nott now fully as hole in hym as we shalle be than." [31:14-16.18-20] Cf.
17:2-4; 81:21. The theme of Christ's thirst will be discussed more fully in chapter
4 (see p. 182-186, below).

144 12:18-19; see also note 138, p. 134, above.
145 Julian compares the flow of blood from Christ's head to the drops of water that
     pour from the eaves of a house after a great rainfall. [7:12-26] In her description
     of the the scourging, she tells us that 'the hote blode ranne out so plentuously that
     ther was neyther seen skynne ne wounde, but as it were all blode.' [12:6-7]
146 12:13-31.
147 61:64-65.
148 Julian describes the plenteous flow of Christ's blood as ready to wash all creatures
     of sin. [12:15-26]
149 "If a child had some disease such that a bath of blood was necessary to its recovery,
     the mother who would provide such a bath would indeed love it greatly. This is
     what Our Lord did for us, when we were so diseased with sin and so marked with
     it that nothing could heal us or cleanse us except His blood. For so He would have
     it. His love makes of it a bath for us." *The Ancrene Riwle,* Part VII, translated by
     M. B. Salu, 175. See also note 49, p. 118, above.

It is a joy, a blysse,[150] an endlesse lyking[151] to me that evyr I sufferd passion for the; and yf I myght suffer more, I wolde suffer more. In thys felyng
my vnderstandyng was leftyd vppe in to hevyn, and ther I saw three hevyns; of
whych syght I was gretly merveyled, and thought: I see iij hevyns, and alle of
the blyssedfulle manhed of Criste. And noone is more, noone is lesse, noone
is hygher, noone is lower, but evyn lyke in blysse. [22:5-11]

The sight of Christ's joy in his passion leads Julian to a christological view
of the beatitude of heaven; the 'joy, bliss, and delight' are clearly Christ's,
linked to his suffering humanity.[152] At the same time, however, Julian
gives a trinitarian scope to Christ's joy in suffering for us.[153]

And in these thre wordes: It is a joy, a blysse and endlesse lykyng to me,
were shewyd thre hevyns, as thus. For the joy, I vnderstode the pleasannce
of the father, and for the blysse the wurshyppe of the soone, and for the
endlesse lykyng the holy gost. The father is plesyd, the sonne is wurschyppyd,
the holy gost lykyth. [23:2-6]

For Julian, the christological reference of each of the three heavens is
maintained: the Father is pleased, the Son is worshipped, and the Holy
Spirit 'delights' — all by virtue of the passion of Christ.[154]

The *joy* of the 'first heaven' is Christ's pleasing of the Father by the
working of our salvation. Julian is not shown the Father directly, but
indirectly, i.e., in his rewarding of Christ.[155]

For the furst hevyn, Crist shewyd me his father, in no bodely lycknesse but
in his properte and in hys wurkyng. That is to sey, I saw in Crist that the
father is. The werkyng of the father is this: that he geavyth mede to hys
sonne Jhesu Crist. . . . For the furst hevyn, that is the plesyng of *the* father,

---

150 In the *Shewings*, 'bliss' always carries the nuance of *blessedness* or *beatitude*.
151 'Delight.'
152 "I see iij hevyns, and alle of the blyssedfulle manhed of Criste." [22:9]   In another
     combination of *joy, blysse,* and *lyke,* Julian maintains the same christological refer-
     ence: "And heer saw I for the thyrde beholdyng in hys blessydfulle passion, that is
     to sey the joy and the blysse that makyth hym to lyke it." [23:6-8]
153 Cf. 23:25-26.32.
154 Cf. 55:2-8.
155 Julian is consistent on this point. Echoing the Book of Exodus, she tells us that
     one cannot see God and live afterwards in this mortal life. [43:55-56] Cf. Exod
     33:20. For Julian, to see Christ is to see the Father; in the parable of the lord and
     the servant, the Father is shown 'homely' as a man (the lord), i.e., in the form of
     Christ's glorified humanity: "But man is blyndyd in this life, and therefore we may
     nott se oure fader god as he is. And what tyme that he of hys goodnesse wyll shew
     hym to man, he shewyth hym homely as man, not *with* stondyng that I saw verely
     we ought to know and beleue that the fader is nott man." [51:140-144] Cf. 47:27-
     28; 51:274-275; John 14:9; 2 Cor 4:6.

> shewyd to me as an hevyn, and it was fulle blyssydfulle. For he is wele plesyde
> *with* alle the dedes that Jh*es*u hath done about our saluacion. [22:12-15.17-20]

The christological reference of the first heaven could not be more clearly stated: the Father's pleasure derives from Christ's passion and is revealed in the rewarding of the Son.

The *bliss* (blessedness) of the 'second heaven' is the honor and worship Christ receives from the Father as a reward for his suffering the passion.[156] By his passion, Christ makes a gift of our humanity to his Father: we come into the presence of God in Christ who bears us up to heaven in his own body. The Father, in turn, gives us to Christ as a reward.

> Crist in his body my*gh*tely beryth vs vp in to hevyn; for I saw that Crist, vs alle
> havyng in hym that shall be savyd by hym, wurschypfully presentyth his fader
> in hevyn *with* vs, whych present fulle thangkfully hys fader receyvyth, and
> curtesly gevyth it vnto his sonne Jhesu Crist. Whych gyfte and werkyng is joy
> to the fader and blysse to the son and lykyng to the holy gost. [55:2-8]

The bliss of the 'second heaven' is the Father's worship of the Son, i.e., the honor that is Christ's by virtue of his passion as the definitive moment of the oneing of humanity to God.

Because we are the gift that the Father gives Christ, Julian tells us that *we* are Christ's bliss, his reward, his worship, his crown.

> [The Father] is wele plesyde *with* alle the dedes that Jh*es*u hath done about
> our saluacion; where for we be nott only hys by his byeng, but also by the
> curteyse gyfte of hys father. We be his blysse, we be his mede, we be hys
> wurshype, we be his crowne. And this was a syngular marveyle and a full
> delectable beholdyng, that we be hys crowne. [22:19-23][157]

Here Julian's theology of oneing leads her to one of her most original insights, a 'singular marvel': we ourselves are Christ's crown of glory. Christ's glory is to be found in his passion, i.e., in the transfiguration of

---

156 Pelphrey relates all three heavens to the mystery of the mutual indwelling of the
Father and the Holy Spirit in Christ. He suggests that, for Julian, the 'second
heaven' is 'an eternal love, which she identifies with the ministry of the Holy Spirit.'
There is, however, no evidence in the text to support Pelphrey's identification of
the 'second heaven' with the Holy Spirit or with the love which prompted Christ
to suffer his passion. See Brant Pelphrey, *Julian of Norwich,* The Way of the
Christian Mystics 7, edited by Noel Dermot O'Donoghue, O.D.C. (Wilmington,
Delaware: Michael Glazier, Inc., 1989) 119.

157 Cf. 23:18-19.50-51; 31:16-17.30-34; 51:317-318; 55:2-8; 79:38-39; cf. 44:2-3; 57:2-3;
71:20-21.

his pain and travail into joy and bliss.[158] Consequently, Christ's garland of thorns is his crown of victory. Moreover, because of our oneing, Christ's pain is our suffering and his reward is our bliss.[159] Thus, we ourselves are his crown of thorns (the suffering due our sins) and his crown of victory (the bliss of our salvation).

> [The Son] stondyth before the fader evyn ryghte rychely clothyd in blyssefull largenesse, with a crowne vpon his hed of precyous rychenes. For it was shewede that we be his crowne, whych crowne is the faders joy, the sonnes wurshyppe, the holy gostys lykyng, and endlesse mervelous blysse to alle that be in hevyn. [51:315-320]

By virtue of our oneing, we are Christ's passion and his crown, and thus the Father's joy, the Son's worship, and the Holy Spirit's delight.[160]

The joy Christ finds in his passion stems from his love of us.[161] He values his reward (us) so much that he 'sets at naught his travail and his passion, his cruel and shameful death.'[162] Christ's wounds are open and 'enjoy' to heal us.[163] His bliss is full because of the fact that the deed of our salvation is done as perfectly as he might have done it.[164] Christ is the 'cheerful giver' whose own happiness rests in our happiness.

> [Christ] brough(t) to my mynd the propyrte of a gladde geauer. Evyr a glade geauer takyth but lytylle hede at the thyng that he geavyth, but alle hys desyr and alle hys intent is to plese hym and solace hym to whome he geavyth it. And yf the receyver take the gyft gladly and thankefully, than the curtesse gevyr settyth at nought alle hys cost and alle hys traveyle, for joy and deleyght that he hath for he hath plesyd and solacyd hym that he lovyth. [23:37-44]

Christ asks nothing for his suffering except that we be satisfied; if we are satisfied, he is satisfied.[165]

Christ's love for us is so strong that he willingly suffers for us, to make us heirs with him in his bliss.[166] Our own joy, our sharing of his bliss, brings us to the meaning of the 'third heaven': we are the locus of

---

158 24:23-25.
159 For Julian, Mary is the perfect example of the soul completely oned to God in Christ, the soul who shares in Christ's joy, bliss (worship), and delight: Julian sees Mary 'as she is now in lykynge, worschyppe and joy.' [25:40-41]
160 22:5-6; 51:317-319; 55:6-8.
161 73:21-22.
162 22:24-26.
163 61:65-66.
164 22:53-57.
165 22:2-5; 23:32-36.
166 20:26-28; 21:23; cf. 82:18-19.

the *delight* which is the Holy Spirit. In other words, we participate in Christ's bliss by the bond of loving union which is the Holy Spirit.

> For we be his blysse, for in vs he lykyth *with*out end; and so schall we in him with hys grace. [23:18-19][167]

Christ's joy becomes our own; conversely, our joy is his joy. Christ's delight is our holiness and endless bliss.[168] Julian explicitly refers to the Holy Spirit as the mutual love (or delight) between the Father and the Son.[169] Now, applying the same image to Christ and the soul, we may say that the 'delight' of the Holy Spirit is the mutual loving gaze of delight between the mother and the child, i.e., between our mother Christ and us.[170]

In summary, Christ's passion is his joy, his bliss, and his delight. The 'joy' of the passion is Christ's pleasing of the Father: we are the gift Christ makes to the Father, i.e., Christ's suffering of our pain is his worship of the Father. The 'bliss' of the passion is the rewarding of the Son by the Father: we are the gift which the Father gives to Christ, the crown with which the Father honors the Son. The 'delight' of the passion is the Holy Spirit, i.e., the mutual delight of the gift-giving: we experience and participate in Christ's joy by virtue of our oneing, which joy is worked in us by the Holy Spirit. We ourselves are both Christ's passion and Christ's crown and, consequently, his joy, his bliss, and his delight.

4. To choose Christ's passion as our joy, our heaven

Julian tells us that the passion is shown to us to make us 'glad and merry' on account of the depth of Christ's love for us which it reveals.[171] Just as the passion is joy for the whole Trinity, so too are we to delight in their joy at our salvation:

---

167 Cf. 24:23-25 (p. 130, above).
168 24:27-28.
169 51:217-218; cf. 44:8-10 (note 115, p. 75, above).
170 "Feyer and swete is our hevenly moder in *th*e syght of oure soule, precyous and louely be *th*e gracyous chyldren in *th*e syght of oure hevynly moder." [63:35] Bradley suggests that this mutual gaze between mother and child is a 'culminating image of mystical loving.' See Ritamary Bradley, "Mysticism in the Motherhood Similitude of Julian of Norwich," *Studia Mystica* 8 (1985) 8.
171 24:29-31.

A, Jhesu, wylle we take hede to thys blysse that is in the blessydfulle trinytie of our saluacion, and that we desyre to haue as much gostly lykyng with his grace, as it is before seyde. That is to say, that the lykyng of our saluacion be lyke to the joy that Crist hath of oure saluation, as it may be whylle we be here. [23:25-29][172]

We are to rejoice with Christ in his passion as he rejoices endlessly in the salvation his passion wrought for us.[173]

Thus it is that Julian chooses Jesus on the cross to be her heaven.

In this tyme I wolde haue lokyde fro the crosse, and I durst nott, for I wyst wele whyle that I behelde the crosse I was suer and safe. . . .

Than had I a profyr in my reason, as it had ben frendely seyde to me: Loke vppe to hevyn to hys father. . . . I answerd inwardly with alle the myght of my soule, and sayd: Nay, I may not, for thou art my hevyn. Thys I seyde for I wolde nott; for I had levyr a bene in that payne tylle domys day than haue come to hevyn other wyse than by hym. . . .

Thus was I lernyd to chese Jhesu for my hevyn, whom I saw only in payne at that tyme. Me lykyd no nother hevyn than Jhesu, whych shalle be my blysse when I come ther. And this hath evyr be a comfort to me, that I chose Jhesu to be my hevyn by his grace in alle this tyme of passion and sorow. And that hath ben a lernyng to me, that I shulde evyr more do so, to chese Jhesu only to my hevyn in wele and in woe. [19:2-3.6-7.10-13.15-20][174]

Julian's choice to keep her gaze fixed on the crucifix was not due to the fact that she felt that the sight of the passion would protect her from perils;[175] Julian chose Jesus crucified as her heaven because she realized that she could know no other heaven. The glory of God is seen in the face of the crucified Christ;[176] Christ reigns from the tree of the cross. This identification of heaven with the suffering humanity of Christ should not surprise us.[177] In her understanding of the transfiguration of Christ's pain to bliss, Julian grasps the unity of the reality of Christ's passion and his joy, his 'wounds' and his 'worships': they are two aspects of the one event of our salvation, viewed respectively from the vantage

---

172 Cf. 23:15-18.32; 55:8-10.

173 23:23-24.

174 Cf. 77:43-48.

175 4:23-27; 19:2-5.

176 2 Cor 4:6; see also p. 130-131, above.

177 As we have seen, the three heavens are all of the humanity of Christ. [22:9-11 (p. 137, above.)] Moreover, the joys of heaven are revealed in the wound of our mother Christ: "The moder may ley hyr chylde tenderly to hyr brest, but oure tender mother Jhesu, he may homely lede vs in to his blessyd brest by his swet opyn syde, and shew vs there in perty of the godhed and the joyes of hevyn, with gostely suernesse of endlesse blysse." [60:38-41] Cf. 24:3-14.

points of time and eternity. Christ reveals our experience, and we experience what Christ reveals, be it pain or joy. Here on earth Christ shows us
his passion, defining our experience of the suffering of sin in himself; in
heaven he shows us his bliss so that we may share his joy.[178] Thus, we
know the joy of heaven in the passion of Christ: while our bodies are
filled with the experience of Christ's passion and death, our substance
(which is in God) is truly rejoicing in the joy and bliss of heaven.[179] We
must look to no other heaven than that which is the cross of Christ.

---

178 Julian's own pain and grief at the sight of Christ's passion vanished when Christ
    was tranfigured on the cross: "And here saw I verely that if he shewde now to vs
    his blyssedfulle chere, there is no payne in erth ne in no nother place *that* shuld
    trobylle vs, but alle thyng shulde be to vs joy and blysse. But for he shewyth vs
    chere of passion as he bare in this lyfe hys crosse, therfore we be in dysees and
    traveyle *with* hym as oure kynd askyth." [21:18-23]
179 55:49-59.

C. Christ Our Mother Comforts Us:
Divine Revelation as Mercy

An explanation of Julian's understanding of divine revelation is best situated within the larger context of her theology of divine mercy. The 'lesson of love' of Julian's shewings is Christ himself. Christ is the 'sight,' the reward, and even the very light by which we see. The gift of divine revelation is part of Christ's motherhood of working, his motherhood of grace. The grace that *is* revelation 'keeps' us, ones us to God, and brings us comfort in our present feeble, sinful condition of being not yet fully oned.

1. Our need for divine revelation

The theme of *sight* (along with its antithesis, *blindness*) permeates the *Shewings*.[180] As Maisonneuve points out, Julian makes the spiritual eye the essential sense by which the soul perceives God.[181] For Julian, sight brings 'knowing' in the biblical sense, that interpersonal relationship which is the basis for our knowledge of God. This relationship with God is always one of our responding to God's prior initiative of love. Sight is crucial in this dialogical relationship; without 'shewing' (revelation) we remain ignorant and therefore unresponsive to God's initiative of love in our regard, i.e., God's mercy.[182] Disabled by the blindness of sin, we stand in absolute need of God's gracious revelation in order to see truly and to respond: to love God and to hate sin.[183]

---

180 To date, Maisonneuve's study of the *Shewings* provides the most complete explication of Julian's treatment of the themes of vision, shewing, and blindness. See Roland Maisonneuve, *L'univers visionnaire de Julian of Norwich,* 125-257. For a comprehensive analysis of Julian's experience of her shewings in terms of 'bodily sight' and various levels of 'ghostly sight,' see Paul Molinari, S.J., *Julian of Norwich,* 31-70.

181 Maisonneuve suggests that, for Julian, 'sight' or 'beholding' may be understood as a synthesis of all the senses: the eye tastes, hears, knows, understands, savors, and touches. Roland Maisonneuve, *L'univers visionnaire de Julian of Norwich,* 143-150. Cf. 36:15-17; 43:49-54; 44:14-21; 52:53-57; 83:2-4.

182 "And thus in ryghtfulnes and in mercy he wyll be know and lovyd, now and withought ende." [35:43-45]

183 The soul that sees and feels the working of love hates nothing but sin. [52:53-56]

a. Sight and oneing

For Julian, even the intratrinitarian joy of God is understood in terms of vision. The Father (sovereign Truth) and the Son (sovereign Wisdom) 'see' each other, and the mutual loving delight which flows from this 'seeing' is the Holy Spirit (sovereign Love).

> Truth seeth god, and wisdom beholdyth god, and of theyse two comyth the thurde, and that is a meruelous delyght in god, whych is loue. Where truth and wysedom is, verely there is loue, verely comyng of them both, and alle of goddes makyng. For god is endlesse souereyne truth, endelesse souereyne wysdom, endelesse souereyne loue vnmade. [44:8-12]

It is not, therefore, surprising that Julian should speak of the joy of our full oneing to God in heaven in terms of 'sight,' the face-to-face vision of God.[184] The highest beatitude is to possess God in clarity of light.

> The hyghest blesse that is is to haue god in cleerte of endlesse lyght, hym verely seyng, hym swetly felyng, hym all peasable havyng in fullhede of joy; and thus was the blessydfulle chere of oure lorde god shewde in perty. [72:6-9]

We are oned to God who is light, by which light and oneing we see.[185] We shall have no rest until we are completely oned, i.e., until we see God in the full clarity and truth of heaven.[186]

The promise inherent in all Julian's shewings is full sight, i.e., the full oneing to God by which we come to know Truth itself.

> And thus oure good lorde answeryd to alle the questyons and dow*gh*tys that I myght make, sayeng full comfortably; I may make alle thyng wele, and I can make alle thyng welle, and I shalle make alle thyng wele, and I wylle make alle thyng welle; and thou shalt se thy selfe *that* alle maner of thyng shall be welle. . . . [And] there he seyth: Thou shalt se thy selfe, I vnderstond the (onyng) of alle man kynde that shalle be sauyd in to the blyssedfulle trynite. [31:2-6.10-12][187]

When we are fully oned to that light and truth which is God, we shall see for ourselves what is now hidden from us;[188] we shall see and know God in the endless bliss of heaven.[189] As for our vision of God here in this

---

184   14:10-12; 43:53-54; 47:29-31; 71:30-38; 72:6-13.29-31; 83:21-23.
185   83:2-7.21-25.
186   47:30-31; 72:18-20.
187   Cf. 1:39-41; 32:14-19; 35:15-17; 63:46-47.
188   We shall return to this notion of God's 'privy counsels' (see p. 148, below).
189   36:29-30; cf. 56:49-51.

life, Julian speaks in paradox: it is impossible for us to see God while we are still weighed down by our earthly existence,[190] but we enjoy a certain 'sight' or 'beholding' of God through God's gracious self-revelation.[191] This divine self-revelation is measured to our 'simpleness,' i.e., to our human capacities and needs.[192]

b. The blindness caused by sin

For Julian, sin is the darkness that contraries the light which is God.[193] We experience the darkness of sin as a spiritual blindness which causes us pain.[194] The parable of the lord and the servant serves to reveal our true situation. The servant exemplifies our blindness, in which blindness we are unable to see God or self.

> And of all this [the servant's fall] the most myschefe that I saw hym in was feylyng of comfort, for he culde nott turne his face to loke vppe on his lovyng lorde, whych was to hym full nere, in whom is full comfort; but as a man that was full febyll and vnwyse for the tyme, he entendyd to his felyng and enduryng in woo, in whych woo he sufferyd vij grett paynes. . . . The iiij was that he was blyndyd in his reson and stonyd in his mynde so ferforth that allmost he had forgeten his owne loue. [51:17-22.25-27]

> This man was hurte in his myghte and made fulle febyll, and he was stonyd in his vnderstandyng, for he was turnyd fro the beholdyng of his lorde, but his wylle was kepte in gods syght. For his wylle I saw oure lorde commende and aproue, but hym selfe was lettyd and blyndyd of the knowyng of this wyll. And this is to hym grett sorow and grevous dysses, for neyther he seeth clerly his lovyng lorde whych is to hym full meke and mylde, nor he seeth truly what hym selfe is in the syght of his louyng lord. [51:104-111]

> But man is blyndyd in this life, and therefore we may nott se oure fader god as he is. [51:140-142]

It is sin that blinds our reason and our judgment, causing us to mourn and suffer in this life because of our lack of understanding of the divine

---

190 43:55-59; 72:35-37; 51:140-142.
191 "God gave me knowyng and vnderstondyng that it was hym selfe that I sawe." [47:27-28] Cf. 51:140-144.
192 43:45-48; 83:16-17; cf. 51:275.
193 The 'night' of sin is the cause of our pain and woe. [83:16-18] Cf. 86:12.
194 "And by Adams fallyng we be so broken in oure felyng on dyverse manner by synne and by sondry paynes, in which we be made derke and so blynde that vnnethys we can take any comforte." [52:13-16]

perspective.[195] Our fallen state produces in us three blindnesses: we do not see God's faithful love for us;[196] we do not see ourselves, i.e., our true identity as God's 'treasure';[197] and, not only are we unable to see God or ourselves, but our blindness is such that we cannot even know the true nature of our sin[198] and our own continued orientation of love towards God even in the midst of our sinning.[199] Moreover, while there is any sin in us, we remain blind; and the greater our sins, the greater our blindness.[200]

The scourge of our blindness escalates in that it actually contributes to the cycle of sin: sin causes blindness and that same blindness weakens us, making us more prone to temptation and fear, leading us to further sin. If we truly enjoyed the vision of God, we would have no inclination to sin.[201] To see God is to be protected from all harm, even the danger of sin.[202] Because sin distorts our perception of our situation,[203] we easily fall prey either to presumption or to despair, i.e., we either fail to see the real horror of our sinning or we fail to see God's love for us.

---

195 "Ther be many dedys evyll done in oure syght and so gret harmes take that it semyth to vs that it were vnpossible that evyr it shuld com to a good end. And vp on thys we loke, sorow and morne therfore so that we can nott rest vs in the blyssedfulle beholding of god as we shuld do. And the cause is this: that the vse of oure reson is now so blynde, so lowe and so symple that we can nott know the hygh marvelous wysdom, the myght and the goodnes of the blyssedfull trynyte." [32:10-16]

196 The darkness of our sin prevents us from seeing God. [72:35-37] Moreover, not only are we harrassed by our own sins, but the sins of others act as a screen (a 'thick mist') that prevents us from seeing God's goodness. [76:15-17]

197 51:185-210; cf. 51:205-207; 86:10.

198 79:11-13; cf. 61:22-23; 78:21-22.

199 Jantzen pursues a more psychological approach in her analysis of the servant's (and our) triple blindness. Grace Jantzen, *Julian of Norwich*, 206-211.

200 "I saw that synne was *the* most contrary, so ferforth *that* as long as we be meddlyd *with* any part of synne we shall nevyr see cleerly *the* b(l)essyd chere of god. And the horyblyer and the grevowser that oure synnes be, the depper are we for that tyme fro this blessyd syghte." [72:9-13] Cf. 72:35-37.

201 "Man is channgeabyll in this lyfe, and by sympylnesse and vncunnyng fallyth in to synne. He is vnmyghty and vnwyse of hym selfe, and also his wyll is ovyr leyde in thys tyme he is in tempest and in sorow and woe. And the cause is blynnes, for he seeth not god; for yf he saw god continually, he shulde haue no myschevous felyng ne no maner steryng, no sorowyng that servyth to synne." [47:16-21] Cf. 52:60-61.

202 In her image of being led down to the bottom of the sea, Julian tells us: "if a man or woman wer there vnther the brode water, and he myght haue syght of god, so as god is with a man contynually, he shoulde be safe in sowle and body, and take no harme." [10:23-26] Cf. 47:19-21.

203 76:40-43; 78:39-41; cf. 11:9-10; 61:22-25; 79:12-13.

In her shewings, Julian usually understood 'sin' to refer to sin in general, but she was given to see two sins in particular: impatience (or sloth) and despair.[204] These two 'sicknesses' are the two that most 'travail and trouble' us, and each is the result of our blindness, i.e., our lack of true judgment about the nature of sin and about God's faithful love in our regard.[205] Julian sees sloth, the 'losing of time,' as the insidious beginning of sin in those who have already given themselves to seeking God.[206] We grow discouraged, and even despondent, giving up our efforts in the struggle against our sinfulness because we do not see results. This discouragement in our battle with sin may lead eventually to despair, a blind fear against which we must be especially alert. A sin against truth (the truth of God's merciful love), despair is most troublesome to us because we do not readily recognize it as sinful; our lack of judgment causes us to mistake fear and depression for meekness.[207] The pain of our sin is such that we think we are already in hell; however, although we are dead to the sight of God by our blindness, we are not dead in God's sight.[208]

The blindness caused by sin is not only the reason for much of our suffering but also one of the greatest obstacles in our struggle against sin. It is our unknowing of God's love that hinders us most.

> And *the* cause why we are traveyled *with* them [our pains] is for vnknowyng of loue. Though the thre persons of *the* blessyd trynyte be alle evyn in the selfe, the soule toke most vnderstandyng in loue. Ye, and he wylle in alle thyng *that* we haue oure beholdyng and oure enjoyeng in loue. And of this knowyng are we most blynde, for some of vs beleue that god is allmyghty and may do alle, and that he is alle wysdom and can do alle, but that he is alle loue and will do alle, there we fayle. And this vnknowyng it is that most lettyth goddes lovers, as to my syght. [73:24-32]

If we were to see God's merciful love, we would be in bliss. Instead, we concentrate on our sins and become discouraged and fearful.[209] Only the light of divine revelation can bring us out of our painful darkness.

---

204 73:9-11; cf. 80:38-39.
205 73:13-18.
206 76:30-39. Julian speaks of sloth (or impatience) in the sense of accidie, i.e., the spiritual restlessness or grudging which causes the soul to lose patience and become negligent in the practice of the spiritual life. Cf. 10:87-90; 64:10-12; 76:30-39.
207 73:37-42. The temptation to depression and fear on account of our sins comes from the devil. [76:30-44]
208 72:14-18; cf. 72:35-40. In chapter 4, we shall return to the problem of despair (see p. 207-210, below).
209 73:32-43; cf. 37:8-9; 61:41-43; 72:36-38; 76:29-39; 82:36-37. Conversely, true knowing of God's love dispels our depression and doubt. [74:13-17]

The fact that we stand in absolute need of divine revelation leads us to another aspect of Julian's understanding of our blindness: while our fallen state accounts for our lack of sight, at the same time our inability to see is not always directly related to our actual sinning. Our blindness may also result from God's free choice to remain hidden from us at times. It is God's goodness that opens the eye of our understanding; when God hides, however, we fall back into our blindness and the pain it brings.[210] Julian recognizes that revelation is the gracious gift of God who chooses to reveal some things while wisely hiding other things from us for the sake of love.[211] We cannot really expect full understanding of the divine perspective here on earth. God's 'privy counsels' will remain hidden from us.[212] We work within the constraints of revelation, satisfied both with what God reveals to us and with what God chooses to keep concealed from our mind's grasp until we are fully oned in heaven.[213] God wants us to rejoice in both the hiding and the showing.[214]

Our relationship with God is dialogical, initiated by God. The task of divine revelation is precisely to begin the intimate, loving dialogue between God and the soul. We would never seek God or love God without some prior 'sight' of God's great desire and love for us.

> For I saw him and sought him, for we be now so blynde and so vnwyse that we can never seke god till what tyme *that* he of his goodnes shewyth hym to vs. And whan we see owght of hym graciously, then are we steryd by the same grace to seke *with* great desyer to see hym more blessedfully. And thus I saw him and sought him, and I had hym and wantyd hym; and this is and should be our comyn workyng in this life, as to my syght. [10:14-20][215]

Without that knowledge of God's love which revelation gives us, we would fail to recognize God as the fullness of life for which we long in our darkness. The light of revelation prompts our longing and desire, leading us to seek our rest and happiness in God. Even our not seeing becomes a form of 'sight' for Julian: when God withdraws the light of

---

210 52:17-29; cf. 47:39-45; 79:31.
211 32:26-32; 46:43-46; cf. 7:60; 10:76-77; 30:2-16; 52:17-20.
212 "It longyth to the ryalle lordschyppe of god to haue hys pryvy connceyles in pees." [30:13-14] Cf. 47:40-48. God's secrets are revealed precisely as hidden [32:26-32; 34:3-4; 36:16-34].
213 27:39-42; 33:30-36; 36:27-33; 85:11-13. Julian tells us that all revelation is 'full of privities.' [51:71-74.270-272] So, while we must continue to probe the mysteries of our faith, we must also respect the limits which God places on our understanding [1:40-42; 30:12-16].
214 33:33-34; 36:23-33; cf. 30:17-19.
215 Cf. 7:55-58; 36:24-26.

consolation (the feeling of weal) and we experience the painful blindness of our human condition of sinfulness (the feeling of woe), we also 'see' our great need for God.[216] Our experience of desolation, the awareness of a presence we no longer experience, increases our longing.[217] Consolation and desolation spring from the one same love,[218] that divine love which desires our response of seeking and trusting.

> For he wyll that we beleue that we see hym contynually, thow that vs thynke that it be but litle; and in the beleue he maketh vs evyr more to gett grace, for he will be seen, and he will be sought, and he will be abyden, and he will be trustyd. [10:27-31]

Thus, sin is not necessarily the immediate cause of our desolation and blindness;[219] sometimes our sight fails for our profit and God's worship, i.e., so that we might honor God by active, faith-filled seeking.[220]

c. God wants us to see

Julian tells us that divine revelation is given to comfort the sinner.[221] God wants us to find solace in the divine perspective of our 'keeping' in Christ so that we will be able to see our sinfulness profitably and without despair.[222] When we see God's love for us, we respond with love and trust.

> It is his [Christ's] office to saue vs, it is his worshyppe to do it, and it is hys wylle we know it; for he wyll we loue hym swetely and trust in hym mekely and myghtly. And this shewde he in these gracious wordes: I kepe the fulle suerly. [61:70-73]

---

216 This insight reflects Julian's experience of her second shewing. Having asked for additional light in order to see more clearly, Julian discovered that her lack of sight was indeed a 'sight' of her own need to trust that God would reveal all that was necessary. [10:11-31]

217 Pelphrey makes an important distinction between our experience of God's absence and the reality of our situation of blindness to God's presence: 'absence' refers to a blindness in ourselves, our own sin, rather than to any genuine absence of Jesus from our lives (which would be impossible). See Brant Pelphrey, *Love Was His Meaning*, 243.

218 15:27-29.

219 Julian learned this through her experience of rapidly alternating shifts from consolation to desolation during which she had no time to sin. [15:26-27]

220 47:37-39.

221 34:22-26.

222 78:15-16; cf. 39:40-42; 79:9-21.

'Our lorde wants us to know (see)' is a refrain that frequently punctuates the *Shewings*.[223] Julian points out three things that God wills us to know, three things that we need to see in order to counteract our three blindnesses.[224]

> It longyth to vs to haue thre manner of knowyng. The furst is *that* we
> know our lorde god. The seconde is that we know oure selfe, what we ar by
> him in kinde and in grace. The thyrde is *that* we know mekely *that* oure selfe
> is a gaynst oure synne and agaynst oure febylnes. And for these thre was alle
> this shewyng made, as to my vnderstandyng. [72:54-58][225]

First, we need to see who God is as our ground of love; secondly, we need to know our own worth in God's sight, i.e., who we are in kind and grace; thirdly, we need to understand the nature of our sin and feebleness, i.e., that our will, our substance is preserved in Christ even in the midst of our sinning. We need to know these three things so that we will not lose heart in our struggle against sin.[226] Divine revelation is God's answer to our need to see.

2. Revelation and mercy: Christ, our remedy for the blindness of sin

Julian's teaching on 'sight' parallels her doctrine on mercy. The basis of our oneing in mercy and the basis of our understanding of God are one and the same: Jesus Christ, the ultimate revelation of divine love and mercy.

---

223 1:33-40; 5:29; 6:60-61; 10:27-31.93-95; 11:31-33; 15:23-24; 20:33-36; 25:29-30; 28:26-
      29; 29:16-17; 32:5-7.8-9.26-30; 33:28-30; 34:7-13; 35:43-45; 36:24-26; 39:43-46; 41:26-
      27; 42:2-3.28-33; 46:42-46; 47:4-5; 53:2.16.52.56.59.62; 55:12-14; 56:47-51; 60:59-60;
      61:70-71; 64:49-55; 65:16-17.23-24.30; 71:3-4; 73:18; 75:36-38; 76:8-9; 77:37-40; 78:6-
      14; 79:24-25.32-33; 80:7-12; 82:25-26; 86:8-9; cf. 1:38-42; 6:53-54; 7:60; 8:37-40;
      10:15-16.76-77; 20:26. 29; 24:9-12; 34:19-20; 36:70-71; 42:36-40; 43:18-19.35; 49:7;
      52:18-20; 55:39-44; 56:9-11.26-29; 61:4-7; 68:2.52.70; 70:30-32; 71:8-10; 82:38-39.
      The fact that Christ wants us to see the divine perspective was borne out for
      Julian; when the 'sight' of the shewings failed her, 'oure lorde Jhesu of his mercy
      wolde nott lett it peryssch,' but showed it again within her soul [70:28-40].
224 See p. 146, above.
225 Cf. 42:34-43; 78:6-14.
226 God wants us to persevere, continuing to be Christ's helpers in the process of our
      existential oneing. [57:56-57]

a. Jesus Christ, the ultimate revelation of God

For Julian, God *is* the light by which we see.[227] Moreover, the light of divine revelation is christological in nature. All of Julian's shewings and consequent insights derive from Christ: he is both their source[228] and their content.[229] While we cannot see the being of God directly, we are able to know God in the incarnate Son. We 'see' the unseeable God precisely as God has chosen to be 'shewn' — in the person of Jesus Christ.[230] Even in heaven, the light which is God is perceived in and through Christ.

> And at *the* end of woe, sodeynly oure eye shalle be opynyd, and in clernes of syght oure lyght shalle be fulle, whych lyght is god, oure maker, fadyr, and holy gost in Crist Jhesu oure savyour. [83:21-23]

We see by the gracious light of Christ himself;[231] he is our light here on earth as well as the vision with which we are rewarded in eternity.[232]

As the saving revelation of divine mercy, Christ himself is God's 'lesson of love.'[233] In Christ our mother we have the remedy for the three blindnesses of sin in that his triple motherhood reveals precisely those three things we need to know: the motherhood of kind reveals Christ to be our substance, i.e., that God's love is our ground; the motherhood of mercy reveals who we truly are in kind and in grace; and the motherhood of working reveals Christ as the existential remedy for our sin, that our will is preserved in Christ while he works our existential oneing by grace. As we have already seen, Christ is the divine remedy for our pain by virtue of his oneing us to God by his motherhood of kind, mercy, and grace; now, understood as God's saving revelation, Christ may again be seen as the remedy for our pain because, by revealing the divine perspective through his incarnation and passion, he overcomes our blindness and gives us reason for joy.

---

227 "If God will shew thee more, he shal be thy light; thou nedyth none but him." [10:12-14] Cf. 44:19-20; 83:22-25; 84:10-15.

228 As we have already seen, the shewing of Christ's passion is the source of all sixteen shewings. [1:2-7 (p. 107, above)]; see also p. 124, above.

229 All the shewings reveal the various aspects of Christ's oneing of us in himself, his taking his place in the human soul. [81:4-8]

230 47:27-28; see also note 155, p. 137, above.

231 42:32-33; 70:30-32; 78:2-5; 82:25-26; cf. 10:35; 71:7-10.

232 64:16-20.47-48.

233 82:24. Julian's shewings of love were given by love for the sake of love. [86:7-12.16-19] Cf. 70:30-32; 82:26.

> This place is pryson, this lyfe is pennannce, and in *the* remedy he wylle that
> we enjoy. The remedy is *that* oure lorde is *with* vs, kepyng vs and ledyng in
> to fulhed of joy. For this is an endlesse joy to vs in oure lordes menyng, that
> he that shalle be oure blesse when we are there, he is oure keper whyle we
> are here, oure wey and oure hevyn in tru loue and feythfulle trust. And of
> this he gaue vnderstandyng in alle, and namely in shewyng of his passion,
> where he made me myghtly to chose hym for my hevyn.
>
> Flee we to oure lorde, and we shalle be comfortyd. Touch we hym, and
> we shalle be made cleene. Cleve we to hym, and we shalle be suer and safe
> from alle manner of peryllys. [77:41-51]

To look at Christ is to see God's love and mercy and to find comfort and
courage in the midst of our pain, whereas to look at our sin and weakness
outside the context of Christ is to move towards despair or presumption.
The revelation of divine love, the sight and knowing of Christ, causes us
to flee to him in whom we have our 'keeping' in love.[234] The 'shewing'
of Christ gives us a secure basis for our hope: we cling to Christ, holding
ourselves in that comfort and safety which is ours in our mother of
mercy.[235]

b. Divine mercy: God's self-revelation saves and 'keeps' us

The ultimate word of revelation God speaks to us is Jesus Christ, God's
Word incarnate.[236] God's self-disclosure[237] in Christ is salvific in nature.
When God discloses Godself in Christ, the divine self is not only 'shewn,'
but is actually given to humanity, oned to us in Christ. Because God is
love (i.e., self-gift), divine self-revelation *is* divine self-communication and,
therefore, salvific; when God reveals self, God communicates self — and
God saves. Thus, not only is Christ himself the revelation of the mercy
by which God wishes to be known and loved,[238] but we can also say
that we are saved and oned to God by God's self-revelation in Christ. In
other words, the nature of divine revelation itself is mercy.

---

234 86:7-10; cf. 77:14-16.

235 Christ's love for us is unchanging, despite our sins; he wills us to cling to him,
      'whether we be foul or clean.' [76:26-29]

236 Cf. Heb 1:1-3.

237 In the self-disclosure model of revelation, the definitive word of divine revelation
      is Jesus Christ who discloses not so much truths *about* God but rather God's very
      self, i.e., Truth itself. The intention and reality of divine revelation is self-manifes-
      tation and self-communication.

238 35:43-45.

For Julian, shewing (or revealing) belongs to Christ's motherhood of mercy. We see by the light of mercy, the light of Christ himself:[239] in Christ is revealed both God's merciful love and our own true identity, our truest self. Moreover, for Julian, it is Christ who gives us sight or shewing by grace.[240] Our own 'seeing' belongs to Christ's 'keeping' us by the working of his motherhood of grace. Of ourselves we cannot know how much and how tenderly our maker loves us, but by grace we stand in 'ghostly beholding'of that divine love.[241] In the same way, because the sight of our sin is so horrible, Christ measures the sight to us by the light of his mercy and grace.[242] (We shall explore further the implications of our seeing by grace when we discuss the 'sight' of faith.)[243]

Julian makes the connection between revelation and mercy. We are 'kept' by our sight—the sight of God's love and the sight of ourselves, including the sight of our sin. Revelation itself is of God's mercy because true self-knowledge 'keeps' us: the sight of our feebleness and sin saves us from pride and presumption,[244] and the sight of God's love and our oneing in Christ saves us from despair, giving us the courage we need to persevere in our struggle against sin.

> And also in *the* same shewyng, ther I saw *that* I shuld synne, ther was I lernyd to be dradfull for vnsykernesse of my selfe, for I wot nott how I shalle falle, ne I know not the mesure ne *the* gretnesse of my synne. . . .
>
> Also oure curteyse lorde, in that same tyme he shewde fulle swetly and fulle myghtely the endleshed and the vnchanngeabylte of his loue, and also his grete goodnesse and his gracious inwardely kepy*n*g, that *the* loue of hym and of oure sowlys shalle nevyr be depertyd vnto wi*t*houten ende. And thus in *the* dred I haue matter of mekenesse, that savyth me fro presumpc*i*on, and in *the* blessyd shewyng of loue I haue mater of true comforte and of joy, that savyth me fro dyspeyer. [79:11-13.15-21]

The shewing of our sin and of our 'keeping' in Christ gives us matter both for meekness and for comfort, for mourning and matter for mirth.[245] Because we need to see our sin in order to become meek, Julian quite naturally attributes the sight of our falling to God's mercy.

---

239 78:2-5.21-22.
240 10:35; 43:18-19.56-57; 70:30-32; 71:7-10.
241 6:49-56.
242 78:2-5.15-22.42-43; cf. 40:2-5.
243 See p. 155-159, below.
244 78:15-19.
245 Cf. 36:40-43; 47:26-34; 52:51-53; 72:32-52; 82:11-15. We shall further consider the roles of meekness and divine comfort when we discuss presumption and despair, especially within Julian's understanding of compassion for self (see p. 160-162, 206-210, below, and note 193, p. 204, below).

> And other [understanding of profit] is the lownesse and mekenesse that we
> shall get by the syght of oure fallyng, for therby we shall hyely be reysyd in
> hevyn, to whych rysyng we my*gh*te nevyr haue comyn *with*out that mekenesse.
> And therfor it nedyt vs to see it; and if we se it not, though we felle it shuld
> not *pro*fyte vs. And comonly furst we falle and sethen we se it; and both is
> of the mercy of god. [61:28-34]

In the same way, because we need the comfort of the sight of God's love
in order not to fall prey to despair, it is Christ's mercy which maintains
the shewing of divine love in our souls and in the faith of the Church.

> Than oure lorde *Jhesu* of his mercy wolde nott lett it [sight] peryssch, but he
> shewde hyt all ageene *with*in my soule, *with* more fullehed *with* the blessyd
> lyght of his precyous loue, seyeng theyse wordes full myghtely and fulle meke-
> ly: Wytt it now welle. . . .
>   This was seyde nott onely for the same tyme, but also to sett there vpon
> the grounde of my feyth, where he seyeth anone folowyng: But take it, and
> lerne it, and kepe thee ther in, and comfort the ther *with,* and trust therto,
> and thou shalt nott be ovyr com. [70:30-33.37-40]

If we hold to the 'sight' of divine revelation, we shall not be overcome by
sin. This sight or knowledge 'keeps' us until we are brought to that fullness of vision which is heaven. Revelation thus represents the working
of divine mercy because, through divine self-revelation, God's perspective
becomes our own; true self-knowledge (i.e., knowledge of ourselves in
Christ) remedies the blindness in us caused by sin.

We can now understand why Julian speaks of revelation in the language of mercy, i.e., as oneing and 'keeping' us. Full sight is synonomous
with salvation (oneing);[246] oneing gives us sight, and sight ones us[247]
and 'keeps' us safe from sin.[248] The sight of Christ's passion is a source
of protection and strength for us.[249] The sight of our sin is the 'time of
mercy and grace'[250] because it gives us the meekness we need in order to
be safe.[251] Julian also ascribes profit (the domain of mercy and grace)[252]
to the sight of our sin and feebleness;[253] moreover, in speaking about her

---

246 See. p. 144-145, above.
247 The 'beholding' of the divine perspective on our situation 'leads us in the right way,
     keeps us in true life, and ones us to God.' [75:38-39] Cf. 68:46-50.
248 47:19-21; cf. 10:23-26.
249 4:23-27.
250 78:34-43.
251 78:34-43; cf. 82:16. Sight of our sin 'meeks' us and makes us cry to God for help
     and grace. [36:64-66]
252 See chapter 2, p. 103-106, above.
253 61:28-34; 78:15-18.

vision of Christ's reigning in our soul, she tells us that the sight of our oneing is of profit ('speed') for us.

> This was a delectable syghte and a restfulle shewyng that is without ende, and the beholdyng of this whyle we are here, it is fulle plesannt to god and fulle grete sped to vs. And the soule that thus beholdyth, it makyth it lyke to hym that is beholde, and ony(th) it in rest and in pease by hys grace. [68:46-50]

We not only see by grace, but our sight also ones us by grace and thus belongs in a special way to Christ's motherhood of working: by the self-knowledge divine revelation brings us, we become Christ's helpers in the process of our existential oneing by grace.

c. Sight and faith: Christ's motherhood of grace

Our 'sight' in Christ embraces both private and public revelation. The sight she gained from Christ in her shewings (private revelation) parallels the sight which is ours in the faith of the Church (the treasury of public revelation).[254] Just as Julian's shewings revealed God's love to Julian, so we too, when we are blinded by sin, are given a shewing of God's love in the faith of the Church. In mercy, Christ reveals to us all we need for our salvation; all that we need to know (and which our blindness hides from our sight) is 'shewn' to us in the Church.

> They are prevytes to vs for oure blyndhed and oure vnknowyng. And therfore hath he grett reuth, and therfore he wylle make them opyn to vs hym selfe, wher by we may knowe hym and loue hym and cleue to hym. For alle that is spedfulle to vs to wytt and for to knowe, fulle curtesly oure good lorde wylle shew vs what it is with alle the prechyng and techyng of holy chyrch. [34:9-14]

Julian assigns to the Church a crucial role: in the faith of the Church we find our 'sight' of Christ, the sight which 'keeps' us safe.

> For a boue the feyth is no goodnesse keppt in this lyffe, as to my syght; and beneth the feyth is no helth of soule. But in the feyth, there wyll oure lorde we kepe vs, for we haue by his goodnesse and his owne werkyng to kepe vs in the feyth. [71:12-15]

---

254 Julian identifies the content of her shewings with the faith of the Church. [7:65-66; 67:22-23] For Julian, the basis of our sight is always the divine self-revelation of Christ, which revelation is 'shewn' to all through the teaching of the Church. Extraordinary visions such as Julian's may serve to heighten one's perception of the mysteries of our faith, but they do not add to the content. For a more detailed discussion of this point, see Paul Molinari, S.J., Julian of Norwich, 134-135.

God wants us to 'keep' ourselves in the faith,[255] yielding to our mother Church as a simple child ought.[256] We find wholeness and safety in the life of faith as it is taught by the Church.[257] Even our wounds are healed in the life of the Church.[258]

For Julian, *sight* (divine revelation) leads to salvation, i.e., *Sight* (our oneing, the beatitude of the vision of God in heaven).

'sight' (the Church's faith)   ⟶   'Sight' (Beatific Vision)
    Divine Revelation   *Salvation*

Faith is our 'sight' on earth, our existential response[259] to God's self-revelation in the person of Jesus Christ. The interim 'sight' of faith 'keeps' us safe and brings us to the full 'Sight' of heaven. We may say that our faith ones us to God because our sight by faith is our subjective participation in the divine self-communication, i.e., the event of revelation, which participation reaches its fulfillment when we enjoy the full vision of beatitude in heaven. Until that time, the sight which is ours in our mother Christ is maintained existentially in the faith of the Church.

> [We] nedyth nott gretly to seke ferre out to know sondry kyndys, but to holy church into oure moders brest, that is to sey in to oure owne soule, wher oure lord dwellyth. And ther shulde we fynde alle, now in feyth and in vnderstand-yng, and after verely in hym selfe clerely in blysse. [62:23-27]

Thus, we see now in the faith of the Church[260] as we await the bliss of full 'Sight' in heaven.[261]

Faith, the exercise of our interim sight by the working of grace, fully accords with our rational nature.

> And oure feyth is a vertu that comyth of oure kynde substannce in to oure sensuall soule by the holy gost, in whych vertu alle oure vertues comyn to vs,

---

255   Cf. 1:40-42; 32:51-55; 33:24-25; 70:5-7.24-27.37-40.
256   46:49-50.
257   Julian herself found safety in the practices of the faith as taught by the Church. E.g., when frightened by the demons, she 'rehearsed' (recited) the creed [70:2-4] and gazed at the crucifix as the curate suggested to her [3:20-32; cf. 19:2-5; 70:2-3].
258   39:7-31.
259   By revelation, God initiates the dialogue to which our faith is the response.
260   We have already said that the faith of the Church ones us to God because it is Christ who is the ground, the substance, the teaching, and the teacher of the Church's faith. [34:17-18; 60:30-37 (p. 120, above); cf. 61:57-64.]
261   Full sight is the 'endles joy and blysse that we shall haue in hevyn, whych god wyll we begynne here in knowyng of his loue.' [56:49-51] Cf. 7:46-64; 43:55-56; 46:10-15.

for *without* that no man may receyue vertues, for it is nou*gh*t eles but a ryght
vnderstandy*n*g *with* trew beleue and suer truste of oure beyng, *that* we be in
god and he in vs, whych we se nott. [54:27-32][262]

Faith is true sight, right understanding; grace brings to perfection our gift
of reason and accords our judgment with the teaching of the Church.[263]
We find true understanding in the faith of the Church.[264] By faith, we
grasp the true meaning of our lives, even when we are not able to see it
clearly by earthly standards of judgment.[265] 'Right' understanding is not
equivalent to 'full' understanding.[266] Faith is grounded on God's word,
not on our ability to perceive.[267] We see and 'rightly understand' when
we accept God's word (i.e., revelation) in faith. Faith enables us to be
well-satisfied ('well apayde'), both with what God chooses to reveal to us
and with those 'privities' God allows to remain hidden from our sight for
the sake of love.[268] By experiencing our inability to see ourselves and our
sin from God's viewpoint, we grow in faith because, as Julian points out,
faith matures by trials;[269] our faith (the 'sight' we exercise when we become aware of our inability to see) grows precisely when we experience
our feebleness and blindness.

Julian's own experience of her shewings taught her that the 'sight' of
faith is not primarily (or even necessarily) a conscious 'seeing'; rather, the
truly salvific 'seeing' by faith is the *virtue* of faith, that gift of the Holy
Spirit which is the basis of our union with God while we are yet here on
this earth. In other words, while private revelations such as Julian's may
enhance one's understanding of the mysteries of our faith, the efficacy of
one's faith is grounded in the gift and action of the Holy Spirit, which
action is evidenced by the life of christian virtue,[270] not by one's con-

---

262 55:14-16.
263 Julian actually describes our salvation in terms of the use of our reason, the common teaching of the Church, and the gifts of the Holy Spirit. [80:2-8]
264 61:57-59; cf. 1:40-42.
265 In our faith we know God and ourselves with that rightful judgment which is based
on our substance. [46:2-12] Cf. 56:32-33; 80:13.
266 E.g., when Julian sought to learn specific details about God's saving will, she was
shown that it is better to accept God's word 'generally' than to be concerned with
full sight here in this life. [35:2-14]
267 Julian tells us that, when her shewings ceased, God left her with 'his owne blessyd
worde in tru vnderstandy*n*g, byddyng me fulle myghtly that I shulde beleue it.'
[70:20-22]
268 35:45-46; 46:43-49; cf. 22:2-3.
269 71:15-18.
270 As we have already seen, faith is the beginning of the life of virtue, the fruit of our
existential oneing by grace. [54:27-37] See p. 80-82, above.

scious awareness of such action. So, while Julian's rather extraordinary shewings gave her a clarity of vision for a time, that clarity lasted only briefly. Such shewings or flashes of insight are only 'for a time'; they pass, leaving us 'without sign or token' of the temporary understanding they gave.[271] Then, it is the hard work of the life lived in faith that keeps us firmly united to God. The virtue of faith 'keeps' the 'sight' of divine revelation until our life's end.[272] For most souls, i.e., those who have never experienced extraordinary shewings like Julian's, the virtue of faith is the only sight they have in this life and the only sight they need. Faith, not extraordinary visions, is the 'seeing' that leads us to full union with God. If we 'keep' ourselves in the faith, we shall not be overcome.[273]

In her teaching on the 'sight' of faith, Julian once again maintains a christological focus in regard to the working of the Holy Spirit. She tells us that our faith is our light in the darkness of sin.

> Oure feyth is a lyght, kyndly comy*n*g of oure endlesse day that is oure fader, god, in whych lyght oure moder, Cryst, and oure good lorde the holy gost ledyth vs in this passyng lyfe. This lyght is mesuryd dyscretly, nedfully stondy(ng) to vs in the nyght. . . . And at *th*e end of woe, sodeynly oure eye shalle be opynyd, and in clernes of syght oure lyght shalle be fulle, whych lyght is god, oure maker, fadyr, and holy gost in Crist Jh*e*su oure savyour.
>
> Thus I sawe and vnderstode that oure feyth is oure lyght in oure nyght, whych lyght is god, oure endlesse day. [83:14-17.21-25]

While trinitarian in its scope, Julian's description of that light of faith points to the fullness of light in heaven, which light shall be found in Christ. The light of faith is God, but God as seen in Christ.[274] It is Christ who does not let the light of faith fail.

> Oure feyth is contraryed in dyverse maner by oure owne blyndnesse and oure gostely enemys wit*h*in and wit*h*oute. And there fore oure precyous louer helpyth vs wit*h* goostely lyghte and tru techyng on dyuerse manner wit*h*in and wit*h*oute, where by *that* we may know hym. [71:6-10][275]

Our faith is 'contraried' by our blindness, but Christ helps us so that we may know him in our faith, both within (through the inspiration of the

---

271 "In alle this blessyde shewyng oure good lorde gave vnderstandyng *that th*e syght shulde passe, whych blessyd shewyng the feyth kepyth wit*h* his owne good wylle and his grace; for he lefte wit*h* me neyther sygne ne tokyn where by I myght know it." [70:17-20]

272 7:63-65; cf. 70:17-20.

273 70:37-40.

274 83:22-25; see also p. 151-152, above.

275 Cf. 70:30-40 (p. 154, above); 84:2-3.

Holy Spirit) and without (through the teaching of the Church).[276] We walk in the light of faith by the working of mercy and grace.[277] Christ, our mother of mercy, is God's self-revelation, and our perception of that revelation is the fruit of Christ's motherhood of grace. The working of grace is the ground of the believer's subjective participation in the event of divine revelation. The Holy Spirit enables us to grasp God's revelation in Christ, according us to the gift of that divine self-revelation: we see by grace.[278] Because divine self-revelation is divine self-communication, a union results between the revealer and the perceiver. That bond of union, the 'sight' of faith, is the domain of grace. Just as the Holy Spirit is the bond of love between Christ and the soul, so too the Holy Spirit is the 'seeing' by which revelation is perceived by the believer. The grace of the Holy Spirit is the condition of possibility for our 'sight' by faith. So while Christ is the light by which the believer sees God, the Holy Spirit may be understood to be present in the subjective dimension of that same light within the believer, the light of faith by which one sees the revelation that is Christ. The light of Christ is a 'gracious light.'[279] (Julian also stresses the role of the Holy Spirit in the communication of divine revelation between believers.)[280]

d. Christ our mother comforts us in our pain

Julian tells us that the shewing of divine mercy, our 'keeping' in Christ, is given in order to solace the sinner.

> Alle thys that I haue now seyde, and more as I shalle sey aftyr, is comfortyng ageynst synne. [34:22-23]

---

276 We are taught inwardly by the Holy Spirit and outwardly by holy Church in the same grace. [30:5-7]
277 83:19-21; cf. 33:25-26.
278 Julian's understanding of our 'sight' by grace parallels her understanding of the relationship between mercy and grace (viz., that we are accorded to Christ's merciful working in us by the action of the Holy Spirit): until we enjoy the full sight of heaven, our spiritual sight or understanding of God's merciful revelation in Christ is the work of grace. [6:53-56; 7:55-65; 10:76-81; 20:26.35-36; 35:32-33.45-46; 36:49-50; 37:4; 43:18-19.35-36.45-59; 45:33-34.36-38; 47:22-24; 49:7-8; 52:53-54.80; 53:10-11; 56:9-10; 64:49-51; 65:35-37; 78:15]
279 42:32-33; 78:2-3; 82:25-26.
280 Julian's appreciation of the importance of sight is reflected in her desire to convey the content of her shewings. She realizes, however, that only the grace of the Holy Spirit can enable her to communicate something of her ineffable experience.[26:11-18] Cf. 10:45-46; 37:10-11; 44:6-7; 47:13-15; 73:7-8; 86:2-3.

All this homely shewynge of oure curteyse lorde, it is a louely lesson and a swete
gracious techyng of hym selfe, in comforthyng of oure soule. [79:22-24][281]

The blindness that is sin intensifies our pain; if that blindness escalates
to the pain of despair (complete blindness to God's love and mercy),[282]
we become inconsolable[283] and lose heart in our struggle against sin.
It is the revelation of God's love for us, especially in the sight of Christ's
passion, which gives us comfort in our pain and need.[284] Moreover, the
shewing of divine mercy is itself a mercy because we are rescued from
fear and despair by the comfort which the sight of our 'keeping' brings us.
The joy[285] we experience in the revelation of Christ eases our pain and
calms our fears.[286] Sight of God's merciful 'keeping' gives us strength
and courage in face of temptation whereas, if we are deprived of the
comfort of revelation, we are 'travailed' by our sin and pain.[287]

At the heart of the message of comfort which Julian received was
God's assurance that 'all shall be well,' despite the way things may appear
to us.[288] As we have seen, true sight and right judgment of our sinful
condition are ours only by the 'light of mercy and grace,' the corrected
vision that is ours in Christ.[289] The merely human perspective of sin is
the changeable judgment of our sensuality and leads to impatience (or
sloth) and despair unless it is balanced with God's higher judgment, the
divine perspective of our substance, whereby we see rightly, i.e., with trust

---

281 Cf. 7:50-52; 23:37-44; 37:10-13; 38:22-23; 40:46-54; 47:35-37; 64:42-46; 68:55-58.60-
      64; 70:26-27.37-40; 79:8; 86:7-12.
282 For Julian, despair is the greatest pain we can suffer, the pain that is hell's pain.
      [17:57] Cf. 76:11-12.
283 Sin deadens us to the comfort of the Holy Spirit. [74:7-8]
284 It is the unknowing of God's love that keeps us in pain. [73:24-32 (p. 147, above)]
      The sight of Christ's pain saves us from despair in the feeling of our own pain.
      [28:26-32; cf. 27:22-24] See also p. 208-210, below.
285 By attentiveness to God's revelation we have 'more enjoyeng in his hole loue than
      sorowyng in oure oftyn fallynges.' [81:14-15] (We shall return to Julian's under-
      standing of joy in chapter 4, p. 209-210, below.)
286 47:35-37.
287 "And the joyng in hys syght with this trew hope of hys mercyfull kepyng made me
      to haue felyng and comfort, so that mornyng and drede were nott grettly paynfull.
      . . . [We] fayle oftymes of the syght of hym, and anon we falle in to oure selfe, and
      than fynde we felyng of ryght nowght but the contraryous that is in oure selfe, and
      that of the olde rote of oure furst synne with all that folowyth of oure owne contyn-
      uance; and in this we be traveyled and temptyd with felyng of synne and of payne
      in many dyverse maner, gostely and bodely, as it is knowyn to vs in this lyfe."
      [47:35-37.40-45]
288 31:2-11; 32:20-22.
289 40:2-5; 78:2-5.

and hope in God's mercy.[290] Divine revelation preserves both judgments, giving us a 'gracious knowing' of our sin, i.e., with meekness and without despair.[291] Moreover, the beholding of the higher truth keeps us in joy and comfort even while we still suffer our sins.[292] Pain is passing and shall be brought to nought; the bliss that shall be the outcome of our pain is the lasting reality.[293] In our pain, we should concentrate on the sight of divine mercy, clinging to God's love and goodness.[294] We are to set our hearts on the higher reality of divine love, turning our attention from the pain that we feel to the bliss that we trust — the healing and salvation that is ours in Christ.[295]

Divine revelation provides us both with 'matter for meekness' and 'matter for love.'[296] We have seen how the sight of the true horror of our sinfulness gives us the meekness we need in order to become Christ's 'helpers' in the process of our existential oneing by grace;[297] however, we also need to appreciate the important role played by the comfort which divine revelation affords us. The comforting sight of our 'keeping' in God's love stirs in us our own love for God, itself a necessary element in that same process of existential oneing because it is love which motivates us to persevere in our struggle with sin. Because the nature of divine revelation is dialogical, the comfort we receive from the shewing of Christ enkindles our desire and love for God: by the vision of divine love as manifested in Christ, we are drawn to that love and oned to God in our response of love by grace. As our sight and knowledge of God's comforting revelation increases, so does our love and trust of God. For this reason, we can say that the comfort we receive in divine revelation is salvific in its effect: as we see God's loving face in the face of Jesus, we are increasingly drawn to God by loving desire and, necessarily, away

---

290 82:29-37; cf. 11:33-39; 45:2-11; 46:2-39; 52:69-70; 72:14-22; 73:39-42.
291 78:15-25.
292 82:29-36; cf. 47:35-37. For Julian, the experience of comfort and joy is more substantial, more trustworthy than the feeling of pain because our pain belongs to our sensuality, our outward bodily existence, while our joy is rooted in our substance, our inner experience — even when that experience does not make itself felt in our consciousness. [55:49-59] (This dual experience of pain and joy is the reason why Julian could choose the crucified Jesus as her 'heaven.' [19:2-20] See p. 140-142, above.)
293 15:29-35; 64:53-59.
294 82:12-15.
295 81:13-27.
296 36:41-43.
297 Self-knowledge produces meekness. (See p. 154, above.)

from sin.[298] The 'sight' of faith heals and ones us: to look at God's love leads to oneing, whereas to concentrate on our guilt leads to despair.

Just as our 'sight' is by grace, so too our seeking in faith, our desire to see God ever more and more, is the work of the Holy Spirit.[299] Moreover, our 'beholding' in faith brings us the grace to seek.

> For I saw him and sought him, for we be now so blynde and so vnwyse that we can never seke god till what tyme *that* he of his goodnes shewyth hym to vs. And whan we see owght of hym graciously, then are we steryd by the same grace to seke *with* great desyer to see hym more blessedfully. And thus I saw him and sought him, and I had hym and wantyd hym; and this is and should be our comyn workyng in this life, as to my syght. . . . [For] he will be seen, and he will be sought, and he will be abyden, and he will be trustyd. [10:14-20.29-31]

Sight of God's love elicits a response of loving desire, itself the work of grace.[300] The more by grace we see God's perspective, the more we shall understand our true nature, and the more by grace we shall long for that bliss for which we have been created.[301] This sight, understanding, and longing belong to the 'beholding' which is prayer. The 'savoring' of prayer brings us to a natural longing and a loving trust rooted in grace.

> For prayer is a ry*gh*twys vnderstandyng of that fulhed of joy that is for to come, *with* tru longyng and very trust. Saworyng or seyng oure blysse that we be ordeyned to, kyndely makyth vs to longe; trew vnderstongdyng and loue *with* swete menyng in oure savyoure[302] graciously makyth vs to trust. And thus haue we of kynde to long and of grace to t(ru)st. [42:55-59]

---

298   When we 'see rightly,' we hate sin [40:33-35; 52:53-54; 76:4-8]; the sight of God's face prevents any stirring to sin [47:20; cf. 10:24-26].

299   "[The soul] may do no more than seke, suffer and trust. And this is wrought in everie soule that hath it by the holy gost. And the clernesse of fyndyng, it is of his speciall grace when it is when it is his will." [10:69-72] Cf. 47:29-31. Julian also speaks about our seeking by hope and charity, the other two theological virtues which are ours by the grace of the Holy Spirit. [10:72-73] (Maisonneuve suggests that the theological virtues are three ways of 'looking': the *regard de vigilance* is faith, the *regard de désir* is hope, and the *regard d'abandon* is charity. See Roland Maisonneuve, *L'univers visionnaire de Julian of Norwich,* 150-153.)

300   43:27-28.

301   45:36-40; cf. 46:5-7; 72:23-25.

302   Colledge and Walsh have emended the Paris MS 'savyoure' to 'savoure,' noting that the emendation is self-evident because of the sentence's opening phrase 'Saworing or seyng.' Glasscoe makes a strong case against such an emendment as self-evident. *A Book of Showings,* notes, p. 473. Marion Glasscoe, "Visions and Revisions: A Further Look at the Manuscripts of Julian of Norwich," *Studies in Bibliography.* Papers of the Bibliographical Society of the University of Virginia 42 (1989) 112-113.

Julian's understanding of the 'beholding' of prayer is perfectly consonant with her theology of revelation.[303] Prayer is a kind of 'seeing' by
grace,[304] a 'seeing' which ones us to God (making us like to that which
we see)[305] and which causes us to seek and desire: the more we see,
the more we shall desire and beseech ('be-seek') God's saving will, i.e.,
our full union with God.[306] Prayer itself is a 'witness that the soul wills
as God wills.'[307] Oned and fastened to God's will by the working of
grace, we beseech God for the accomplishment of that divine will, our
salvation in Christ,[308] who is himself the ground of our prayer, our beseeching.[309] Consequently, Julian can say that true prayer or beseeching
is marked by rightfulness and trust: if our prayer is rightful, i.e., if we
seek that which God wills us to have and which God makes us to desire,
then we may pray with full trust that God will accomplish that will.[310]
Finally, the notion of trust implies that, like the 'sight' of our faith, our
beseeching is not a full, conscious 'seeing'; if we were enjoying full vision
we would no longer be trustfully seeking, because we would already have
the object of our beseeching, the full sight of God to whom we make our
prayer.[311] We exercise the 'sight' of prayer (like that of faith) precisely
when we are unable to see clearly.[312] If and when, by grace, one is giv-
en the rather uncommon experience of a clear 'vision' of God's presence
in mystical union, quite naturally that soul ceases its conscious beseeching
(seeking) and gives its full attention to the beholding itself ('clearness of
finding').[313] At the same time, however, the soul's desire and seeking
for God grows because of its increased 'sight';[314] so, while its beseech-

---

303 See Paul Molinari, S.J., *Julian of Norwich*, 73-145, for a comprehensive analysis of
     Julian's doctrine on prayer.
304 43:45-49.
305 By grace, prayer makes us like to Christ in condition as we are in kind. [41:40-41;
     43:2-4.17]
306 41:27-28; 43:27-28.
307 43:4-17.
308 "Besechyng is a trew and gracious lestyng wylle of the soule, onyd and fastenyd in
     to the wylle of oure lorde by the swet prevy werkyng of the holy gost." [41:30-32]
     From her definition, it is clear that, for Julian, beseeching is not a mere petitioning
     of 'things' from God, but a more unitive type of prayer, i.e., the evidence of a
     oneing of wills (the soul's with God's).
309 41:10-14; cf. 41:64-67; 42:4-6.18-20.65-66; 43:8-9.25-26.
310 41:3-5; cf. 42:15-22.
311 43:18-26.
312 43:27-35.
313 43:18-21. Seeking is our common experience of prayer; 'clearness of finding' is a
     gratuitous gift of God's grace, a gift which may or may not be given. [10:68-77]
314 43:27-28.

ing may be 'imperceptible,'[315] its prayer does continue until the soul reaches the full vision of God in the bliss of heaven.

Julian's image of Christ as our mother is a most eloquent portrait of the word of divine comfort which God addresses to us in the person of the incarnate Son. In his motherhood of merciful 'keeping,' Christ brings us to spiritual birth, comforting us in the pain of that birthing.

> Ande in oure gostly forth bryngyng he vsyth more tendernesse in kepyng without ony comparyson, by as moch as oure soule is of more pryce in his syght. He kyndelyth oure vnderstondyng, he prepareth oure weyes, he esyth oure consciens, he confortyth oure soule, he lyghteth oure harte and gevyth vs in party knowyng and louyng in his blessydfull godhede, with gracyous mynde in his swete manhode and his blessed passyon, with curtesse mervelyng in his hye ovyr passyng goodnesse, and makyth us to loue all that he louyth for his loue, and to be well apayde with hym and with alle his werkes. And whan we falle, hastely he reysyth vs by his louely beclepyng and his gracyous touchyng. And when we be strenthyd by his swete werkyng, than we wylfully chose hym by his grace to be his seruanntes and hys lovers, lestyngly without ende. [61:2-14]

Christ comforts us, encourages us to rise whenever we have fallen, and increases our desire for full union with him in love. We are to flee to Christ as children flee to their mother for solace and healing[316] — and we shall find our comforting mother Christ in the faith of the Church.[317] There, in that faith, our mother of mercy mercifully eases the pain of our blindness by being who he is: the saving self-revelation of God.

---

315 43:21-22.
316 61:41-51; 77:49; see also p. 118-119, above.
317 61:57-64 (p. 120-121, above); cf. 67:22-24.

4 The Compassion of God in Christ: the Face of Divine Mercy

For Julian, Jesus Christ is the compassion of God. In his incarnation, passion, death and resurrection, Jesus Christ is the saving revelation of God's compassion for humankind. It is only in Christ that divine compassion is properly situated and expressed.[1]

Julian uses the words 'compassion,' 'ruth,' and 'pity' to describe God's compassionate love towards humankind.[2] We shall analyze her use of these three words within the context of three themes of the *Shewings*, each of which underscores the characteristically christocentric nature of her thought: (a) the compassion of God as revealed in the parable of the lord and the servant — a 'chere'[3] of God's merciful love; (b) the compassion of Christ within the context of his triple chere; and (c) human compassion as the fruit of Christ's compassion in us. We shall then explore Julian's understanding of compassion as it accords with the scriptural concept of divine compassion.

Julian is even more precise in appropriating the word 'compassion' to Christ than she was in regard to the word 'mercy.' While Julian uses 'compassion,' 'ruth,' and 'pity' as equivalent terms in reference to Christ,[4] she restricts herself to the use of the words 'ruth' and 'pity' when she describes God's attitude towards humankind, consistently reserving the word 'compassion' to refer to Christ[5] or to the human person inserted

---

1   As we have already noted, Julian is careful to note that by 'Christ' the fullness of Trinity is implied. [4:14-16] Thus, the compassion of Christ can be understood as the divine compassion proper. See p. 29-30, above.
2   In the Long Text, *compassion* appears 22 times [2:13-14.42; 3:46.49; 18:2; 20:35; 28:2.4.4.11.21.23;30:17;31:50.51;39:23.25-26; 64:44; 71:29; 76:18.20-21; 80:27]; *ruth*, 15 times [28:35; 31:41.51; 34:10; 48:13; 51:40.130.132.134; 52:43.74.90; 61:54; 71:28. 35]; and *pity*, 34 times [28:11.35; 30:17; 31:41.45.46; 48:13.18.25.28; 51:40.125.131. 132.132.133.138.139;52:44.75.91;55:18;59:33.35;61:54; 71:28.35;72:9; 75:3.3;77:31. 33; 80:32; 82:9]. N.b., the references for 'pity' include 72:9 (see note 35, p. 171, below).
3   'Chere' may be translated as *face, mien, demeanor, manner,* etc.
4   For the most clearly parallel examples, cf. 28:11.35; 30:17; 31:50.51; 71:29.
5   While the word 'lorde' in 64:43-44 ('For in this behest I saw a mercyfulle compas-sio*n* that oure lorde hath in vs for oure woo') may appear to be at least ambiguous, the change from the use of the antecedent 'God' in the Short Text [xx:9] to 'oure curteyse lorde' in the Long Text [64:13] seems to point to the possibility of a conscious attempt to situate divine compassion properly in Christ. (N.b., the

into Christ, i.e., the christian.[6] Thus, to discover Julian's understanding
of divine compassion, we must begin by looking at the words 'ruth' and
'pity' as she uses them in reference to God. Only then may we move on
to a consideration of their usage in reference to divine compassion as
proper to Christ.[7]

---

specific reference to compassion [64:44] does not appear in the Short Text.) The
other uses of the word 'lorde' as the subject of compassion [viz., 28:10-11; 30:17;
31:50.51] have 28:2ff [the 'shewyng of compassion' in Christ] as their general
context, suggesting a christological interpretation. Cf. note on 76:20, *A Book of
Showings*, p. 686.

6 The nature of the relationship between divine compassion and the exercise of
compassion to which every christian is called will be discussed later in this chapter
(see p. 203-205, below).

7 See p. 175ff, below.

A. Divine Compassion: the Chere of God's Merciful Love

In isolating Julian's statements on God's compassionate stance towards humankind, we find that her most concentrated use of the words 'ruth' and 'pity' occur in either direct or indirect references to the parable of the lord and the servant.[8] 'Pity/ruth'[9] is used to refer to God's compassion nineteen times in explicit references to the parable[10] and an additional ten times in implicit references.[11] Moreover, apart from the references to God's compassion which find their basis in the parable, there are only two other passages in the *Shewings* that speak directly of God's pity and ruth.[12] This fact alone suggests the significance of the parable in Julian's understanding of divine compassion. Having already seen how the parable of the lord and the servant is central to the meaning of the *Shewings* as a whole, we shall now explore some aspects of the parable which shed light on the nature of divine compassion as rooted in the mystery of Christ's incarnation.

1. The lord's double chere: the mystery of suffering and sin

In the parable of the lord and the servant, the lord responds tenderly to the servant's falling (and to the consequent pain he endures) in two ways: with pity (or ruth) because of the servant's sufferings, and with rejoicing because of the great reward that will eventually come to the servant because of his ordeal.

> And ryght thus contynuantly his loueyng lorde full tenderly beholdyth hym; and now wyth a doubyll chere, oone owtwarde, full mekly and myldely, with grett rewth and pytte, and this was of the furst; another inwarde, more gostly, . . . [in] whych I saw hym hyely enjoy for the wurschypfull restyng and noble

---

8   It may be noted that some of the references to Christ's compassion, ruth, and pity also contain elements which can be traced to the parable of the lord and the servant, e.g., 28:11.35.35; 31:41.41.45.46; 64:44; 71:28.28.35.35.

9   References to the terms 'pity' and 'ruth' will be combined because there seems to be no discernible distinction between the two in Julian's usage. She often pairs them (e.g., 28:35; 31:41; 48:13; 51:40.130.131.132.134; 52:43.44.74.75.90.91; 61:54; 71:28.35).

10   51:40.40.125.130.131.132.132.132.134.134.138.139;52:43.44.74.75.90.91; 82:9.

11   28:11.35.35; 48:13.13.18.25; 72:9; 75:3.3.

12   See p. 184-185, below, for a discussion of 31:41-52 and 75:2-8.

that he wyll and shall bryng his seruannt to by his plentuous grace. [51:38-
41.42-44]

The lord's chere of 'ruth and pity' is Julian's way of describing God's
compassion for us in the midst of the pain we suffer because of our sins.

The parable presents a poignant, detailed description of the pain and
suffering of the servant:

> And anon he fallyth in a slade, and takyth ful grett sorow; and than he
> gronyth and monyth and wallowyth and wryeth, but he may nott ryse nor help
> hym selfe by no manner of weye. And of all this the most myschefe that I saw
> hym in was feylyng of comfort, for he culde nott turne his face to loke vppe
> on his lovyng lorde, whych was to hym full nere, in whom is full comfort; but
> as a man that was full febyll and vnwyse for the tyme, he entendyd to his
> felyng and enduryng in woo, in whych woo he sufferyd vij grett paynes. The
> furst was the soore brosyng that he toke in his fallyng, whych was to hym
> moch payne. The seconde was the hevynesse of his body. The thyrde was
> fybylnesse that folowyth of theyse two. The iiij was that he was blyndyd in his
> reson and stonyd in his mynde so ferforth that allmost he had forgeten his
> owne loue. The v was that he myght nott ryse. The vj was payne most
> mervelous to me, and that was that he leye aloone. I lokyd alle about and
> behelde, and ferre ne nere ne hye ne lowe I saw to hym no helpe. The vij[th]
> was that the place whych he ley in was alang, harde and grevous. [51:15-31]

Although the lord was 'full near' to him in his sufferings, the servant was
unable to look up to the lord for comfort. Disconsolate and terrified by
the hopelessness of his situation, he could see only his own pain and
separation from his gracious lord. Indeed, his greatest pain was his
isolation; and, without someone to help him, he was unable to make his
way back to his kind lord in whom alone his comfort lay. Sorely injured,
the servant was left blinded and enfeebled, so overwhelmed by his pain
and misery that he was very close to forgetting his own love for his lord.

Julian is surprised by the servant's meek acceptance of his painful
situation, but even more so by the fact that the lord addressed no blame
to the servant for his falling.

> I merveyled how this seruannt myght thus mekely suffer all this woo; and
> I behelde with avysement to wytt yf I culde perceyve in hym ony defaughte, or
> yf the lorde shuld assigne in hym ony maner of blame; and verely there was
> none seen, for oonly hys good wyll and his grett desyer was cause of his
> fallyng. And he was as vnlothfull and as good inwardly as he was when he
> stode before his lorde, redy to do his wylle. [51:32-37]

Julian searches but finds no fault or evidence of blameworthiness in the
servant; rather the servant's eagerness to perform the lord's will seems to
be the cause of his falling.

Since, as we have already noted, the fall of the servant represents

Since, as we have already noted, the fall of the servant represents Adam's fall from paradise,[13] we can say that sin is the cause of human suffering: the servant 'falls,' and all his woes are a result of that fall. Because she identifies the fall of the servant with the fall of Adam, Julian is left with the startling conclusion that God's attitude towards the sinner is one of compassion and pity, not blame.[14] Moreover, the lord does not merely view the servant with pity; he joyfully plans a wonderful reward and blissful rest for the servant because of the sufferings he endured, a reward much greater than what he would have received had he not fallen.

> Than seyde this curteyse lorde in his menyng: Lo my belouyd servant, what harme and dysses he hath had and takyn in my servys for my loue, yea, and for his good wylle. Is it nott reson that I reward hym his frey and his drede, his hurt and his mayme and alle his woo? And nott only this, but fallyth it nott to me to geve hym a yyfte that be better to hym and more wurschypfull than his owne hele shuld haue bene? . . . I saw that it behovyth nedys to be standyng his grett goodnes and his owne wurschyppe, that his deerworthy servannt, whych he lovyd so moch, shulde be hyely and blessydfully rewardyd withoute end, aboue that he shulde haue be yf he had nott fallen. [51:47-53.55-59][15]

In Julian's account of the servant's blindness and pain, we recognize an accurate description of our own experience of the sufferings caused by sin, even to the 'failing of comfort' which leaves the sinner prone to depression and even despair.[16] We suffer our sins, i.e., we live in pain because we live in the context of sin. As Pelphrey points out, every sin (every willful decision to participate in what is *not God*) brings about its own pain because it results in an erosion of our very nature, an attack on our being.[17] In other words, suffering is the inevitable hallmark of lives not yet existentially oned to God.

The parable illustrates the nature of God's loving compassion for us in our sinning. As we have already seen, it is our oneing in Christ which explains why, when God looks at Adam (and us), God sees Christ.[18]

---

13 51:67-68.100-101.
14 82:9-10; cf. 27:35-36; 28:32-35; 39:35-37; 45:15-16; 50:7-15; 51:34-35; 80:42-43.
15 Cf. 52:46-49.
16 "And by Adams fallyng we be so broken in oure felyng on dyverse manner by synne and by sondry paynes, in which we be made derke and so blynde that vnnethys we can take any comforte." [52:13-16]
17 Brant Pelphrey, *Love Was His Meaning*, 256. See also chapter 2, p. 96-97, above.
18 "In the servant is comprehendyd the seconde person of the trynyte, and in the seruannt is comprehendyd Adam, that is to sey all men. And therfore when I sey the sonne, it menyth the godhed whych is evyn with the fader, and whan I sey the servannt, it menyth Crystes manhode whych is ryghtfull Adam . . . . Wher fore this

The two cheres of the parable are directly linked to this identification of Adam with Christ.

> And thus in the servant was shewde the blyndnesse and the myschefe of Adams fallyng; and in *the* servant was shewde *the* wysdom and the goodnesse of goddys son. And in the lorde was schewde the rewth and the pytte of Adams woo; and in the lorde was schewde the hye noblyte and the endlesse wurschyppe that mankynde is come to by the vertu of the passyon and the deth of his deerwurthy son. [52:41-46][19]

The pain suffered by the servant is caused by sin and evokes God's compassion, while the worship of Christ's oneing us by his incarnation evokes God's endless joy. God addresses no more blame to us than to Christ;[20] rather, because the pain we experience as a result of our sins is identified with the Christ's suffering on the cross,[21] God views us with compassion, i.e., with the chere of ruth and pity.[22] This chere of pity is accompanied by the second chere, the chere of bliss,[23] i.e., God's rejoicing ('enjoying') at the reward which will be ours for suffering sin's pain.[24] Not only are we excused in our sins, but God will also bring us to an honorable nobility, turning all our blame into endless worship and glory, in which all our suffering and woes are destroyed.[25]

The two cheres of the parable reiterate what Julian has already puzzled over, i.e., that in God she could see no wrath, no manner of blame for us in our sinning.[26] The compassionate face of the lord reveals that, not only is there no wrath on God's part, but God does not even address blame to us in our sins; instead, God excuses us, seeing only our good will and desire to give loving service.[27] Our sin evokes com-

---

menyng was shewed in vnderstanding of the manhod of Crist. For all mankynde that shall be savyd by the swete incarnacion and the passio*n* of Crist, alle is the manhode of Cryst . . . . For J*h*esu is in all that shall be safe, and all that (shall) be sa(fe) is in J*h*esu, and all of the charyte of god." [51:211-215.253-256.265-266] See also p. 38-39, above.

19 Cf. 51:134-136 (note 39, p. 172-173, below).
20 51:232-234; cf. 51:222-224.
21 See notes 222 (p. 92-93, above) and 257 (p. 97, above).
22 51:40.130-140; cf. 82:9-10.
23 Elsewhere, God's 'blessydfulle chere' [14:11; 72:8.45.49; cf. 71:30-31.38; 72:20.30].
24 52:46-49; cf. 51:47-59 (p. 169, above). Julian tells us that God actually thanks us for the travail we suffer here on earth as a result of sin. [14:3-20]
25 52:94-96; cf. 28:33; 51:22-224; 80:42-43.
26 The parable itself was the response to Julian's plea to understand why she could see in God no manner of blame for us in our sinning. [45:27-32; cf. 50:7-18].
27 As we have seen, there can be no wrath, i.e., opposition to peace and love [48:8], in God because of the unchangeability of his love; God is love and peace [46:29-36;

passion and help from God who seems to concentrate, not on our blame-worthiness, but rather on the pain we suffer in our falling.[28] God sees our lives as a penance we suffer[29] and our sins as sorrow and pain to us.[30]

The key role of the parable of the lord and the servant in under-standing God's compassion becomes clear. The lord's 'double chere' reveals the depth of God's steadfast love: not only are our sins excused, but we are also rewarded (for enduring the sufferings they inflict upon us) by our compassionate God who, seeing us in our pain and misery, sees the Son who has oned humanity in himself by his incarnation. Through the imagery of the parable, Julian discovers that God's judgment on our sinning is grounded on God's loving purpose — the whole of God's plan of salvation, i.e., our oneing in Christ. God's unfailing love accounts for the fact that, even when we judge our sins as deserving punishment, God continues to love us tenderly in spite of our guilt.[31] This compas-sionate love that excuses us is the same love that rewards us. God's double chere, the 'sweet eye of pity'[32] and 'marvelous joy,'[33] are actually two 'workings' of the one same love.[34] Indeed, the chere of bliss is shown us *in* loving compassion.[35]

---

cf. 49:9-16]. Therefore, Julian locates wrath in us: "We by synne and wrechydnesse haue in vs a wrath and a contynuant contraryousnes to pees and to loue; and that shewed he full ofte in his louely chere of ruth and pytte." [48:11-13] Cf. 40:5-6.

28 51:115-119.

29 77:26-46; 81:16-27; 82:4-7.

30 "For [God] beholdyth synne as sorow and paynes to his louers, in whom he assign-yth no blame for loue." [39:35-37] God welcomes repentant sinners as if they had been in pain and in prison. [40:9-12; cf. 77:41.]

31 "I knowe wele I haue deservyde payne; but oure lorde is almyghty, and may p-onyssch me myghtly, and he is all wysdom, and can ponyssch me wysely, and he is alle goodnesse, and lovyth me tendyrly." [77:16-19]

32 48:25; cf. 51:125.

33 52:93.

34 52:82-96.

35 "[And] thus was *the* blessydfulle chere of our lorde god shewde in pite." [72:8-9] Note the use of 'in pite' from the two Sloane MSS in preference to 'in perty' ('in part') from the Paris MS. Colledge and Walsh argue for the superiority of the Paris MS 'in perty,' citing 71:37-38: "[Christ] shewyth to us in this lyfe . . . his blessyd chere lyke in perty as it shalle be in hevyn." Glasscoe, however, presents a sound argument for the acceptability of the Sloane MSS 'in pite.' According to Glasscoe, the chere of pity preserves us in our sin and is mingled with the chere of bliss which serves as a light to inform our faith by grace [71:36-43]. Elsewhere, Julian herself refers to this mingling of the two cheres, telling us that Christ rejoic-es in our tribulations with pity and ruth [28:10-11]. *A Book of Showings*, notes, p. 660; Marion Glasscoe, "Visions and Revisions: A Further Look at the Manuscripts

God's response to our sufferings, then, is one of endless and steadfast love, a love that is expressed in compassion. The unchangeability of this divine love[36] is demonstrated, above all, in God's chere of ruth and pity in the face of our sinning.

> And here I vnderstode *that the* lorde behelde *th*e servannt w*ith* pytte and nott w*ith* blame; for this passyng lyfe askyth not to lyue alle w*ith*out synne. He lovyth us endlessly, and we synn customeably, and he shewyth it vs fulle myldely. [82:9-12]

We are not expected to live this 'passing life' without sinning. The context of our earthly existence *is* sin.[37] Yet God does not punish us, but remains always in an attitude of compassionate love, comforting us in our pain.[38] By the light of the parable, we discover that God's compassion for us in our sufferings is really compassion for us in our sins.

2. The 'homeliness' of God's love and its basis in Christ

Julian's understanding of divine compassion is thoroughly christological: God's 'chere of ruth and pity' is shown to us precisely because of our oneing in Christ. The compassion of the Father for the Son belongs properly to Christ but is extended to us because, by embracing humanity in his incarnation, Christ has oned us to God in himself. Compassion is the chere, the *face* of divine love shown to us because of the event of divine mercy, Christ's incarnation; therefore, in a real sense, we can say that compassion is the face of God's mercy. The merciful chere of divine compassion is ours in Christ and continues to be shown to us until our oneing is complete in the bliss of heaven.[39]

---

of Julian of Norwich," 115.

36 79:16; cf. 11:44-45. God's fidelity cannot be broken by our offenses. [61:26-27; cf. 68:61-63.]

37 82:10-11; cf. 36:6; 37:2.8; 52:57-58; 79:6-7.11; 82:5.14-15.27-28.

38 "And this [the parable] was a begynnyng of techyng whych I saw in the same tyme, wherby I myght come to knowyng in what man*n*er he beholdeth vs in oure synne. And then I saw that oonly payne blamyth and ponyschyth, and oure curteyse lorde comfortyth and socurryth, and evyr he is to the soule in glad chere, lovyng and longyng to bryng vs to his blysse." [51:115-19]

39 "The rewth and the pytte of the fader was of the fallyng of Adam, whych is his most lovyd creature. The joy and the blysse was of the fallyng of his deerwurthy son, whych is evyn w*ith* the fader. The mercifull beholdyng of his louely chere fulfyllyd all erth, and descendyd downe w*ith* Adam into helle, w*ith* whych contyn-

Julian's insight into the christological nature of divine compassion is perhaps nowhere more clearly demonstrated than in her theme of God's homely[40] love. By describing divine love as 'homely,' Julian attempts to convey the extraordinary familiarity[41] with which God loves humankind.

> [Full] greatly was I a stonned for wonder and marvayle that I had that he that is so reuerent and so dreadfull will be so homely *with* a synnfull creature liueing in this wretched flesh. [4:17-19]

A homely love implies that, between God and the human person, there exists the familiarity proper to an intimate intersubjective relationship. From a human standpoint, such a relationship of intimacy remains completely unattainable because of the great chasm that separates divinity and humanity; a homely love between God and the human person only becomes possible through Christ's incarnation. Because we share the humanity assumed by the Second Person of the Trinity, we participate in that intimate bond of love that exists between the Father and the Son. Indeed, it is precisely for the sake of God's homely love, this relationship of intimacy, that Christ took on sensuality: Christ himself is sovereign homeliness,[42] and his homeliest home is in us.[43]

The mystery of Christ's incarnation, then, is central to Julian's understanding of God's compassion for humankind and stands as the definitive revelation of God's homely love.[44] God has compassion for the sufferings of the Son and compassion for us because we are oned in the Son.

(u)ant pytte Adam was kepte fro endlesse deth. And this mercy and pytte dwellyth *with* mankynde in to the tyme that we come vppe in to hevyn." [51:134-140] (N.b., although ruth and pity do have temporal reference, they are nevertheless properly in God. [31:41])

40 'Homely'" is best translated as *familiar* or *intimate*.

41 Julian juxtaposes the idea of homeliness (or familiarity) with the medieval courtly ideal of courtesy, e.g., 7:46-48. As Riehle rightly points out, Julian does not equate the 'homeliness' of God with any notion of an unrestrained familiarity in our relationship with God. She is careful to balance *homeliness* with the notion of *courtesy*: "be we ware that we take not so rechelously this homelyhed for to leue curtesye." [77:53-54] See Wolfgang Riehle, *The Middle English Mystics*, 99.

42 77:54; cf. 7:52-55.

43 "The place that Jhesu takyth in oure soule he shall nevyr remoue *with*outen ende, as to my syght, for in vs is his homelyest home and his endlesse dwellyng." [68:15-17]

44 As Julian tells us in her oft-quoted closing chapter, love alone is the meaning, intent, and content of divine revelation: "What, woldest thou wytt thy lordes menyng in this thyng? Wytt it wele, loue was his menyng. Who shewyth it the? Loue. (What shewid he the? Love.) Wherfore shewyth he it the? For loue. Holde the therin, thou shalt wytt more in the same. But thou schalt nevyr witt therin other *with*outn ende." [86:15-19]

In his incarnation, Jesus Christ bridges the otherwise unbridgeable chasm which exists between divinity and humanity, making possible the relationship of homely love between God and humankind. Without Christ's incarnation, we would remain outside the sphere of God's homely love, that same faithful love from which divine compassion flows.[45]

In summary, Julian's parable of the lord and the servant reveals that, while God's love is the source of divine compassion, that same compassion is thoroughly christological. By virtue of Christ's incarnation, we are oned in Christ and brought into that homely love relationship between the Father and the beloved Son so that God's compassion for Christ in his sufferings also embraces us. Moreover, as we shall see in the next section, it is only in Christ that we are actually able to see the chere of God's compassion.

---

45   52:82-96.

B. The Compassion of Christ: the Triple Chere of Christ

Julian's statements about the compassion of Christ closely parallel what she has to say about God's compassion. For example:

> And here I vnderstode *that the* lorde [God] behelde *the* servannt *with* pytte and nott *with* blame. [82:9-10]

> And of hys gret curtesy he [Christ] doth away alle oure blame, and beholdeth vs *with* ruth and pytte, as chyldren innocens and vnlothfulle. [28:33-35][46]

We notice, however, that in referring to Christ she uses not only the words 'ruth' and 'pity'[47] (the words to which she restricts herself in reference to God), but also 'compassion.'[48] This usage suggests that Julian situates divine compassion proper (i.e., compassion in its true meaning as a *suffering with*) in Christ.

Nowhere is Julian's parallelism as evident as in her doctrine of the triple chere of Christ. Whereas God looks at the sinner with a 'double chere' of pity/ruth and bliss, Christ has a 'triple chere' towards humankind: the passion, pity/ruth (which Julian identifies with compassion), and bliss.

> I haue menyng of th(re) manner of cherys of oure lorde. The furst is chere of passion, as he shewde whyle he was *with* vs in this lyfe dyeng; and though this beholdyng be mornyng and swemfulle, yet it is glad and mery, for he is god. The seconde manner of chere, it is pitte and ruth and compassion, and this shewyth he to all his louers *with* sekernesse of kepyng that hath nede to his mercy. The thyrde is *the* blessydfulle chere as it shalle be *with* outyn ende, and this was oftenest shewyd and longeste contynuyd. [71:25-32]

For Julian, the triple chere of Christ is the incarnated counterpart to God's double chere.

---

46 For other examples, compare 8:11-12 with 52:43-44; 71:28-29 with 51:130-131 and 52:73-75.

47 28:11.35.35;30:17;31:41.41.45.46.51;34:10;55:18;59:33.35;61:54.54;71:28.28.35.35; 77:33; 80:32.

48 28:2.4.11.23; 30:17; 31:50.51; 71:29; 76:20; 80:27.

1. Christ's passion

The shewing of Christ's passion is the focal point and ground from which all of Julian's shewings follow.[49] Consequently, the 'shewing of Christ's compassion'[50] must also be seen to derive from his passion. The passion of Christ is Julian's entry into an understanding of divine compassion, i.e., Christ's passion is the tangible manifestation of God's compassion for humankind, God's 'suffering with' us. Christ in his passion *is* the chere of divine compassion.[51]

Julian ascribes to the standard medieval doctrine of the impassibility of the Godhead. Because God as God is impassible, God can 'suffer with' us only through the humanity of Jesus.[52] But Julian is very clear: it is God who suffers in Christ.

> For he that is hyghest and worthyest was foulest co(n)dempnyd and vtterly dyspysed; for the hyest poynt that may be seen in his passion is to thynke and to know that he is god that sufferyd, seeyng after these other two poyntes whych be lower. That one is what he sufferyd; and that other for whom that he sufferyd. [20:8-13][53]

For Julian, divine compassion for humankind (i.e., true 'suffering with' us) requires the mystery of Christ's incarnation. By taking on sensuality Christ suffers and sorrows with us—as one of us. His humanity gives Christ his passibility.

---

49 1:2-7 (p. 107, above); see also p. 124-126, above. Our discussion of the passion here will be limited to those aspects which relate specifically to Christ's compassionate 'suffering with' us and to his showing the chere of his passion to us. See p. 123-142, above, for other aspects of Julian's understanding of Christ's passion.

50 Julian clearly identifies the thirteenth shewing of the pains Christ suffered in his passion [27:16-38] as the 'shewing of compassion' [28:2; 31:50; 76:20; 77:33].

51 As we have already noted, we have no sight of God other than in Christ. See note 155 (p. 137) and p. 151-152, above.

52 According to Aquinas, the subject of Christ's human acts is divine, so God truly suffers when Christ suffers. This is not because Christ suffers as God (i.e., in the divine nature), but because that which is both human and divine (the person, the *suppositum*') suffers as human. "The union of the human nature with the Divine was effected in the Person . . . yet observing the distinction of natures . . . . The Passion is to be attributed to the *suppositum* of the Divine Nature, not because of the divine nature which is impassible, but by reason of the human nature." Thomas Aquinas, *Summa Theologiae*, 1a, q.46, a.12.

53 Cf. 51:280-282.287-288. Julian elsewhere tells us that 'alle that is good oure lorde doyth, and *that* is evyll oure lord sufferyth.' [35:21-22]

And in thys he brought to mynd in parte the hygh(t) and the nobylyte of the glorious godhede, and ther *with* the precioushede and the tendyrnesse of the blessydfulle body whych be to gether onyd, and also *the* lothfullnesse that in our kynde is to suffer peyne. For as moch as he was most tendyr and clene, ryght so he was most strong and myghty to suffer. . . . And more over, in as mech as the swete manhed of hym was wurthyer in kynde, for as long as he was passyble he sufferde for vs and sorowde for vs. And now he is vppe resyn and no more passibylle; yett he sufferyth *with* vs as I shalle sey after. [20:14-19.22-26]

Julian expands further on the impassibility of the risen Christ, explaining that, just as God suffered in Christ's passion, now the risen Christ suffers in us, his members.[54]

For as aneynst that Crist is oure hede, he is glorifyed and vnpassible; and as anenst his body, in whych alle his membris be knytt, he is nott yett fulle glorifyed ne all vnpassible. [31:34-36]

Jesus suffered in solidarity with the whole of humankind, taking on the sufferings of his passion for love of every man and woman.

And for every mannys synne that shal be savyd he sufferyd; and every mannes sorow, desolacion and angwysshe he sawe and sorowd, for kyndnes and loue. [20:19-21][55]

Moreover, the suffering of Christ in his passion was a perfect suffering; in other words, were it possible to have suffered more, Christ would have done so for the love which he bears us.

It is a joy, a blysse, an endlesse lykyng to me that evyr I sufferd passion for the; and yf I myght suffer more, I wolde suffer more. [22:5-7]

Julian tells us that Christ's suffering in his passion is greater than any and all other human suffering,[56] and once again demonstrates the centrality of Christ's incarnation to her thought. His incarnation is not only the *sine qua non* for Christ's passibility, but also the cause of his more perfect suffering: the oneing of Christ's humanity to the Godhead gave him more strength to suffer.

---

54 The theme of Christ's suffering in us will receive more extensive consideration later in this chapter. (See p. 192ff, below).
55 Julian is very clear that Christ's willingness to suffer for us is an expression of his love [22:5-7.32-53; cf. 60:23-26]. Because of his love for us, Christ suffers the passion meekly with great joy [20:28; cf. 51:32] and patience [73:20-22].
56 20:2-9.29-30; 27:22-24; 60:21-22.

And thus saw I oure lorde Jhesu languryng long tyme, for the vnyng of the godhed gaue strenght to the manhed for loue to suffer more than alle man myght. I meene nott oonly more payne than alle man myght suffer, but also that he sufferd more payne than all man of saluacion that evyr was from the furst begynnyng in to the last day myght telle or fully thynke, havyng regard to the worthynes of the hyghest worshypful kyng and the shamfulle dyspyteous peynfull deth. For he that is hyghest and worthyest was foulest co(n)dempnyd and vtterly dyspysed. [20:2-8][57]

Julian gives us two meanings or intentions for Christ's 'suffering with' us in his passion: our salvation and our comfort. First, Christ's passion is our salvation. We are oned to God,[58] redeemed from Adam's sin,[59] washed clean by the passion — a flood of mercy.

For the flode of mercy that is his deerworthy blode and precious water is plentuous to make vs feyer and clene. [61:64-65]

There is a unity of suffering[60] between Christ and humankind; because of his oneing us in himself as his members, Christ is the true subject of our pain, i.e., the locus of the sufferings of humanity is the cross of Christ.[61] It is not that Christ has assumed *our* sufferings; rather, we participate in *his* sufferings. Indeed, Julian explains that Christ's showing us the chere of his passion *is* our experience of pain, of being in 'dis-ease and travail' with him.[62] All our sufferings are with Christ; we have suffered nothing that he does not suffer with us.[63] We are with him on his cross, dying with him in our pains.[64] All our sufferings are turned to our worship and profit by virtue of his passion.[65] This is the fruit of the passion: we become heirs with Christ to bliss because our sufferings are

---

57 Cf. 20:14-19.22-24 (p. 177, above).
58 Christ, 'by the vertu of his passion, his deth and his vprysyng onyd vs to oure substannce.' [58:47-48]
59 Christ's suffering for our sins by his passion 'is more plesyng to the blessyd godhed and more wurschypfulle for mannys saluacion with oute comparyson than evyr was the synne of Adam harmfulle.' [29:12-14]
60 Cf. 18:14-38.
61 18:14-24.36-37. See also p. 132-133, above; cf. Gal 2:20 and Col 1:24.
62 21:21-22.
63 Christ suffered 'all mans payne' [51:287-288] and wills that we 'wytte that we sufferyd ryght nought aloone, but with hym, and see hym oure grownde.' [28:28-29] Cf. 18:15-16.
64 "I vnderstode that we be now in our lordes menyng in his crosse with hym in our paynes and in our passion dyeng, and we willfully abydyng in the same crosse with his helpe and his grace in to the last poynt." [21:11-14]
65 20:30-32; cf. 28:27-28; 56:35-37.

oned.[66] The passion ones us in Christ in such a way that we cannot be separated from God.[67] The devil is overcome by virtue of the passion.

Then he *with*out voys and openyng of lyppes formyd in my sowle these wordes: Here *with* is the feende ovyr come. This worde sayde our lorde menyng his blessyd passyon, as he shewed before. [13:6-8][68]

The consequence of Christ's conquering the devil is that we who are oned in Christ are saved: we shall not be overcome by the 'fiend.'

And ryght as in the furst worde *that* oure good lorde shewde, menyng his blessyd passyon: Here *with* is the fende ovyr come, ryght so he seyde in the last worde *with* full tru feythfullnes, menyng vs alle: Thou shalt not be ovyr come. . . . And this worde: Thou nott be ovyrcom, was seyde fulle sharply and full myghtly, for sekernesse and comfort agaynst all trybulacyons that may come. He seyde nott: Thou shalt not be trobelyd, thou shalt not be traveyled, thou shalle not be dyssesyd; but he seyde: Thou shalt not be ovyrcom. [68:60-63.66-70]

This 'comforting word'[69] is actually the second meaning or intention of the passion: the chere of Christ's passion is a source of strength for us, saving us from 'grudging and despair' in our situation, because we see that his sufferings were much greater than our own.

And that we see his paynes and hys trybulac*i*on passe so ferre alle that we may suffer, that it may nott be full thought. And the well beholdyng of thys wylle doth saue vs from grugyng and despeyer in the felyng of our paynes. [28:29-32]

And thus in the tyme of oure payne and oure woo he shewyth to vs chere of his passion and his crosse, helpyng vs to beer it by his owne blessyd vertu. [71:32-34]

The chere of the passion is thus shown to us in the time of our pains to give us strength in our woe, as an example for us to follow.[70]

---

66 "And the cause why that he sufferyth is for he wylle of hys goodnes make vs the eyers *with* hym in hys blysse." [21:23-25]
67 Christ never leaves the place he has taken in our soul [68:15-17; cf. 51:145-146; 55:30-31; 57:55-56; 81:9-12]. Therefore, nothing comes between our soul and God because 'where the blessyd soule of Crist is, there is the substance of alle the soules that shall be savyd by Crist.' [54:6-8] Cf. 46:38-39; 53:47-49; 54:2-6.
68 Cf. 68:61-62; 70:14-16.
69 Cf. 68:57-58; 70:38-40; see also p. 159-164, above.
70 73:20-24. See also note 55, p. 177, above.

In summary, divine compassion must be seen in the light of the passion of Christ, the central shewing from which all of Julian's insights are developed. Christ's incarnation allows God to 'suffer with' us (compassion proper), making possible the passion as the human expression of divine compassion. By presenting the passion as God's compassion incarnated, Julian situates divine compassion properly in Christ. Moreover, it is his incarnation, the union of his divinity with his humanity, that enables Christ to suffer perfectly, assuming in himself all the sufferings of the whole of humankind. Oneing us in himself, Christ saves us, making us heirs with him to bliss by his passion. He shows us the chere of his passion in order to comfort us in our own sufferings and woes.

2. Christ's compassion

Julian's presentation of the compassion of Christ is in clear correspondence to her portrayal of God's compassion in the parable of the lord and the servant. God has pity and ruth on us in our sufferings, i.e., in our sins. Christ shows us his chere of compassion 'in the time of our sinning.'

> And in tyme of oure synnyng he shewyth to vs chere of reuth and pytte, myghtely kepyng vs and defending agaynst all oure enmys. [71:34-36][71]

Indeed, Julian actually identifies the 'shewing of compassion' with the thirteenth revelation, i.e., Christ's compassion in our sinning.

> Thus I saw how Crist hath compassyon on vs for the cause of synne. [28:2][72]

Christ's compassion is the divine response to us in our sinfulness.

Like the lord of the parable, Christ too keeps us from blame in his sight, excusing us and seeing us as though we were innocent children.

> [Christ's] loue excusyth vs. And of hys gret curtesy he doth away alle oure blame, and beholdeth vs with ruth and pytte, as chyldren innocens and vnlothfulle. [28:33-35][73]

---

71 Cf. 28:33-35; 80:32-34.
72 Colledge and Walsh note that 'the shewing of compassion' [77:33; cf. 31:50] and of 'pytte' [76:20] both refer to 28:2ff. See *A Book of Showings,* notes, pp. 686, 692.
73 Cf. 80:42-43. The allusion to ourselves as innocent children recalls Julian's motherhood imagery (e.g., 63:35-38).

And, as we have seen in the previous section, Christ does more than that. He actually takes on our blame, i.e., the pain of our sins.[74] Christ's passion stands as the ultimate expression of God's 'suffering with' us in compassion for us in our sins; by virtue of his oneing us by his incarnation, Christ 'suffers with' us on his cross, and our pain becomes, in reality, our participation in his pain.[75] We shall now explore Julian's understanding of divine compassion as proper to Christ, i.e., that the chere of compassion derives from his passion and incorporates the mystery of his continuing to 'suffer with' us as we experience the pain brought on by our sins.

a. Christ's compassion is occasioned by our suffering: the human misery and blindness caused by sin

The two understandings assigned to Christ's compassion parallel those given to his passion, i.e., to bring us to bliss (by virtue of his passion) and to comfort us in our pain.[76]

> Ych maner noughtyng that he shewde in hys passion, it was shewde ayene in thys compassion, wher in were two maner of vnderstondynges in oure lordes menyng. That one was the blysse that we be brought to, wher in he wille that we enioye. That other is for comfort in oure payne, for he wille that we wytt that it alle shalle be turned vs to wurschyp and to profyghte by the vertu of hys passyon, and *that* we wytte that we sufferyd ryght nought aloone, but *with* hym, and see hym oure grownde. [28:21-29]

These two understandings follow logically from the fact that Christ's compassion is occasioned by sin in that they correspond to the two effects of sin in our lives: human misery (from which he delivers[77] us by bringing us into bliss by his passion) and spiritual blindness (which he removes by the comfort of revelation). In his compassion for us in our need,[78] Christ not only saves us when we are harrassed and oppressed by sin, but

---

74 For Julian, only pain blames and punishes. [51:115-119 (note 38, p. 172, above)]
75 See p. 178-179, above.
76 See p. 178-179, above.
77 As we have seen, Julian's clearest image of compassionate deliverance is found in the fifteenth shewing—a fair, pure child rising from a bloated mass of stinking mud: "For in this behest I saw a mercyfulle compassion that oure lorde hath in vs for oure woo, and a curtesse behytyng of cleene delyuerance; for he wylle that we be comfo(r)tyd in the ovyr passyng joy." [64:43-46] See also p. 66-67, above.
78 His pity lasts as long as we be in need. [31:46-49; cf. 75:2-4.]

he is also our solace in our sufferings.[79] We are comforted in our pain
by the very revelation of Christ's compassion for us in that pain. What
is important to note is that the revelation that flows from Christ's compassion is Christ himself, i.e., Christ is the compassionate response to our
need. In other words, divine compassion is both the motive and the
content of the revelation that is Christ.[80]

Our blindness evokes the same compassion from Christ as do our
sins. Christ responds compassionately to our need to see,[81] comforting
us with the teaching and preaching of the Church.

> They are prevytes to vs for oure blyndhed and oure vnknowyng. And therfore
> hath he grett reuth, and therfore he wylle make them opyn to vs hym selfe,
> wher by we may knowe hym and loue hym and cleue to hym. For alle that is
> spedfulle to vs to wytt and for to knowe, fulle curtesly oure good lorde wylle
> shew vs what it is *with* alle the prechyng and techyng of holy chyrch. [34:9-14]

Even when it is necessary for us to remain in darkness, Christ has compassion on us in our struggle to understand.[82]

b. Christ's compassion continues in his thirst and longing

Christ's passion was ended by his death on the cross, but his compassion
continues even now. Julian adopts the Johannine image of *thirst*:[83]
Christ's bodily thirst[84] ended with his death on the cross, but his compassionate 'suffering with' us, i.e., his spiritual 'thirst' and 'love-longing,'
continues until all are 'gathered,' completely one with him in heaven.

> For thys is the goostly thyrst of Cryst, the loue longyng *that* lastyth and evyr
> shall tyll we se that syght at domys day; for we that shalle be safe, and shalle
> be Crystes joy and hys blysse, ben yet here, and some be to come, and so shall
> some be in to that day. Therfore this is his thurste and loue longyng of vs, all

---

79 This theme of Christ's comforting us by revelation has already been treated in
    depth in chapter 3 (see p. 143-164, above).
80 For example, it is out of compassion for Julian in her searching that God chooses
    to reveal the incredible depth of divine compassion in Christ through the parable
    of the lord and the servant, thus providing her with the solution to the dilemma
    which 'travailed her reason.' [50:15-16]
81 We need revelation so as to 'keep' ourselves where we can be safe: in the faith of
    the Church. [71:13-14]
82 "Oure lorde hath pitte and compassion on vs for *that* some creatures make them
    so besy therin [the divine privy counsels]." [30:17-18]
83 John 19:28.
84 17:2-49.

to geder here in hym to oure endlesse blysse, as to my syght. For we be nott now fully as hole in hym as we shalle be than. [31:14-20]

[Christ] gaue the vnderstandyng of the gostely thurst that is the loue longyng that shalle last tylle domys day. [63:26-27][85]

Later in the *Shewings*, Julian also refers to God's thirst.

For *the* thurst of god is to haue the generalle man in to hym, in whych thurst he hath drawyn his holy soules, *that* be now in blysse. And so gettyng his lyvely me*m*bris, evyr he drawyth and dryngkth, and yett hym thursthyth and longyth. [75:5-8]

In the above passages we again see the christocentricity of Julian's doctrine on compassion. Although 75:5-8 clearly has some trinitarian allusions, christological overtones still dominate the passage. God's thirst is in and through Christ,[86] and it is Christ who gathers us into himself in the bliss of heaven.[87] Morever, while Colledge and Walsh hold that 'drawyth' alludes to the Father,[88] Julian herself uses the word in clear reference to Christ, maintaining her link to Johannine vocabulary.[89]

He is *with* vs in hevyn, very man in his owne person, vs vpdrawyng; and that was shewd in *the* gostely thyrst. [52:36-37][90]

Elsewhere, Julian does speak of God's drawing us by love, but that 'drawing' is in the context of our 'sight' by prayer.[91] (It is possible to

---

85 Cf. 71:20.

86 Colledge and Walsh note: "Theologically, the Father's thirst is through Christ — 'no man comes to the Father except through me' (John 14.6) — yet the first *colon* refers to the whole Trinity. The second plainly refers to the Son as savior, the thirst to him as head of his Church; but there is also, in *lyvely,* allusion to the life of the Spirit. In the fourth there is in *drawyth* allusion again to the Father — 'no man comes to me unless the Father draw him' (John 6.44), and the last *colon* again refers to the whole Trinity. Furthermore, the *conduplicatio* in *drawyth and dryngk-yth, thursthyth and longyth* refers to the two natures of the Incarnate Word." *A Book of Showings,* notes, p. 678.

87 The notion of gathering ('to geder' [31:190]) also appears three chapters before in reference to Christ's compassion: "I shalle gader yow and make yow meke and mylde, clene and holy by onyng to me." [28:19-20] Cf. Matt 23:37; 11:28-29; Eph 5:25-26, all referring to Christ.

88 See note 86, above.

89 "And I, when I am lifted up from the earth, will draw all things to myself." [John 12:32]

90 Cf. 31:47-49.

91 43:36-37; cf. 46:40.

argue that, since Christ is the ground of our prayer,[92] that 'drawing' also maintains a christological reference.) A christological interpretation is further supported by the final chapter of the *Shewings* where Julian speaks of Christ's drawing our hearts from sorrow and darkness by his self-revelation of love.[93]

Keeping in mind the christological allusions of 75:5-8, we may now examine the three lines which precede it for their christological content in reference to divine pity.

> I saw that god may do alle that vs nedyth; and theyse thre *that* I shall say (vs) nede: loue, longyng (and pytte). Pytte (in) love kepyth vs in the tyme of oure nede; and longyng in *the* same loue drawyth vs in to hevyn. [75:2-4]

Colledge and Walsh note that these opening sentences of chapter 75 are much corrupted and are thus open to wide variations in interpretation.[94] While the text speaks of God as the subject of the pity and longing, the 'pity that keeps us in our time of need' has a clearly christological antecedent in chapter 71 where Julian tells us that Christ shows his chere of pity and ruth and compassion in his sure 'keeping' of those who need his mercy.[95] Moreover, as we shall see below, the 'longing' that 'draws' us into heaven again points to Christ who is the subject of our longing.[96]

The christological overtones of 75:2-8 also shed light on 31:41-52, the only other passage in the *Shewings* which speaks of God's ruth and pity, without at least an implicit reference to the parable of the lord and the servant.

> For as truly as ther is a propyrte in god of ruth and pyte, as verely ther is a properte in god of thurst and longyng; and of the vertu of this longyng in Crist we haue to long ayene to hym, *with*out whych no soule comyth to hevyn. And this *p*roperte of longyng and thyrst comyth of the endlesse goodnes of god, ryght as the propyrte of pytte comyth of his endlesse goodnesse. And thow*g*h he haue longyng and pytte, they ben sondry pro*p*yrtees, as to my syght; and in thys standyth the poynte of gostly thyrst, whych is lastyng in hym as long as we be in need, vs drawyng vppe to his blysse.
>
> And alle this was seen in shewyng of compassion, for that shalle ceacyn at domyes day. Thus he hath ruthe and compassion on vs, and he hath longyng to haue vs, but hys wysdom and hys loue suffer nott the ende to come tylle the best time. [31:41-52]

---

92 41:11; 42:19.
93 86:11-12.
94 *A Book of Showings*, notes, p. 678.
95 71:28-30; cf. 80:32 (note 112, p. 188, below).
96 See p. 185-186, below, for the development of this point.

Because of their context here (i.e., the 'shewing of compassion') and their relationship to Christ's thirst and longing (and to the 'pity,' 'longing,' and 'updrawing' of 75:2-8 with their christological antecedent in 71:28-30), the divine 'properties of pity and ruth' have, in fact, a christological reference. God's pity and longing continue as compassion proper in Christ until the day of eschatological judgment ('domyes day').

The concept of Christ's continuing thirst and longing brings us back to the question of his impassibility. As we have already noted, the risen Christ suffers in his members.[97] Even though Christ is in glory, he continues to moan and mourn with us until we are existentially oned.[98] While impassible in his glorious state, Christ is truly present and compassionate to us in our sufferings. This insight explains Julian's assertion that Christ's thirst and longing find their existential expression in our own painful longing for union with God.

> [For] the kyndly desyer of oure soule is so gret and so vnmesurable that if it were yeve vs to oure joy and oure comfort, alle the nobley *that* evyr god made in hevyn and in erth, and we saw nott *the* feyer blessydfulle chere of him selfe, yett shuld we nevyr leue mornyng ne of gostely wepyng, *that* is to sey of paynfull longyng, tyll whan we see verely the feyer blessedfull chere of oure maker. [72:42-48]

> [And] there I sey he abydyth vs, monyng and mornyng, it menyth all *the* trew felyng *that* we haue in oure selfe, in contricion and in compassion, and alle monyng and mornyng for we are nott onyd *with* oure lorde. And such as is spedfull, it is Crist in vs; and though some of vs feele it sylden, it passyth nevyr fro Crist tylle what tyme he hath brought vs oute of alle our woo. [80:25-31][99]

> For kynde longyng in vs to hym is a lastyng pennance in vs, whych penannce he werkyth in vs, and mercyfully he helpyth vs to bere it. [81:19-21]

The parable of the lord and the servant also situates all human longing in Christ.

> And all that be vnder hevyn, whych shall come theder, ther way is by longyng and desyeryng; whych desyeryng and longyng was shewed in the seruant stondyng before the lorde, or ellys thus in the son stondyng afore the fadyr in Adam kyrtyll. For the longyng and desyer of all mankynd that shall be safe aperyd in Jhe*s*u. [51:260-265]

---

97 See p. 177, above.
98 "[Christ] stondyth alle aloone, and abydyth vs contynually, monyng and mornyng tylle whan we come." [79:38-40]
99 Cf. 79:38-40 (note 98, above); 40:23-26.

Thus, in compassion, Christ patiently suffers in us that painful thirst and longing which is 'speedful' to us, for as long as we are in need,[100] i.e., until that day when we are whole in him.[101] Christ's compassion, his 'suffering with' us, marks the interim until that great day, which will not come until the 'best time' on account of the love he bears us.[102]

c. Christ, our tender and compassionate mother

Julian's christocentric focus reappears in her development of the theme of Christ's motherhood as an image of divine compassion. The compassion of God takes the form of our tender protection and guidance by Christ, our mother of mercy and pity.[103] Although Julian uses 'ruth' and 'pity' only seven times in explicit references to Christ's motherhood[104] and three times in implicit references,[105] the concept of Christ's compassion is integral to the motherhood similitude in the *Shewings*.[106] An overview of her doctrine of Christ's motherhood as it relates to divine compassion will help to situate the more explicit references to Christ's pity and ruth in her treatment of this theme.[107]

Compassion is implicit and integral to the notion of Christ's motherhood, even if Julian's explicit references are few, because motherhood is of its very nature a relationship of compassion. The mother suffers for and with the child—in the act of childbirth itself but also in many other ways until that day when the child reaches maturity. With great tenderness and pity, Christ our mother suffered for us on the cross to bring us to our spiritual birth. In his compassion, he continues to suffer thirst and longing for us until we be fully borne in him to the bliss of heaven. As a wise mother, he 'suffers with' us in our fallings as we learn and mature from our mistakes, not only protecting his children from harm but also turning our wounds to good.

---

100 31:46-49. Christ's compassion bears the same quality of patience as his passion. [73:20-21]
101 31:18-20.
102 31:50-53 (p. 184, above).
103 59:32-33.
104 48:18.25.28; 55:18; 59:33; 61:54.54.
105 75:3.3; 80:32.
106 N.b., Julian never uses the actual word 'compassion' in reference to the 'motherhood' of Christ.
107 For the complete discussion of Julian's doctrine of Christ's motherhood of kind, mercy, and grace, see chapter 3, p. 111-122, above.

Within the motherhood imagery, Julian's direct references to Christ's pity/ruth fall into two areas within the framework of his motherhood of working (i.e., of grace): in her understanding of Christ as our 'mother of mercy and pity' and in her development of the image of the motherhood of working as Christ's tender service to his children.

In considering Christ as our mother of mercy and pity, we are brought back to the fact that, for Julian, divine mercy and compassion are integrally related within the concept of God's 'keeping' us in tender love. Christ's motherhood of mercy is inextricably bound to compassion (or 'pity').

> Mercy is a swete gracious werkyng in loue, medlyd *with* plentuous pytte, for mercy werkyth vs kepyng. [48:17-18]

> Mercy is a pyttefull properte, whych longyth to moderhode in tender loue;
> . . . . Mercy werkyth kypyng, sufferyng, quyckyng and helyng, and alle is of tendyrnesse of love. [48:28-29.30-32]

Julian explicitly attributes to Christ that pity which 'keeps' us in love in the time of our need.[108] It is Christ, our mother of mercy and pity,[109] whose tender 'keeping' brings us to full spiritual birth.[110] Until that day when we are brought to bliss in heaven, Christ protects and preserves us in all tenderness.

> The kynde lovyng moder that woot and knowyth the neyde of hyr chylde, she kepyth it full tenderly, as the kynde and condycion of moderhed wyll.[60:51-53]

Moreover, Julian's frequent use of the word 'tender' in her discussion of Christ's motherly love further suggests the notion of compassion.[111]

Since Julian's image of the motherhood of mercy and grace implies her doctrine of Christ's oneing us by his incarnation, Christ's motherhood can be understood as an image of divine compassion because, by taking on our sensuality, he is able to 'suffer with' us, as one of us. However, we must turn to Christ's motherhood of working to find the clearest references to divine compassion within the motherhood similitude.

---

108 75:2-4; 80:32; see p. 184, above.
109 59:32-33.
110 61:2-3.
111 E.g., 36:45; 48:29.30; 60:31.38.38.53; 61:2; cf. 62:6; 72:26; 80:42; 81:20. Julian's usage of 'tender' reveals her affinity with the scriptural notion of compassion; the Hebrew *raḥᵃmîm* (from *rāḥam*, 'womb'), a word which means the instinctive love of a mother for her child, is translated as *compassion* or *tenderness*. See also p. 211-213, below.

The tender, compassionate mother who suffers for and with her children is Julian's image *par excellence* for Christ's motherhood of working. Christ continues to 'suffer with' us, even after giving us birth by his passion. This compassionate suffering of Christ is the forth-spreading of his motherhood of mercy, i.e., the motherhood of grace or working, Christ's unceasing labor in our endless spiritual birth.

> But mekely make we oure mone to oure derewurthy mother, and he shall all besprynkyl vs in his precious blode, and make oure soule full softe and fulle mylde, and heele vs fulle feyer by processe of tyme, ... And of this swete feyer werkyng he shalle nevyr ceese nor stynte, tylle all his deerworthy chyldren be borne and brought forth; and that shewde he where he gaue the vnderstandyng of the gostely thurst that is the loue longyng that shalle last tylle domys day. [63:20-27]

Here Julian links Christ's motherhood with that divine compassion which continues in Christ's thirst and longing.

Julian describes this 'working' or service of Christ's motherhood of mercy by pointing to various aspects of human motherhood, each of which serves to illustrate different facets of divine compassion. The selfless love of a mother always involves pain, i.e., suffering *for* and suffering *with*.[112] A mother suffers the pains of labor,[113] bearing us to pain and death.[114] Christ bears us to joy and endless bliss by carrying us within himself through his passion and death on the cross.[115] Now that he can die no more,[116] he continues to work as mother, tenderly feeding and sustaining us with the food of his very life in his Church just as the mother feeds her child with her milk.[117] Furthermore, Christ's feeding of his children is truly the fruit of his 'suffering for' us: he leads us to his breast by the wound in his side.[118]

As her child grows, a mother suffers when the child suffers; a mother's wisdom, however, allows her children to suffer for their greater good, e.g., if they might receive virtues and graces by chastisement.[119] So too does Christ 'suffer with' us in ruth and pity if it be of profit to us.

---

112 "For loue sufferyth hym nevyr to be wit*h*out pytte." [80:32]
113 In Julian's day, a mother's risk of death in childbirth was extremely high. This fact heightens the impact of her motherhood imagery.
114 60:19.
115 60:19-24; 63:31-32.
116 The measure of Christ's suffering was perfect. [60:24-27] See p. 177-178, above.
117 60:29-33; cf. 63:32-34.
118 "The moder may ley hyr chylde tenderly to hyr brest, but oure tender mother Jhe*s*u, he may homely lede vs in to his blessyd brest by his swet opyn syde." [60:38-39]
119 60:55-57.

And if we feele vs nott than esyd, as sone be we suer *that* he vsyth the condycion of a wyse moder. For yf he see that it be for profyte to vs to morne and to wepe, he sufferyth *with* ruth and pytte in to *the* best tyme for loue. [61:52-55]

Mercy for loue sufferyth vs to feyle by mesure; and in as moch as we fayle, in so moch we falle, and in as much as we falle, in so moch we dye. For vs behovyth nedys to dye in as moch as we fayle syghte and felyng of god that is oure lyfe. . . . But yet in all this the swet eye of pytte and of loue deperteth nevyr from vs. [48:19-23.25-26][120]

Furthermore, our suffering prompts us to seek help and comfort from the compassionate Christ so that even our falling becomes an occasion for mercy.[121] We are 'kept' and do not perish.

In summary, Julian's christocentric vision of divine compassion is clearly demonstrated in the motherhood similitude of the *Shewings*. It is Christ who is our compassionate mother: he 'keeps' us in his tender love, bearing us to joy by the labor of his passion and 'suffering with' us as we are brought to our full spiritual birth in him.

3. Christ's blessydfulle chere

The two cheres that Christ commonly shows to us in this life are those of his passion and his compassion; but there is yet a third chere of Christ, his 'blessydfulle[122] chere,' which we will truly know only in our full un-ion with him in heaven. Even now, however, by grace we are able to see this blessydfulle chere of Christ present in the two 'common cheres,' but only as a partial foreshadowing of the bliss that will be ours in heaven.

And theyse two be *the* comyn cherys whych he shewyth to vs in this lyfe, ther*with* meddelyng *the* thyrde, and that is his blessyd chere lyke in perty as it shalle be in hevyn; and that is by gracyous toucchyng of swete lyghtenyng of goostly lyfe, wher by that we ar kept in true feyth, hope and cherite, *with* contrycion and devotion and also *with* contemplacion and alle manner of tru joyes and swete comfortes. The blessydfull chere of oure lorde god werkyth it in vs by grace. [71:36-43][123]

---

120 N.b., in this passage we have Julian's only reference to mortification. See *A Book of Showings*, notes, p. 501.
121 See p. 119, above.
122 'Blissful.'
123 Cf. 71:19-25.

Christ's blessydfulle chere can be known by us only in part in this life
because God's mysterious plan for humanity includes our suffering. If we
were to have full sight of Christ's blessydfulle chere here on earth, our
pains would cease and earthly existence would no longer be as God has
planned it.

> And here saw I verely that if he shewde now to vs his blyssedfulle chere, there
> is no payne in erth ne in no nother place *that* shuld trobylle vs, but alle thyng
> shulde be to vs joy and blysse. [21:18-21]

> [For] in *that* precious syght ther may no woo abyde nor wele feyle. [72:30-31]

> And if we were in all the payne that hart may thyngk or tong may telle, and
> we myght in that tyme se his blessydfull chere, alle this payne shule vs nott
> greve. Thus is *that* blessydful syght ende of alle manner of payne to louyng
> soules, and fulfyllyng of all manner joy and blysse. [72:48-52]

Full sight of Christ's blessydfulle chere necessarily ends the darkness and
pain of sin.[124] Julian herself experienced something of this sight of
Christ's blessydfulle chere in the ninth shewing. She had been looking at
Christ's dying on the cross when, suddenly, his face changed from the
chere of the passion to his blessedfulle chere, at which sight her anguish
ceased and she herself became 'glad and merry.'[125]

Like his chere of compassion, the sight of Christ's blessydfulle chere
(i.e., our union with him in heaven) flows from the merits of his passion.
Julian speaks of the

> . . . manyfolde joyes that folowen of the passion of Crist. . . . [One] is that he
> brought vs vp in to hevyn and made vs for to be hys crowne and hys endlesse
> blysse. [23:47.50-51]

Because these 'manifold joys' are Christ's, there is a mutuality implied in
Julian's concept of Christ's blessydfulle chere. While our reward and
bliss consists precisely in the full vision of the blessydfulle chere of Christ
in heaven, we ourselves are the source of Christ's own bliss.[126] Christ's
compassion implies that he not only suffers our pains, but he also 'enjoys'
our joys. Conversely, we stand not only in Christ's passion but also in his
bliss. When he shows us his pain, we are in pain; when he shows us his

---

124 While we are yet on this earth, the darkness of sin prevents us from seeing clearly
the blessydfulle chere so we continue to mourn. [72:32-40] Cf. 51:109-110.
125 21:2-10.
126 'We be his blysse, we be hys mede, we be hys wurshype, we be his crowne.' [22:21-
23] Cf. 22:15-17; 23:18.46.50-51; 31:17.33-34; 51:317-318. See p. 138-140, above.

bliss, we are in bliss (as Julian's experience of the ninth shewing demonstrated).

Not only is Christ's blessydfulle chere present in the cheres of his passion and his compassion,[127] but his blessydfulle chere also bears the mark of his compassion in two ways. First, it is shown to us 'in pity' to solace us in our sufferings.[128] Indeed, this desire of Christ to comfort us in our pain may be the reason why, of the three cheres shown to Julian, the blessydfulle chere was 'oftenest shown and longest continued.'[129] The sight of Christ's face, his blessydfulle chere, comforts us and gives us courage in our sufferings.[130] Secondly, the 'suffering with' of Christ's compassion accompanies his 'rejoicing with us' in our salvation (i.e., the bliss that has been won for us) because we ourselves do not fully experience this bliss until we have reached heaven. Julian uses the symbol of Christ's blood to suggest how Christ continues to 'suffer with' us in our need, even while rejoicing in our future salvation.

> The precious plenty of his dereworthy blode ascendyth vp into hevyn in the blessed body of our lorde Jesu Crist, and ther is in hym, bledyng, preyeng for vs to the father, and is and shal be as long as vs nedyth. And ovyr more it flowyth in all heauen, enjoying the saluacion of all mankynd that be ther and shall be, fulfylling the number that faylyth. [12:26-31]

Thus, until the day of our full union with him in heaven, the hallmark of Christ's bliss is compassion: he is 'with us' in both our suffering and our joy. While we remain in the pains and tribulations of this life, Christ rejoices in our reward—but in pity and compassion for us who still mourn and long[131] for the sight of that blessydfulle chere which will be ours only when we reach heaven.[132]

---

127 Cf. 71:36-38 (p. 189, above).
128 Cf. 72:6-9 in terms of God's blessydfulle chere (see note 35, p. 171, above).
129 72:31-32.
130 71:36-43.
131 72:42-48.
132 "[Oure] lord enjoyeth of the tribulacions of hys sarvanntes with pyte and compassion." [28:10-11]

C. Human Compassion: the Compassion of Christ in Us

Julian begins the *Shewings* by describing her desire to feel compassion for the sufferings of Christ, and she goes on to develop an understanding of human compassion that includes compassion for oneself and for others. For Julian, however, the origin and nature of human compassion cannot be understood apart from the compassion of God in Christ.

In regard to human compassion, Julian uses the word 'compassion' twelve times: nine times in reference to our compassion for Christ[133] and three times in reference to our compassion for others.[134] The word 'pity' is used only twice: once in reference to our compassion for Christ[135] and once in reference to our compassion in general, i.e., without a specific object.[136] The notion of our compassion as a 'suffering with' is also evident in many passages which do not, however, use the actual word 'compassion.'[137]

Julian's notion of the 'wound of compassion' is the logical starting point for a discussion of her understanding of human compassion. She uses the word 'compassion' no less than eight times in either explicit or implicit reference to this 'wounding' of the soul by God.[138] As a result of that wounding (our oneing in Christ), our compassion finds expression in three ways: our compassion for Christ (our love of God); our compassion for others (oned to Christ, we love all whom Christ loves); and our self-compassion (the trust in God which replaces despair).

1. The wound of compassion

Julian opens the second chapter of the *Shewings* by telling us that, sometime prior to her illness, she had desired three gifts 'by the grace of God': 'mind of the passion,' a bodily sickness,[139] and three 'wounds.'

---

133 2:13.42; 3:46.49; 18:2; 20:35; 28:4; 39:23; 80:27.
134 28:4.21; 76:18.
135 59:35.
136 77:31.
137 E.g., 2:11-16; 3:51; 17:50.61-63; 28:28-29.
138 2:42; 3:46.49; 20:35; 39:23.25; 76:18; 80:27.
139 Julian wished to have an experience of illness similar to dying in order to come to terms with death so that she might then live 'more to the worshippe of god by cause of that sicknes.' [2:30-31]

The furst was mynd of the passion. The secund was bodilie sicknes. The thurde was to haue of godes gyfte thre woundys. . . . For the third, by the grace of god and teeching of holie church I conceiued a mightie desyre to receive thre woundes in my life, that is to say, the wound of verie contricion, the wound of kynd compassion and the wound of willfull longing to god. [2:4-6.40-43]

Of these three gifts, Julian attached the greatest importance to the third. Because she considered the first two to be 'outside the common use of prayer,'[140] she had desired them only on the condition that they be, in fact, God's will for her. This was not the case for the third desire, i.e., her desire for the wounds of contrition, compassion and true longing for God. Julian felt that a request for these wounds was well within the orthodox tradition of prayer in the Church and, therefore, in accord with God's will for her.[141] Indeed, she saw the three wounds as prerequisite stages or 'means' of salvation.

And also whom oure lord wylle he vysyteth[142] of his specialle grace with so grett contricion, and also with compassion and tru longyng to god that they be sodeynly delyverde of synne and of payne, and taken vp to blysse and made evyn with seyntes. By contryscion we be made clene, by compassion we be made redy, and by tru longyng to god we be made wurthy. Theyse be thre menys, as I vnderstode, wher by that alle soules com to hevyn, that is to sey that haue ben synners in erth and shalle be savyd. [39:21-29]

Julian thus placed no condition on this desire,[143] and, while her first two desires eventually passed from her mind, this third wish for the three wounds did not fade but 'dwelled with her continually.'[144]

---

140 2:35-36.

141 2:40-43. Julian's request for these particular wounds was consonant with medieval piety. Tugwell notes that Julian's three wounds coincide with the three things which James of Milan (*Stimulus Amoris,* ch. 4) regarded as the essential factors leading to contemplation. Ward likens them to Anselm's three 'piercings' of contrition, compassion, and longing (*Prayers and Meditations*). Pelphrey points out that, while Julian may have been influenced directly or indirectly by Anselmian thought, she gives a different content to his vocabulary. See Simon Tugwell, "Julian of Norwich," in *Ways of Imperfection,* 187; Benedicta Ward, S.L.G., "'Faith Seeking Understanding': Anselm of Canterbury and Julian of Norwich," in *Julian of Norwich: Four Studies to Commemorate the Sixth Centenary of the Revelations of Divine Love,* Fairacres Publication No. 28 (Oxford: SLG Press, 1973) 27-28; and Brant Pelphrey, *Love Was His Meaning,* 207.

142 God 'visits' the soul with the gift of compassion. The wound of compassion is not something of our own doing; rather, we are wounded by God.

143 2:43-45.

144 2:45-46.

When Julian felt herself to be at the point of death, she was suddenly inspired to ask God for one of these wounds, the gift of compassion.

> Then cam sodenly to my mynd that I should desyer the second wound of our lordes gifte and of his grace, that my bodie might be fulfilled *with* mynd and feeling of his blessed passion, as I had before praied, for I would that his paynes were my paynes, *with* compassion and afterward langyng to god. Th(u)s thought me that I might *with* his grace haue the woundes that I had before desyred; but in this I desyred never no bodily sight ne no maner schewing of god, but compassion as me thought that a kynd sowle might haue *with* our lord Jesu, that for loue would become a deadly man. With him I desyred to suffer, liuyng in my deadly bodie, as god would giue me grace. [3:43-52]

In this passage, we have Julian's definition of the wound of compassion: that her body would be filled with the mind and feeling of Christ's passion, that his pains would be her pains.[145]

Julian's request for the wound of compassion is not unrelated to her first 'desire' for 'true mind of the passion.'[146]

> For the furst, me thought I had sumdeele feelyng in the passion of Christ, but yet I desyred to have more by *the* grace of god. Me thought I would haue ben that tyme *with* Magdaleyne and *with* other that were Christus louers, that I might haue seen bodilie the passion that our lord suffered for me, that I might have suffered with him, as other did that loved him. And therfore I desyred a bodely sight, wher in I might haue more knowledge of the bodily paynes of our sauiour, and of the compassion of our lady and of all his true louers that were lyuyng that tyme and saw his paynes; for I would haue be one of them and haue suffered with them. [2:7-16]

Julian wanted to 'suffer with' Christ after the example of Mary and the disciples; she obviously attached great significance to the fact that they were actually present at Christ's passion.[147] However, Julian's understanding of the nature of our compassion for Christ was dramatically amplified by the experience of her shewings.

In response to her request for the wound of compassion, Julian was shown the passion of Christ in vivid detail. As we have already seen, the passion of Christ was the focal point and ground of Julian's shewings; but Julian was also shown Mary, exemplar of all who will be saved.[148] In

---

145 Cf. 17:50-53; 28:3-4. As Jantzen points out, Julian's desire to identify with Christ's passion was consonant both with scriptural tradition (e.g., Matt 16:24; Gal 2:20; Phil 3:10-11; Col 1:24) and with the affective medieval piety of her day. Grace Jantzen, *Julian of Norwich*, 53-57.

146 2:5.19; cf. 77:31.

147 Cf. 2:12-15; 77:30-32.

148 See chapters 4, 18, 25 of the *Shewings*.

pondering the meaning of her shewings, Julian came to her first insight
into the nature of our compassion: she saw that the compassion of Mary,
the compassion of a mother, was the most perfect 'suffering with' Christ
because hers was the most perfect love for him.

> Here I saw in parte the compassion of our blessed lady sainct Mary; for
> Crist and she was so onyd in love that the grettnes of her loue was cause of
> the grettnes of her peyne. For in this I saw a substance of kynde loue contyn-
> ued by grace that his creatures haue to hym, whych kynde loue was most
> fulsomly shewde in his swete mother, and ovyrpassyng, for so much as she
> louyd hym more then alle other, her peyne passyd alle other. For ever the
> hygher, the myghtyer, the swetter that the loue is, the more sorow it is to the
> lover to se that body in payne that he lovyd. [18:2-10]

Julian saw love as the basis of all compassion.[149] Because Mary was
so oned in love to Christ, she suffered more than all others.[150] No pain
equals that of seeing one's beloved suffer.[151] The more we are oned to
Christ, the greater is our love for him and the more we 'suffer with' our
beloved in his pains. This understanding of the compassion of Mary led
Julian to a second insight into the very origin and nature of compassion:
compassion, *suffering with*, is the result of being oned to Christ in love.

> Here saw I a grett onyng betwene Crist and vs, to my vnderstondyng; for
> when he was in payne we ware in payne, and alle creatures that myght suffer
> payne sufferyd *with* hym. [18:14-16]

Julian penetrates to the heart of the wound of compassion: Christ's
oneing us in love *is* the wound of compassion.[152] When we are oned,
Christ makes our soul his dwelling;[153] we no longer suffer alone, but

---

149 Cf. 80:32 (note 112, p. 188, above).
150 Cf. 25:3-37 for a description of Christ's incomparable love for and delight in his
     mother, whom he loves above all other creatures.
151 "But of alle peyne *that* leed to saluacion, thys is the most, to se the louer to suffer.
     How myght ony peyne be more then to see hym that is alle my lyfe, alle my blysse
     and alle my joy suffer? Here felt I stedfastly that I louyd Crist so much aboue my
     selfe that ther was no peyne that myght be sufferyd lyke to that sorow that I had
     to see hym in payne." [17:58-63]
152 Here we must disagree with Panichelli who suggests that the wound of compassion
     refers to God's sending the shewings and that the Long Text is the 'voice which
     speaks from that wound. (In Panichelli's analysis, the wound of contrition is prayer
     and the wound of longing is Julian's experience of reliving the shewings after her
     denial.) Debra Scott Panichelli, "Finding God in the Memory: Julian of Norwich
     and the Loss of the Visions," 303-304.
153 68:15-17; cf. 51:145-146; 55:30-31; 81:9-12.

with him who is our ground.[154] We are so oned that there is a unity of
suffering[155] between Christ and us. As our ground, not only is Christ
the subject of our sufferings, but he is by that very fact also the subject
of our compassion, our 'suffering with'; our compassion is truly a participation in the compassion of Christ, i.e., the working of 'Christ in us.'

> And than saw I that ech kynde compassion that man hath on hys evyn
> cristen *with* charyte, it is Crist in hym. [28:21-22][156]

Julian's trinitarian theology confirms this teaching. Our virtues are
attributed to the operations of the three divine persons within us: our
mildness to the Father, our patience and pity (or compassion) to our
mother Christ, and our hating of sin and wickedness to the Holy Spirit.

> [It] longyth to vs to loue oure god in whome we haue oure beyng, hym rever-
> ently thankyng and praysyng of oure makyng, myghtly prayeng to oure moder
> of mercy and pytte, and to oure lorde *the* holy gost of helpe and grace. For
> in these iij is alle oure lyfe, kynd, mercy and grace, werof we haue myldeheed,
> paycyence and pytte, and hatyng of synne and wyckydnesse. [59:30-35][157]

As the subject of our compassion, Christ suffers even our 'suffering
with' him. Any suffering we experience, including our compassion for *his*
sufferings, is truly his for he 'suffers with' us all that we suffer.

> [Every] mannes sorow, desolacion and angwysshe he sawe and sorowd, for
> kyndness and loue. For in as mech as our lady sorowde for his paynes, as
> mech sufferde he sorow for her sorowse. [20:20-22][158]

---

154 28:28-29.
155 See p. 178-179, above.
156 Cf. 80:26-28 (p. 198, below).
157 Colledge and Walsh interpret this passage differently by assigning our pity to the
operation of the Holy Spirit, arguing that it, too, is part of the *inclusio* of the
phrase which follows it ('for it longyth properly to vertuse to hat synne and wyckyd
nesse'). However, in 76:4-6, Julian attributes the hatred of sin to the teaching of
the Holy Spirit, in a possible reference to John 16:7-8. Moreover, while Colledge
and Walsh relate the virtue of mildness to the lord/Father's disposition to the
servant/Adam/Christ and the virtue of patience to the hard travail of the servant/
Son, they make no attempt to justify the relationship of pity to the Holy Spirit;
indeed, it would seem that pity flows much more logically from 'our moder of
mercy and pytte,' i.e, Christ, than from the Holy Spirit. Cf. *A Book of Showings*,
notes, p. 592.
158 Julian's choice of the word 'kyndness' in this passage is significant. The ambiguity
of meaning in the word 'kyndness' (meaning 'compassion' as well as 'nature') allows
the interpretation that the reason why compassion is possible is that there is a unity
of kind (or nature) between the two parties. Christ's compassion for us is possible

In the shewing of Mary's compassion, Julian saw that the more we are oned to Christ in love, the more we will 'suffer with' him, and the greater his own suffering will be at the pain we experience because we suffer nothing that he does not 'suffer with' us. This insight was perhaps the seed of the motherhood similitude which only appeared in the Long Text, written almost twenty years after the experience of the shewings. Julian first saw that the mother of Christ suffered with her son in all his pains, but only after long years of reflection did she come to see that Christ suffered even Mary's 'suffering with' him. Because Christ's compassion is more perfect than even the compassion of his own mother, Julian understood that Christ is more truly 'mother' to Mary than Mary is to Christ.[159] He bears us and our sufferings in the 'womb' of his own suffering, i.e., his passion.[160]

As the wound of our oneing in love, compassion is an experience of mutuality in love, a compassionate sharing of both pain and joy with the beloved; because we are oned, we suffer what the beloved suffers and rejoice in the beloved's joys.[161] This mutuality in love also explains the fact that our earthly experience finds its ground in Christ. For example, our wounds by sin are Christ's worship, i.e., Christ's suffering the pain of our sins becomes the form his worship of the Father takes.[162] In other words, our experience corresponds to Christ's experience, although existentially it may be felt quite differently because we are not yet fully oned; they are two faces, as it were, of one reality. Consequently, Julian's three wounds are but existential counterparts to various aspects of Christ's love for us. Christ's faithful love is experienced by us as contrition (we perceive his unconditional love as forgiveness);[163] his pains become our own in compassion[164] (we mirror Christ's compassion by sharing his pain as he shares ours); his thirst for us, his drawing us to himself in love, is experienced by us as painful desire or longing for full union with God (we mourn that we are not yet oned).[165]

---

because of his incarnation: he shares our kind.

159 57:47-50; 60:45-47.

160 Julian speaks of the wound in Christ's side almost in terms of a womb [24:3-7]. See also p. 133-134, above.

161 This aspect of compassion was explored in our discussion of Christ's three cheres: when Christ shows us chere of the passion, we are in pain with him; and when he shows us his blessydfulle chere, we are in bliss. See p. 178, 189-191, above.

162 See p. 129-131, above.

163 80:27-31 (p. 198, below).

164 17:52-53.

165 31:42-44; 40:22-26; 51:261-265. The correspondence of our longing to divine longing is made explicit in 75:9-10: "I saw thre manner of longyng in god, and alle

[He] abydyth vs, monyng and mornyng, it menyth alle *the* trew felyng *that* we haue in oure selfe, in contricion and in compassion, and alle monyng and mornyng for we are nott onyd *with* oure lorde. And such as is spedfull, it is Crist in vs; and though some of vs feele it sylden, it passyth nevyr fro Crist tylle what tyme he hath brought vs oute of alle our woo. [80:26-31]

The three wounds are our experience of Christ's love. In our not-yet-oned state of separation from God by sin, we suffer the pain of Christ's wound of love, the wound of compassion; when our oneing is complete, this same wound of love will be experienced, not as suffering, but as the bliss of heaven.

2. Human compassion: fruit of our oneing in Christ

Human compassion is a participation in divine compassion, i.e., God's compassion as expressed in Jesus Christ. Oned to God in Christ, we become compassionate persons — with the very compassion of God; we become true incarnations of the gospel injunction to be compassionate as God is compassionate.[166]

Our compassion takes three forms: (a) compassion for Christ (love of God); (b) compassion for others (love of all those whom Christ loves); and (c) self-compassion (trust in God). Because we are oned to him in love, the sight of Christ's passion fills us with loving compassion for him. Moreover, the sight of Christ's compassion for us in our sin comforts us, leading us to self-compassion[167] and filling us with compassion for other sinners. Oned to Christ, we love all whom he loves.

Julian had hoped that the sight of the passion (Christ's first chere) would deepen her compassion for Christ, as indeed it did.[168] What she did not realize was that she would also experience another form of compassion as a result of the sight of Christ's second chere of compassion; and, as we shall see, in a certain sense our self-compassion springs from Christ's third blessydfulle chere. Thus, there is a real, even if not strict, correlation between Christ's three cheres and the three forms which our compassion takes: our compassion for Christ is prompted by sight of his

---

to one ende, (of which we have the same in vs, *and* of the same vertue, *and* for the same end)."

166 Luke 6:36.
167 By the term 'self-compassion' we mean that one replaces fear and despair with trust in God and thus allows oneself to be healed by by one's very suffering in love.
168 28:3-4; cf. 17:50-63.

sufferings, our compassion for others springs from our being oned to Christ's 'suffering with' others, and self-compassion is the fruit of our trust in the promise of his blessydfulle chere.

a. Compassion for Christ: acceptance of our sufferings for love of God

Our compassion for Christ is his 'working' in us,[169] a result of his oneing us in love. The greater the oneing, the greater is our love and the more we 'suffer with' Christ in his passion. This was seen in Mary's compassion as well as in the compassion of the disciples.[170] However, all creatures 'suffer with' Christ — even if they are unaware of him.

> Here saw I a grett onyng betwene Crist and vs, to my vnderstondyng; for when he was in payne we ware in payne, and alle creatures that myght suffer payne sufferyd *with* hym. That is to say, alle creatures that god hath made to oure servys, *the* fyrmamente and erth, feylyd for sorow in ther kynd in the tyme of Cristes dyeng, for it longyth kyndly to ther properte to know hym for ther lorde, in whom alle ther vertuse stondyth. And whan he feylyd, then behovyd nedys to them for kyndnes[171] to feyle *with* hym, in as moch as they myght, for sorow of hys paynes. And thus tho that were hys fryndes suffered payne for loue, and generally alle; that is to sey, they that knew hym nott sufferde for feylynge of all maner comfort. [18:14-24][172]

While it is our being oned to Christ which makes possible our 'suffering with' him (even if we do not know him), our conscious experience of compassion for Christ flows from true 'sight' of the passion, i.e., from insight into the deepest meaning of his suffering for us. Julian tells us that it is God's will that, as we contemplate Christ's passion, we should feel compassion for him because of the hard pain he suffered for us.[173] The sight of pain alone, however, will never bring us to real compassion; love, not pain, is the ground of compassion. We 'suffer with' because we love the one who is suffering. Thus, true 'sight' or understanding of the passion takes us beyond the bodily pains of Christ on the cross to a

---

169 59:30-35; 80:26-28; cf. 28:21-22; 39:21-29; see also p. 196, above.
170 Along with the example of Mary's compassion [18:7], Julian also presents the disciples as models of compassion for Christ: "And so alle hys dyscyples and alle his tru lovers sufferyd more payn than ther awne bodely dyeng, for I am suer by my awne felyng that the lest of them lovyd hymn so farre abovyn them selfe that it passyth alle that I can sey." [18:10-13] Cf. 2:12-15; 18:22; 77:32.
171 Cf. 20:20-21; see note 158, p. 196-197, above.
172 Cf. 18:34-38.
173 20:33-36.

glimpse of the infinite love which prompted him to endure such pain for us in his 'suffering with' us in his humanity.[174]

> And heer saw I for the seconde beholding in his blessyde passion. The loue that made hym suffer it passith as far alle his paynes as hevyn is aboue erth; for the payne was a noble precious and wurschypfulle dede done in a tyme by the workyng of loue. And loue was without begynnyng, is and shall be without ende. For whych loue he seyde fulle swetely thys worde: If I myght suffer more, I wolde suffer more. [22:45-51]

It is the revelation of Christ's passion that shows us the depth of God's love for us.

This 'sight' of the passion (i.e., the love of God which gives meaning to Christ's suffering and death on the cross for us)[175] evokes our response of love: our compassion for Christ in his suffering.[176] Love is the reason for the pain of our conscious 'suffering with' Christ, even as our oneing makes this same 'suffering with' possible. Our compassion for Christ is the 'face' of our love for God. We see this in Julian's realization that only love could explain the pain she herself experienced at the sight of Christ's passion.

> The shewyng of Cristes paynes fylled me fulle of peynes, for I wyste welle he suffyryde but onys, but as he wolde shewe it me and fylle me with mynde, as I had before desyerde. And in alle thys tyme of Cristes presens, I felte no peyne, but for Cristes paynes; . . . . For me thought my paynes passyd ony bodely deth . . . . But of alle peyne that leed to saluacion, thys is the most, to se the louer to suffer. How myght ony peyne be more then to see hym that is alle my lyf, all my blysse and alle my joy suffer? Here felt I stedfastly that I louyd Crist so much aboue my selfe that ther was no peyne that myght be sufferyd lyke to that sorow that I had to see hym in payne. [17:52-53.56.58-63][177]

---

174 Julian tells us that Christ's willingness to suffer for us is the greatest proof of his love: "And in these wordes: If I myght suffer more I wolde suffer more, I saw truly that as often as he myght dye, as often he wolde, and loue shulde nevyr lett hym haue rest tille he hath done it . . . . For though the swete manhode of Crist myght suffer but oonse, the goodnes of hym may nevyr seese of profer. Every day he is redy to the same, yf it myght be. For yf he seyde he wolde for my loue make new hevyns and new erthys, it ware but lytylle in regarde, for this myght he do ech day, yf that he wolde, without any traveyle. But for to dye for my loue so often that the nomber passyth creatures reason, thys is the hyghest profer that our lorde god myght make to mannes soule, as to my syght." [22:25-28.34-41]

175 See p. 135-136, above, on this second way of 'beholding' Christ's passion.

176 28:3-4.

177 Cf. 18:10-13 (note 170, p. 199, above).

The 'sight' of the passion also necessarily produces in us a hatred of sin, the cause of Christ's suffering.[178] As the only thing that hinders us from union with God,[179] our sin is precisely the obstacle that Christ overcomes in his oneing of us through his passion. As such, it inflicts the pain of the crucifixion. For the person who has 'seen' Christ's passion, the very thought of sin brings Christ's sufferings to mind.

> In *this* nakyd worde: Synne, oure lorde brou*gh*te to my mynde generally alle that is nott good, and the shamfull despyte and the vttermost trybulation that he bare for vs in thys lyfe, and hys dyeng and alle hys paynes, and passion of alle hys creatures gostly and bodely . . . . And (with) the beholdyng of thys, *with* all the paynes that evyr were or evyr shalle be, I vnderstode the passion of Criste for the most payn and ovyr passyng. [27:14-18.22-24]

As we grow in our understanding of sin, our approach to our own suffering changes. The more we understand Christ's passion (i.e., the depth of God's love and the role sin plays as the cause of Christ's sufferings), the more we love God and hate sin,[180] and the more willingly we choose suffering over sin—because sin causes us greater pain.

> For the same tru loue that touchyth vs alle by hys blessyd comfort, the same blessyd loue techyth vs that we shalle hate syn only for loue. And I am suer by my awne felyng, the more that ech kynde soule seeth this in the curtesse loue of our lorde god, the lother is hym to synne, and the more he is asschamyd. For if it were leyde before vs, alle the payne *that* is in hell and in purgatory and in erth, deed and other, than synne we shulde rather chese alle that payne than synne. For syn is so vyle and so mekylle for to hate that it may be lyconnyd to no payne whych payne is not syn*n*e. And to me was shewed none harder helle than synne, for a kynd soule hatyth no payne but synne; for alle is good but syn, and nought is yvell but synne. [40:31-41][181]

We hate sin because we love God, and we are willing to suffer any pain rather than sin against God's love for us.

Thus, in compassion, we willingly embrace Christ's sufferings. This 'embracing' is the fruit of the wound of compassion. It is because of our oneing, i.e., the wound of compassion, that we have a way of sharing in

---

178 "And thus we haue mater of mornyng, for oure synne is cause of Cristes paynes." [52:51-52].

179 27:3-4.

180 In 59:30-36, Julian uses an *inclusio* which explicitly links love of God to the hatred of sin and wickedness. See note 157, p. 196, above.

181 Cf. 63:14-18; 76:5-6.

Christ's sufferings; because of our oneing, our own pains and dying are
one with his.[182]

> I vnderstode that we be now in our lordes menyng in his crosse *with* hym in
> our paynes and in our passion dyeng, and we willfully abydyng in the same
> crosse *with* his helpe and his grace in to the last poynt. [21:11-14]

We are able to 'suffer with' Christ, to share in his passion by the humble,
even joyful,[183] acceptance of our own sufferings.

> We shulde mekely and pacyently bere and suffer *that* pennawnce *that* god hym
> selfe gevyth vs, *with* mynde of hys blessyd passion. For whan we haue mynde
> of his blessyd passion, *with* pytte and loue, then we suffer *with* hym lyke as his
> frends dyd that saw it. [77:28-32]

Our sufferings continue throughout our life until we are completely oned
in the bliss of heaven. Indeed, our very life is a penance which Christ
works in us: our longing for him and the pain that longing brings is
Christ's drawing us to himself.[184]
    Whatever we suffer is fruitful and redemptive because we 'suffer with'
Christ.[185] In our suffering for love of God, Christ works in us the debt
of love we owe to God:

> [And] in this I sawe that alle dett that we owe by gods byddyng to faderhod
> and moderhod is fulfyllyd in trew lovyng of god, whych blessyd loue Cryst
> werkyth in vs. [60:62-63]

Oned to Christ, our suffering increases.[186] As we have seen, the
more we are oned, the greater our 'suffering with'; but, just as Christ's
divinity gave strength to his sensuality to suffer,[187] so our oneing to
Christ gives us strength because Christ becomes our 'ground' in our
suffering.[188] Julian tells us that, paradoxically, the more we are willing

---

182 We stand in Christ's pain; when he was in pain, we were in pain. [18:14-24.34-38]
     See note 117 (p. 129-130) and p. 199, above.
183 Julian gives us example of Christ who suffers for us as a 'cheerful giver.' [23:34-43]
     See also note 55, p. 177, above.
184 "For kynde longyng in vs to hym is a lastyng penannce in vs, whych penannce he
     werkyth in vs, and mercyfully he helpyth vs to bere it." [81:19-21] Cf. 80:26-31 (p.
     198, above); 40:24.
185 Although Julian carefully attributes the fruitfulness of our suffering to Christ, she
     also stresses the importance of our *working with* Christ as his 'helpers' in our oned
     activity by our intention and desire. [57:56-59]
186 As Christ was most sinless, he was most strong to enter into suffering. [20:17-19]
187 20:2-8.17-19 (p. 178, above).
188 28:26-29.

to suffer for love of God, not counting the cost of our sufferings, the less pain there will be in our experience of those sufferings—and the greater will be our reward.

> It is goddys wylle that . . . we take oure abydynges and oure dyssesys as lyghtely as we may take them, and sett them at nought. For the lyghtlyer that we take them, and *the* lesse pryce that we sett at them for loue, lesse payne shalle we haue in *the* feelyng of them, and the more thanke and mede shalle we haue for them. [64:61-67]

> And for this lytylle payne that we suffer heer we shalle haue an hygh endlesse knowyng in god, whych we myght nevyr haue wi*th*out that. And the harder oure paynes haue ben wi*th* hym in hys crosse, the more shalle oure worsch(y)ppe be wi*th* hym in his kyngdom. [21:24-28]

We truly 'suffer with' Christ in our pains on earth. Our oneing to God in Christ does not eliminate our suffering; rather, our suffering increases as we become more oned, but joy replaces sorrow.[189] We find 'heaven' in sharing the sufferings of Christ.[190]

b. Compassion for others: our love for all whom Christ loves

Just as the chere of Christ's passion was the source of Julian's compassion for Christ, so too Christ's second chere, his compassion, evoked a second response of love in Julian: compassion for her 'even christians.'

> Thus I saw how Crist hath compassyon on vs for the cause of synne; and ryght as I was before in the passion of Crist fulfyllyd wi*th* payne and compassion, lyke in thys I was in party fulfylled wi*th* compassion of alle my evyn cristen, for fulle wele he lovyth pepylle that shalle be savyd, that is to seye goddes servanntes. [28:2-6][191]

---

189 Cf. 21:3-16; 15:30-32.

190 Only by taking our stand in the cross of Christ are we safe from the power of sin. This insight caused Julian to choose not to raise her eyes from the crucifix when she was tempted to look up to heaven for comfort. She chose Christ and his sufferings as her heaven: "For I wyst wele that he that bounde me so sore, he shuld vnbynd me whan he wolde. Thus was I lernyd to chese Jh*e*su for my hevyn, whom I saw only in payne at that tyme. Me lykyd no nother hevyn than Jh*e*su, whych shalle be my blysse when I come ther." [19:13-17] Cf. 77:47-48. See also p. 140-142, above.

191 Julian's compassionate concern for her 'evyn cristen,' i.e., all men and women who share her condition as *saved* sinner, is reflected throughout the *Shewings*. E.g., 8:22-24; 9:9-19; 13:27-28; 37:5-13; 68:63-73; 79:1-10.

When we have true 'sight' of Christ's compassion,[192] we share his understanding of the scourge of sin. With such insight, we cannot help but to feel compassion for all men and women who share our painful condition of sinfulness.[193] Our own experience of sin's pain teaches us to recognize that same pain in others — and we 'suffer with' them in their pain. Oned to Christ, we incarnate his own compassion for sinners.

> And than saw I that ech kynde compassion that man hath on hys evyn cristen with charyte, it is Crist in hym. [28:21-22]

Christ himself is the charity with which we love our 'even christians.'[194] The good that we do in the face of evil, i.e., the love of neighbor that we demonstrate in the midst of pain and even rejection, is the working of Christ in us. Because Christ himself is the measure of our love for others, our compassion for sinners must know no bounds.[195]

Just as our compassion for Christ brings with it a hatred for sin,[196] our compassion for sinners also implies a hatred for sin.[197] We 'suffer with' others in their pain — pain that is caused by sin. Like Christ, we hate the sin that causes the suffering, but we have a compassionate love and understanding of the sinner who suffers, not unlike the compassion of a mother for her suffering child. Compassion is the filter through which we must view the sinner.

---

192 Christ 'suffers with' us in the pain and misery our sins cause us. This was Julian's thirteenth shewing, the 'shewing of compassion' [chapters 27-40]. See p. 180-182, above.

193 Seeing ourselves in the light of the Creator who 'keeps' us, we find that the knowledge of our sinfulness and of God's mercy makes us meek and fills us with compassionate love for other sinners: "For of alle thyng the beholdyng and the lovyng of the maker makyth the soule to seme lest in his awne syght, and most fyllyth hit with reuerent drede and trew meknesse, and with plente of charyte to his euyn crysten." [6:64-67] Cf. 36:6-7.40-41; 44:15-21.

194 Here again Julian echoes John: God's presence in us is reflected in our love of neighbor. Cf. 1 John 4:12.16.

195 "For Crist hym selfe is ground of alle the lawes of cristen men, and he taught vs to do good ayenst evylle. Here we may se that he is hym selfe thys charite, and doyth to vs as he techyth vs to do; for he wylle that we be lyke hym in hoolhed of endlesse loue to oure selfe and to oure evyn cristene. No more than hys loue is brokyn to vs for oure synne, no more wylle he that oure loue be broken to oure selfe nor to our evyn cristen; but nakydly hate synne, and endlesly loue the soule as god louyth it. Than shulde we hate synne lyke as god hateth it, and loue the soule as god loueth it." [40:45-53]

196 See p. 201, above.

197 See 40:49-53 (note 195, above).

For *the* beholding of other m(a)nnes synne, it makyth as it were a thyck myst afore *the* eye of *the* soule, and we may nott for *the* tyme se the feyerhede of god, but yf we may beholde them *with* contrycion *with* him, *with* compassion on hym, and *with* holy desyer to god for hym. For *with* out this it noyeth and trobelyth and lettyth the soule that beholde them; for this I vnderstande in *the* shewyng of *the* compasssion. [76:15-21]

We see that Julian goes even further in regard to our compassionate view of our 'even christians.' She warns that we should be looking at our own sins and not at the sins of others unless it might contribute in some way to their help or comfort in their suffering.[198]

In her 'sight' of Christ's compassion, Julian realized that everything God had revealed about divine compassion for her in her sinfulness applies not just to herself, but to all her 'even christians.'[199] She understood her unity with all men and women, both here on earth and in heaven, as one body in Christ.[200] To be oned in Christ means to be oned in love with all of humankind.

[The] charyte of god makyth in vs such a vnitie that when it is truly seen, no man can parte them selfe from other. [65:18-20]

What may make me more to loue myn evyn cristen than to see in god that he louyth alle that shalle be savyd, as it were alle one soule? [37:13-15]

The chere of Christ's compassion brings us to a deeper understanding of our unity with all who open themselves to Christ's saving action. We see that his compassion for us embraces all of humankind and that, oned to Christ, we must love all whom he loves. We become reflections of his compassion to all our 'even christians.'[201]

c. Self-compassion: our trust in God

The phrase 'compassion for self' does not actually appear in the *Shewings*; however, while not explicitly articulated, the notion of 'self-compassion'

---

198 "And ther was I lernyd that I shulde se my awne synne and nott other mennys, but if it may be for comfort or helpe of my evyn crysten." [79:9-10]

199 37:5-13.

200 9:5; 30:24; 61:60-61. Here, and below, our references to 'all men and women' (or 'all humankind') must be interpreted within the parameters Julian consistently maintains: she confines her reflections to 'all those who shall be saved.'

201 Indeed, in the the very writing of the *Shewings*, Julian reflected Christ's compassion. In her compassion for her 'even christians,' she wanted them to be comforted as she had been comforted. Cf. 8:22-24; 9:9-19; 13:27-28; 37:5-13; 68:63-73; 79:1-10.

is implied in what Julian has to say about our compassion for others. Oned in Christ, we are also oned with all men and women who share our sinful human condition. Our compassion for others necessarily includes compassion for ourselves as members of one same body.

Like our compassion for others, self-compassion also finds its source in Christ's chere of compassion. We are invited to extend to ourselves the same love that Christ extends to us.

> [Christ] wylle that we be lyke him in hoolhed of endlesse loue to oure selfe and to oure evyn cristene. No more that hys loue is brokyn to vs for oure synne, no more wylle he *that* oure loue be broken to oure selfe nor to our evyn cristen; but nakydly hate synne, and endlesly loue the soule as god louyth it. Than shulde we hate synne lyke as god hateth it, and loue the soule as god loueth it. [40:47-53]   ,

Accordingly, to love ourselves as Christ loves us requires a compassionate love;[202] we must adopt his chere of compassion for us in our sinning.[203] As Christ loves sinners while hating their sin, so too self-compassion (like our compassion for others) requires that we love ourselves even while hating our sin.[204] This kind of self-love presumes self-knowledge.

True self-knowledge is to see ourselves as our Creator sees us, i.e., as sinners — but always in the light of divine compassion for us in our sinning.[205] We see both our sin (with our inability to repair the damage we cause by it) and God's everlasting love and plenteous mercy.[206] With such self-knowledge we discover our true value, and that we must love and respect the self because God made us and loves us and 'keeps' us — despite our sinning.[207] Without this self-knowledge, we fall prey either to presumption (we fail to see our sin)[208] or to despair (we see only our sin and fail to see God's compassion and mercy).[209]

---

202 Christ's love 'sufferyth hym nevyr to be wi*th*out pytte.' [80:32]

203 Cf. 28:33-35; 71:34-35.

204 40:42-53; see also p. 204-205, above.

205 "Owre lorde of his mercy shewyth vs oure synne and oure feblynesse by the swete gracious lyght of hym selfe, for oure synne is so foule and so horryble that he of his curtesy wylle not shewe it vs but by *the* lyght of his mercy." [78:2-5] Cf. 40:2-5; 79:22-39.

206 52:76-80.

207 5:17-19.44-46; 44:19-21.

208 Julian tells us that if we see only God's love for us and not our own sinfulness, we are tempted to be 'more reckless in our living or in the keeping of our heart.' [79:26-29]

209 The remedy for despair is true 'sight' of our situation. See p. 146-147, above. Without 'sight,' we become weighed down by depression and doubt. [42:45-46]

Hating our sin is not the same as hating ourselves. It is right that we should hate our sins. True 'sight' of the horror of our sin makes us ashamed and breaks us of our pride and presumption.[210] If, however, we lack understanding of the divine perspective on sin, we so fear God's judgment[211] that we despair at the sight of our sins: instead of being compassionate to ourselves, we hate ourselves so much that we cannot allow ourselves to accept help and healing — even from God. An extreme form of self-hatred, despair is the very antithesis of self-compassion and is also incongruous with our compassion for Christ. Hating ourselves causes Christ additional pain since he suffers that anguish with us.[212]

Self-compassion, then, means that we adopt Christ's attitude towards us. Christ hates our sin as the cause of our pain and separation from him; however, he does not condemn us but bears our suffering with us until we are fully oned with him in the bliss of heaven. The self-compassionate response to the sight of our sin reflects this compassion of Christ: we do not condemn ourselves because of our sins, but patiently[213] and meekly suffer the pain they bring, trusting God to deliver in mercy.[214] If we look only at our sins, self-hatred (despair) is the result; if we look

---

210 "For sothly vs nedyth to see it [our synne], and by *the* syghte we shulde be made ashamyd of oure selfe, and br(o)kyn downe as agay*n*st oure pryde and oure presumpcion. For vs behovyth verely to see *that* of oure selfe we are ryght nought but synne and wrechydnesse." [78:16-19] Cf. 79:11-14.19-20.

211 76:36-39. Julian categorizes both depression and despair as manifestations of 'doubtful dread.' [73:11.37-38] When we look at our sins, it seems to us that we deserve to be cast away and forsaken by God [39:18-19]; in our 'useless depression' [73:46-47; cf. 76:40-43; 77:35-36; 79:35-36] over our 'oft and grievous falling,' we are prone to despair [39:41]. Julian warns that such doubtful dread is a sickness [73:9-11] and should be rooted out, especially when it masquerades as humility [73:39]. In the light of her own experience, Julian asserts that it is the devil that actually prompts one to doubtful dread [69:7-8; cf. 76:30-44; 78:38-42; 79:25-26].

For Julian, fear (doubtful dread) is the basis of despair because it causes us to doubt the unchangeability of God's goodness. [74:12-16; 76:30-39] The only dread that is to our benefit is that which comes with seeing our own insignificance in the light of the greatness of the Creator. This is the 'drede of our lorde to which meekenes is knyt' [65:10-11], the dread that saves us from presumption [79:11-14.19-20]. Julian gives Mary as an exemplar of this meekness. [4:35-37; cf. 44:15-21; 75:30-45.]

212 20:20-21.

213 Besides despair, impatience is the only specific sin Julian warns us against. [73:9-10; cf. 10:87-90; 64:10-12; 76:30-39.] This is not surprising, given the fact that she lived at a time in history when patience was severely tested by such horrors as the Black Death, frequent famines, and the Hundred Years War. Cf. 64:13-26; 73:20-24; 74:3-6.

214 77:20-23. God wants us to trust [10:95-96], which trust is 'never in vain.' [74:48:50].

at our sins in the light of God's love and mercy, we are led to trust. Trust in God is the self-compassionate response to one's own sinful human condition.

Trust in God, i.e., the true self-compassion that springs from self-knowledge, is always recognizable by two characteristics: meekness and joy.[215] *Meekness,* the result of knowing the terrible reality of our sin,[216] manifests itself in our willingness to enter into the process of continual conversion, i.e., we fall neither into despair nor presumption. Instead, meekly accepting the fact that we will fall continuously, we rise willingly and quickly whenever we fall.

> And if we by oure blyndnesse and oure wrechydnesse ony tyme falle, that we redely ryse, . . . and go forth *with* god in loue, and neyther on that one syde fall ovyr lowe, enclynyng to dyspeyrs, ne on that other syde be ovyr rechelesse, as yf we geue no forse; but mekely know oure febylnes, wyttyng that we may nott stonde a twynglyng of an ey but *with* kepyng of grace, and reverently cleue to god, in hym oonly trustyng. [52:60-68][217]

Thus, knowledge of our sin and weakness produces meekness, and meekness makes us safe[218] because it causes us to cling to Christ, our 'salve'[219] in our woundedness. This is the heart of self-compassion: to cling to the Lord in trust. In our sinful state, the wisest and most self-compassionate thing we can do is to cling to Jesus.[220] The most foolish and least self-compassionate course of action is to despair and remain in our sins.[221] Thus, to cling to Christ means to rise quickly when we fall.

While the sight of our sin and weakness are 'matter for meekness,' our knowledge of God's love and compassion for us produces the second characteristic of our trust in God: our *joy.*[222] In a certain sense, the joy that pervades our trust in God is actually the result of our 'sight' of Christ's blessydfulle chere, i.e., the joy of our union with him in heaven. Even as we suffer in our sins, we are comforted and strengthened by the assurance of our faith, that partial 'sight' we have now of the bliss that

215 36:40-43; 79:19-21.
216 6:64-67;36:40-43.64-66;52:75-81;61:10-34;75:30-45;78:16-19.36-38;79:11-14,19-20; see also p. 153-154, 160-162, and note 193, p. 204, above.
217 Cf. 76:10-11; 77:6-8.
218 78:36-38; cf. 61:30-31.
219 79:39.
220 76:24-30; cf. 77:14-15.50-51; 82:9-15.
221 76:30-43.
222 79:15-21; cf. 24:20-31; 36:40-43; 52:51-53.

will be ours in Christ in heaven. We rejoice more in the love of God manifest in Christ than we sorrow in our many and frequent fallings.[223]

Paradoxically, the very joy we experience in Christ's blessydfulle chere causes us to mourn that we are not yet completely oned. Because of the wound of compassion, Christ's action of drawing us to himself is experienced in us as a longing for him.[224] The more Christ reveals his blessydfulle chere to us, i.e., the more Christ draws us to himself, the more painful our longing for union becomes in us.[225] Because we have seen the promise contained in Christ's blessydfulle chere, however, we joyfully await the full bliss of heaven in hope, even while we are mourning and longing for Christ.

Our mourning is, thus, itself a form of self-compassion because it is done in trust, not in despair, and because it is the result of the wound of compassion, i.e., it is Christ in us, 'thirsting and longing' for us,[226] who is the subject of our mourning until we are fully oned with him:

[Christ] stondyth alle aloone, and abydyth vs contynually, monyng and mornyng tylle whan we come. [79:36-38]

[And] there I sey he abydyth vs, monyng and mornyng, it menyth alle *the* trew felyng *that* we haue in oure selfe, in contricion and in compassion, and alle monyng and mornyng for we are nott onyd *with* oure lorde. [80:25-28]

Moreover, when we are blinded by our sin and unable to take solace and courage from his cheres, Christ maintains our self-compassion all alone, mourning our sin until we return to him in trust from our despair.

For loue sufferyth hym nevyr to be *with*out pytte; and what tyme *that* we falle in to synne and leue *the* mynde of hym and *the* kepyng of oure owne soule, than beryth Cryst a loone alle *the* charge of vs. And thus stondyth he monyng and mornyng. Than longyth it to vs for reverence and kyndnesse to turne vs hastely to oure lorde, and lett hym nott aloone. He is here aloone

---

223 81:14-15.
224 See p. 197-198, above.
225 "And evyr the more clerly that the soule seeyth the blyssefull chere by grace of lovyng, the mor it longyth to se it in fulhed, that is to sey in his owne lycknes. For not*with*stondyng that oure lorde god dwellyth now in vs, and is here *with* vs, and colleth vs and beclosyth vs for tendyr loue, that he may nevyr leue vs, and is more nere to vs than tonge may telle or harte may thyngke, yet maye we nevyr stynte of mornyng ne of wepyng nor of sekyng nor of longyng, tyll whan we se hym clere in his blessydfulle chere." [72:23-30]
226 "He is *with* vs in hevyn, very man in his owne person, vs vpdrawyng; and that was shewd in *the* gostely thyrst." [52:36-37] Cf. 31:14-20; 63:26-27; see also p. 182-186, above.

with vs alle; that is to sey, only for vs he is here. And what tyme I be straunge
to hym by synne, dyspeyr or slowth, then I lett my lorde stonde aloone, in as
moch as he is in me. [80:32-39]

The wound of compassion is medicine for the wound of our sin.[227]
Because we are oned to Christ who is our 'salve,'[228] the pain we suffer in
our woundedness becomes a sign of hope: as our very scars bear witness,
our pain is the pain of healing. Ultimately, self-compassion means that
we allow ourselves to be healed. When we are truly self-compassionate,
meekness replaces presumption and joy replaces despair: we hate our
sins and mourn that we are not yet oned fully, but we do so in trust,
meekly clinging to Christ and joyfully bearing the sufferings caused by our
sin.[229] As we grow in self-knowledge,[230] so too should we grow in self-
compassion, for self-knowledge is nothing more than the understanding
of the truth of our human situation, which truth *is* the compassion of
Christ for us in our sinning. Oned to Christ, we become bearers of his
same compassion to ourselves. We allow ourselves to trust in his healing
love, despite our temptation to despair at the sight of our sinfulness. We
allow ourselves to rejoice in the sight of Christ's blessydfulle chere for us,
even while we mourn the sin that still separates us from the fullness of
that union with him, which mourning is the way we experience Christ's
own thirst and longing for us. Our self-compassion is the very compassion of Christ for us — *in* us.

---

227 39:25-32; cf. 39:7-9.

228 79:39; cf. 82:12-14.

229 Our meekness and joy in suffering mirror that of Christ's. See note 55, p. 177, and
note 183, p. 202, above.

230 Like our sight of Christ's blessydfulle chere, the self-knowledge we have in this life
is always incomplete. Thus, we only know ourselves in faith (see p. 157, above).
When we know and see clearly what our true 'selves' are, we shall also know God
in fullness of joy. [46:2-5.10-12] Self-knowledge comes from knowing Christ, who
reveals in himself the true meaning of humanity (see p. 49-50, 79, above).
Moreover, Julian tells us that the reason she was shown Mary was so she might
know herself, i.e., the virtues and meekness to which humanity is called. [25:18-22;
cf. 7:2-11]

Excursus: Scripture, Compassion, and Julian's Theology

Julian's understanding of divine compassion is closely related to the biblical concept of compassion. Scholars are in general agreement that Julian's theology and language reflect a strong scriptural influence. In their analysis, Colledge and Walsh cite hundreds of references or allusions to scriptural texts and even conclude that Julian made her own translations from the Vulgate.[231] A more conservative approach to the question of Julian's familiarity with scripture is rightly taken by Reynolds who holds that the most significant single influence on the *Shewings* is the Bible (both Old and New Testaments)[232] and attributes Julian's direct references to scripture and her many allusions to and borrowings from scripture (both its ideas and phraseology) to a mind steeped in scriptural language and thought.[233] This would not be unexpected as Julian lived in a culture whose art, entertainment, and education was dominated by religious and biblical themes. In any case, it is obvious to even the casual reader of the *Shewings* that Julian was familiar with biblical characters (e.g., Mary, Peter, Mary Magdalen, Pilate) and often incorporated scriptural themes, phraseology, and allusions. Moreover, her theology stands squarely within the scriptural tradition, especially Pauline and Johannine thought.[234] We shall now examine the remarkable degree of correspondence between Julian's theology of divine compassion and the biblical understanding of God's compassion.

The scriptural vocabulary of compassion is richly nuanced. The meaning of the word 'compassion' carries with it elements of mercy, tenderness, pity, graciousness, and faithful love, within the context of a relationship of piety.[235] The Hebrew *rah*ᵃ*mîm* (from the root *rāham*,

---

231 Edmund Colledge, O.S.A. - James Walsh, S.J., *A Book of Showings*, 43, 779-788; "Editing Julian of Norwich's Revelations: A Progress Report," 408-411.
232 Sister Anna Maria Reynolds, C.P., "Some Literary Influences in the Revelations of Julian of Norwich," 20.
233 *Ibid.*, 20-22.
234 See also Sr. M. Dulcidia, "Dame Julian and St. Paul," *Cross and Crown* 7 (1955) 100-106; Sr. Mary Paul, *All Shall Be Well, Julian of Norwich and the Compassion of God*, 4-7, 20-23; and "Julian of Norwich and the Bible," in *Julian of Norwich: Four Studies to Commemorate the Sixth Centenary of the Revelations of Divine Love*, Fairacres Publication No. 28 (Oxford: SLG Press, 1973) 11-23; Brant Pelphrey, *Love Was His Meaning*, 331-349; James Walsh, S.J., "God's homely loving: St. John and Julian of Norwich on the divine indwelling," *The Month*, NS 19 (1958) 164-172; and note 78, p. 16, above.
235 *Piety* is here understood in its biblical meaning: at the level of human relations, it

the 'womb' or maternal bosom) and the Greek *oiktirmos* (the 'feeling' of compassion) and *splanchna* (the 'bowels' — by which is meant the seat of the emotions, i.e., the heart, that which is moved to pity) are all used to denote various facets of compassion. *Eleos*, commonly translated 'mercy,' is the usual Greek translation of the Hebrew *ḥeseḏ* (the relationship of piety which implies fidelity, loving kindness, grace), but it is also used as a translation of *raḥᵃmîm*; the verb form *eleēmosynē* is used to render the Hebrew *sᵉḏāqâh*, the righteousness that has, as its standard, God's merciful fidelity to the covenant.[236] In summary, divine compassion is best understood as divine love concretely expressed in history in acts of mercy/grace within the context of a relationship: God's covenant with Israel (which, in the New Testament, becomes the Church). God's compassion is an intimate relationship of tenderness translated into action. Similarly, human compassion is human love manifested in outward acts for others within the context of a faithful relationship — family, tribe, or community.

The connections between scriptural vocabulary and Julian's theology of compassion may be summarized as follows:

1. Divine compassion is divine love concretely expressed in history in acts of mercy/grace within the context of a intimate relationship.

Scripture	*Shewings*
a. Relationship (*ḥeseḏ* or piety) is the ground of compassion. In the Old Testament, this relationship is God's covenant with Israel; in the New Testament, the relationship is grounded in Christ our brother, head of the Church and her spouse.	Christ is mother, brother, and spouse. We are oned to God in Christ; treasured in Christ, we share in the intra-trinitarian love of God. Christ is our head, our ground; we participate in his humanity — and share his pain.
Num 14:19; Hos 2:19-23; Rom 8:29; Rom 8:29; 12:5; Eph 5:31-32.	*18:14-16; 28:28; 51:255-257; 53:32-40; 54:2-8; 56:4; 58:15.26-27.*

---

is the mutual relationship of compassionate goodness which unites relatives, friends, and allies; in relations with God, piety denotes the covenantal relationship God establishes with Israel, i.e., God's merciful love for Israel and Israel's filial attachment of loving obedience and worship of God. Christ becomes the source and model of piety for the christian. See Marc-François Lacan, "Piety," in *Dictionary of Biblical Theology*, edited by Xavier Léon-Dufour (London: Geoffrey Chapman Publishers, 1973) 429-430.

236 Hans-Helmut Esser, "Mercy, Compassion," in *The New International Dictionary of New Testament Theology*, Vol. 2, edited by Colin Brown (Grand Rapids: The Zondervan Corporation, 1986) 593-601.

Scripture	Shewings
b. Divine compassion is *rah^amîm* — the intimate, tender, and instinctive love of a mother[237] for her child (or the brotherly/sisterly love that exists between those born from the same womb). This compassion has its seat in the maternal bosom (*splanchna,* the 'bowels' or heart of a father/ brother). God's compassion is like the instinctive 'suffering with' of the mother/brother/sister.	God has pity/ruth on us in our sin (and the suffering it causes us) because, when God looks at us, God sees Christ and extends to us the same compassion that is reserved properly to the Son. Christ 'suffers with' us because, by virtue of his incarnation, he shares his humanity with us. Christ is our mother who 'suffers with' us in our pain until we are borne to full bliss in him.
Gen 43:30; 1 Kgs 3:26; Jer 31:20; Luke 1:78.	*20:14-26; 31:34-36; 51:100-140; 51:254-256; 52:41-46; 57:42-46; 60:19-20; 61:2-3; 80:32.*
c. Divine compassion is *ḥesed/eleos,* a freely-given relationship of tenderness translated into historical acts of mercy (protection/deliverance/providence and forgiveness/restoration). Compassion is occasioned by human misery: God is moved by our appeals for mercy, our cries for help in our distress. We must admit our sinfulness in order to be beneficiaries of divine mercy.	Divine mercy is God's plan for our salvation/oneing in Christ; mercy defines our nature and is experienced in time as God's free gift of grace. We are 'kept' (protected) and delivered from our pain by Christ who restores us by his passion, bearing us to heaven in himself. We must meekly know/accuse ourselves as sinners and flee to Christ, our 'keeper' and savior.
Exod 3:7; 33:19; Isa 63:7; Jer 3:11-13; Rom 11:32; Heb 2:17.	*5:44-45; 52:30-31.70-80; 55:2-6; 58:24-26; 68:43-45; 77:14-16.49.*
d. God's compassion is more than familial affection; it is God's fidelity to self, a merciful maintaining of the covenant (*ṣ^edāqâh/eleēmosynē*). Divine compassion is always freely given because God retains sovereign freedom to make the covenant with whomever God wills.	Christ's motherhood has made him 'debtor' to us for the sake of love: as with the covenant, all of the obligation on God's part is freely chosen for love. God is never wroth with us, but 'ever the same in love.' In God's unchangeable love we have our 'sureness of keeping.'
Exod 33:19; 34:6-7; Pss 25:6-7; 51:1.	*11:44-45; 48:7-16; 49:4-13; 53:26-35; 60:28-29; 85:7-10.*

---

237 See also note 10, p. 110, above, for additional references to the scriptural theme of divine motherhood.

Scripture	*Shewings*
e. Divine compassion is not bound by finite, human limitations. God's tender compassion triumphs over sin: God's justice *is* mercy in the economy of salvation. Divine justice has particular reference to the poor and the afflicted.	Our salvation derives from God's 'rightful' judgment which is based on our substance 'kept whole and safe' in Christ. This is a 'hard and marvelous love' which cannot be broken by offenses. We shall not escape affliction, but we shall be rewarded for our pains.
Pss 5:7-8; 33:4-5; 40:10-11; 98:2-3; 103:8-10; Isa 54:7-8; Hos 11:8-9; Rom 1:16-17; 9:22-23.	*14:2-36; 38:4-6; 39:40-48; 45:2-12; 51:49-58; 61:27; 68:66-70.*
f. Divine mercy and compassion become part of Israel's eschatological hope; in the New Testament, they are linked to the final consummation in Christ.	On the last day, 'all shall be well'and we shall see it for ourselves. The compassionate work of mercy and grace finished,we shall be fully, existentially oned to God in Christ in bliss.
Isa 14:1; 49:13; Jer 12:15; 2 Tim 1:18; Jude 21.	*31:2-12.50-52; 36:2-7.*

2. God's compassion is perfectly expressed in the person of Jesus Christ.

Scripture	*Shewings*
a. Jesus' compassion reveals the heart of the Father of mercies. Christ is the merciful high priest whose solidarity with humankind assures us of his mercy and compassion. His passion and death open the gates of mercy.	Jesus is divine compassion incarnated: we have no vision of the Father except in Christ. Having oned us in himself, Christ 'suffers with' us as our ground. The blood of his cross is a 'flood of mercy.'
2 Cor 1:3; Heb 2:17; 4:14-16.	*22:12-14; 28:29; 51:140-44; 61:64.*
b. Christ is moved to compassion in the deepest, inner seat of his emotions *(splanchnizomai),* which compassion gives rise to outward acts: healing the sick, teaching and feeding the hungry masses, raising the widow's son.	Christ is moved by love to suffer for us; if he could suffer more for us, he would suffer more. He leads us to bliss through his pierced heart, the open wound of his side. We flee to the Church, 'our mother's breast.'
Mark 1:41; 6:34; 8:2; Luke 7:13.	*22:25-28.45-53; 24:3-25; 60:38-40.*

3. Our relationship to God grounds the debt/duty of human compassion.

Scripture	*Shewings*
God's covenant binds us to the members of the covenant community in a relationship of compassion. In the New Testament, the covenant community becomes the Church, the Body of Christ. Moreover, Christ extends the debt/duty of compassion universally and without limitation: all are neighbors. We are to be 'compassionate as our heavenly Father is compassionate,' having heartfelt sympathy/compassion *(oiktirmos)* for one another, i.e., the the very compassion of the heart *(splanchna)* of Christ.	We are one body in Christ; he is the head and we are his members. Oned to God in Christ, we cannot see ourselves apart from all men and women — our 'even christians.' We are all one in love. Christ himself is the charity and compassion we have for our 'even christians.' *9:5; 28:2-6.21-22; 31:34-36; 40:45-53 61:60-61; 65:18-20; 51:255-257; 76:15-21.*
Matt 18:33; Luke 6:36; Rom 12:5; 2 Cor 1:3-4; Phil 1:8; Col 3:12.	

Having noted so many clear parallels between scripture and the *Shewings,* we may now consider once again the thorny question of Julian's understanding of divine wrath, this time in relationship to the biblical perspective.[238] According to the Old Testament, sin provokes the wrath of God; instances of divine anger and chastisement punctuate the history of Israel.[239] The New Testament records many occasions on which the anger of Jesus flared,[240] and Paul tells us that the wrath of God is set against human wickedness.[241] Julian, on the other hand, insists that there is no wrath in God, but rather an unchanging stance of compassionate mercy and love towards sinners. Wolters suggests that Julian's doctrine on divine wrath must be considered, at the very least, heterodox in terms of the scriptural tradition.[242] A more insightful analysis is offered by Pelphrey who interprets Julian to use 'wrath' to refer to the way of the 'fiend' (the destructive anger that characterizes all that is not of God) in

---

238 See also p. 33-36, 43, above.
239 E.g., Isa 30:27-33; Num 12:9-15; Exod 32:1-35; Ezek 20:33-38.
240 E.g., Matt 11:20-24; 12:34-37; 23:29-36; Mark 3:1-5; John 2:13-17.
241 Rom 1:18.
242 Clifton Wolters, ed., *Revelations of Divine Love,* 36-37.

contrast to the steadfast love and gentleness of God.[243] Pelphrey, however, does not really address adequately the problem of the seeming
contradiction between Julian's position and the scriptural accounts of
divine wrath.

While not agreeing with Wolters' assessment, we must also assert that
any attempt to judge Julian as orthodox by simply reducing the biblical
notion of divine wrath to a mythical portrayal of human experience (or
to a projection of our experience on God) would be to deny the gravity
of the problem of sin and human responsibility. As Sr. Mary Paul points
out, wrath is neither a property of God nor a description of a divine
mood; wrath is the name given to God's judgment of sin.[244] As divine
Love itself, God is absolutely opposed to evil and sin; however, as Julian
might say, God's love is the higher truth.[245] Divine wrath, then, is always for the sake of divine love; by virtue of that love, God stands opposed to all that is harmful to us. It is precisely this divine opposition to
evil that is experienced, in us, as wrath (i.e., wrath as defined in the
Shewings). Julian does not deny that this opposition to evil exists in God;
on the contrary, she affirms it[246] and insists that God is ever the same

---

243 Pelphrey argues: "If we take the bald statement that 'there is no wrath in God' by
     itself, we may indeed doubt that Julian was very orthodox at all—even less that she
     knew something of the accounts of God's wrath in the Old Testament. On the
     other hand, her argument is really quite different. In ch. 13 she is taught how the
     'Fiend' is overcome by the passion of Christ. The malice and wrath of Satan is
     contrasted with the love and gentleness of God, who has the best interest of his
     beloved in mind. Julian hardly denies that God despises sin, even the sinfulness
     of mankind; but she wishes to show how the humiliation of the Son of God is more
     powerful than the wrath of the Fiend. 'Wrath', in this passage, refers to the way
     of evil, the destructive anger that characterizes all that is not of God. Seen in its
     context, her statement is not at all what it may appear to be. In ch. 45, 48, 49, 51
     and others Julian develops the concept of the steadfast love of God, the love which
     is God (cf. especially ch. 46), who created and sustains all that is (ch. 11), who
     means to 'one' us to Himself in love (ch. 84-84) and who does not forgive, in the
     ordinary sense, because in him there is no condemnation in the first place (ch. 49)."
     Brant Pelphrey, Love Was His Meaning, 339-340.
         Unfortunately, Pelphrey goes on to cite 40:5-6 as an example of a place where
     Julian does say that God is angry with us for our sin. In context, however, the
     meaning of this passage is that, seeing ourselves 'so foul' in our sinning, we mistak-
     enly think that God is wroth with us. Ibid., 340.
244 "When [the human person's] sin flies in the face of the God who is goodness, what
     the prophet sees revealed is the wrath or judgement of God." Sr. Mary Paul, All
     Shall Be Well, Julian of Norwich and the Compassion of God, 13-14.
245 Even within the biblical tradition, God's wrath is always seen in service of God's
     love for Israel, that Israel might turn away from sin and return to the Lord.
246 "For wyckydnesse hath ben sufferyd to ryse contrary to that goodnesse; and the

in love towards us.[247] She does, however, reserve the use of the word 'wrath' to connote contradiction or opposition to love and peace rather than love's opposition to evil. Simply put, the reality of God's absolute opposition to evil is experienced by us as wrath.[248] It is not so much that Julian's doctrine lacks orthodoxy; rather, in choosing to highlight one particular aspect of God's attitude towards us (God's steadfast and unconditional love), she does not, perhaps, do full justice to the concept of God's unwavering and total opposition to sin, i.e., to all that hinders our fully experiencing that love.

In summary, we can say that Julian's theology of divine compassion is completely orthodox. While it is not clear whether she always does so consciously, Julian embraces basic scriptural concepts (e.g., compassion as *raḥᵃmîm, ḥesed, ṣᵉdāqâh, eleos, splanchna, oiktirmos*) and develops them with great originality within the framework of her fundamental christological insight: by virtue of his incarnation, Christ 'suffers with' us as one of us, and we 'suffer with' him by virtue of our oneing. Because Christ is our mother who shares with us his humanity, we stand in his pain; our suffering becomes a participation in his redemptive suffering on the cross. Julian's creative use of biblical themes results in striking parallels to the scriptural vocabulary of compassion: the motherhood of Christ *(raḥᵃmîm)*; 'sureness of keeping' *(ḥesed)*; and God's 'rightfulness' *(ṣᵉdāqâh)*. Undoubtedly, her comprehensive development of the motherhood theme remains her most notable contribution to a scriptural understanding of divine compassion.

---

goodnesse of mercy and grace contraryed agaynst that wyckydnesse, and turnyd all to goodnesse and wurshyppe to all that shall be savyd. For it is that properte in god whych doth good agaynst evylle." [59:5-8]

247 43:33; 46:17-18.36; 49:4-13; 61:26-27; 78:12-14; 79:16.

248 Julian's doctrine that wrath is situated in us, not in God, resonates with Paul's teaching that vessels of wrath (ourselves) can become vessels of mercy. Rom 9:23.

5 Conclusions

The most striking characteristic of Julian's treatment of the mercy and compassion of God is the christocentricity of her approach. For Julian, Jesus Christ *is* the event of divine mercy; he is the very incarnation of divine compassion, the saving revelation of God's compassion for suffering humankind. Julian's theology of oneing provides a solid basis for exploring the mystery of the human person's union with God in Christ.[1] Hers is the voice of a mystic whose personal, immediate experience of God's love led her to embrace theology, that disciplined reflection by which the faith-enlightened intellect works to make the mystery intelligible. With her reason she struggled to understand and in love she sought to respond to the mystery of God's love as it was 'shewn' to her in the visions themselves, in the 'touchings' of the Holy Spirit during the years following her shewings, and in the teachings of the Church.

Julian's years of reflection on her shewings resulted, not in an abstract theological system, but in an understanding of God's love which addresses the real dilemmas of christian experience and offers comfort and encouragement to her 'even christians.'[2] We are now led us to do as Julian did, i.e., to relate the results of our study to christian praxis and, more specifically, to christian spirituality. In this concluding chapter, we shall highlight those insights which may serve as beacons for all who strive to understand and live more fully the christian 'spiritual life'—life in Christ.

---

1   As noted in the *Introduction* (see p. 17, above), Julian's message and teachings must always be seen in the light and context of the theology and spirituality of the fourteenth century. Julian's teachings touch upon various problems in the field of dogmatic theology, doctrinal issues that were explored and defined only in later centuries (e.g., the metaphysical constitution of the human person and resulting implications with regard to the human moral activity; grace, justification, and predestination; etc.). These areas within Julian's theological vision deserve further study in the light of contemporary dogmatic and spiritual theology.

2   8:22-24. Although she herself had the extraordinary experience of her shewings, throughout the *Shewings* Julian identifies herself more with the simple 'even christian' whose spiritual journey is marked by darkness and 'often fallings' rather than mystical favors. She reminds her readers that love, not visions, is the true measure of one's goodness. [9:2-9]

A. Divine Mercy and a Spirituality of 'Keeping'

Three key elements of Julian's understanding of divine mercy shed light on the christian spiritual life: her christological doctrine of our oneing by kind, mercy, and grace; her understanding of 'keeping' as one's existential experience of divine mercy; and her teaching on sin, the problem which assails every christian in his or her spiritual journey.

1. Julian's christological understanding of divine mercy

Julian's theology and anthropology are thoroughly christological. The revelation that is Christ gives us our knowledge of God and of ourselves; not only is Christ the divine self-disclosure of love, but he also defines our humanity in himself. Just as God sees us in terms of Christ's humanity, we too know ourselves only in Christ who reveals our true nature. We participate in his humanity and, consequently, have a share in that intratrinitarian love reserved properly for the beloved Son. We are Christ's 'crown,' the fruit of his passion; we are a loved and oned humanity, sinners who have been restored and redeemed by Christ's sufferings.

Julian centers her theology of salvation around the concept of oneing or union with God. We are oned to God in Christ by virtue of his incarnation. Our oneing in Christ is a single event of divine love, accomplished in three distinct, but inseparable 'moments': kind, mercy, and grace. We are saved by our kind, our nature, in that from all eternity the Father has ordained our salvation in Christ for whom and in whom our nature is created as *capax dei*. In the second moment, our salvation enters the realm of time and space, mercifully worked by Christ who, doing the will of the Father, defines humanity in himself by oneing our substance to our sensuality. The event of Christ's incarnation is mercy proper, i.e, the oneing of substance to sensuality, of in-God-ness to God-separateness. Grace, the third moment of our oneing, is the extension of mercy in time. We are individually, existentially oned to God in Christ by the working of grace. What has been accomplished once for all in Christ is confirmed in the christian as he or she accords to grace and moves towards wholeness, i.e., full union with God. By grace we truly become ourselves, oned in Christ who is perfect humanity, our truest 'self.' Thus, we are saved by kind, mercy, and grace; our salvation is ordained by the Father, worked by the Son, and confirmed and perfected by the

Holy Spirit. While this oneing is trinitarian in scope, Julian stresses the christological nature of the working of our salvation: we are saved in and through Christ. It is in Christ that the coincidence of opposites is most dramatically realized: we who are 'not God' are oned to God in Christ.

Julian's theology of oneing suggests, first of all, a positive and holistic spirituality. Her teaching on substance and sensuality does not dichotomize the human person into body and soul by 'spiritualizing' substance; rather, our substance is our 'self' (the truth of who we are in Christ) while our sensuality is our way of experiencing our self/substance. It is the whole person who is saved when our sensuality is fully oned to our substance. We are to love our human nature. The body is sacred because it is oned to God in Christ's own body. Moreover, grace is not to be seen over against nature; rather, mercy holds the key to the relationship between nature and grace. Nature is defined by mercy (Christ's incarnation), and grace is the working of mercy in time, our existential oneing. What the Son is by nature, we are by participation, i.e., by grace. Julian's anthropology suggests that the human person's 'divinization' in Christ is actually implied in Christ's defining humanity in himself.[3] It is precisely by virtue of his divinity that Christ is able to be human (the oneing of God-separateness with in-God-ness). In other words, if Christ were not divine, he could not be truly human; similarly, if we are not in Christ, we cannot achieve our full humanity.

Mercy proper is the *mystērion*, God's plan for our salvation, our oneing in Christ.[4] Christ is both the event of mercy and the saving revelation of that same mercy. Defining us by his incarnation, Christ is truly *logos* for us, i.e., the 'meaning' of our experience.[5] He is our ground: the ground of humanity, the ground of the Church (his Body), the ground even of our prayer. We mirror Christ. We only truly know ourselves when we know Christ. Of course, our 'sight' of God and of ourselves will not be full until we reach the bliss of heaven; here on earth, our 'sight' takes the form of faith. By faith we have right understanding: we recognize and accept the truth, the good news of our oneing as revealed in Christ. Having recognized Christ as the truth of humanity, we begin the life of virtue, the work of conforming our lives to his by grace.

---

3 Julian's theology resonates with the standard Orthodox doctrine of the human person's *theosis* (deification) in Christ. We have already noted Julian's affinity with Irenaeus' insight that Christ's incarnation was for the purpose of our divinization (see note 233, p. 94-95, above). For scriptural examples of the theme of our divinization, see 2 Pet 1:3-4; 1 John 3:1-2; cf. Gen 1:26.

4 Eph 1:9-10; 3:9-12; Col 1:15-20.24-27.

5 Julian, like Paul, sees Christ as the true image of God, the true *logos* or meaning of creation, the true purpose of all things. [Col 1:15-20] Cf. John 1:1-14.

2. 'Keeping': our existential experience of divine mercy

For Julian, divine mercy is also our existential 'keeping,' the same event of our salvation but as we experience it in time: we are oned to God in Christ existentially by the 'working of mercy and grace.' Like every theologian, Julian was faced with the paradox of the 'already' and the 'not yet' of our salvation, our oneing in Christ. Although Christ has definitively oned us to God by virtue of his incarnation, we experience ourselves as not yet fully oned existentially. For Julian, oneing is primarily an ontological reality, not a psychological experience. Our will is 'kept' in Christ; Christ works in us, maintaining our will even when we do not experience it existentially. 'Keeping' is Julian's term for the psychological reality, our perception of God's ongoing working of mercy in our existential lives; because we live in the context of sin, we experience oneing as 'keeping,' i.e., as a 'being kept safe' in Christ.

Julian's concept of divine mercy as 'keeping,' reveals once again the harmony between nature (kind) and grace. In nature, we have our ontological 'keeping'; in grace, we have our existential 'keeping.' In the Father, we have our 'keeping' in regard to our 'kindly substance.' We are 'kept' safe and whole in God (in Christ). In grace, on the other hand, we have our existential 'keeping': by grace, we ourselves become events of God's mercy, i.e., the oneing accomplished by Christ. Grace does not intervene into nature; on the contrary, the natural order realizes its potential through the grace of Christ. Christ himself suffers our existential lives, and grace accords us to Christ's living in us in such a way that our nature is fulfilled. By grace, we recognize our true nature in Christ and embrace it, becoming Christ's 'helpers' in the work of our salvation. Thus, both our ontological 'keeping' and our existential 'keeping' have a christological reference. This is demonstrated perhaps most effectively in Julian's image of Christ as our mother of mercy: we are 'kept' in Christ, enclosed and protected in love, endlessly borne to life in him. Divine mercy as a 'sureness of keeping' also implies fidelity, indicating the interpersonal and continual nature of our relationship with God. Of course, it is our experience of temporality which gives us the notion of fidelity; divine fidelity is more accurately God's rightfulness translated into terms of time. Here again, Julian suggests a christological interpretation of our 'sureness of keeping' when she tells us that it is the mother's love that is 'surest.'[6]

Julian's theology of oneing gives us a second key insight into our experience of being not yet fully oned. When she develops the theme of

---

6   60:14-17.

our wounds as 'worships,' she indicates that our experience corresponds to Christ's experience even though, existentially, they may be experienced quite differently because our oneing is not yet complete. They are, as it were, two faces of one reality. For example, the wounds of our sins are, in reality, Christ's worship of the Father, i.e., Christ's suffering the pain of our sins is the form his worship of the Father takes. In other words, the horror of sin is, at the same time, Christ's passion, the ultimate revelation of divine love and mercy. The three painful 'wounds' of contrition, compassion, and longing are the existential counterparts to the various aspects of Christ's love for us: Christ's faithful love is experienced by us as contrition (we perceive his unconditional love as forgiveness); Christ's passion becomes our own in compassion (we mirror Christ's compassion by sharing his pain as he shares ours); Christ's 'thirst' for us, his drawing us to himself in love, is experienced by us as painful desire or longing for full union with God (we mourn that we are not yet oned). The three 'wounds' are our experience of Christ's love. In our not-yet-oned state of separation from God by sin, we suffer the pain of Christ's wound of love; when our oneing is complete, this same wound of love will be experienced, not as suffering, but as the bliss of heaven. Once again, Christ is *logos* for us, explaining the meaning of our experience of suffering.

Julian's understanding of the essential unity between our wounds and Christ's worship touches upon the realm of eschatology.[7] She suggests a continuity between this life and our life in glory; our scars shall be our honors, i.e., we shall be 'thanked' for what we have suffered. What shall be is already present in what we experience now. 'All is well' represents Julian's basic eschatological insight into those things to come that are 'already now' (but not fully): she recognizes that 'all is well' even if, from our perspective, 'all shall be well' seems to be more accurate. For the mystic such as Julian, the eschaton breaks through linear time, revealing the timeless 'all is well' that God's love insures. Christ is in eschatological glory, yet one with us in our sufferings here and now, in time. Were we to have full eschatological 'sight' now, we too would experience Christ's glory; for now, we remain blinded and thus perplexed by sin's presence in our world. Thus, while we are still on earth, we experience

---

7   Julian devotes little time probing the more usual topics of eschatology with the exception of her mention of a 'secret deed' that God will do on the 'last day,' the deed by which we shall see for ourselves that 'all is well' indeed. Julian relegates this 'secret deed' to the realm of God's privy counsels, telling us that we cannot know anything about its nature other than the fact that God shall do it. [32:23-60] Julian concentrates her energies instead on what is revealed about our salvation.

God's 'well' as promise, as 'sureness of keeping.' When the last day shall come, 'all shall be well' and 'we shall see that all is well.'

Julian's doctrine of divine mercy as 'keeping' also provides a basis for a holistic spirituality of growth or maturing which she characterizes as 'forth-spreading' and 'increasing.' This is not, however, a self-validating, step-by-step, measurable kind of piety. Julian does not employ the standard terminology of 'stages' of spiritual growth,[8] preferring instead to concentrate on the progressive nature of our oneing in terms of the ever-expanding dimensions of Christ's acting in us through the working of grace in our lives — an endless spiritual birthing process. Spiritual growth is our maturation in Christ; our outer experience (sensuality) is oned more and more to our inner truth (substance) by the working of grace. We grow ('increase') to full maturity, i.e, we become wholly ourselves in Christ. The notion of the continuity between the 'already' and the 'not yet' is also reinforced by Julian's concept of oneing as growth. Salvation as healing, transfiguration, and even deliverance necessarily implies that what one is now (or what one shall be finally) is substantially what one has been from the beginning. Our weakness is healed, not destroyed; our 'wounds' are transfigured into 'worships.' Julian's image of deliverance[9] serves to demonstrate this continuity in her unique insight that we are taken, removed from pain rather than simply having the pain taken from us. This deliverance symbolizes the soul's continuity of identity in moving from the realm of time (in which pain may make a reappearance) into the realm of eternity (in which our scars are our glory). Finally, Julian's concept of oneing as growth must be seen within the context of the interpersonal nature of the relationship of love between God and the human person. Because this relationship has an ontological basis, our growth is a growth in love. As a result of God's free and gratuitous love in our regard, we have been created as those creatures with a capacity to return God's interpersonal love. The more we are oned to God in love, the more we become that which God communicates in that relationship of love: we further incarnate God's own love for us and, having grown in

---

8 Julian does not use designations such as *beginner, proficient, perfect,* etc. In the Short Text, she does make one comparison between 'men and women who desire to live contemplatively' and those who 'busy themselves with earthly business,' but the fact that she suppresses this reference in the Long Text suggests that Julian herself came to see that such distinctions as 'contemplative' and 'active' may distract her readers from the universal character of her message. [iv:41-56] Unlike her contemporaries, she even avoids the word 'contemplation' and uses more ordinary words such as 'sight' or 'beholding,' words that would be understood by all her 'even-christians.'

9   64:31-46.

love, are able to love more fully in return. Our truest 'self' (Christ) is God's love incarnate; our growth is growth in love and in relationship.

The concept of our 'keeping' in Christ does much to explain the paradox we experience as we live in this world. 'Keeping' allows for our being oned in time and for the real tension involved in that existential oneing. We experience the tension between our 'outward' part (our sensuality which is bound up with time) and our 'inward' part (our substance *sub specie aeternitatis*). Our life on earth is the process of our being oned, the inward part's mastering of the outward by grace. Christ, acting in our sensuality by grace, gives meaning to our existence in this world, to our struggle to become ourselves in him. To enter into Julian's spirituality of 'keeping' is to realize that we need not become depressed or despondent because of our blindness and sinfulness. Our subjective experience (wrath or 'unpeace') must give way to the objective truth of our situation (our 'merciful keeping' in Christ). We are to hope and trust in the truth that we are treasured in Christ, whole and safe in him, regardless of what we may experience existentially. In other words, we are to live by faith, the 'sight' wherein we see our true selves — ourselves in Christ. Moreover, Julian insists that to seek in pure faith is as good as to be granted vision. Vision is in itself a passive reality, i.e., we are 'shewn' the truth by a special gift of God's grace. Our 'sight' by faith is an active reality: by grace we believe and embrace what we cannot see because of our blindness. Julian's own approach to her experience of her shewings encourages us to take an active stance towards our faith. She understood that faith does not oppose human reason, but informs it. Julian did not skirt dilemmas;[10] as a result of her perseverance in reflection, she was able to throw light on some of the great paradoxes of our faith for us, even if she leaves us, at times, as perplexed as she was herself.[11] Julian's example teaches us to value the gift of reason, using it to

---

10 In trying to reconcile the content of her shewings with what she knew from her own experience and from the teaching of the Church, Julian probed such apparent contradictions as: the existence of an all-powerful, all-loving God whose purpose cannot be thwarted vs. the fact that our choices have meaning and consequences; 'all is well' vs. all is manifestly 'not well' (sin, suffering); God's transcendent majesty vs. God's homely, courteous love; Christ's passion as evil/horror vs. Christ's passion as his joy/bliss/delight; sin as evil/horror and ourselves as blameworthy vs. sin as 'behovely,' our sins as our 'worships,' and ourselves as receiving no blame from God.

11 What is impossible for us is not impossible for God. [32:49-50] Cf. Matt 19:26; Luke 1:37.

work with what we have learned from experience and with what we know from revealed doctrine.[12]

Finally, Julian's doctrine of 'keeping' raises the question of the role of free will. As we have already pointed out, Christ wishes us to be his 'helpers' in the process of our oneing. We are not simply passive to the work of grace; rather, by grace we actively accord to the life of Christ in us. We work with Christ in our oned activity by our intention and desire. It is an active embracing of Christ's life, an embracing made possible by grace. The virtues we embrace are gifts of grace given to us as we mature in Christ (those same gifts which are treasured in him until we be fully grown, i.e., until we come into our full humanity). We are 'kept' in Christ by grace, but at the same time we 'keep' ourselves in the faith by our life of virtue. Within the theological perspective of the *Shewings,* true freedom is that which allows us to become our true selves, a freedom from all that hinders our oneing. True freedom is that freedom to do what we truly will (in the sense of our 'godly will' which is preserved in Christ) – not a 'freedom' to do anything at all that may occur to us. By grace we are freed to become who we truly are: sin is never allowed to pursue us unchecked by the working of mercy and grace.

3. 'Keeping' as protection from sin

The concept of 'keeping' brings us back to Julian's primary dilemma, the question of sin. By its very nature, 'keeping' implies the presence of sin (that from which we are protected until we are fully oned). The milieu of mercy is precisely that of sin: mercy is about the salvation of sinners.

For Julian, sin is separatedness from God and, consequently, alienation from our true self; moral sin consists in those things that we do to promote that alienation, that illusion that our real identity lies somehow apart from God. Whereas grace is an embracing of our true nature (that 'according' to the life of Christ in us), all else is unnatural, an 'unkindness' (sin), which unkindness or 'contrarying' is the source of our pain, our suffering. Indeed, sin is only known by the pain it causes. Julian seems to understand that the proper response to pain is comfort. One does not rebuke pain; one comforts pain. We suffer our sins, and God addresses comfort to us in our pain. This solace, the revelation that is

---

12 As she herself asserts, private revelations such as Julian's shewings serve merely to amplify and restate truths which have already been given in the public revelation, i.e., the faith of the Church. See p. 155-158, above.

Jesus Christ, is the comforting 'good news' of the *Shewings*: we may be troubled, distressed ('dis-eased'), and travailed by sin and pain in this life, but we shall not be overcome.[13]

We began this study with the question: how does God view sin? The imagery of Julian's parable of the lord and the servant teaches us that God views sinners with mercy, i.e., in the light of Christ's incarnation, and that the 'face' of that mercy is divine compassion. God shows us our sins by light of that same mercy. We are shown that both 'judgments' of sin are true: we are truly blameworthy, yet God looks at us with pity, not blame, because our humanity is that of Christ, the beloved Son, in whom there is no guilt. Our rightfulness depends on our being oned to God in Christ, not on the merit of our own actions. We are asked to believe in God's love more than in our own blameworthiness.

To see the truth of both 'judgments' of sin is to experience the 'wound' of contrition. Because we see our blameworthiness, we assume that God is wroth with us. In reality, however, God is 'ever the same in love' towards us. Our contrition is our coming to rest in the experience of the truth of God's judgment: we no longer see God as wroth with us, but as loving us. We experience this unchanging, unconditional divine love as God's 'forgiving' us, whereas it is more accurately a 'giving up' of our own unpeace. Moreover, because love calls forth a response of love, our experience of God's love in our contrition takes the form of our growth in love; conversely, as long as we feel that God is judging us blameworthy, we are hindered in loving. We might make the comparison to the experience of human love. When someone loves me, I am given more of myself; a part of me comes to life that had not been alive before. I become more fully myself in loving. In the same way, when I experience God's love, I grow in my capacity to return that love; I become more myself, my true 'self,' i.e., that loving response to the Father that is the Son. In this sense, sin is 'behovely' for it brings us to contrition and growth. If we did not face the obstacles and pain sin represents, we would not grow. Just as a child learns to walk by falling, so we 'adjust our balance' through our experience with sin. To deny the reality of the unsteady child is to deny the growth that the mature adult represents. To deny the reality of sin is to trivialize the miracle of our oneing.

Julian's doctrine on sin does present us with the problem that her theology seems to allow no real place for forgiveness: because there is no wrath in God, there is no need for forgiveness. We have already seen that it is God's unconditional love that we experience as forgiveness. We discover that we are loved, but that we were always loved; that we are

---

13   68:68-70; cf. John 16:33.

forgiven, but that we were always forgiven. Forgiveness, however, is not simply a subjective reality; there does exist a *moment of forgiveness,* that embrace of mutual love between God and the penitent, like that between the prodigal son and his father.[14] When we are shown both the horror of our sin and God's unconditional love, we experience sin's reality (separation from God) as suffering — and we turn back. This 'moment' may also be understood as conversion: we 'come to ourselves,' as, the prodigal son 'came to himself'[15] and returned to the arms of his loving father. As we are oned, our attitude towards sin is also converted: we 'come to ourselves,' recognizing that true exercise of freedom lies, not in sinning (which contradicts our nature), but in choosing to accord ourselves to the life of Christ in us. While the possibility of sinning is psychologically inevitable for human freedom to be possible, sin is really the antithesis of freedom. As we are oned, we hate sin the more — not out of fear but because it hinders us from what we truly will, the union with God for which we long. For this reason, sin is itself a penance: we suffer our lives in 'love-longing' until we be fully oned and freed from sin's grasp. This conversion of our attitude towards sin prevents us from falling into the error of thinking that, if our sins are our 'worships,' we ought to sin more in order to have more reward.[16]

As christians we learn, not 'to forgive and forget,' but to forgive — and to remember more gracefully. That 'graced' way of remembering *is* divine mercy. We do not 'give up' our unpeace and forget our sin; rather, we give it up and *remember* our sin, but always in the light of God's mercy and grace. We ought to accuse ourselves and then cling to Christ. Julian is not naïve. She teaches that we do indeed sin, and sin grievously at times. Objectively, we must recognize sin as evil and wrong, and ourselves as blameworthy; subjectively, however, what ought we do when we find sin and wrath in ourselves? Julian's answer to that question is that we should place our trust in God rather than engage in self-hatred. We are to accept God's love and mercy in Jesus Christ.

---

14 Luke 15:20.
15 Luke 15:17.
16 Like Paul, Julian herself warns us against such a conclusion. [40:28-30] Cf. Rom 6:1-2. See p. 105-106, above.

B. Jesus Christ: the Compassion of God and Our Compassion

An analysis of Julian's vocabulary has revealed two distinct though related understandings of divine compassion. First, she sees God's compassion as a 'chere,' a mien or attitude towards us as we suffer the pain of our sins. Divine compassion is the 'face' of divine mercy, i.e., the face of Jesus Christ. Whereas we usually identify Christ's passion as the historical event of mercy, Christ's compassion is our perception of God's ongoing stance of mercy towards us in response to our condition of human sinfulness. Julian's second understanding is that of compassion proper, i.e., as a true 'suffering with' us. Because Christ shares our humanity, Julian situates divine compassion proper in Christ.

We shall now review briefly the distinctive elements in Julian's theology of compassion before considering their significance in terms of consequences for spiritual theology. The following summary statements highlight the main theses which emerge in Julian's development of the theme of compassion in the *Shewings*.

1. The compassion of God for *us in Christ*: divine compassion is grounded in Christ's incarnation.

For Julian, compassion proper means to 'suffer with,' which suffering presumes a relationship in which both persons share the same nature. God the Father could have compassion for the Son (who shared the divine nature), but there is, from a human standpoint, an unbridgeable chasm separating God from us, i.e., separating divinity from humanity. Divine compassion for us would be possible only if God shared our humanity. Jesus Christ, by virtue of his incarnation, is that union of humanity and divinity; he bridges the chasm, allowing for the 'homely' relationship of love between God and humankind, which relationship is implied in compassion.

The parable of the lord and the servant reveals that God's compassion for Christ (the servant) is also God's compassion for *us in Christ* because, by virtue of Christ's incarnation, the servant also represents Adam — and us. Divine compassion is explained in the essential unity between the first and second Adam. The compassion of God for the Son in the human suffering he assumed in his incarnation is transferred to us in our sufferings because we have been oned to God in Christ. Christ himself is our true humanity, 'rightful Adam.' In Christ, we enter into the intimacy of a filial relationship with God, a relationship which explains God's compassion for us. When God looks at our humanity, God sees the beloved Son; thus, when God sees our sufferings, they are identified with the sufferings of the Son.

2. The *compassion of God in Christ* for us: divine compassion is proper to Christ.

Julian's use of the words 'compassion,' 'ruth,' and 'pity' suggests a conscious attempt to situate divine compassion properly in Christ. While she uses all three words equivalently in reference to Christ, it is significant that she restricts herself to the use of the words 'ruth' and 'pity' when she describes God's attitude towards humankind. The word 'compassion' is consistently reserved for references to Christ or to the human person inserted into Christ, i.e., the christian. God's 'pity' for us becomes compassion proper in Jesus Christ. This conclusion is borne out in Julian's theology as well as in her use of vocabulary.

The parable of the lord and the servant reveals that God views us with the chere of compassion because of our oneing in the Son. However, the parable also reveals that God does indeed truly 'suffer with' us in the humanity of Christ. To see God's compassion, therefore, we must look not only at the lord, but also at the servant whose suffering is God's 'suffering with' us. Here, Julian takes up the question of divine impassibility. Because God as God is impassible, God 'suffers' the passion only in the humanity of Jesus. In the same way, Julian situates divine compassion, God's 'suffering with' us, in Christ's humanity.

Thus, in Christ, divine compassion acquires a human ground: the compassion of God in Christ is a human *suffering with*. Christ 'suffers with' us by virtue of his incarnation. It is precisely in his oneing of humankind by taking on our sensuality that Christ suffers and sorrows with us, as one of us. Sharing our life with us, suffering 'with us' in the totality of what it means to be human, Christ is himself the definitive expression of divine compassion. While our suffering is the result of our sins, Christ's suffering is the expression of his compassion: he suffers *with us* and *for us* for love. Our sins are the cause of his suffering, which suffering he gladly bears for love of us.

3. The passion of Christ is divine compassion incarnated.

In the parable of the lord and the servant, Julian describes the compassionate 'double chere' of God: not only are our sins excused by God's chere of pity and ruth, but our compassionate God also looks at us with 'joy' in anticipation of the blissful reward that will be ours for the suffering we endure, the suffering our sins inflict upon us.

The crucial significance of Julian's notion of God's 'double chere' becomes clear when she speaks of Christ's 'triple chere.' The three cheres of Christ, i.e., his passion, his compassion for us in our sinning, and his 'blessydfulle chere,' are the incarnated counterparts to God's two cheres. Whereas Christ's cheres of compassion and of blissful rewarding are in clear correspondence to God's double chere, the chere of the passion is proper only to Christ.

Again, the centrality of Christ's incarnation in Julian's theology emerges: only by virtue of the incarnation could the passion (Christ's suffering) be possible. In his incarnation, Christ took on our sensuality — and our suffering; the passion and death of Christ on the cross is the culminating point of his 'suffering with' us. Thus, Christ's passion reveals the deepest meaning of his incarnation: God becomes one of us in order to share our suffering, and in so doing, to bring us to bliss through our oned sufferings. The chere of Christ's passion is the incarnation of God's compassion; God 'suffers with' us in and through the humanity of Christ.

Julian's image of Christ as the perfect, archetypal mother also reflects her understanding of the passion of Christ as an expression of divine compassion. Motherhood, by its very nature, is a relationship of compassion. Already our mother in creation, the Eternal Word becomes our mother in mercy and in grace: oneing us in himself in his incarnation, the Word made flesh bears us to spiritual birth by virtue of his suffering and death on the cross. Christ's passion is his labor for his children.

4. Divine compassion is occasioned by the human misery caused by sin.

Perhaps the most consoling aspect of the parable of the lord and the servant is Julian's understanding of God's chere of pity in the face of our 'falling' into sin: our sins evoke compassion, not wrath from God. Adopting a traditional metaphysics of sin, Julian tells us that sin in itself is a nought; we only know sin by the pain and suffering it causes. God views our sins as so much pain and sorrow to beloved children. Sin harasses us by blinding our reason; we are unable to see God or self clearly and fall prey to despair over our situation. Thus, sin escalates: blinded by sin, we fall into more sin. God's response to our sinning is compassion for us in this harassment by sin. There is no need for despair when we see our true situation: yes, our sins are terrible and the source of the worst harm possible, but God's steadfast love is infinitely greater than our sins.

This insight is also reflected in the motherhood similitude. Christ our mother 'keeps' us; in his 'motherhood of working' (motherhood of grace), Christ tenderly protects us when we fall, never suffering us to be lost. We are to trust in his steadfast and compassionate love, to rise quickly when we fall, fleeing to him for mercy as a child flees to its mother.

5. Divine compassion continues in us.

Julian's motherhood similitude presents us with yet another aspect of divine compassion, i.e., its continuing nature in Christ's 'motherhood of working': Christ exercises the tender office of a mother, guiding and 'keeping' us in the existential realization of our salvation in him. This guidance and protection is often experienced by us as pain and suffering, not unlike the pain and chastisement by which a child comes to maturity. Such suffering, although painful, eventually leads to a fuller and happier existence for the child. Christ, the archetype of the wise mother, continues to 'suffer with' us as we mature until we are borne to full spiritual birth in the bliss of our union with him in heaven.

The clearest image Julian uses to explain this continuing compassion is that of Christ's 'thirst and 'love-longing.' In his thirst and longing for our full union with him, Christ 'suffers with' us the pain we experience in our separation from him until the best time to deliver us; even though our suffering increases his own, he waits for the sake of love. His longing and drawing us to himself is experienced in us as suffering and mourning for the separation that still exists because of our sin. Divine compassion thus continues in Christ's thirst and longing for us — *in* us: he draws us to himself, which action is experienced in us as painful suffering and mourning for the sin that still separates us from him.

In her treatment of Christ's continuing compassion for us in his thirst, Julian also confronts again the question of divine impassibility. Just as God suffers in the humanity of Christ, so too the risen Christ suffers in our humanity, i.e., the humanity of his members. Our sufferings are united to him by virtue of our oneing; thus, Christ continues to 'suffer with' us until the glorification of the *Totus Christus* is fully realized.

6. Our compassion is Christ's working in us.

For Julian, our compassion is God's doing: the 'wound' of compassion for which Julian prayed *is* Christ's oneing us in his incarnation. Christ 'suffered with' us in his passion by virtue of his incarnation, and he continues even now to 'suffer with' us in us (e.g., our experience of his 'thirst' as a painful longing in us). However, when we are oned to Christ, not only does he 'suffer with' us, but we also have compassion for him: we 'suffer with' him by virtue of that same oneing. Our own suffering is truly his. In a very real sense, Christ is the true subject of our sufferings. We are oned to Christ's suffering in our own pain. We 'suffer with' Christ by accepting the pain of our own lives, which suffering he bears with us. Our suffering becomes a true 'suffering with.'

Our compassion for others (and even for ourselves) is also Christ's as a result of his incarnation. Oned in Christ, we are oned to each other's sufferings through Christ's 'suffering with' all men and women. To 'suffer with' our brothers and sisters is to 'suffer with' Christ. Our compassion for Christ finds expression in our compassion for others and for ourselves, as part of his body. Moreover, Christ in us, 'suffering with' us, also ones us to his 'suffering for' sinners. Thus, our 'suffering with,' our compassion for ourselves and for others, becomes redemptive. This mutuality of suffering finds its natural complement in a mutuality of joy. We are so identified in the oneing accomplished by Christ's incarnation that our suffering is his, our bliss is his: we are his bliss.

The gospel mandate to be 'compassionate as God is compassionate' takes on new meaning in the light of Julian's understanding of the nature of our compassion.[17] Our compassion for Christ, for others, and for self are the fruit of our union with Christ. The 'wound' of compassion moves us to desire not only to bear our own sufferings for love of Christ, but also to bear one another's burdens for the sake of that same love. The realization that our 'suffering with' is oned to Christ's own redemptive suffering gives meaning and purpose to the sufferings we endure in life.

7. Human compassion implies a hatred of sin.

Sin is the only thing which hinders us from union with God; therefore, sin is precisely the obstacle which Christ overcomes in his oneing of us through his passion and, as that obstacle, is the source of the pain of the

---

17 Luke 6:36.

crucifixion. Thus, the 'sight' of the passion not only evokes our compassion for Christ in his suffering, but also necessarily produces in us a hatred of sin, the cause of his suffering.

Like our compassion for Christ, compassion for self and for others also implies a hatred for the sin which causes us that pain and suffering. When we have true 'sight' of Christ's compassion for us in our sinning, we share his understanding of the scourge of sin in our own lives and in the lives of all who share our painful condition of sinfulness. We 'suffer with' them in their pain, which pain is caused by sin. Oned to the compassion of Christ, we hate the sin while we love and 'suffer with' the sinner — even when the sinner is oneself.

8. Divine revelation flows from divine compassion.

Because sin is the cause of our inability to see the truth of our situation, we need divine revelation in order to be freed from the bondage of sin. Jesus Christ is the revelation of God's compassion: the incarnation and, most especially, the passion of Christ reveal the divine perspective on sin. Without the revelation of God's compassion in Christ, we easily fall prey either to presumption or to despair because of our inability to see ourselves as God sees us, i.e., to recognize the terrible reality of our sinfulness (and our inability to repair the damage caused by our sins) but to see that sinfulness always and only in the light of God's unchangeable love and mercy. In compassion, God reveals to us in Christ all that we need to know for our salvation. At the same time, God's revelation is also for our solace. God has compassion on us in our blindness because of the anguish and pain our ignorance causes us. We are truly 'self-compassionate' when we allow ourselves to accept God's revelation in trust, finding both our salvation and solace in Christ. We 'keep' ourselves in the 'sight' which is faith, i.e., in the truth which is revealed to us in the Church.

In these two intentions or 'meanings' of revelation (our salvation and our comfort), we see a clear parallel to the two meanings which Julian assigns both to Christ's passion and to his compassion. Christ 'suffers for' us and 'suffers with' us in order that we might be both saved and comforted in our own sufferings. We are saved in that our oned sufferings bring us to bliss: oned to Christ's victory, we cannot be overcome by sin. We are comforted in that Christ's suffering is a source of strength for us: we are saved from despair in our own sufferings because we see that Christ's pain is always greater than our own and that we suffer not alone, but with him who will turn all of our pain to profit by virtue of his passion. In this correspondence between the 'meanings' of revelation and the 'meanings' of the cheres of Christ's passion and compassion, Julian highlights the fact that divine revelation is itself an expression of divine compassion. Accordingly, Jesus Christ, as the revelation of God, is the definitive revelation of divine compassion.

C. Consequences for Spiritual Theology

This final section will explore briefly the consequences of this present study for spiritual theology. In other words, what does Julian's christocentric vision of divine mercy and compassion have to contribute to an understanding of the nature of the 'spiritual life,' i.e., our life in Christ?

1. The spiritual life: growth in compassion

Julian's understanding of salvation as 'health' or 'wholeness' suggests that the deepest meaning of christian holiness is to come to oneself, i.e., one's true 'self' who is Christ. Consequently, spiritual growth can be understood as a process of our coming to wholeness through our being existentially oned in Christ; in other words, we become 'holy' by becoming wholly ourselves in Christ. This theology of oneing is the basis for any reflection on the relationship between divine compassion and the christian spiritual life; our being oned in Christ is the very ground of possibility for the 'homely' relationship with God which is presumed in the notion of a christian spiritual life. For Julian this oneing *is* the 'wound' of compassion. Thus, in a real sense, the wound of compassion is the basis of the spiritual life. Christ, the definitive expression of God's compassion, ones us in himself. This 'wounding' unites us to Christ's own compassion, which compassion becomes operative and redemptive in our own lives. Oned to God in Christ, we too become events of mercy, and reveal in our lives the 'face' of that mercy by our own exercise of compassion. We become compassionate with God's own compassion.

According to Julian, our oneing (wounding) is completed only when Christ bears us to full union with him in the bliss of heaven. The spiritual life is, therefore, a continual growth in compassion; our becoming compassionate *is* the process of coming to deeper union with God, and it is God's doing, in and through Christ. This is not to say, however, that the human person's response to the wound of compassion is a passive reality. Julian advocates receptivity, not passivity, on our part; we are actively receptive to the grace of Christ, working with him as his 'helpers' in our oned compassion. The intention and desire of our wills remain important elements of our response by grace to the wound of true compassion.

2. The hallmarks of compassion in the life of the christian

The effects of the 'wounding' by divine compassion are the manifestations of compassion in the life of the christian. In a real sense, the deepening of true compassion in the life of the christian is a sign of spiritual growth. The more we progress in the spiritual life, the more our lives will evidence the qualities of christian compassion: (a) willingness to enter into one's own suffering; (b) willingness to share the burdens of others; and (c) trust in God (meekness and joy).

a. Willingness to enter into one's own suffering

The willingness to accept one's own suffering is the most fundamental hallmark of christian compassion. When we have been 'wounded' by divine compassion, we do not flee the suffering of our lives; rather we willingly embrace our suffering for the sake of the loved one who 'suffers with' us *in* us. Oned to Christ, we meet him in our sufferings *because they are his.* Because God's self-disclosure has taken the form of Christ crucified, we choose his cross to be our heaven; therefore, our maturing involves conformation to his passion. Consequently, we come to ourselves in the face of evil and pain: just as gold is tested by fire, so too we discover ourselves in our sufferings. Our mettle is tested, and we learn who we are and what we truly will.

This particular aspect of Julian's understanding of christian compassion is a most comforting one for the ordinary christian: we need not seek extraordinary penances in order to demonstrate our love for Christ. Life itself is the penance Christ works in us. The sufferings of our ordinary, daily existence are our way to enter Christ's passion — to 'suffer with' him. Oned to Christ, we 'suffer with' him by touching our own pain. We discover real meaning for our earthly existence, with all its suffering and travail: it is our sharing of Christ's sufferings and, consequently, our entry into his eschatological glory.[18] Our wounds become our 'worships.'

Because we are oned in Christ, our 'suffering with' is also oned to his 'suffering for' sinners. Thus, when we accept the suffering of our lives in compassion for Christ, our suffering becomes redemptive, fruitful. Even our longing for full union with him is a redemptive suffering because it is Christ's own 'suffering with' us, Christ's working in us as he continues to draw us to himself.

---

18 Cf. Col 1:24.

The willingness to enter into the pain of our own sufferings is also a way of rejecting sin. As we are oned in love to Christ, we see the nature of sin ever more clearly and, consequently, our attitude towards suffering changes. Hatred for sin, which is the cause of the pains Christ endured on the cross (and the cause of our own pain), is necessarily implied in our compassion for Christ in his suffering; and, just as Christ our mother sees our sins as so much sorrow and pain to his beloved children, so we see our sins as the cause of Christ's pain. We choose suffering over sin because sin pains our beloved.

b. Willingness to share the burdens of others

Compassion for Christ leads us to consider what is perhaps the most obvious hallmark of true christian compassion: a willingness to share the burdens of others. Oned to Christ, we extend to others that same compassionate love that God has extended to us in Jesus. Although Julian does not explicitly develop the theme of love of neighbor, her theology of oneing does have significant ramifications in terms of christian compassion. Oned in Christ, we are also oned to all men and women as members of one body; their pain becomes our own pain and our 'suffering with' them is Christ's own work in us. Moreover, the wound of compassion opens our eyes to see that to 'suffer with' the members of Christ's body is to 'suffer with' Christ; because we see Christ in them, we embrace their suffering as Christ's own. Our compassion for our brothers and sisters is, thus, an expression both of Christ's compassion working in us and of our compassion for Christ.

We become more ourselves in compassion. Sensing that the other remains incomplete without our entering into his or her suffering and that our own human wholeness lies in that embrace of compassion, we choose to become ourselves by being compassionate to others. We recognize that, while we live in this world, the authentic mark of a christian life is not the absence of sin, but the presence of redemptive compassion in the midst of the suffering that sin brings. Such compassion (and not mere virtue for its own sake) is the real measure of our spiritual growth and, therefore, of our humanity.

c. Trust in God: meekness and joy

A profound trust in God is the third hallmark of christian compassion, a sign that we are able to extend the compassion of Christ to ourselves as

well as to others. Our trust in God is the alternative to the self-hatred
of despair. As such, trust in God is the heart of self-compassion because,
by accepting in trust the revelation of God's compassion in Christ, we are
freed from our fear and from that destructive self-condemnation which
is incompatible with God's mercy. Trust in God allows us to accept
ourselves and our sinfulness in compassion.

For Julian, our trust in God, i.e., our self-compassion, manifests itself
in two qualities: meekness and joy. Meekness is the fruit of the self-
knowledge we gain from the revelation of God's compassion in Jesus.
The perfect suffering of Christ demonstrates the compassion of God: we
see in Christ that God will do all that needs to be done in order to save
us. The 'sight' of the passion reveals to us the truth of our situation: we
come to know the horror of our sin, but we also see that God's mercy is
infinitely greater than our sins. Seeing the truth of our situation makes
us meek, but it is also a source of joy and comfort for us; we need never
fear, even when we feel overwhelmed by our sins. To be compassionate
to self means to allow ourselves to be comforted and freed from our fear;
we choose to permit ourselves to accept the revelation of God's compassion in faith. We place our trust in God's love and mercy rather than in
our own strength. Oned to Christ, we love ourselves with Christ's own
compassion. Although we hate our sin, we are able to love ourselves
even while we are still sinners.[19]

Trusting in God's mercy, in meekness we rise quickly when we fall.
We are compassionate to ourselves: we do not allow ourselves to be
paralyzed by the self-hatred of depression or despair at the sight of our
sins. Just as God's love overcomes our sinning, so our joy overcomes our
depression. We experience more joy in God's love than sorrow in our
own fallings. We replace self-hatred (which only increases the pain of
Christ who suffers all of our pain with us) with the joy that comes from
trusting in God. Paradoxically, while joy overcomes sorrow, suffering
continues. In self-compassion, however, we see our sufferings to be a
form of chastisement that will lead us to greater glory. Because Christ
'suffers with' us, helping us to bear it, we meekly and joyfully accept the
pain our sins bring, trusting always in God's mercy to deliver us at the
'best time.'

Trust in God also implies a life of prayer. In self-compassion, we flee
to Christ, our tender, protective mother, for strength and comfort amidst
the sufferings of our lives. Our pain and the sight of our weakness make
us cry out meekly to Christ for mercy, as a child cries to its mother for
help. Moreover, for us as for Julian, prayerful meditation on Christ's

---

19 Cf. Rom 5:8.

passion becomes our entry into an ever deeper participation in Christ's working of self-compassion within us. Our trust in God is renewed and strengthened by the chere of Christ's passion, the concrete manifestation of God's 'suffering with' us.

3. Concluding remarks

The message of the *Shewings* of Julian of Norwich is a message of comfort and solace for the sinner. Jesus Christ is the saving event of divine mercy, the definitive revelation of God's compassion. Sin has been overcome, once for all, in the person of Christ by virtue of his incarnation; we need not fear, but only trust in God's mercy.

Julian's christocentric vision of divine compassion gives christians a way to make sense of their own sufferings and reason to take up the burdens of others in compassion. Christ's incarnation has oned us to God by virtue of his passion and death on the cross. This oneing is itself the 'wound' of compassion. Oned in Christ, who is our true humanity, we become the compassion of Christ incarnate in our world. In our own lives, we 'suffer with' Christ. Our suffering becomes redemptive and fruitful because it is oned to the 'suffering with' and 'suffering for' of Christ.

We are to be Christ's 'helpers' in this working of mercy in our lives. We cannot abdicate our role in Christ's compassionate 'suffering with' humankind if we are to become our truest selves, i.e., completely oned to God in Christ in love. Our compassion for Christ, for ourselves, and for others is our path to full union with God in love. Just as God's love is expressed to us in the compassion of Christ, so our love for God finds its most perfect expression in the working of Christ's compassion in and through us. By accepting the suffering which sin brings to our lives, we 'suffer with' Christ whose own pain it truly is. By embracing the sufferings of Christ in others, we love God as God has loved us: at the price of suffering.[20] For Julian, Christ himself is the measure of our compassion, the measure of our humanity, the measure of our love. Jesus Christ is the compassionate 'face' of divine mercy; our human compassion is the 'face' of our existential oneing in Christ, our participation in the event of divine mercy. In our lives as christians, compassion becomes the true measure of our oneing, the measure of our spiritual growth.

---

20 Cf. 1 John 4:9-11.

As we enter more fully into the mystery of divine mercy and compassion, we come to learn what Julian herself discovered in her years of reflection on her shewings: <u>love is always God's meaning</u>.

> What, woldest thou wytt thy lordes menyng in this thyng? Wytt it wele, loue was his menyng. Who shewyth it the? Loue. (What shewid he the? Love.) Wherfore shewyth he it the? For loue. Holde the therin, thou shalt wytt more in the same. But thou schalt nevyr witt therin other *wi*thoutyn ende. [86:15-19]

Jesus Christ is the compassion of God and our compassion, i.e., the love of God for us and the reflection in us of that same love. Oned to Christ, we enter that mystery of divine compassion, the mystery of God's love as revealed in Jesus. Christ, our mother of mercy, is our healing 'salve' as we suffer the pain of our sins; in him we find our 'sureness of keeping,' the sureness of a mother's gratuitous, unconditional love. With this image of Christ as our mother, Julian provides us with her most touching portrait of divine mercy: <u>we are given our humanity, enclosed in love, and borne to bliss in Christ, our mother of mercy and grace, in whose sure 'keeping' we shall truly know that 'all is well.'</u>

Bibliography

1. Manuscripts of Julian's *Shewings*

London, MS British Museum, Additional 37790 ('Amherst')
Paris, MS Bibliothèque Nationale, Fonds anglais 40
London, MS British Museum, Sloane 2499
London, MS British Museum, Sloane 3705
London, Westminster Archdiocesan Archives MS
MS St. Joseph's College, Upholland

2. Editions of Julian's *Shewings* (Arranged chronologically)

Cressy, R. F. Serenus, Benedictine. *XVI Revelations of Divine Love, Shewed to a Devout Servant of our Lord called 'Mother Juliana,' An Anchorete of Norwich: Who lived in the Dayes of King Edward the Third.* 1670, copy in Trinity College Library, Cambridge. [From Paris MS.]

Parker, G. H., ed. *Sixteen Revelations of Divine Love, showed to a devout servant of our Lord called Mother Juliana of Norwich.* Leicester, 1843. [From Paris MS.]

Collins, Henry, ed. *Revelations of Divine Love Shewed to a Devout Anchoress by Name, Mother Julian of Norwich.* London: Thomas Richardson and Sons, 1877. [From Sloane MS 2499.]

Warrack, Grace, ed. *Revelations of Divine Love.* London: Methuen and Co., 1901. [From Sloane MS 2499.]

Tyrrell, George, ed. *XVI Revelations of Divine Love Shewed to Mother Juliana of Norwich 1373.* London: Kegan Paul, Trench, Trübner and Co. Ltd., 1902. [From Paris MS.]

Harford, Dundas, ed. *Comfortable Words for Christ's Lovers, Being the Visions and Voices Vouchsafed to Lady Julian Recluse at Norwich in 1373.* London: H. R. Allensen, 1911. [From Shorter Version, Brit. Mus. Add. MS 37790.]

Hudleston, Dom Roger, O.S.B., ed. *Revelations of Divine Love.* London: Burns, Oates and Washbourne Ltd., 1927. [From Sloane MS. 2499.]

Reynolds, Frances (Sister Anna Maria, C.P.), ed. *An Edition of Ms. Sloane 2499 of Sixteen Revelations of Divine Love By Julian of Norwich.* Unpublished M.A. thesis, Leeds University, 1947.

Chambers, Percy Franklin, ed. *Juliana of Norwich: An Introductory Appreciation and an Interpretive Anthology.* London: Gollancz, 1955. [Selections from all known MSS.]

Reynolds, Frances (Sister Anna Maria, C.P.), ed. "A Critical Edition of the *Revelations* of Julian of Norwich (1342–c. 1416), Prepared from All Known Manuscripts." Unpublished Ph.D. thesis, Leeds University, 1956.

Reynolds, Anna Maria, C.P., ed. *Julian of Norwich: A Shewing of God's Love.* London: Sheed and Ward, 1958. [From Shorter Version, Brit. Mus. Add. MS 37790.]

Walsh, James, S.J., ed. *Revelations of Divine Love.* Glasgow: Anthony Clarke Books, 1961. [From Sloane MSS 2499 and 3705, and Paris MS.]

Wolters, Clifton, ed. *Revelations of Divine Love*. Harmondsworth: Penguin Books, 1966. [From Sloane MS 2499.]

Glasscoe, Marion, ed. *Julian of Norwich, A Revelation of Love*, rev. ed. M. J. Swanton, gen. ed. Exeter Medieval English Texts and Studies. Exeter: University of Exeter, 1986. [From Sloane MS 2499.]

Del Mastro, M. L., ed. *Revelations of Divine Love*. Garden City, New York: Image Books, 1977. [From Sloane MS 2499 with Sloane MS 3705 as a corrective "where necessary."]

Beer, Frances Fitzerald, ed. *Julian of Norwich's 'Revelations of Divine Love': The Shorter Version*. M. Gorlain, gen. ed. Middle English Texts 8. Heidelberg: Carl Winter Universitätsverlag, 1978. [From Brit. Mus. Add. MS 37790.]

Colledge, Edmund, O.S.A. - James Walsh, S.J., eds. *A Book of Showings to the Anchoress Julian of Norwich*. Studies and Texts, 35. Toronto: Pontifical Institute of Mediaeval Studies, 1978. [Critical edition of both versions from all available MSS.]

————. *Julian of Norwich, Showings*. New York: Paulist Press, 1978. [Both versions, using all available MSS.]

Swanson, John-Julian, O.J.N., ed. *A Lesson of Love, The Revelations of Julian of Norwich*. London: Darton, Longman and Todd, Ltd., 1988. [From Sloane MS 2499.]

3. Other primary sources

Anselm of Canterbury. *The Prayers and Meditations of St. Anselm*. Translated by Benedicta Ward, S.L.G. Harmondsworth: Penguin, 1973.

Aquinas, Thomas. *Summa Theologiae*, 60 Vol. Edited by Blackfriars. London: Eyre & Spottiswoode, 1963.

Augustine of Hippo. *Contra secundam Iuliani responsionem opus imperfectum*. *Patrologia Latina*, 45. Edited by J.-P. Migne. Paris, 1844-64.

————. *De peccatorum meritis et remissione et de baptismo parvulorum ad Marcellinum libri tres*. *Patrologia Latina*, 44. Edited by J.-P. Migne. Paris, 1844-64.

Bernard of Clairvaux. *Bernard of Clairvaux: On the Song of Songs I*. Translated by Kilian Walsh, O.C.S.O. Cistercian Fathers Series 4. Kalamazoo: Cistercian Publications, Inc., 1979.

Dionysius. *Divine Names*. *Patrologia Graeca*, 3. Edited by J.-P. Migne. Paris, 1857-66.

Eliot, T. S. *Four Quartets*. New York: Harcourt, Brace and Company, 1943.

Hilton, Walter. *The Goad of Love*. Translated by Clare Kirchberger. London: Faber and Faber Ltd., 1951.

————. *The Stairway of Perfection*. Translated by M. L. Del Mastro. New York: Image Books, 1979.

Irenaeus of Lyons. *Adversus Haereses*. *Patrologia Graeca*, 7. Edited by J.-P. Migne. Paris, 1857-66.

Kempe, Margery. *The Book of Margery Kempe*. Edited by Sanford Brown Meech and Hope Emily Allen. The Early English Text Society 212. London: Oxford University Press, 1940.

The Ancrene Riwle. Translated by M. B. Salu. London: Burns & Oates, 1955.

The Cloud of Unknowing. Translated by James Walsh. New York: Paulist Press, 1981.

Rolle, Richard. *Richard Rolle, the English Writings*. Translated by Rosamund S. Allen. New York: Paulist Press, 1988.

4. Studies

Albert, Sr. M. "God Is Our Mother," *Life of the Spirit* 2 (1945) 49-53.
_____. "The Motherhood of God," *Life of the Spirit* 7 (1952) 85-96.
_____. "Spiritual Childhood and Mother Julian," *Life of the Spirit* 2 (1945) 81-83.
Allchin, Arthur M. "Julian of Norwich and Hildegarde of Bingen," *Mount Carmel* 37 (1989) 128-143.
_____. "Julian of Norwich and the Continuity of Tradition," in *The Medieval Mystical Tradition in England,* Exeter, 1980. Edited by Marion Glasscoe. Exeter: University of Exeter, 1980, 72-85.
_____. "Julian of Norwich for Today," in *Julian of Norwich: Four Studies to Commemorate the Sixth Centenary of the Revelations of Divine Love.* Fairacres Publication No. 28. Oxford: SLG Press, 1973, 33-38.
Allen, Christine. "Christ Our Mother in Julian of Norwich," *Studies in Religion* 10 (1981) 421-428.
Armstrong, Elizabeth Psakis. "Motives of Charity in the Writing of Julian of Norwich and St. Teresa of Avila," *Mystics Quarterly* 16 (1990) 9-26.
Baker, Albert E. "The Lady Julian of Norwich," in *Prophets for a Day of Judgment.* London: Eyre and Spottiswoode, Ltd., 1944, 39-55.
Baker, Derek, ed. *Medieval Women.* Ecclesiastical History Society. Oxford: Blackwell, 1978.
Bancroft, Anne. *The Luminous Vision, Six Medieval Mystics.* London: Allen & Unwin, 1984.
Barker, Paula S. Datsko. "The Motherhood of God in Julian of Norwich's Theology," *The Downside Review* 100 (1982) 290-304.
Benedictine of Stanbrook. "English Spiritual Writers, XII. Dame Julian of Norwich," *The Clergy Review,* NS 44 (1959) 705-720.
Benvenuta, Sr. Mary, O.P. "Juliana of Norwich," *Dublin Review* 176 (1923) 81-94.
Birrell, T. A. "English Catholic Mystics in Non-Catholic Circles," I, II, III, *The Downside Review* 94 (1976) I, 60-81; II, 99-117; III, 213-231.
Biscoglio, Frances M. "Julian of Norwich's Reconciliation of Love and Sin," *Review for Religious* 47 (1988) 413-424.
Bolton, J. L. *The Medieval English Economy 1150-1500.* London: J. M. Dent, 1980.
Børreson, Kari Elizabeth. "Christ nôtre mère, la théologie de Julienne de Norwich," *Mitteilungen und Forschungsbeiträge der Cusanus-Gesellschaft* 13 (1978) 320-329.
Bradford, Clare M. "Julian of Norwich and Margery Kempe," *Theology Today* 35 (1978) 153-158.
Bradley, Ritamary. "Christ the Teacher in Julian's Showings, The Biblical and Patristic Traditions," in *The Medieval Mystical Tradition in England,* Dartington, 1982. Edited by Marion Glasscoe. Exeter: University of Exeter, 1982, 127-142.
_____. "Julian of Norwich on Prayer," in *Spätmittelalterliche Geistliche Literatur in der Nationalsprache 1.* Edited by James Hogg. Analecta Cartusiana 106:1. Salzburg: Institut für Anglistik und Amerikanistik, 1983, 136-154.
_____. "Julian of Norwich: Writer and Mystic," in *An Introduction to the Medieval Mystics of Europe.* Edited by Paul Szarmach. Albany, New York: State University of New York, 1984, 195-216.
_____. "Julian on Mary," *Anima* 15 (1989) 108-112.

Bradley, Ritamary. "Julian on Prayer," in *Peaceweavers*. Edited by Lillian Thomas Shank and John A. Nichols. Medieval Religious Women, Vol. 2. Kalamazoo: Cistercian Publications, Inc., 1987, 291-304.

_____. "Julian's 'doubtfull drede,'" *The Month* 242 (1981) 53-57.

_____. "The Motherhood Theme in Julian of Norwich," *Fourteenth Century English Mystics Newsletter* 2 (1976) 25-30.

_____. "Mysticism in the Motherhood Similitude of Julian of Norwich," *Studia Mystica* 8 (1985) 4-14.

_____. "Patristic background of the motherhood similitude in Julian of Norwich," *Christian Scholar's Review* 8 (1978) 101-113.

_____. "Perception of Self in Julian of Norwich's Showings," The *Downside Review* 104 (1986) 227-239.

_____. "Present-Day Themes in the Fourteenth-Century English Mystics," *Spiritual Life* 20 (1974) 260-267.

_____. "The Speculum Image in Medieval Mystical Writers," in *The Medieval Mystical Tradition in England*, Dartington, 1984. Edited by Marion Glasscoe. Cambridge: D. S. Brewer, 1984, 9-27.

Brockett, Lorna, R.S.C.J. "Traditions of Spiritual Guidance. The Relevance of Julian for Today," *The Way* 28 (1988) 272-279.

Busshart, Helen M. "Christ as Feminine in Julian of Norwich in the Light of the Psychology of C. G. Jung." Unpublished dissertation, Fordham University, 1985.

_____. "Julian of Norwich — God's Love and the Experience of Dying," *Contemplative Review* 12 (1979) 6-13.

Bynum, Caroline Walker. *Jesus As Mother: Studies in the Spirituality of the High Middle Ages*. Berkeley: University of California, 1982.

_____. "Jesus as Mother and Abbot as Mother: Some Themes in Twelfth Century Cistercian Writing," *Harvard Theological Review* 70 (1977) 257-284.

Cabassut, Andre, O.S.B. "Une dévotion médiévale peu connue, la dévotion a 'Jésus notre Mère,'" *Revue d'Ascétique et de Mystique* 25 (1949) 234-245.

Cambier, Jules - Léon-Dufour, Xavier. "Mercy," in *Dictionary of Biblical Theology*. Edited by Xavier Léon-Dufour. London: Geoffrey Chapman Publishers, 1973, 351-354.

Carfagna, Rosemarie. "A Spirituality of Suffering," *Review for Religious* 47 (1988) 255-263.

Clark, John P. H. "Fiducia in Julian of Norwich," I and II, *The Downside Review* (1981) I, 97-108; II, 214-229.

_____. "Nature, Grace and the Trinity in Julian of Norwich," *The Downside Review* 100 (1982) 203-220.

_____. "Predestination in Christ According to Julian of Norwich," *The Downside Review* 100 (1982) 79-91.

Clay, Rotha Mary. *The Hermits and Anchorites of England*. London: Methuen and Co., 1914.

Cohn, Ricki Jean. "God and Motherhood in *The Book of Margery Kempe*," *Studia Mystica* 9 (1986) 26-35.

Colledge, Edmund, O.S.A. "The Julian Manuscripts," in *Julian and her Norwich. Commemorative essays and handbook to the Exhibition "Revelations of Divine Love."* Edited by Frank Dale Sayer. Norwich: Julian of Norwich 1973 Celebration Committee, 1973, 39.

Colledge, Edmund, O.S.A. "This blessed teaching," in *Julian and her Norwich. Commemorative essays and handbook to the Exhibition "Revelations of Divine Love."* Edited by Frank Dale Sayer. Norwich: Julian of Norwich 1973 Celebration Committee, 1973, 34-35.

Colledge, Edmund, O.S.A. - James Walsh, S.J. "Editing Julian of Norwich's Revelations: A Progress Report," *Mediaeval Studies* 38 (1976) 408-427.

_____. "Julienne de Norwich," *Dictionnaire de Spiritualité ascétique et mystique,* Vol. 8. Edited by Marcel Viller *et al.* Paris: Beauchesne, 1974, 1606-1611.

Colledge, Eric. "Early English Spirituality," I and II, *The Month* 216 (1963) I, 22-32; II, 108-120.

_____. "The English Mystics and Their Critics," *Life of the Spirit* 15 (1961) 554-559.

_____. *Medieval Mystics of England.* London: John Murray, 1961.

Collier-Bendelow, Margaret. *Gott Ist Unsere Mutter, Die Offenbarung der Juliana von Norwich.* Translated by Maria-Sybille Bienentreu. Freiburg: Herder, 1989.

Congar, Yves. "The Spirit as God's Femininity," *Theology Digest* 30 (1981) 129-132.

Cooper, Austin, O.M.I. *Julian of Norwich: Reflections on Selected Texts.* Kent: Burns & Oates, 1987.

Corless, Roger. "The Dramas of Spiritual Progress: The Lord and the Servant in Julian's Showings 51 and the Lost Heir in Lotus Sutra 4," *Mystics Quarterly* 11 (1985) 65-75.

Cummings, Charles, O.C.S.O. "God's Homely Love in Julian of Norwich," *Cistercian Studies* 13 (1978) 68-74.

_____. "The Motherhood of God According to Julian of Norwich," in *Peaceweavers.* Edited by Lillian Thomas Shank and John A. Nichols. Medieval Religious Women, Vol. 2. Kalamazoo: Cistercian Publications, Inc., 1987, 305-314.

_____. "Wounded in Glory," *Mystics Quarterly* 10 (1984) 73-76.

Darwin, Francis D. S. *The English Medieval Recluse.* London: Society for Promoting Christian Knowledge, 1944.

Deanesly, Margaret. *The History of the Medieval Church, 590-1500.* London: Methuen and Co. Ltd., 1925.

Del Mastro, M. L. "Julian of Norwich: Parable of the Lord and Servant – Radical Orthodoxy," *Mystics Quarterly* 14 (1988) 84-94.

Dickman, Susan. "Julian of Norwich and Margery Kempe: Two Images of 14th-Century Spirituality," in *Spätmittelalterliche Geistliche Literatur in der Nationalsprache 1.* Edited by James Hogg. Analecta Cartusiana 106:1. Salzburg: Institut für Anglistik und Amerikanistik, 1983, 178-194.

Dinnis, Enid. "Julian's Bread," *New Catholic World* 116 (1923) 605-619.

Dorgan, Margaret. "Julian of Norwich," *Spiritual Life* 22 (1976) 173-178.

Doyle, Teresa Anne. "Classical and Baroque Elements of Spirituality in Medieval Didactic Works for Women." Unpublished dissertation, Fordham University, 1948.

Dreyer, Elizabeth. "'And All Shall Be Well': Julian of Norwich," in *Manifestation of Grace.* Theology and Life Series 29. Wilmington, Delaware: Michael Glazier, Inc., 1990, 104-125.

_____. "Julian of Norwich: Her Merry Counsel," *America* 139 (1978) 55-57.

Dulcidia, Sr. M. "Dame Julian and St. Paul," *Cross and Crown* 7 (1955) 100-106.

Dunn, F. I. "Hermits, anchorites and recluses: a study with reference to medieval Norwich," in *Julian and her Norwich. Commemorative essays and handbook to the Exhibition "Revelations of Divine Love."* Edited by Frank Dale Sayer. Norwich: Julian of Norwich 1973 Celebration Committee, 1973, 18-26.

Durka, Gloria. *Praying with Julian of Norwich*. Winona, MN: St. Mary's Press, 1989.

Durley, Maureen Slattery. "Guilt and Innocence: The Coincidence of Opposites in Julian of Norwich's Parable of the Lord and the Servant," *Revue de l'Université d'Ottawa* 50 (1980) 202-208.

Eileen Mary, S.L.G., Sr. "The Place of Lady Julian of Norwich in English Literature," in *Julian of Norwich: Four Studies to Commemorate the Sixth Centenary of the Revelations of Divine Love*. Fairacres Publication No. 28. Oxford: SLG Press, 1973, 3-9.

Ellis, Roger. "A Literary Approach to the Middle English Mystics," in *The Medieval Mystical Tradition in England*, Exeter, 1980. Edited by Marion Glasscoe. Exeter: University of Exeter, 1980, 99-119.

_____. "The Choices of the Translator in the Late Middle English Period," in *The Medieval Mystical Tradition in England*, Dartington, 1982. Edited by Marion Glasscoe. Exeter: University of Exeter, 1982, 18-46.

_____. "Revelation and the Life of Faith: The Vision of Julian of Norwich," *Christian* 6 (1980), 61-71.

Esser, Hans-Helmut. "Mercy, Compassion," in *The New International Dictionary of New Testament Theology*, Vol. 2. Edited by Colin Brown. Grand Rapids: The Zondervan Corporation, 1986, 593-601.

Faulkner, Mara, O.S.B. "Julian of Norwich and the Power and Peril of Silence," *Sisters Today* 57 (1986) 278-288.

Flindall, Roy Philip. "The Lady Julian and her City: a meditation on religion and society," in *Julian and her Norwich. Commemorative essays and handbook to the Exhibition "Revelations of Divine Love."* Edited by Frank Dale Sayer. Norwich: Julian of Norwich 1973 Celebration Committee, 1973, 10-17.

Flood, H. R. *St. Julian's Church Norwich and Dame Julian*. Norwich: Wherry Press, 1936.

Foss, David B. "From God as Mother to Priest as Mother: Julian of Norwich and the Movement for the Ordination of Women," *The Downside Review* 104 (1986) 214-226.

Furness, Jean. "Teilhard de Chardin and Julian of Norwich: A Rapprochement," *Mystics Quarterly* 12 (1986) 67-70.

Gatta, Julia. *A Pastoral Art, Spiritual Guidance in the English Mystics*. London: Darton, Longman and Todd, 1987.

_____. "Julian of Norwich: Theodicy as a Pastoral Art," *Anglican Theological Review* 63 (1981) 173-181.

Gilchrist, Jay. "Unfolding Enfolding Love in Julian of Norwich's Revelations," *Fourteenth Century English Mystics Newsletter* 9 (1983) 67-88.

Glasscoe, Marion. "Means of Showing: An Approach to Reading Julian of Norwich," in *Spätmittelalterliche Geistliche Literatur in der Nationalsprache 1*. Edited by James Hogg. Analecta Cartusiana 106:1. Salzburg: Institut für Anglistik und Amerikanistik, 1983, 155-177.

_____. "Visions and Revisions: A Further Look at the Manuscripts of Julian of Norwich," *Studies in Bibliography*. Papers of the Bibliographical Society of the University of Virgina, 42 (1989) 103-120.

Glasscoe, Marion, ed. *The Medieval Mystical Tradition in England*, Exeter, 1980. Exeter: University of Exeter, 1980.

_____. *The Medieval Mystical Tradition in England*, Dartington, 1982. Exeter: University of Exeter, 1982.

Glasscoe, Marion, ed. *The Medieval Mystical Tradition in England*, Dartington, 1984. Cambridge: D. S. Brewer, 1984.

Gray, Douglas. *Themes and Images in the Medieval English Religious Lyric*. London: Routledge & Kegan Paul, 1972.

Grayson, Janet. "The Eschatological Adam's Kirtle," *Mystics Quarterly* 11 (1985) 153-160.

Hanshell, Deryck. "A Crux in the Interpretation of Dame Julian," *The Downside Review* 92 (1974) 77-91.

Heimmel, Jennifer Perone. "God Is Our Mother: Julian of Norwich and the Medieval Image of Christian Feminine Divinity." Unpublished dissertation, St. John's University, 1980.

Hodgson, Geraldine. *English Mystics*. London: Mowbray and Co. Ltd., 1922.

Hodgson, Phyllis. *Three 14th Century English Mystics*. London: Longmans, Green & Co., 1967.

Homier, Donald F. "The Function of Rhetoric in Julian of Norwich's Revelations of Divine Love," *Fourteenth Century English Mystics Newsletter* 8 (1982) 162-178.

Hussey, S. S. "Editing the Middle English Mystics," in *Spiritualität Heute und Gestern* 2. Edited by James Hogg. Analecta Cartusiana 35:2. Salzburg: Institut für Anglistik un Amderikanistik, 1983, 160-173.

Inge, William Ralph. *Studies of English Mystics*. St. Margaret's Lectures, 1905. London: John Murray, 1921.

Israel, Martin. "A Meditation on Dame Julian's Revelations of Divine Love," *Fourteenth Century English Mystics Newsletter* 6 (1980) 6681.

Jantzen, Grace. *Julian of Norwich: Mystic and Theologian*. London: Society for Promoting Christian Knowledge, 1987.

Jewson, Charles B. *People of Medieval Norwich*. Norwich: Jarrold and Sons Ltd., 1955.

Jones, Catherine. "The English Mystic: Julian of Norwich," in *Medieval Women Writers*. Edited by Katharina M. Wilson. Athens: University of Georgia Press, 1984, 269-296.

Kilroy, Phil, R.S.C.J. "Julian of Norwich — her experience of God," *Doctrine and Life Supplement* 19 (1979) 115-123.

King, Margot H. "The Desert Mothers: From Judith to Julian of Norwich," *Fourteenth Century English Mystics Newsletter* 9 (1983) 12-25.

Knowles, Dom David. *The English Mystical Tradition*. New York: Harper and Brothers, 1961.

_____. *The Evolution of Medieval Thought*. London: Cambridge University Press, 1962.

Knowlton, Mary Arthur. *The Influence of Richard Rolle and of Julian of Norwich on the Middle English Lyrics*. The Hague: Mouton, 1973.

Koenig, Elizabeth K. J. "Imagination in Julian of Norwich," *New Catholic World* 225 (1982) 260-262.

Lacan, Marc-François. "Piety," in *Dictionary of Biblical Theology*. Edited by Xavier Léon-Dufour. London: Geoffrey Chapman Publishers, 1973, 429-430.

Lagorio, Valerie. "New Avenues of Research in the English Mystics," in *The Medieval Mystical Tradition in England*, Exeter, 1980. Edited by Marion Glasscoe. Exeter: University of Exeter, 1980, 234-249.

_____. "Variations on the Theme of God's Motherhood in Medieval English Mystical and Devotional Writings," *Studia Mystica* 8 (1985) 15-37.

Lagorio, Valerie Marie - Ritamary Bradley. *The 14th-Century English Mystics, A Comprehensive Annotated Bibliography.* New York: Garland Publishing, Inc., 1981.

Lang, Judith. "'The Godly Wylle' in Julian of Norwich," *The Downside Review* 102 (1984) 163-173.

Lant, Denis. "Devotional and Pastoral Classics: Mother Julian's 'Revelations of Divine Love,'" *The Expository Times* 68 (1957) 372-374.

Lash, Nicholas. "All Shall Be Well: Christian and Marxist Hope," *New Blackfriars* 63 (1982) 404-415.

Lawlor, J. "A Note on the Revelations of Julian of Norwich," *Review of English Studies,* NS 2 (1951) 255-258.

Leclercq, Jean. "Solitude and Solidarity: Medieval Women Recluses," in *Peaceweavers.* Edited by Lillian Thomas Shank and John A. Nichols. Medieval Religious Women, Vol. 2. Kalamazoo: Cistercian Publications, Inc., 1987, 67-83.

Leech, Kenneth. "Hazelnut Theology: Its Potential and Perils," in *Julian Reconsidered.* Edited by Kevin Leech and Benedicta Ward, S.L.G. Fairacres Publication No. 106. Oxford: SLG Press, 1988, 1-9.

Levasti, Arrigo. "St. Catherine of Siena and Dame Julian of Norwich," translated by Dorothy M. White, *Life of the Spirit* 7 (1953) 332-334.

Lewis, Gertrud Jaron. "God's Femininity: Medieval Precursors of a Current Theological Issue," *Vox Benedictina* 2 (1985) 245-281.

Lewis, Muriel. "After Reflecting on Julian's Revelations of Behovabil Synne," *Studia Mystica* 6 (1983) 41-57.

Lichtmann, Maria R. "I desyrede a bodylye syght": Julian of Norwich and the Body," *Mystics Quarterly* 17 (1991) 12-19.

————. "Julian of Norwich and the Ontology of the Feminine," *Studia Mystica 13* (1990) 53-65.

Llewelyn, Robert. *Love Bade Me Welcome.* London: Darton, Longman and Todd, 1984.

————. *With Pity, Not Blame.* London: Darton, Longman and Todd, 1982.

Llewelyn, Robert, ed. *Julian, Woman of Our Day.* London: Darton, Longman and Todd, 1985.

Logarbo, Mona. "Salvation Theology in Julian of Norwich: Sin, Forgiveness, and Redemption in the Revelations," *Thought* 61 (1986) 370-380.

Lorenzo, Bernadette. "The Mystical Experience of Julian of Norwich, with Reference to the Epistle to the Hebrews (ch. IV). Semiotic and Psychoanalytic Analysis," translated by Yvette LeGuillou, in The *Medieval Mystical Tradition in England,* Dartington, 1982. Edited by Marion Glasscoe. Exeter: University of Exeter, 1982, 161-181.

Lucas, Elona K. "Psychological and Spiritual Growth in Hadewijch and Julian of Norwich," *Studia Mystica* 9 (1986) 3-20.

MacDonald, Donald, S.M.M. "Mary and Our Reconciliation in Christ," *Review for Religious* 46 (1987) 321-330.

Madore, Marion. "Julian of Norwich on God's Homely Love," *Review for Religious* 42 (1983) 261-271.

Maisonneuve, Roland. "Julian of Norwich and the Prison of Existence," *Studia Mystica* 3 (1980) 26-32.

————. *L'univers visionnaire de Julian of Norwich.* Paris: O.E.I.L., 1987.

————. "The Visionary Eye and Its Pluridimensional Perception," *Studia Mystica* 9 (1986) 15-20.

Maisonneuve, Roland. "The Visionary Universe of Julian of Norwich," in *The Medieval Mystical Tradition in England,* Exeter, 1980. Edited by Marion Glasscoe. Exeter: University of Exeter, 1980, 86-98.

Marshall, D. E. "St. Thomas Aquinas and Mother Julian on Charity," *Life of the Spirit* 7 (1953) 335-341.

Mary Paul, S.L.G., Sr. *All Shall Be Well, Julian of Norwich and the Compassion of God.* Oxford: SLG Press, 1976.

_____. "Julian of Norwich and the Bible," in *Julian of Norwich: Four Studies to Commemorate the Sixth Centenary of the Revelations of Divine Love.* Fairacres Publication No. 28. Oxford: SLG Press, 1973, 11-23.

Mayeski, Marie Anne. "Creation Motifs in the Spirituality of Julian of Norwich," in *The Journey of Western Spirituality.* Edited by A. W. Sadler. The College Theology Society. Ann Arbor: Edwards Brothers, Inc., 1981, 107-118.

McCaslin, Susan. "Vision and Revision in Four Quartets: T. S. Eliot and Julian of Norwich," *Mystics Quarterly* 12 (1986) 171-178.

McIlwain, James T. "The 'Bodelye Syeknes' of Julian of Norwich," *Journal of Medieval History* 10 (1984).

McLaughlin, Eleanor. "'Christ My Mother': Feminine Naming and Metaphor in Medieval Spirituality," *Nashotah Review* 15 (1975) 228-248.

_____. "Julian's Death Into Life," *Living Prayer* 20 (1987) 28-35.

McLean, Michael. *Guidebook to St. Julian's Church and Lady Julian's Cell.* Norwich, 1979. Revised, 1981.

McNamer, Sarah. "The Exploratory Image: God as Mother in Julian of Norwich's Revelations of Divine Love," *Mystics Quarterly* 15 (1989) 21-28.

Meany, Mary Frances Walsh. "The Image of Christ in the Revelations of Divine Love of Julian of Norwich." Unpublished dissertation, Fordham University, 1975.

Medcalf, Stephen. "Medieval Psychology and Medieval Mystics, " in *The Medieval Mystical Tradition in England,* Exeter, 1980. Edited by Marion Glasscoe. Exeter: University of Exeter Press, 1980, 120-155.

Merton, Thomas. *Seeds of Destruction.* New York: Farrar, Straus and Cudahy, 1964.

_____. "The English Mystics," in *Mystics and the Zen Masters.* New York: Farrar, Straus and Giroux, 1967.

Moffitt, John. "God as Mother in Hinduism and Christianity," *Cross Currents* 28 (1978) 129-133.

Molinari, Paul, S.J. *Julian of Norwich. The Teaching of a 14th Century English Mystic.* London: Longmans, Green & Co., 1958.

_____. "Love Was His Meaning: Julian of Norwich – Six Centuries Later," *Fourteenth Century English Mystics Newsletter* 5 (1979) 1233.

Nutting, Geoffrey. "The Enlightenment of Mother Julian: A Fourteenth Century Vision of Reconciliation," *The Tyndale Paper* 30 (1985), 1-14.

O'Donoghue, Noel Dermot, O.D.C. "Visions and System: The Contribution of theMystical Tradition to Understanding God," *Irish Theological Quarterly* 44 (1977) 90-104.

Panichelli, Debra Scott. "Finding God in the Memory: Julian of Norwich and the Loss of the Visions," *The Downside Review* 104 (1986) 299-317.

Pantin, William Abel. *The English Church in the Fourteenth Century.* Cambridge: Cambridge University Press, 1955.

Peloquin, Carol Marie. "All Will Be Well: A Look at Sin in Juliana's *Revelations,*" *Contemplative Review* 13 (1980) 9-16.

Pelphrey, Brant. *Julian of Norwich*. Edited by Noel Dermot O'Donoghue, O.D.C. The Way of the Christian Mystics 7. Wilmington, Delaware: Michael Glazier, Inc., 1989.

_____. *Love Was His Meaning, The Theology and Mysticism of Julian of Norwich*. Edited by James Hogg. Elizabethan and Renaissance Studies 92:4. Salzburg: Institut für Anglistik und Amerikanistik, 1982.

_____. "Spirituality in Mission: Lessons from Julian of Norwich," *Cross Currents* 34 (1984) 171-190.

_____. "'Uncreated Charity': The Trinity in Julian of Norwich," *Sobornost* 7, Series 7 (1978) 527-535.

Pepler, Conrad, O.P. "Mother Julian Herself," *Life of the Spirit* 3 (1948/49) 450-454.

_____. *The English Religious Heritage*. London: Blackfriars, 1958.

_____. "The English Spirit," *Life of the Spirit* 11 (1956) 52-65.

_____. "The Ground of Union," *Life of the Spirit* 4 (1949) 249-255.

_____. "The Mystical Body in the English Mystics," *Clergy Review,* NS 23 (1943) 49-59.

_____. "The Soul of Christ," *Life of the Spirit* 4 (1949) 149-156.

_____. "The Soul of a Mystic," *Life of the Spirit* 4 (1949) 56-64.

_____. "Visions and Shewings," *Life of the Spirit* 3 (1948/49) 486-493.

Peters, Brad. "The Reality of Evil within the Mystic Vision of Julian of Norwich," *Mystics Quarterly* 13 (1987) 195-202.

Pezzini, Domenico. "Giuliana di Norwich"; "I grandi temi delle rivelazioni"; and "Giulana oggi," in *Libro delle rivelazioni*. Translated by Domenico Pezzini. Milan: Editrice Ancora, 1984, 7-94.

_____. "The Theme of the Passion in Richard Rolle and Julian of Norwich," in *Religion in the Poetry and Drama of the Late Middle Ages in England*. Edited by Piero Boitani and Anna Torti. Cambridge: D. S. Brewer, 1990, 29-66.

Renaudin, Paul. *Quatre Mystiques Anglais*. Paris: Les Éditions du Cerf, 1945.

Reynolds, Anna Maria, C.P. "'Courtesy' and 'Homeliness' in the Revelations of Julian of Norwich," *Fourteenth Century English Mystics Newsletter* 5 (1979) 12-20.

_____. "Julian of Norwich," *The Month* 24 (1960) 133-144.

_____. "Julian of Norwich: Woman of Hope," *Mystics Quarterly* 10 (1984) 118-125.

_____. "Love Is His Meaning," *Clergy Review* 58 (1973) 363-369.

_____. "Some Literary Influences in the Revelations of Julian of Norwich," *Leeds Studies in English and Kindred Languages* 7-8 (1952) 18-28.

_____. "Woman of Hope," in *Julian. Woman of Our Day*. Edited by Robert Llewelyn. London: Darton, Longman and Todd, 1985, 11-26.

Riehle, Wolfgang. *The Middle English Mystics*. Translated by Bernard Standring. London: Routledge & Kegan Paul, 1981.

Rogers, Daniel J. "Psychotechnological Approaches to the teaching of the Cloud-author and to the Showings of Julian of Norwich," in *The Medieval Mystical Tradition in England*, Dartington, 1982. Edited by Marion Glasscoe. Exeter: University of Exeter, 1982, 143-160.

Rosof, Patricia J. F. "The Anchoress in the Twelfth and Thirteenth Centuries," in *Peaceweavers*. Edited by Lillian Thomas Shank and John A. Nichols. Medieval Religious Women, Vol. 2. Kalamazoo: Cistercian Publications, Inc., 1987, 123-144.

Ryder, Andrew, S.C.J. "A Note on Julian's Visions," *The Downside Review* 96 (1978) 299-304.

Ryder, Andrew, S.C.J. "The English Spiritual Writers of the Fourteenth Century," I-V, *Mount Carmel* 26-27 (1978-1979) I, 199-209; II, 25-34; III, 72-82; IV, 138-148; V, 192-203.

Sayer, Frank Dale. "Who was Mother Julian?" in *Julian and her Norwich. Commemorative essays and handbook to the Exhibition "Revelations of Divine Love."* Edited by Frank Dale Sayer. Norwich: Julian of Norwich 1973 Celebration Committee, 1973, 5-9.

Shank, Lillian Thomas, O.C.S.O. "Theological Trends: Ordinary Mysticism and Ordinary Mystics," *The Way* 30 (1990) 231-244.

Sitwell, Gerard. "Julian of Norwich," *Sponsa Regis* 32 (1960) 12-18.

Stone, Robert Karl. *Middle English Prose Style, Margery Kempe and Julian of Norwich.* The Hague: Mouton and Co., 1970.

Swanson, John-Julian, O.J.N. "Guide for the Inexpert Mystic," in *Julian. Woman of Our Day.* Edited by Robert Llewelyn. London: Darton, Longman and Todd, 1985, 75-88.

_____. "Thankyng in Julian," *Mystics Quarterly* 15 (1989) 70-74.

Tanner, Norman P. *The Church in Late Medieval Norwich. 1370-1532.* Studies and Texts, 66. Toronto: Pontifical Institute of Mediaeval Studies, 1984.

Thouless, Robert H. *The Lady Julian: A Psychological Study.* London: Society for Promoting Christian Knowledge, 1924.

Tugwell, Simon, O.P. "Julian of Norwich As a Speculative Theologian," *Fourteenth Century English Mystics Newsletter* 9 (1983) 199-209.

_____. "Julian of Norwich," in *Ways of Imperfection: An Exploration of Christian Spirituality.* London: Darton, Longman and Todd, 1984, 187-207.

Tuma, George Wood. *The Fourteenth Century English Mystics: A Comparative Analysis.* 2 Vol. Edited by James Hogg. Elizabethan and Renaissance Studies, 61 and 62. Salzburg: Institut für Englische Sprache und Literatur, 1977.

Tyrrell, George, S.J. "Julian of Norwich," in *The Faith of the Millions.* London: Longmans, Green & Co., 1901.

Underhill, Evelyn. "Medieval Mysticism," in *The Cambridge Medieval History,* Vol 7. Edited by J. R. Tanner *et al.* Cambridge: University Press, 1932, 777-812.

_____. *The Essentials of Mysticism and other Essays.* London: J. M. Dent & Sons Ltd., 1920.

Upjohn, Sheila. *In Search of Julian of Norwich.* London: Darton, Longman and Todd, 1989.

Vann, Gerald, O.P. "Juliana of Norwich on the Love-Longing of Christ," *The Month* 160 (1932) 537-541.

Vinje, Patricia Mary. *An Understanding of Love According to the Anchoress Julian of Norwich.* Edited by James Hogg. Elizabethan and Renaissance Studies 92:8. Salzburg: Institut für Anglistik und Amerikanistik, 1983.

Walsh, James, S.J. "A New Thérèse," *The Month* 206 (1958) 150-159.

_____. "A Note on Sexuality and Sensuality," *The Way, Supplement* 15 (1972) 86-92.

_____. "God's homely loving: St. John and Julian of Norwich on the divine indwelling," *The Month,* NS 19 (1958) 164-172.

Walsh, James, S.J., ed. *Pre-Reformation English Spirituality.* London: Burns & Oates, 1965.

Ward, Benedicta, S.L.G. "'Faith Seeking Understanding': Anselm of Canterbury and Julian of Norwich," in *Julian of Norwich: Four Studies to Commemorate the Sixth Centenary of the Revelations of Divine Love.* Fairacres Publication No. 28. Oxford: SLG Press, 1973, 26-31.

Ward, Benedicta, S.L.G. "Julian the Solitary," in *Julian Reconsidered*. Edited by Kevin Leech and Benedicta Ward, S.L.G. Fairacres Publication No. 106. Oxford: SLG Press, 1988, 11-29.

Ward, James M. "Mercy, Merciful; Compassion; Pity," in *The Interpreter's Dictionary of the Bible*, Vol. 3. Edited by George Arthur Buttrick *et al*. Nashville: Abingdon Press, 1962, 352-354.

Warren, Ann K. *Anchorites and Their Patrons in Medieval England*. Berkeley: University of California Press, 1985.

————. "The Nun as Anchoress: England 1100-1500," in *Distant Echoes*. Edited by Lillian Thomas Shank and John A. Nichols. Medieval Religious Women, Vol. 1. Kalamazoo: Cistercian Publications, Inc., 1984, 197-212.

Watkin, E. I. "Dame Julian of Norwich," in *The English Way*. Edited by Maisie Ward. New York: Sheed and Ward, 1933, 128-158.

————. "Revelations of Divine Love," *New Catholic World* 131 (1930) 174-182.

Watkins, Renée Neu. "Two Women Visionaries and Death. Catherine of Siena and Julian of Norwich," *Numen* 30 (1983) 174-196.

Webb, Geoffrey. "The Person and the Place — II: At Old St. Julian's," *Life of the Spirit* 15 (1961) 549-554.

Webster, Alan Brunskill. "Julian of Norwich," in *Julian and her Norwich. Commemorative essays and handbook to the Exhibition "Revelations of Divine Love."* Edited by Frank Dale Sayer. Norwich: Julian of Norwich 1973 Celebration Committee, 1973, 28-31.

Webster, Alan Brunskill, ed. *Julian of Norwich: A Light in the Darkness*. London: Lawrence Rivington, 1980.

Windeatt, B. A. "The Art of Mystical Loving: Julian of Norwich," in *The Medieval Mystical Tradition in England*, Exeter, 1980. Edited by Marion Glasscoe. Exeter: University of Exeter, 1980, 55-71.

————. "Julian of Norwich and Her Audience," *Review of English Studies*, NS 28 (1977) 1-17.

Wolters, Clifton C. "Two Spiritualities: A Superficial Survey," *Fourteenth Century English Mystics Newsletter* 5 (1979), 16-27.

Wright, Robert E. "The 'Boke Performyd': Affective Technique and Reader Response in the Showings of Julian of Norwich," *Christianity and Literature* 36:4 (1987) 13-32.

Index

Christianity
and Modern Politics

Edited by
Louisa Sue Hulett

1992. Large-octavo. Approx. 400 pages.
Cloth approx. DM 104,— ISBN 3-11-013462-4
Paperback approx. DM 50,— ISBN 3-11-013461-6

Anthology of writings on Religion and Politics in the United
States of America.

Sample contents: Definitions of Christianity, Civil Religion, and
Politics · Separation of Church and State in America · Religious
Freedom and the Supreme Court · The Rise of Christian Funda-
mentalism · Fundamentalism versus Secular Humanism · Just War
Doctrine · Pacifism and Nuclear Ethics · Liberation Theology.

The editor is an Associate Professor of Political Science at Knox
College (USA, Illinois), contributor of numerous articles and
several books on international relation, nuclear strategy, and Law
and Religion.

Price is subject to change

Walter de Gruyter · Berlin · New York

Gregory of Nyssa: Homilies on Ecclesiastes

Proceedings of the Seventh International Colloquium on Gregory of Nyssa
(St. Andrews, 5—10 September 1990)

Edited by
Stuart George Hall and Rachel Moriarty

1992. Large-octavo.
Approx. 340 pages. Cloth approx. DM 128,—
ISBN 3-11-013586-8

An English version of the eight Homilies on Ecclesiastes by a leading theologian of the fourth century, with supporting introductory and expository studies.

The translation is based on the text in Gregorii Nysseni Opera V (ed. P. Alexander, 1986). Leading scholars from various countries provide exegetical studies of each homily and wider researches on the Christian interpretation of Ecclesiastes.

Proceedings of the Seventh International Colloquium on Gregory of Nyssa, St. Andrews, 5—10 September 1990, under the chairmanship of Stuart G. Hall, Professor of Ecclesiastical History, King's College London.

Price is subject to change

Walter de Gruyter Berlin · New York

DATE DUE